ADVANCES
IN CHILD DEVELOPMENT
AND BEHAVIOR

POSITIVE YOUTH DEVELOPMENT

VOLUME 41

Contributors to This Volume

Kristine M. Baber

Janette B. Benson

Peter L. Benson

Ciprian Boitor

Edmond P. Bowers

Michelle J. Boyd

Drew Carr

Paul A. Chase

Julie Dobrow

Steinunn Gestsdóttir

Julie Going

Kei Kawashima-Ginsberg

Pamela Ebstyne King

Reed W. Larson

Jacqueline V. Lerner

Richard M. Lerner

Selva Lewin-Bizan

Yibing Li

Emily S. Lin

Shane Lopez

Jenni Menon Mariano

Michelle M. Martel

Megan Kiely Mueller

Christopher M. Napolitano

Adam Rainer

Natalie Rusk

Peter C. Scales

Kristina L. Schmid

Amy K. Syvertsen

Jennifer Brown Urban

Alexander von Eye

Jonathan F. Zaff

ADVANCES
IN
CHILD DEVELOPMENT
AND
BEHAVIOR

POSITIVE YOUTH DEVELOPMENT

edited by

Richard M. Lerner
Institute for Applied Research in Youth Development
Tufts University, Medford, Massachusetts, USA

Jacqueline V. Lerner
Counseling, Developmental, and Educational Psychology
Department, Boston College, Chestnut Hill
Massachusetts, USA

Janette B. Benson
Department of Psychology, University of Denver
Denver, Colorado, USA

VOLUME 41

AMSTERDAM • BOSTON • HEIDELBERG • LONDON
NEW YORK • OXFORD • PARIS • SAN DIEGO
SAN FRANCISCO • SINGAPORE • SYDNEY • TOKYO
Academic Press is an imprint of Elsevier

ELSEVIER

Academic Press is an imprint of Elsevier
32 Jamestown Road, London NW1 7BY, UK
Radarweg 29, PO Box 211, 1000 AE Amsterdam, The Netherlands
225 Wyman Street, Waltham, MA 02451, USA
525 B Street, Suite 1900, San Diego, CA 92101-4495, USA

First edition 2011

Recognizing the importance of preserving what has been written, Elsevier prints
its books on acid-free paper whenever possible.

Library of Congress Cataloging-in-Publication Data
A catalogue record for this book is available from the Library of Congress

British Library Cataloguing in Publication Data
A catalog record for this book is available from the British Library

ISBN: 978-0-12-386492-5
ISSN: 0065-2407 (Series)

For information on all Academic Press publications
visit our website at elsevierdirect.com

Printed in the United States of America

11 12 13   10 9 8 7 6 5 4 3 2 1

Contents

Positive Youth Development: Research and Applications for Promoting Thriving in Adolescence

RICHARD M. LERNER, JACQUELINE V. LERNER, AND
JANETTE B. BENSON

The Development of Intentional Self-Regulation in Adolescence: Describing, Explaining, and Optimizing its Link to Positive Youth Development

CHRISTOPHER M. NAPOLITANO, EDMOND P. BOWERS, STEINUNN
GESTSDÓTTIR, AND PAUL A. CHASE

Religion, Spirituality, Positive Youth Development, and Thriving

PAMELA EBSTYNE KING, DREW CARR, AND CIPRIAN BOITOR

The Contribution of the Developmental Assets Framework to Positive Youth Development Theory and Practice

PETER L. BENSON, PETER C. SCALES, AND AMY K. SYVERTSEN

Youth Activity Involvement and Positive Youth Development

MEGAN KIELY MUELLER, SELVA LEWIN-BIZAN, AND
JENNIFER BROWN URBAN

Media Literacy and Positive Youth Development

MICHELLE J. BOYD AND JULIE DOBROW

Advances in Civic Engagement Research: Issues of Civic Measures and Civic Context

JONATHAN F. ZAFF, KEI KAWASHIMA-GINSBERG, AND EMILY S. LIN

Shortridge Academy: Positive Youth Development in Action within a Therapeutic Community

KRISTINE M. BABER AND ADAM RAINER

Integrating Theory and Method in the Study of Positive Youth Development: The Sample Case of Gender-specificity and Longitudinal Stability of the Dimensions of Intention Self-regulation (Selection, Optimization, and Compensation)

ALEXANDER VON EYE, MICHELLE M. MARTEL, RICHARD M. LERNER, JACQUELINE V. LERNER, AND EDMOND P. BOWERS

Contributors

KRISTINE M. BABER
University of New Hampshire, Emeritus, New Hampshire, USA
JANETTE B. BENSON
Department of Psychology, University of Denver, Denver, Colorado, USA
PETER L. BENSON
Search Institute, Minneapolis, Minnesota, USA
CIPRIAN BOITOR
School of Psychology, Fuller Theological Seminary, Pasadena, California, USA
EDMOND P. BOWERS
Eliot-Pearson Department of Child Development, Tufts University, Medford, Massachusetts, USA
MICHELLE J. BOYD
Institute for Applied Research in Youth Development, Tufts University, Medford, Massachusetts, USA
DREW CARR
School of Psychology, Fuller Theological Seminary, Pasadena, California, USA
PAUL A. CHASE
Eliot-Pearson Department of Child Development, Tufts University, Medford, Massachusetts, USA
JULIE DOBROW
Communications and Media Studies Program, Tufts University, Medford, Massachusetts, USA
STEINUNN GESTSDÓTTIR
School of Education, University of Iceland, Reykjavík, Iceland
JULIE GOING
University of South Florida S-M, Sarasota, Florida, USA
SHANE J. LOPEZ
Gallup & Clifton Strengths School, Omaha, Nebraska, USA
KEI KAWASHIMA-GINSBERG
Tufts University, Medford, Massachusetts, USA

PAMELA EBSTYNE KING
School of Psychology, Fuller Theological Seminary, Pasadena, California, USA
REED W. LARSON
Department of Human and Community Development, University of Illinois, Urbana, Illinois, USA
JACQUELINE V. LERNER
Counseling, Developmental, and Educational Psychology Department, Boston College, Chestnut Hill, Massachusetts, USA
RICHARD M. LERNER
Institute for Applied Research in Youth Development, Tufts University, Medford, Massachusetts, USA
SELVA LEWIN-BIZAN
Tufts University, Medford, Massachusetts, USA
YIBING LI
Education, Human Development, and the Workforce, American Institutes for Research, Washington, District of Columbia, USA
EMILY S. LIN
Tufts University, Medford, Massachusetts, USA
JENNI MENON MARIANO
University of South Florida S-M, Sarasota, Florida, USA
MICHELLE M. MARTEL
University of New Orleans, New Orleans, USA
MEGAN KIELY MUELLER
Tufts University, Medford, Massachusetts, USA
CHRISTOPHER M. NAPOLITANO
Eliot-Pearson Department of Child Development, Tufts University, Medford, Massachusetts, USA
ADAM RAINER
Shortridge Academy, Milton, New Hampshire, USA
NATALIE RUSK
Eliot-Pearson Department of Child Development, Tufts University, Cambridge, Massachusetts, USA
PETER C. SCALES
Search Institute, Minneapolis, Minnesota, USA
KRISTINA L. SCHMID
Eliot-Pearson Department of Child Development, Tufts University, Medford, Massachusetts, USA
AMY K. SYVERTSEN
Search Institute, Minneapolis, Minnesota, USA

JENNIFER BROWN URBAN
Montclair State University, Montclair, New Jersey, USA
ALEXANDER VON EYE
Michigan State University, East Lansing, Michigan, USA, and University of Vienna, Austria
JONATHAN F. ZAFF
Tufts University, Medford, Massachusetts, USA

Preface

Interests in the strengths of youth, the plasticity of human development, and the concept of resilience coalesced in the 1990s to foster the development of the concept of positive youth development (PYD). Several different models of the developmental process believed to be involved in PYD have been used to frame descriptive or explanatory research across the adolescent period. However, all of the models of the PYD process reflected ideas associated with relational, developmental systems conceptions of human development. Accordingly, a key goal of this volume is to present the features of the relational, developmental systems theoretical model of the PYD process and through the several chapters included in this volume, to describe the breadth of contemporary scholarship pertinent to understanding and promoting PYD.

Relational, developmental systems theory stresses that mutually influential relations between the developing individual and his or her complex and changing ecology (represented as individual ↔ context relations) provide the fundamental process of human development. Because humans are embedded in ecologies that change constantly with time (history), these individual ↔ context relations may change as well; as such, there is always the potential for systematic change, or plasticity, in human development. Plasticity represents, then, a key strength of human development, and because adolescence is a period of profound individual and ecological change, one may be optimistic that if the strengths of youth are aligned with resources in the ecology that can nurture or support positive change (termed "developmental assets"), then all youth may be placed on a more positive path across adolescence.

This optimistic idea is the key hypothesis of the PYD perspective, and the relational process of development linked to this hypothesis involves the study of mutually beneficial individual ↔ context relations (termed "adaptive developmental regulations") that may result in the thriving of young people across the adolescent years. Thriving has often been operationalized by the development of five positive characteristics among youth—Competence, Confidence, Character, Connection, and Caring—and the development of these Five Cs of PYD has, in turn, been linked to the growth of a young person's commitment to contribute positively to his or her context, for instance, through civic engagement. In addition, thriving has been linked to lower probabilities of risk and problem behaviors.

These facets of the PYD developmental process are reflected in the contributions to this volume, contributions that reflect the range of scholarship involved in the contemporary study of PYD. The chapters reflect scholarship that focuses on different components of the PYD process, but nevertheless, all chapters provide evidence about the empirical usefulness of the PYD perspective and discuss how—in the areas of youth development of concern within a given chapter—research consistent with the model has important implications both for future adolescent development research and for the application of developmental science.

For instance, as explained in the opening chapter by Lerner, Lerner, and Benson, the foreground of several chapters in this volume focuses on the strengths that youth bring to the individual ↔ context relations that constitute the basic, relational process of development within the PYD model. Napolitano, Bowers, Gestsdóttir, and Chase discuss the role of intentional self-regulation skills in promoting thriving in adolescence, and in turn, Mariano and Going describe the nature of youth purpose and discuss research that shows that many young people develop their potentialities in conjunction with a positive purpose in life.

Although intentional self-regulation skills and the possession of positive purposes are necessary components of youth contributions to adaptive developmental regulations, they may not be sufficient to assure PYD. Two chapters in this volume address the issue of the motivational characteristics that need to be present among youth for either the use of the self-regulation skills they possess or the actions required to pursue their positive purposes. Schmid and Lopez discuss the role of hope in adolescents' constructions of their futures, of their acting to engage their contexts in ways that place them on pathways toward positive adulthoods. In turn, Larson and Rusk present and evaluate the idea that intrinsic motivation is a powerful engine of development and learning. Without such motivation, youth would only be directed into actions through extrinsic factors, and there would be at best only a low probability that adaptive developmental regulations predicated on purpose and hope would be prominent parts of the developmental repertoire of youth.

When the strengths of youth are used in adaptive developmental regulations, then young people effectively engage their contexts in ways that support both them and their settings. A key setting of youth is schools, and Li describes why, from a relational, developmental systems perspective, focusing on cognitive, emotional, and behavioral school engagement is important for understanding the adaptive individual

↔ context relations that are fundamental to human development. In turn, constructs other than school engagement reflect the dynamic relation between the developing adolescent and the institutions of his or her world. King, Carr, and Boitor note that, across the United States and around the world, a ubiquitous instance of such individual ↔ context relations is reflected in the spirituality and religiosity of individuals. They discuss data that indicate the individual and contextual conditions through which spirituality and religiosity place young people on a thriving pathway.

In turn, many of the chapters in this volume focus on features of the ecology that, in integration with the strengths of the person, create the adaptive individual ↔ context relations that constitute the basic, relational process of development within the PYD model. The chapter by Benson, Scales, and Syvertsen epitomizes this focus. It describes the foundational theory and research of Search Institute about the strengths of both individuals and their ecologies (their respective developmental assets) that foster thriving. One of the key ecological developmental assets identified by Benson et al. is out-of-school-time (OST) programs, and Mueller, Lewin-Bizan, and Urban discuss theory and research that underscores that involvement by youth in OST activities is an asset in the development of youth. In addition, in contemporary society, a growing and seemingly ubiquitous facet of youth activity is engagement with media. The chapter by Boyd and Dobrow reviews the literature that documents the growing presence of the use of media among youth and points to the links among media literacy, PYD, and a key outcome of the adaptive individual ↔ context relations that are associated with PYD, that is, youth community contribution, as exemplified by civic engagement. Consistent with the work of Boyd and Dobrow, Zaff, Kawashima-Ginsberg, and Lin present a model of active and engaged citizenship and explain how this concept integrates motivation to be engaged civically, civic participation, social connection, and self-efficacy in regard to civic contributions. They use a relational, developmental systems approach to argue that information about civic functioning can no longer focus primarily on Western democracies.

Across the chapters in this volume, authors point to the implications of theory and research about PYD for applications to programs or policies. The chapter by Baber and Rainer presents an example of the implementation of a PYD model within an actual program, that is, a therapeutic boarding school, Shortridge Academy in New Hampshire. Baber and Rainer note that the PYD-based ecology present at Shortridge Academy increases the likelihood of greater consistency in students' interactions at school and in their families, and has been shown to promote positive change in the youth.

Finally, across the chapters in this volume, authors have pointed to the importance of research methods that integrate individuals and contexts in manners that may elucidate the individual ↔ context relations fundamental to the model of the PYD process. Innovations in relational and change-sensitive analyses may be required to accomplish such work and, as such, von Eye, Martel, Lerner, Lerner, and Bowers use a study of gender specificity and of longitudinal stability of intentional self-regulation skills to illustrate the nature of such methodological innovations in research about the PYD process.

In sum, the chapters in this volume provide support for the use of a relational, developmental systems PYD model perspective in framing research that enhances understanding of the intricacies of individual ↔ context relations, relations that—when mutually beneficial to both individual and context—put young people on a thriving journey across the adolescent period. Moreover, as readers review the scholarship included in this volume, they will find considerable evidence in support of the ideas that there is a diversity of youth strengths and of ecological developmental assets that may be integrated: to foster PYD; to enhance the likelihood of the contributions of youth, such as active and engaged citizenship; and to decrease the likelihood of risk/problem behaviors.

To the extent that the readers of this volume find its chapters of value they will be indebted, as we certainly are, to the extraordinary scholarship of the colleagues who contributed to this work. Their excellence as developmental scientists and their commitment to conducting good research and application in the service of promoting PYD are contributions that we greatly admire and for which we are deeply grateful.

We are also grateful to the National 4-H Council, the Altria Corporation, the Thrive Foundation for Youth, the John Templeton Foundation, and the National Science Foundation for supporting the scholarship of Richard M. Lerner and Jacqueline V. Lerner during the period in which they worked on this volume. Much of the research they supported is represented in this volume. Much of the research about PYD more generally would not exist without their support.

We are deeply appreciative of the work of the managing editor within the Institute for Applied Research in Youth Development, Jarrett M. Lerner. His substantive, editorial, and organizational skills; his capacity to engage efficiently and simultaneously in the multiple tasks associated with the development and production of this book; and his ability to remain cordial and effective with the diverse personalities encountered in academic work are truly extraordinary. His talents enabled this book to move from idea to reality in a very short period of time. We are also very grateful to Jarrett's assistant, Yael Tzipori. She was a creative and indefatigable collaborator in all facets of the development and production of this book, and we admire greatly her impressive abilities.

Finally, we are pleased to express our greatest gratitude to Donald T. Floyd, Jr., president and CEO of the National 4-H Council, to whom we are honored to dedicate this book. Don's vision, values, and courage created the field of PYD research. His leadership moved PYD from being a heuristic concept to an empirically powerful approach to understanding and enhancing the lives of diverse young people in the United States and around the world. We, the scholars who have contributed to this volume, our scientific and practitioner colleagues working in the field of PYD, and literally millions of young people around the world owe to Don Floyd the deepest appreciation for enabling a new conception of young people to be born, to flourish, and to enrich the lives of youth.

Richard M. Lerner
Medford, Massachusetts, USA
Jacqueline V. Lerner
Chestnut Hill, Massachusetts, USA
Janette B. Benson
Denver, Colorado, USA

POSITIVE YOUTH DEVELOPMENT: RESEARCH AND APPLICATIONS FOR PROMOTING THRIVING IN ADOLESCENCE

Richard M. Lerner,* Jacqueline V. Lerner,[†] and Janette B. Benson[‡]

* INSTITUTE FOR APPLIED RESEARCH IN YOUTH DEVELOPMENT, TUFTS UNIVERSITY, MEDFORD, MASSACHUSETTS, USA
[†] COUNSELING, DEVELOPMENTAL, AND EDUCATIONAL PSYCHOLOGY DEPARTMENT, BOSTON COLLEGE, CHESTNUT HILL, MASSACHUSETTS, USA
[‡] DEPARTMENT OF PSYCHOLOGY, UNIVERSITY OF DENVER, DENVER, COLORADO, USA

Abstract

Interests in the strengths of youth, the plasticity of human development, and the concept of resilience coalesced in the 1990s to foster the development of the concept of positive youth development (PYD). This chapter presents the features of the relational developmental systems theoretical model of the PYD developmental process, and then uses this model to describe the scholarship in the present volume. These contributions suggest that all young people have strengths that may be capitalized on to promote thriving across the adolescent years. We conclude that the findings reported in this volume provide a basis for optimism that evidence-based actions can be taken to enhance the chances for thriving among all young people.

1

I. Introduction

Interests in the strengths of youth, the plasticity of human development, and the concept of resilience coalesced in the 1990s to foster the development of the concept of positive youth development (PYD) (Lerner, Phelps, Forman, & Bowers, 2009; Lerner et al., in press). As discussed by Hamilton (1999), the concept of PYD was understood in at least three interrelated but nevertheless different ways: (1) as a developmental process, (2) as a philosophy or approach to youth programming, and (3) as instances of youth programs and organizations focused on fostering the healthy or positive development of youth.

In the decade following Hamilton's (1999) discussion of PYD, several different models of the developmental process believed to be involved in PYD were used to frame descriptive or explanatory research across the adolescent period (e.g., Benson, Scales, Hamilton, & Semsa, 2006; Damon, 2004; Larson, 2000; Lerner et al., 2005) and, as well, to shape programs designed to promote PYD (e.g., Catalano, Berglund, Ryan, Lonczak, & Hawkins, 2004, Catalano, Hawkins, Berglund, Pollard, & Arthur, 2002; Flay, 2002; Flay & Allred, 2003). This literature was marked by a diversity of specific ideas about the substance of PYD, that is, about the particular set of manifest individual-level variables to be studied in elucidating thriving across the adolescent period (e.g., positive purpose, intentional self-regulation, intrinsic motivations, religiosity or spirituality, hope for the future, school engagement, or active and engaged citizenship (AEC)), or about the manifest contextual-level variables that, in interrelation with the individual, promoted PYD, for example, ecological developmental assets (associated with individuals or with institutions, such as the family or school, media influences, or community-based, out-of-school-time (OST) youth development programs).

Despite this diversity of manifest variable foci, all the models of the PYD developmental process found commonality at the level of latent or, even more abstractly, at the metatheoretical level: All models reflected ideas associated with relational, developmental systems conceptions of human development (e.g., Overton, 2010; see also Lerner et al., in press). The fit between theory and application has not been perfect. For example, it has not always been clear that any of these models of the PYD developmental process have served as theoretical frames for either of the other two instances of the PYD concept Hamilton (1999) discussed (see also Lerner et al., in press), that is, for different approaches to PYD programming or for the elements of actual PYD-focused youth development programs (Lerner et al., in press). Nevertheless, there is increasing evidence—some of it presented in this volume—that relational, developmental systems ideas are being more precisely and consistently employed in, at least, discussions of the framing of approaches to youth programming pertinent to PYD (e.g., Chapter 12; Gray, in press; Kurtines et al., 2008; Lerner & Overton, 2008; Zaff, Boyd, Li, Lerner, & Lerner, 2010).

Accordingly, a key goal of this chapter is to describe the features of the relational, developmental systems theoretical model of the PYD developmental process. This presentation will allow us to describe the breadth of contemporary scholarship pertinent to understanding and promoting PYD and, as such, to frame the scholarship that is represented in the present volume. These contributions reflect the range of theory-predicated research and applications pertinent to this relational, developmental systems conception of PYD.

II. Features of the PYD Process: The Relational, Developmental Systems "Lens"

Developmental science seeks to describe, explain, and optimize intra-individual change and interindividual differences in intraindividual change across the life span (Baltes, Reese, & Nesselroade, 1977). The contemporary, cutting-edge theoretical frame for such scholarship involves relational, developmental systems theoretical models (Overton, 2010). Examples of these models include Bronfenbrenner's bioecological theory (e.g., Bronfenbrenner & Morris, 2006), action theory models of intentional, goal-directed behaviors (e.g., Baltes, 1997; Brandtstädter, 1998, 2006; Heckhausen, 1999, 2000), Elder's (1998; Elder & Shanahan, 2006) life-course theory, the Thelen and Smith (1998, 2006) dynamic systems theory, Magnusson's (1999; Magnusson & Stattin, 1998, 2006) holistic person-context interaction theory, and the Ford and Lerner (1992) and the Gottlieb (1997, 1998) developmental systems formulations.

All these instances of developmental systems models emphasize that the basic process of human development involves mutually influential relations between the developing individual and the multiple levels of his/her changing context. These bidirectional relations may be represented as individual ↔ context relations. These relations regulate (i.e., govern) the course of development (i.e., its pace, direction, and outcomes). When these "developmental regulations" involve individual ↔ context relations benefiting both the person and his or her ecology, they may be termed "adaptive developmental regulations" (Brandtstädter, 1998, 1999).

History, or temporality, is part of the ecology of human development that is integrated with the individual through developmental regulations. As such, there is always change and, as well, at least some potential for systematic change (i.e., for plasticity), across the life span (Baltes, Lindenberger, & Staudinger, 2006; Lerner, 1984). This potential for change represents a fundamental strength of human development. Of course, plasticity means that change for the better or worse can characterize any individual's developmental trajectory. Nevertheless, a key assumption of relational developmental systems theories—and, as we will note, of the use of these theories to understand both adolescent development in general and to frame the PYD conception of developmental processes more specifically—is that the developmental system is sufficiently diverse and complex such that some means may be found (by researchers and/or practitioners) to couple individual and context in manners that enhance the probability of change for the better, of promoting more positive features of human development (Lerner, 2002, 2004; Lerner et al., 2009).

There are an enormous number of individual and contextual changes characterizing the adolescent period. Moreover, in adolescence, the individual has the cognitive, behavioral, and social relational skills to contribute actively and often effectively to his/her own developmental changes (Lerner, 1982; Lerner & Busch-Rossnagel, 1981; Lerner & Walls, 1999). Accordingly, adolescence is an ideal "ontogenetic laboratory" for studying the plasticity of human development and for exploring how coupling individual and contexts within the developmental system may promote positive development during this period.

III. The Study of Adolescence within the Relational, Developmental System

Multiple dimensions of profound changes are prototypic of the adolescent period, involving levels of organization ranging from the physical and physiological, through the cognitive, emotional, and behavioral, and to the social relational and institutional. As already noted, plasticity represents a fundamental strength of the adolescent period (Lerner, 2005, 2009), in that it reflects the potential that systematic changes may result in more positive functioning. Indeed, if adaptive developmental regulations emerge or can be fostered between the plastic, developing young person and features of his context (e.g., the structure and function of his/her family, school, peer group, and community), then the likelihood will increase that youth may thrive (i.e., manifest healthy, positive developmental changes) across the adolescent decade.

Indeed, predicated on developmental systems theory, the links among the ideas of plasticity, adaptive developmental regulations, and thriving suggest that all young people have strengths that may be capitalized on to promote thriving across the adolescent years. For instance, one example of the emerging strengths of adolescents is their ability to contribute intentionally to the adaptive developmental regulations with their context (Gestsdóttir & Lerner, 2008). Such intentional self-regulation may involve the selection of positive goals (e.g., choosing goals that reflect important life purposes), using cognitive and behavioral skills (such as executive functioning or resource recruitment) to optimize the chances of actualizing ones purposes and, when goals are blocked or when initial attempts at optimization fail, possessing the capacity to compensate effectively (Baltes & Baltes, 1990; Freund & Baltes, 2002).

Simply, through the lens of relational, developmental systems theory, it is possible to assert that youth represent "resources to be developed" (Roth & Brooks-Gunn, 2003a,b). Increasingly, this strength-based view of adolescents has been used to study PYD within the United States (e.g., Lerner et al., 2009) and internationally (e.g., Gestsdóttir & Lerner, 2007; Silbereisen & Lerner, 2007). As we have noted, this research has been framed at a "meta-level" by the ideas of individual ↔ context relations of focus within relational, developmental systems models; in addition, this research has been influenced by interest in the characteristics of PYD that emerge from this relational process, by the individual and ecological bases of the development of these characteristics, and by interest in theoretically expected outcomes of the PYD process, for example, youth community contribution or AEC (e.g., Zaff et al., 2010).

Together, these interests by scholars in the PYD process reflect the first emphasis within the PYD field that was identified by Hamilton (1999). Accordingly, it is useful to discuss in more detail the relational, developmental systems theory-based conception of the thriving process across adolescence.

IV. The PYD Developmental Process Focuses on Individual ↔ Context Relations

There are several different theoretical views of the PYD process (e.g., Baltes et al., 2006; Benson, 2008; Damon, 2004, 2008; Eccles, 2004; Eccles & Wigfield, 2002; Larson, 2000; Lerner, 2004, 2005; Masten, 2001; Spencer, 2006; see also Lerner et al., 2009). However, as we have noted, these conceptions of PYD share, at the metatheoretical level, an emphasis on relational, developmental system's thinking and an interest in adaptive individual ↔ context relations. The model of the PYD process used by Lerner et al. (2005, in press) explicitly draws on this relational conception. Accordingly, to illustrate the role of this individual ↔ context relational view of the PYD process within the PYD field, we draw on the Lerner and Lerner model and, as well, on the research they have conducted that is pertinent to it.

Lerner, Lerner, and colleagues have conducted longitudinal research—the 4-H Study of PYD (e.g., Lerner et al., 2005)—that seeks to identify the individual and ecological relations that may promote thriving and that, as well, may have a preventive effect in regard to risk/problem behaviors. Within the 4-H Study, thriving is seen as the growth of attributes that mark a flourishing, healthy young person, for example, the characteristics termed the "Five Cs" of PYD—competence, confidence, character, connection, and caring (Eccles & Gootman, 2002; Lerner et al., 2005; Roth & Brooks-Gunn, 2003a,b). A key hypothesis tested in this approach to the developmental process of PYD is that, if:

(a) the strengths of youth (e.g., a young person's cognitive, emotional, and behavioral engagement with the school context, having the "virtue" of hope for the future, or possession of the intentional self-regulation skills of Selection [S], Optimization [O], and Compensation [C] (SOC));

(b) can be aligned with the resources for positive growth found in families, schools, and communities—for instance, the capacities of adults to provide for young people a nurturing, positive milieu in which their strengths may be enhanced and positively directed (e.g., DuBois & Rhodes, 2006; Karcher, Davis, & Powell, 2002; Lewin-Bizan, Bowers, & Lerner, 2010; Rhodes & Lowe, 2009);

(c) then young people's healthy development may be optimized (Lerner, 2004).

In addition, given that positively developing youth should be involved in adaptive developmental regulations, then a thriving young person should act to contribute to the context that is benefiting him or her; there should be contributions to self, family, community, and civil society (Jelicic, Bobek, Phelps, Lerner, & Lerner, 2007; Lerner et al., 2005). In other words, if positive development rests on mutually beneficial relations between the adolescent and his/her ecology, then thriving youth should be positively engaged with and act to enhance their world. As well, they should be less prone to engage in risk/problem behaviors. Figure 1 presents an illustration of the Lerner and Lerner conception of the PYD developmental process.

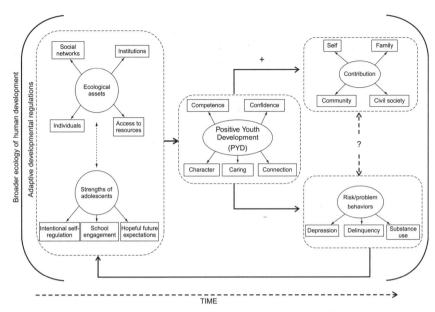

Fig. 1. The relational, developmental systems model of the individual ↔ context relations involved in PYD used by Lerner et al. (2005, in press).

As indicated in the figure, the developmental process envisioned by Lerner and Lerner (e.g., Lerner et al., 2005) to be involved in PYD involves adaptive developmental regulations between the strengths of youth and the developmental assets present in their ecologies. These mutually beneficial individual ↔ context relations are depicted as being associated with PYD (and the Five Cs associated with this construct) and, in turn, with the enhanced probability of youth contributions to their ecology and with lowered probabilities of risk/program behaviors. The outcomes of these adaptive developmental regulations feed back to the individual and his/her context and thus create a nonrecursive basis for further adaptive developmental regulations. The figure illustrates as well that these adaptive developmental regulations and their positive and problematic sequelae exist within the broader ecology of human development. This ecology includes cultural and, as well, historical (temporal) variation, and thus introduces change at all levels of organization within the developmental system (Bronfenbrenner & Morris, 2006; Elder, 1998). Such changes are manifested by intraindividual change, by interindividual differences in intraindividual change, and by normative and nonnormative contextual variation (Baltes et al., 1977).

These facets of the PYD developmental process represented in Figure 1 may be used to summarize the contributions to this volume, contributions that reflect the range of scholarship involved in the contemporary study of PYD. The chapters reflect scholarship that focuses on different components of the model of the PYD process illustrated in Figure 1. Nevertheless, all chapters provide evidence about the empirical usefulness of the PYD perspective and discuss how—in the areas of youth development of concern within a given chapter—research consistent with the model has important implications for both adolescent development research and for the application of developmental science.

V. An Overview of this Volume

The foreground of several chapters in this volume focuses on the strengths that youth bring to the individual ↔ context relations that constitute the basic, relational process of development within the model depicted in Figure 1. Napolitano, Bowers, and Gestsdóttir discuss the role of intentional self-regulation skills in promoting thriving in adolescence. Focusing on the intentional self-regulation model of SOC that was developed by Baltes, Freund, and colleagues (e.g., Baltes, 1997; Baltes & Baltes, 1990; Baltes et al., 2006; Freund & Baltes, 2002), Napolitano et al. review research that indicates that, at particular points within adolescence, one or more of the skills involved in SOC combine with assets in the ecology of youth to put youth on positive developmental trajectories. To illustrate the potential use of these data for promoting positive development, Napolitano et al. describe their preliminary work in "translating" findings about the links between SOC skills and PYD into tools (e.g., rubrics) that mentors, coaches, or teachers may use to foster both intentional self-regulation skills and thriving among diverse youth.

Selection of positive goals is one key manifestation of the adaptive use of SOC skills in adolescence. Such selections reflect that adolescents possess purposes that engage them positively with their ecology. Mariano and Going discuss the nature of youth purpose and review research that shows that many young people develop their potentialities in conjunction with a positive purpose in life. Their interest is in examining a more positive, agency-inclusive, and individual ↔context relational view of purpose. Although this view has generally been neglected in the youth development literature, Mariano and Going describe their research and the work of Damon and colleagues (e.g., Damon, 2004, 2008; Damon, Menon, & Bronk, 2003) in providing theory and research documenting the power of such a conception. Accordingly, Mariano and Going discuss purpose as a tool, or medium, through which adolescents can employ their distinct talents, gifts, interests, and strengths in the adaptive developmental regulations we discussed earlier.

Intentional self-regulation skills and the possession of positive purposes are necessary components of youth contributions to adaptive developmental regulations. However, they are not sufficient. Two chapters in this volume address the issue of the motivational characteristics that need to be present among youth for either the use of the self-regulation skills they possess or the actions required to pursue their positive purposes. Schmid and Lopez discuss the role of hope in adolescents' constructions of their futures, of their acting to engage their contexts in ways that place them on pathways toward positive adulthoods. Without hope for the future, there would be little rationale for the adolescent to articulate a positive purpose or to pursue it through enacting his/her intentional self-regulation skills. Accordingly, Schmid and Lopez discuss hope as an emotional concomitant of intentional self-regulation and present theory and research that points to links between hope, PYD, and youth contributions to their communities. In turn, Larson and Rusk present and evaluate the idea that intrinsic motivation is a powerful engine of development and learning. Without such motivation, youth would only be directed into actions through extrinsic factors, and there would be at best only a low probability that adaptive developmental regulations predicated on purpose and hope would be prominent parts of the developmental repertoire of youth. As such, Larson and Rusk synthesize research from different conceptual paradigms (theories of interest, self-determination, flow, effectance motivation, and mastery orientation) into a composite conception of intrinsic motivation as a single psychological system: a system that can mobilize positive development. In a sense, their chapter constitutes a conceptual umbrella for the ideas presented by Napolitano et al., Mariano and Going, and Schmid and Lopez in regard to the intrinsic (person-centered) characteristics of youth involved in adaptive individual ↔ context relations.

If the strengths of youth—for instance, their positive purposes, their hopes for the future, their intentional self-regulation skills, and their intrinsic motivations—are used in adaptive developmental regulations, then young people effectively engage their contexts in ways that support both them and their settings. A key setting of youth is schools, in that school engagement is critical for youth to draw from the context those resources that enable them to attain the knowledge and skills needed to traverse positive paths across adolescence and into adulthood (and therefore to become productive citizens who maintain and perpetuate the institutions of society—such as schools). In a sense then, school engagement is an instance of how the strengths of youth coalesce to enable the young person to thrive in (and ultimately contribute to) a key setting of his/her life. Accordingly, Li describes why, from a relational, developmental systems perspective, focusing on school engagement is important for understanding the adaptive individual ↔ context relations that are fundamental to human development. In addition, she explains why it is important to fuse behavior, emotion, and cognition in conceptualizing school engagement. She presents theory and research that documents the importance of all three components of school engagement in the promotion of PYD. Moreover, she presents evidence that characteristics of cognitive, emotional, and behavioral school engagement are inversely related to problematic youth development. As such, she proposes promising directions for future research and application.

Constructs other than school engagement reflect the dynamic relation between the developing adolescent and the institutions of his/her world. Indisputably, across the USA and around the world, a ubiquitous instance of such individual ↔ context relations is reflected in the spirituality and religiosity of individuals, that is, of the cognitive, emotional, and behavioral features of individual functioning that may be involved in a young person's sense of spirituality (e.g., of transcendence), of his or her religiosity, and of engagement with cultural and religious concepts of the sacred and with religious institutions. King, Carr, and Boitor discuss these ideas. They note that youth are engaged at high rates in religion and with issues of spirituality. They review the different conceptions that exist of youth spirituality and religiosity and, as well, they discuss the data that exist about the individual and contextual conditions through which spirituality and religiosity place young people on a thriving pathway.

Many of the chapters in this volume put the strengths of youth into the foreground of their presentations; other chapters focus on the individual ↔ context relations involved in engagement with schools or community programs, or in respect to the roles of spirituality and religiosity, pertaining to thriving. However, still other chapters in this volume focus on features of the ecology that, in integration with the strengths of the person, create the adaptive individual ↔ context relations that constitute the basic, relational process of development within the model depicted in Figure 1. The chapter by Benson, Scales, and Syvertsen epitomizes this focus.

Across several decades, Benson and his colleagues at Search Institute have presented foundational theory and research that stresses that both individuals and their ecologies have strengths that foster thriving. As noted earlier in this chapter, these strengths are termed "developmental assets," and Benson et al. describe past and recent research at Search Institute that documents that when the strengths of youth are integrated with the developmental assets of their ecology, youth thrive. Benson et al. point also to the important implications of their research for applications that, through the enhancement of the presence of developmental assets, can promote positive development among diverse young people living within diverse communities.

One of the key ecological developmental assets identified by Benson et al. is OST programs. Mueller, Lewin-Bizan, and Urban discuss theory and research that underscores that involvement by youth in OST activities is an asset in the development of youth. They describe the links among activity involvement, the strengths of youth (for instance, related to intentional self-regulation skills), and PYD. They present a model that both organizes existing research and points to areas that require new or further study. In addition, they discuss the role of OST involvement in applications designed to enhance thriving in adolescence.

In contemporary society, a growing and seemingly ubiquitous facet of youth activity is engagement with media. Reviewing the literature that documents the growing presence of the use of media among youth, Boyd and Dobrow explore the links among media literacy, PYD, and a key outcome of the adaptive individual ↔ context relations that are associated with PYD, that is, youth community contribution, as exemplified by civic engagement. Boyd and Dobrow discuss issues involved in promoting PYD and media literacy in the home as well as in educational and extracurricular settings. They consider how media literacy about news might become an important indicator of PYD as a significant predictor of civic engagement among young people.

As noted in regard to the chapter by Boyd and Dobrow, and as illustrated in the model of the PYD process presented in Figure 1, contribution to the community, as instantiated for instance through AEC, is a key, positive outcome of the development of PYD. Accordingly, Zaff, Kawashima-Ginsberg, and Lin present a model of AEC and explain how this concept integrates motivation to be engaged civically, civic participation, social connection, and self-efficacy in regard to civic contributions. They use a relational, developmental systems approach to argue that information about civic functioning can no longer focus primarily on Western democracies. They emphasize that culturally relevant civic measures need to be developed. In addition, they discuss the ways that civic engagement can be encouraged across a breadth of contexts.

Across the chapters in this volume, all authors point to the implications of theory and research about PYD for applications to programs or policies. The chapter by Baber and Rainer switches field and ground and presents an example of the implementation of a PYD model within an actual program, that is, a therapeutic boarding school, Shortridge

Academy in New Hampshire. Shortridge is private and residential and includes both clinical and academic services, thereby providing a setting where a PYD-framed approach can be pervasively instituted into the environment of the students' day-to-day lives. Reflecting the integration of the youth with all facets of his/her ecology, and an interest in building sustained, adaptive developmental regulations, education, and support for parents are integral parts of the school's agenda. Baber and Rainer note that the PYD-based ecology present at Shortridge Academy increases the likelihood of greater consistency in students' interactions at school and in their families, and has been shown to promote positive change in the youth.

Finally, across the chapters in this volume, authors have pointed to the importance of research that integrates individual and contexts in manners that may elucidate the individual $\leftrightarrow$ context relations fundamental to the model of the PYD process. Such research rests on using methods that afford such integration within the context of studying changes in these relations. These relational and change-sensitive analyses may require innovations in developmental methodology, and as such, von Eye, Martel, Lerner, Lerner, and Bowers use a study of gender specificity and of longitudinal stability of the SOC intentional self-regulation skills to illustrate the nature of such methodological innovations in research about the PYD process. A key point made by von Eye and his colleagues is that both person-centered and variable-centered methods may need to be integrated in order to understand the complex individual $\leftrightarrow$ context relations involved in thriving across adolescence.

VI. Conclusions

The chapters in this volume provide support for the use of a relational, developmental systems theory-based, PYD perspective in framing research that enhances understanding of the intricacies of individual $\leftrightarrow$ context relations, relations that—when mutually beneficial to both individual and context—put young people on a thriving journey across the adolescent period. Moreover, as readers review the scholarship included in this volume, they will find considerable evidence in support of the ideas that there is a diversity of youth strengths and of ecological developmental assets that may be integrated: To foster PYD; to enhance the likelihood of the contributions of youth, such as AEC; and to decrease the likelihood of risk/problem behaviors.

As the theory-predicated research presented in this volume continues to evolve, and as other work pertinent to the study and enhancement of

PYD continues (Lerner, et al., in press), developmental science will become increasing able to specify what sorts of individual and contextual resources need to be linked to maximize the probability that all young people will be given a greater chance to thrive. As such, in underscoring the vital connection between research and application, the chapters in this volume pertain to another, larger point associated with the PYD perspective. The potential to change youth development for the better—a potential illustrated by the findings reported in this volume—is a reason for all people concerned with the health and welfare of adolescents to be optimistic that evidence-based actions can be taken to enhance the chances for thriving among all young people.

These actions will of course require the collaboration of researchers and practitioners. Our hope is that the scholarship presented in this volume will further the progress of such collaborations. If so, then the three goals of the developmental science of adolescence (Baltes et al., 1977)—that is, to describe, to explain, and to optimize youth development—will be advanced by the work of the colleagues contributing to this volume. Our hope is also that this volume will be regarded by members of the PYD field as facilitating such advances.

Acknowledgment

The preparation of this chapter was supported in part by grants from the National 4-H Council and the Thrive Foundation for Youth.

REFERENCES

Baltes, P. B. (1997). On the incomplete architecture of human ontogeny: Selection, optimization, and compensation as foundations of developmental theory. *The American Psychologist, 52*, 366–380.

Baltes, P. B., & Baltes, M. M. (1990). Psychological perspectives on successful aging: The model of selective optimization with compensation. In P. B. Baltes & M. M. Baltes (Eds.), *Successful aging: Perspectives from the behavioral sciences.* (pp. 1–34). New York: Cambridge University Press.

Baltes, P. B., Lindenberger, U., & Staudinger, U. M. (2006). Lifespan Theory in Developmental Psychology. In W. Damon & R. M. Lerner (Editors-in-chief) & R. M. Lerner (Ed.), *Theoretical models of human development. Handbook of child psychology* (Vol. 1), Hoboken, NJ: Wiley.

Baltes, P. B., Reese, H. W., & Nesselroade, J. R. (1977). *Life-span developmental psychology: Introduction to research methods.* Monterey, CA: Brooks/Cole.

Benson, P. L. (2008). *Sparks: How parents can help ignite the hidden strengths of teenagers.* San Francisco, CA: Jossey-Bass.

Benson, P. L., Scales, P. C., Hamilton, S. F., & Semsa, A. Jr., (2006). Positive youth development: Theory, research, and applications. In R. M. Lerner (Ed.), *Theoretical models of human development. Handbook of child psychology* (6th ed., Vol. 1). Hoboken, NJ: Wiley.

Brandtstädter, J. (1998). Action perspectives on human development. In W. Damon & R. M. Lerner (Eds.), *Handbook of child psychology: Vol. 1. Theoretical models of human development.* (5th ed., pp. 807–863). New York: Wiley.

Brandtstädter, J. (1999). The self in action and development: Cultural, biosocial, and ontogenetic bases of intentional self-development. In J. Brandtstädter & R. M. Lerner (Eds.), *Action and self-development: Theory and research through the life-span.* (pp. 37–65). Thousand Oaks, CA: Sage.

Brandtstädter, J. (2006). Action perspectives on human development. In W. Damon & R. M. Lerner (Editors-in-chief) & R. M. Lerner (Ed.), *Theoretical models of human development. Handbook of child psychology* (6th ed., Vol. 1). Hoboken, NJ: Wiley.

Bronfenbrenner, U., & Morris, P. A. (2006). The bioecological model of human development. In W. Damon & R. M. Lerner (Editors-in-chief) & R. M. Lerner (Ed.), *Theoretical models of human development. Handbook of child psychology* (6th ed., Vol. 1). Hoboken, NJ: Wiley.

Catalano, R. F., Berglund, M. L., Ryan, J. A. M., Lonczak, H. S., & Hawkins, J. D. (2004). Positive youth development in the United States: Research findings on evaluations of youth development programs. *The Annals of the American Academy of Political and Social Science, 591*(Special issue), 98–124. Positive Development: Realizing the Potential of Youth.

Catalano, R. P., Hawkins, J. D., Berglund, M. L., Pollard, J. A., & Arthur, M. W. (2002). Prevention science and positive youth development: Competitive or cooperative frameworks? *The Journal of Adolescent Health, 31*, 230–239.

Damon, W. (2004). What is positive youth development? *The Annals of the American Academy of Political and Social Science, 591*, 13–24.

Damon, W. (2008). *The path to purpose: Helping our children find their calling in life.* New York, NY: Free Press, Simon & Schuster, Inc.

Damon, W., Menon, J., & Bronk, K. C. (2003). The development of purpose during adolescence. *Applied Developmental Science, 7*(3), 119–128.

DuBois, D., & Rhodes, J. (2006). Introduction to the special issue: Youth mentoring: Bridging science with practice. *Journal of Community Psychology, 34*(6), 647–655.

Eccles, J. S. (2004). Schools, academic motivation, and stage-environment fit. In R. M. Lerner & L. Steinberg (Eds.), *Handbook of adolescent psychology.* (2nd ed., pp. 125–153). Hoboken, NJ: John Wiley & Sons, Inc.

Eccles, J., & Gootman, J. (Eds.), (2002). *Community programs to promote youth development.* Washington, DC: National Academy Press.

Eccles, J. S., & Wigfield, A. (2002). Motivational beliefs, values, and goals. *Annual Review of Psychology, 53*, 109–132.

Elder, G. H., Jr. (1998). The life course and human development. In W. Damon (Series Ed.) & R. M. Lerner (Vol. Ed.), *Handbook of child psychology: Vol. 1 Theoretical models of human development* (5th ed., pp. 939–991). New York: Wiley.

Elder, G. H., Jr.,& Shanahan, M. J. (2006). The life course and human development. In W. Damon & R. M. Lerner (Editors-in-chief) & R. M. Lerner (Ed.), *Theoretical models of human development. Handbook of child psychology* (6th ed., Vol. 1). Hoboken, NJ: Wiley.

Flay, B. R. (2002). Positive youth development requires comprehensive health promotion programs. *American Journal of Health Behavior, 26*(6), 407–424.

Flay, B. R., & Allred, C. G. (2003). Long term effects of the *Positive Action* program. *American Journal of Health Behavior, 27*(1), S6–S21.

Ford, D. H., & Lerner, R. M. (1992). *Developmental systems theory: An integrative approach.* Newbury Park, CA: Sage Publications.

Freund, A. M., & Baltes, P. B. (2002). Life-management strategies of selection, optimization and compensation: Measurement by self-report and construct validity. *Journal of Personality and Social Psychology, 82,* 642–662.

Gestsdóttir, S., & Lerner, R. M. (2007). Hlutverk sjálfstjórnar í æskilegum þroska barna og unglinga. *Sálfræðiritið, 12,* 37–55.

Gestsdóttir, G., & Lerner, R. M. (2008). Positive development in adolescence: The development and role of intentional self regulation. *Human Development, 51,* 202–224.

Gottlieb, G. (1997). *Synthesizing nature-nurture: Prenatal roots of instinctive behavior.* Mahwah, NJ: Erlbaum.

Gottlieb, G. (1998). Normally occurring environmental and behavioral influences on gene activity: From central dogma to probabilistic epigenesis. *Psychological Review, 105,* 792–802.

Gray, C. (in press). Invited commentary: A practitioner's view. *Journal of Adolescence.*

Hamilton, S. (1999). *A three-part definition of youth development.* Ithaca, NY: Cornell University College of Human Ecology. Unpublished manuscript.

Heckhausen, J. (1999). *Developmental regulation in adulthood: Age-normative and sociostructural constraints as adaptive challenges.* New York, NY: Cambridge University Press.

Heckhausen, J. (Ed.), (2000). *Motivational psychology of human development: Developing motivation and motivating development.* In: *Advances in psychology* (Vol. 131), New York, NY: Elsevier Science.

Jelicic, H., Bobek, D., Phelps, E. D., Lerner, J. V., & Lerner, R. M. (2007). Using positive youth development to predict contribution and risk behaviors in early adolescence: Findings from the first two waves of the 4-H Study of Positive Youth Development. *International Journal of Behavioral Development, 31*(3), 263–273.

Karcher, M., Davis, C., & Powell, B. (2002). The effects of developmental mentoring on connectedness and academic achievement. *The School Community Journal, 12*(2), 35–50.

Kurtines, W. M., Ferrer-Wreder, L., Berman, S. L., Lorente, C. C., Silverman, W. K., & Montgomery, M. J. (2008). Promoting positive youth development: New directions in developmental theory, methods, and research. *Journal of Adolescence Research, 23*(3), 233–244.

Larson, R. W. (2000). Towards a psychology of positive youth development. *The American Psychologist, 55,* 170–183.

Lerner, J. V., Phelps, E., Forman, Y., & Bowers, E. P. (2009). Positive youth development. In R. M. Lerner & L. Steinberg (Eds.), *Handbook of adolescent psychology: Vol. 1. Individual bases of adolescent development.* (3rd ed., pp. 524–558). Hoboken, NJ: Wiley.

Lerner, R. M. (1982). Children and adolescents as producers of their own development. *Developmental Review, 2,* 342–370.

Lerner, R. M. (1984). *On the nature of human plasticity.* New York: Cambridge University Press.

Lerner, R. M. (2002). *Concepts and theories of human development* Mahwah, NJ: Erlbaum.

Lerner, R. M. (2004). *Liberty: Thriving and civic engagement among American youth.* Thousand Oaks, CA: Sage.

Lerner, R. M. (2005). *Promoting Positive Youth Development: Theoretical and Empirical Bases.* Washington, DC: National Academies of Science White paper prepared for the Workshop on the Science of Adolescent Health and Development, National Research Council/Institute of Medicine.

Lerner, R. M. (2009). The positive youth development perspective: Theoretical and empirical bases of a strength-based approach to adolescent development. In C. R. Snyder & S. J. Lopez (Eds.), *Oxford handbook of positive psychology*. (2nd ed., pp. 149–163). Oxford, England: Oxford University Press.

Lerner, R. M., & Busch-Rossnagel, N. A. (Eds.), (1981). *Individuals as producers of their development: A life-span perspective*. New York: Academic Press.

Lerner, R. M., Lerner, J. V., Almerigi, J., Theokas, C., Phelps, E., Gestsdóttir, S., et al. (2005). Positive youth development, participation in community youth development programs, and community contributions of fifth Grade adolescents: Findings from the first wave of the 4-H Study of Positive Youth Development. *Journal of Early Adolescence*, *25*(1), 17–71.

Lerner, R. M., & Overton, W. F. (2008). Exemplifying the integrations of the relational developmental system: Synthesizing theory, research, and application to promote positive development and social justice. *Journal of Adolescent Research*, *23*(3), 245–255.

Lerner, R. M., & Walls, T. (1999). Revisiting individuals as producers of their development: From dynamic interactionism to developmental systems. In J. Brandtstädter & R. M. Lerner (Eds.), *Action and self-development: Theory and research through the life-span*. (pp. 3–36). Thousand Oaks, CA: Sage.

Lerner, R. M., Lerner, J. V., Lewin-Bizan, S., Bowers, E. P., Boyd, M. J., Mueller, M. K., Schmid, K. L., & Napolitano, C. M. (in press). Positive youth development: Processes, programs, and problematics. *Journal of Youth Development: Bridging Research and Practice*.

Lewin-Bizan, S., Bowers, E., & Lerner, R. M. (2010). One good thing leads to another: Cascades of positive youth development among American adolescents. *Development and Psychopathology*, *22*, 759–770.

Magnusson, D. (1999). Holistic interactionism: A perspective for research on personality development. In L. Pervin & O. John (Eds.), *Handbook of personality: Theory and research*. (2nd ed., pp. 219–247). New York, NY: Guilford Press.

Magnusson, D., & Stattin, H. (1998). Person-context interaction theories. In W. Damon & R. M. Lerner (Eds.), *Handbook of child psychology: Vol. 1: Theoretical models of human development*. (5th ed., pp. 685–759). Hoboken, NJ: John Wiley & Sons Inc.

Magnusson, D., & Stattin, H. (2006). The person in the environment: Towards a general model for scientific inquiry. In W. Damon & R. M. Lerner (Editors-in-chief) & R. M. Lerner (Ed.), *Theoretical models of human development. Handbook of child psychology* (6th ed., Vol. 1). Hoboken, NJ: Wiley.

Masten, A. S. (2001). Ordinary magic: Resilience processes in development. *The American Psychologist*, *56*, 227–238.

Overton, W. F. (2010). Life-span development: Concepts and issues. In R. M. Lerner & W. F. Overton (Eds.), *The handbook of life-span development: Vol. 1. Cognition, biology, and methods*. (pp. 1–29). Hoboken, NJ: Wiley.

Rhodes, J., & Lowe, S. (2009). Mentoring in adolescence. In R. M. Lerner & L. Steinberg (Eds.), *Contextual influences on adolescent development. Handbook of adolescent psychology* (3rd ed., Vol. 2, pp. 152–190). Hoboken, NJ: John Wiley & Sons Inc.

Roth, J. L., & Brooks-Gunn, J. (2003a). What is a youth development program? Identification and defining principles. In F. Jacobs, D. Wertlieb & R. M. Lerner (Eds.), *Enhancing the life chances of youth and families: Public service systems and public policy perspectives: Vol. 2 Handbook of applied developmental science: Promoting positive child, adolescent, and family development through research, policies, and programs* (pp. 197–223). Thousand Oaks, CA: Sage.

Roth, J. L., & Brooks-Gunn, J. (2003b). What exactly is a youth development program? Answers from research and practice. *Applied Developmental Science, 7,* 94–111.

Silbereisen, R. K., & Lerner, R. M. (Eds.), (2007). *Approaches to positive youth development.* London: Sage Publications.

Spencer, M. B. (2006). Phenomenology and ecological systems theory: Development of diverse groups. In W. Damon (Series Ed.) & R. M. Lerner (Vol. Ed.), *Handbook of child psychology: Vol. 1. Theoretical models of human development* (6th ed., 829–893). Hoboken, NJ: John Wiley & Sons.

Thelen, E., & Smith, L. B. (1998). Dynamic systems theories. In W. Damon & R. M. Lerner (Eds.), *Theoretical models of human development. Handbook of child psychology* (5th ed., Vol. 1, pp. 563–634). Hoboken, NJ: John Wiley and Sons Inc.

Thelen, E., & Smith, L. B. (2006). Dynamic systems theories. In W. Damon & R. M. Lerner (Editors-in-chief) & R. M. Lerner (Ed.), *Theoretical models of human development. Handbook of child psychology.* Hoboken, NJ: Wiley.

Zaff, J., Boyd, M., Li, Y., Lerner, J. V., & Lerner, R. M. (2010). Active and engaged citizenship: Multi-group and longitudinal factorial analysis of an integrated construct of civic engagement. *Journal of Youth and Adolescence, 39*(7), 736–750.

THE DEVELOPMENT OF INTENTIONAL SELF-REGULATION IN ADOLESCENCE: DESCRIBING, EXPLAINING, AND OPTIMIZING ITS LINK TO POSITIVE YOUTH DEVELOPMENT

Christopher M. Napolitano,* Edmond P. Bowers,* Steinunn Gestsdóttir,[†] and Paul A. Chase*

* ELIOT-PEARSON DEPARTMENT OF CHILD DEVELOPMENT, TUFTS UNIVERSITY, MEDFORD, MASSACHUSETTS, USA

[†] SCHOOL OF EDUCATION, UNIVERSITY OF ICELAND, REYKJAVÍK, ICELAND

Abstract

Intentional self-regulation (ISR) skills are key assets promoting healthy and positive development across the life span. In this chapter, we describe the development of ISR in adolescence, offer explanations for the development of these skills and their relation to positive youth development among diverse youth in diverse contexts, and provide suggestions for future research and programs seeking to optimize youth outcomes through the promotion of ISR skills. Primarily drawing from data from the 4-H Study of Positive Youth Development, we discuss research using the Selection,

Advances in Child Development and Behavior

Richard M. Lerner, Jacqueline V. Lerner and Janette B. Benson : Editors

Optimization, and Compensation model of Baltes, Freund and colleagues, measures of which have been linked to a variety of positive developmental outcomes in adolescence. In addition to providing a review of the literature and relevant recent research, an applied program designed to promote ISR — termed Project GPS — is also discussed.

I. Introduction

Evidence from several fields suggests that intentional self-regulatory, or goal-directed, skills become especially important to healthy development during adolescence (e.g., Cunha & Heckman, 2007; Cunha, Heckman, & Schennach, 2010; Freund & Baltes, 2002; Gestsdóttir & Lerner, 2007, 2008; Lerner, Freund, De Stefanis, & Habermas, 2001; Perels, Dignath, & Schmitz, 2009). The emergence of the particular salience of intentional self-regulation (ISR) during adolescence is grounded in the dynamic nature of the multifaceted changes that mark the second decade of life. Such changes include the development of the prefrontal cortex (Paus, 2009), the emergence of new drive states (Freud, 1969; Susman & Dorn, 2009), and cognitive changes, such as an expanded ability to engage in metacognitions (Kuhn, 2009), and an increased prioritization of values and a refinement of long-term planning skills (Brandtstädter, 1989; Keating, 2004; McClelland, Ponitz, Messersmith, & Tominey, 2010). This suite of structural and functional changes provides the foundations for the importance of ISR in adolescence (Geldhof, Little, & Colombo, 2010).

At the same time, contextual changes typical in Western societies emphasize adolescents' need to develop and effectively employ their ISR skills. These changes include school transitions (e.g., Eccles & Roeser, 2009), increased relevance of peer pressure for risk taking (e.g., Gardner & Steinberg, 2005), access to drugs and alcohol (Johnston, O'Malley, Bachman, & Schulenberg, 2009), initiation of sexual activity (Diamond & Savin-Williams, 2009), and exposure to serendipitous events (Bandura, 1982, 1998; Krumboltz, 2009; Rand & Cheavens, 2009). Just as ISR skills are important assets during other periods of the life span characterized by marked contextual changes (e.g., Jopp & Smith, 2006; Wiese, Freund, & Baltes, 2002), they are also important for healthy, positive development during adolescence (Gestsdóttir & Lerner, 2008; Lerner et al., 2001).

As such, the purpose of this chapter is to describe the development of ISR in adolescence, and in turn, to depict how an adolescent's ISR is related to his or her thriving, as characterized by mutually beneficial, person ↔ context relations termed adaptive developmental regulations (Brandtstädter, 1998,

2006). To accomplish this goal, we first operationalize ISR through each of its component words—intentionality, the self, and regulation. We use a developmental systems-based, action–theoretical lens for these definitions (Brandtstädter, 2006). We then review the literature about ISR in adolescence, with a particular focus on the model of Selection, Optimization, and Compensation (SOC; Baltes, 1997; Freund & Baltes, 2002). We next discuss research that relates an adolescent's SOC skills to his or her levels of positive development, as indexed by a measure of the Five Cs Model of Positive Youth Development (PYD; Lerner et al., 2005; Lerner, Phelps, Forman, & Bowers, 2009). We then discuss Project GPS, a recently launched initiative to translate the research findings about SOC skills into useful tools for promoting ISR through mentoring. We conclude this chapter with a discussion of some current limitations to the study of ISR in adolescence, specifically focusing on issues of methodology and theory. We offer suggestions for future work.

II. Adolescent Intentional Self-regulation: Operationalization and Theoretical Context

There is a substantial theoretical and empirical literature regarding the development of ISR across the life span, including conceptualizations or operationalizations of the self-controlled actions of children (e.g., Kochanska, Murray, & Harlan, 2000; Mischel, Shoda, & Rodriguez, 1989), the goal-directedness of adults (e.g., Carver & Scheier, 1981; Heckhausen, 1997), and the resource-loss minimization of the elderly (e.g., Baltes & Baltes, 1990; Baltes, Lindenberger, & Staudinger, 2006). To date, however, there is comparatively less ISR work focusing on adolescents (e.g., Gestsdóttir & Lerner, 2008; Moilanen, Shaw, & Fitzpatrick, 2010). Why? Given the above-noted salience of ISR in adolescence, the relative lack of information about the second decade of life is problematic.

A possible reason for the relative paucity of research on adolescent ISR might be due to the still-predominate perspective of adolescence as a time of "storm and stress" (Hall, 1904), developmental disturbance (Freud, 1969), or crisis (Erikson, 1968). Over the past century, theoretical, empirical, and applied work has often viewed adolescence as a period of risk taking, conflict, and difficulties. Positive development during adolescence has typically been conceptualized as the absence of negative behaviors rather than the growth of positive behaviors (Benson, Scales, Hamilton, & Sesma, 2006; Lerner, 2009). Adolescents, within this view, were problems to be managed (Roth & Brooks-Gunn, 2003). The pervasive influence of the "deficit perspective" on research aims, policy, and practice is reflected in the prevalence of measures of risk and problematic behaviors that are most often collected by researchers and by program and service organizations. Rather than identifying and measuring the strengths and skills of youth to make positive choices, and to pursue those goals through adaptive developmental regulations, that is, positive individual ↔ context relations, researchers and practitioners focused on youth substance use, delinquent behavior, and risky sexual practices.

An alternative conception of adolescence has emerged across the past two decades, one that views adolescents as "resources to be developed" (Roth & Brooks-Gunn, 2003). Termed the PYD perspective, this model of adolescent development focuses on the strengths believed to exist among all youth and on how youth thriving can be promoted by aligning youth strengths with ecological developmental assets (Benson et al., 2006; Larson, 2000). Although several versions of the PYD perspective exist, (see Lerner et al., 2009 for a review), this chapter uses the Five Cs Model of PYD (Lerner et al., 2005) because of its prevalence in the literature of youth development (e.g., see Eccles & Gootman, 2002; Roth & Brooks-Gunn, 2003), and discusses in detail, findings from the 4-H Study of PYD, a longitudinal study that assesses the Five Cs Model through data from nearly 7000 youth from Grades 5 through 12 (Bowers et al., 2010; Phelps et al., 2009). Work using this 4-H data set has linked the ISR skills of adolescents to a variety of healthy, positive outcomes (e.g., Gestsdóttir & Lerner, 2007; Gestsdóttir, Bowers, von Eye, Napolitano, & Lerner, 2010; Gestsdóttir, Lewin-Bizan, von Eye, Lerner, & Lerner, 2009) and points to the critical role of ISR as an individual strength involved in the healthy, positive development of adolescents.

To best discuss the development of ISR in adolescence, it is useful to operationalize our use of the term. To do so, we focus on each word in this construct. First, *intentional* actions (or self-regulations) may be distinguished from organismically based actions (or self-regulations; Gestsdóttir & Lerner, 2008). The latter actions (or instances of self-regulation) are the relatively stable, physiologically textured processes, such as digestion, respiration, or circadian rhythms that occur largely outside the realm of self-awareness and are concerned with maintaining or improving functioning throughout the body-as-system (Hooker & McAdams, 2003; Shonkoff & Phillips, 2000). Alternatively, intentional actions occur within the realm of conscious behavior and include goal setting, decision-making, and related behaviors (e.g., strategizing). These actions involve purposeful responses to stimuli and are intrinsically motivated (Geldhof et al., 2010). Intentionality, therefore, is concerned with one's chosen actions.

Given the breadth of research and reviews that have considered the definition of the *self* (e.g., Harter, 2006, 2011; James, 1890), we approach the study of self during adolescence here by focusing on perceptions of the self and on the use of self-definitions as they relate to one's valued goals or purposes (e.g., Lerner et al., 2001). These goals or purposes, contribute to the development of one's identity, that is, a stable, predictable representation of one's behavioral characteristics, interests, values, attitudes, and abilities (Côté, 2009), and influence the development of one's self-perceptions and self-definitions (Lerner et al., 2001). In reference to ISR, then, the self can be defined, in part, through the goals, purposes, and actions that result as a consequence of actions the actor sees as meaningful, important, or valuable.

Finally, *regulation* can be defined as the "rules" governing the organization of emotional, cognitive, or behavioral actions toward some desired end or state within the bounds of specific contextual conditions (Lerner, in press). Regulation is concerned with the organization of a person's actions-in-context. Taking these definitions together, we can define ISR as *an individual's chosen, organized actions-in-context that further self-defined, valued goals or purposes.*

This operationalization is embedded in an action–theoretical perspective. Action theory emphasizes that the individual's actions, and control of those actions, have a chief influence on his or her development (Geldhof et al., 2010). Within an action–theoretical perspective, the individual, through his or her ISR, attempts to influence or adjust elements within the self and/or within the context to promote positive and minimize negative goal-related outcomes (Heckhausen & Schulz, 1995). Rooting our definition of ISR in action theory is important, in that it enables us to envision the individual as having the ability to influence and promote his or her own positive development through his or her actions (Lerner, 1982; Lerner & Busch-Rossnagel, 1981).

This ability to promote one's own development is a central concept in a relational, developmental systems theory (DST) approach (e.g., Overton, 2010). Indeed, this approach frames action theory (Lerner, 2002). DSTs hold that each level of the individual's developmental system is characterized by the interpenetrating, fused influence of every other level. Further, DST holds that mutually influential relations between an individual and his or her context, which we have noted is represented as individual ↔ context relations, create the potential for systemic change (for plasticity) across ontogeny. Such plasticity makes multiple developmental trajectories possible for any individual, given the affordances and constraints present in any developmental system (Lerner, 2006). A DST approach, therefore, is optimistic about the possibility that the actions of the individual and the characteristics of his environment, even if either or both are limited, can be arrayed in ways that may promote healthier, more positive development for an individual.

We began this chapter by explaining why ISR was especially pertinent to adolescence. Consistent with other discussions of ISR that have been framed by DST-based action–theoretical ideas (e.g., Geldhof et al., 2010; McClelland et al., 2010; Chapter 11), we pointed to the fact that the development of ISR in adolescence is especially important because of the major physiological, cognitive, emotional, social, and behavioral, and contextual changes that are emerging during this period (Steinberg, 2011). As do other theorists, we have also noted that ISR skills are *essential* in the successful navigation of these major changes (Lerner et al., 2001). Given these points, recent research has begun to investigate the development of ISR in adolescence. Much of this research utilizes the SOC model (Baltes & Baltes, 1990; Baltes et al., 2006; Freund & Baltes, 2002). We review next the theoretical foundations of this model.

III. The Selection, Optimization, and Compensation Model

The SOC model is one of several key action–theoretical models that describe an individual's attempts to influence his or her positive development through ISR. This model is derived from the work of Baltes and colleagues, who sought to understand the "fundamental pragmatics of life" through the study of an individual's goal-related actions and investments across the life span (Baltes, 1997). The SOC model has been utilized extensively to understand successful aging in adult and elderly populations (e.g., Ebner, Fruend, & Baltes, 2006; Freund & Baltes, 1998; Wiese et al., 2002) and has been proposed as a means to understanding ISR in adolescence as well (Gestsdóttir & Lerner, 2008; Lerner et al., 2001).

Baltes and colleagues proposed that an individual's ISR could be understood through three distinct, but interrelated processes. The first of these processes involves the selection of goals. In giving direction to development, actions must be organized in efforts toward specific goal selections. The SOC model includes two types of these selections. The first, *elective selection* (S) refers to the selection of a goal from a pool of other goals, or alternative developmental pathways (Baltes et al., 2006). An elective selection organizes one's goal-related energies into long-term, goal-based action sequences (Brandtstädter, 2006) that guide and organize one's actions, thereby facilitating efficient interactions within a context (Gestsdóttir & Lerner, 2008). Typical instances of elective selection include the selection of a goal, the setting of a goal system or goal hierarchy, and commitment or energy investment in a goal (Baltes et al., 2006). An example of an elective selection may be choosing to apply for a job at a restaurant to earn extra income, even if the potential job may come at the expense of limited time with friends.

The aims of *loss-based selection* (LBS) are similar to those of elective selection; however, a LBS occurs as a consequence of loss or diminishment of functioning or resources at the individual or contextual level. LBS involves the choices one makes after his or her first goals appear to be permanently blocked. Typical instances of LBS include focusing on the most important goals, adapting personal goal standards, and searching for new goals. An example of LBS might be applying for construction jobs if one cannot find employment in a restaurant.

Simply choosing a goal does not guarantee one's success. Individuals must identify, allocate, refine, and deploy internal and external resources as means or strategies for goal achievement. In other words, *optimization* (O) behaviors are the strategies and resources that individuals use to achieve their goals (Freund & Baltes, 1998). Typical instances of optimization include acquiring new skills/resources; seizing the right moment for action, persistence, practicing skills; and modeling successful others. An example of optimization might be scouring the classified section for job postings, or developing a strong résumé.

Of course, the first choice of optimization strategies may be insufficient for goal attainment. This insufficiency may be due to the strategies themselves being inappropriate or inefficient, or it may occur in relation to the decline of individual or contextual resources. Whatever the reason, the individual must employ new or adapted strategies if he/she wishes to attain a goal. These new strategies are termed *compensation* (C) behaviors, and they differ from LBS in that the individual still strives toward the same (or closely-related) goal. One compensates for a loss through changing strategies toward the same end, rather than changing the goals themselves. Typical instances of compensation include substituting old strategies for new ones, using external aids and/or the help of others, acquiring new skills and/or resources, or increasing effort. An example of compensatory strategies may be to ask a family member or teacher to help practice for a job interview after a first interview went poorly.

IV. Intentional Self-Regulation in Adolescence: Research Finding

We have described that the profound changes that characterize adolescence influence the development and importance of ISR during this period. In addition, we have described the SOC model as a key action–theoretical model of ISR. Freund and Baltes (2002) contended that, through the course of adolescence and early adulthood, individuals refine their SOC skills and begin to show increased preference for SOC-related behaviors in tasks that require ISR. Based on this contention, as well as indications that SOC is potentially applicable to the changes involved in adolescence (Lerner et al., 2001), the literature has recently begun to explore these issues in detail.

Using data from the 4-H Study of PYD, researchers have documented the development of SOC strategies across much of the adolescent period, as well as the relations between an adolescent's levels of SOC and his or her levels of PYD and risk or problem behaviors. In general, these studies suggest that an adolescent's SOC skills undergo significant change throughout adolescence and play an important, positive role in promoting his or her thriving. Initial research indicated that in 5th and 6th graders, SOC existed as a global construct, rather than as the tripartite construct found in adult and aged samples and as described above (Gestsdóttir & Lerner, 2007). This globality of SOC structure suggested that younger adolescents, while still possessing ISR strategies in some capacity, had not yet fully developed the distinct and independent components that comprise the SOC model. Younger adolescents had simply "strong SOC" or "weak SOC," rather than a complex combination of these skills. Results indicated that higher SOC scores were positively related to PYD and negatively related to risk or problem behaviors in 5th, 6th, and 7th graders, and as well, predicted placement in the most-optimal developmental trajectories across the same age range (Gestsdóttir & Lerner, 2007; Zimmerman, Phelps, & Lerner, 2007).

Subsequent research involving the 4-H Study indicated that SOC did exist as a tripartite, differentiated, adult-like construct in adolescents in Grades 8 through 10 (Gestsdóttir et al., 2009). Consistent with Werner's orthogenetic principle (Werner, 1957), which holds in part that development progresses, across life, to states of greater differentiation, older adolescents now presented complex combinations of S, O, and C, and, in other research with Grade 10 youth, LBS behaviors (Gestsdóttir et al., 2010). While overall SOC scores of adolescents from Grades 8 to 10 were positively correlated with PYD, there were differences in relations with PYD when examining the individual components of SOC. That is, high levels of O, C, and LBS—but not S—were strongly associated with PYD (Gestsdóttir et al., 2009, 2010). Studying the influences and outcomes related to these complex patterns of S, O, C, and LBS, development among older adolescents will be an important research project for the coming years.

Some recent examples of this nascent research include investigations of the influence of contextual resources on the relation between SOC (or S, O, C, and LBS separately) and PYD in adolescence. For example, Urban, Lewin-Bizan, and Lerner (2010) found that, within disadvantaged settings, youth aged 12–14 with the highest levels of SOC skills benefited the most from extracurricular activity involvement. These results indicated that only youth with high levels of SOC scores were able to extract the maximum benefit from the proximal contextual resources in their constrained environments. In addition, Napolitano (2010) found that, using a select sample of youth, adolescents from resource-restricted environments, as characterized by lower levels of maternal education and lower levels of family per-capita income, benefited more strongly from having high levels of Selection skills, when compared to their more well-advantaged peers.

It is useful to summarize how the findings from the 4-H Study have informed the literature regarding the development of ISR in adolescence by using the three goals of developmental science (Lerner, 2002), which are to describe, explain, and optimize human behavior and development. What research has *described*—that having high SOC skills is associated with higher PYD—and what some initial, more *explanatory* research has suggested—that contextual factors influence the development and efficacy of SOC strategies, and that high levels of SOC skills may be particularly important in contexts with limited resources—has lead to the development of an applied project which attempts to *optimize* youth outcomes through the improvement of SOC skills through participation in a mentoring program.

V. Applying SOC Research to the Mentoring Context: Project GPS

High-quality, community-based, programmatic youth-serving organizations are regarded as key resources that promote positive development among adolescents (Li, Bebiroglu, Phelps, & Lerner, 2009; Mahoney, Vandell, Simkins, & Zarrett, 2009). Youth-serving organizations that are based in youth mentoring (e.g., Rhodes & Dubois, 2008) may, in particular, provide ISR-building experiences to large numbers of adolescents. Despite the prominence of mentoring programs in the USA (Rhodes & Lowe, 2009), not all programs of this genre are created equal. For instance, the highest quality mentoring programs are characterized by what research labels the "Big Three" (Lerner, 2004); that is, (1) positive and sustained mentor-youth relations (for more than 1 year; Rhodes, 2002); (2) activities that build life skills (such as ISR); and (3) a focus on youth participation in and leadership of valued community activities (Zaff, Hart, Flanagan, Youniss, & Levine, 2010). Programs that incorporate the "Big Three" provide a structured environment and serve as a developmental asset that develops life skills and improves PYD for participating youth (Balsano, Phelps, Theokas, Lerner, & Lerner, 2009; Eccles & Gootman, 2002; Larson, 2000; Mahoney, Larson, Eccles, & Lord, 2005; Chapter 9).

Mentoring programs characterized by the "Big 3" may be ideal settings for the development of ISR in youth. Mentoring may provide structured activities to develop life skills such as ISR through the facilitation of a committed, invested adult mentor (Rhodes & Lowe, 2009). One example of such a structure can be found in the Boy Scouts of America. Starting in Grade 6, boys can enter the Scouts, and they can participate as Scouts until their 18th birthday. The boys are mentored by adult leaders, termed Scoutmasters, who tutor the youth in various outdoor skills (e.g., camping, hiking, archery) and life skills (e.g., personal financial management, public speaking, and leadership). Youth participating in programs that share a similar mentoring profile to Scouting have higher levels of PYD and other positive outcomes (Balsano et al., 2009; Chapter 9).

Given this potential impact of high-quality mentoring programs on the development of an adolescent's ISR, and through a grant from the Thrive Foundation for Youth, a mentoring-based applied project—"Project GPS"—is currently being implemented to develop tools to-be-used by mentors to improve the chances of youth to thrive through the development of their ISR skills. Project GPS is also aimed at allowing researchers to ascertain which characteristics of which mentoring programs best lead to the development of ISR for which adolescents from which contexts.

The core components of Project GPS are based on a translation of SOC theory and research into appropriate, useful tools for youth development programs. The project uses the metaphor of a car's GPS navigation system—you "choose your destination" and the GPS (your SOC skills in this case) provides "strategies" to arrive at your destination (in this case, at achieving a goal). In Project GPS, "G" stands for "*G*oal Selection," and reflects Selection skills; "P" stands for "*P*ursuit of Strategies," and reflects Optimization skills; and "S" stands for "*S*hifting Gears," and reflects Compensation skills. There are three main foci in the project: measurement, activities, and video exemplars.

The measurement tools for Project GPS are designed to be well suited to the mentoring context. In the 4-H Study, SOC skills are indexed through scores from the 24-item SOC Questionnaire (Freund & Baltes, 2002). Despite being a well-validated measure, the SOC Questionnaire may not be an ideal measurement tool for mentoring programs, as the self-report design may not facilitate the conversation and development of skills central to many high-quality mentoring programs. Therefore, Project GPS utilizes a series of rubrics to assess both an adolescent's SOC skills and his or her levels of PYD. Rubrics are simplified scoring tools to assess a product or performance based on standards or criteria. In this case, the criteria are the skills emphasized in the SOC model and in the SOC research findings from the 4-H Study (e.g., Gestsdóttir et al., 2010).

In Project GPS, assessments of an adolescent's SOC skills and levels of PYD are being triangulated to improve the validity of the tool. Youth self assess their abilities, and mentors assess the behavior of youth as well. This triangulation also addresses a limitation in the research, in which assessments of an adolescent's SOC only comprise self-reported data. Each rubric in Project GPS, which includes self- and mentor-assessed levels of SOC and each of the Five Cs of PYD, has a comparable structure to expedite responding and to minimize scoring error. The rubrics were also designed to be especially sensitive to developmental change; for instance, a youth can improve her score on "Making a plan," an O skill, by showing initiative at making and completing to-do lists for a week; whereas in previous weeks, the mentor had to remind her to make to-do lists, or had to convince her that to-do lists were useful for achieving goals. Currently, these rubrics are being empirically validated in a pilot study, assessing whether youth and mentors are providing scores on the new measures that correspond to already-validated scores on SOC Questionnaire items. An example of these rubrics, indexing an older adolescent's self-assessed "Goal Selection," is presented here, in Figure 1.

While measurement is central to Project GPS, simply completing measures may not be sufficient to build an adolescent's SOC skills. Accordingly, to support the mentoring process, mentors can elect to use portions of a suite of SOC-building activities and/or watch SOC skill-specific videos of exemplary young people narrating their life stories and highlighting the importance of their SOC skills to their success. The use of these resources in the pilot study, and in a subsequent evaluation program, is voluntary, as the needs and schedules of programs vary widely. However, if analysis indicates that using a particular activity, such as "Puzzle Pieces" (an activity to show the importance of selecting goals with identifiable short-term steps that may be put together in a manner analogous to completing a jigsaw puzzle), leads to higher SOC, then final versions of Project GPS may suggest incorporating the activity into the mentoring plan.

Following a longitudinal assessment of the efficacy of the SOC-related tools, Project GPS should benefit each set of stakeholders in the process: youth, mentors, organizations, and researchers. Providing youth with a program context within which to develop their ISR skills should both improve their long-term positive development and also help them achieve important, meaningful goals. Project GPS may provide these youth with tools that they can carry with them into the future, charting new "destinations" as they develop. Mentors, often looking to take the "next step" with youth, may benefit from the tools and measures in Project GPS, which will provide support and scaffolding for conversations and

"Where am I going?"
Rubric for Goal Selection

Scoring Levels	Choosing Your Destination	Choosing Goals That Help Others / Community	Breaking Down Long Term Goals "Vertical Coherence"	Identifying Relations Among Goals "Horizontal Coherence"
5 Consistent initiative; skill mastery	Consistently shows initiative and initiative by choosing meaningful, realistic and demanding goals. Focuses on one or small number of goals at a time.	Consistently shows mastery and initiative at choosing goals that benefit self and community.	Consistently shows mastery & initiative at breaking down long term, goals into short-term steps. Consistently identifies potential obstacles and solutions.	Consistently shows mastery & initiative at choosing goals that help in multiple ways and make meeting other goals easier.
4 "On and off" initiative; skill competence	Shows competency and takes initiative —about half the time—to choose meaningful, realistic and demanding goals. May pursue "too many" goals at once.	Shows competency & takes initiative—about half the time—to choose one or a small number of goals that benefit self and community.	Shows competency & takes initiative —about half the time—to break down long-term goals into short-term steps. Will sometimes identify potential obstacles and solutions.	Shows competency & takes initiative —about half the time—to choose goals that help in multiple ways and make meeting other goals easier. Sometimes chooses goals that help only a particular part of life (e.g., social).
3 Emerging initiative; basic skill	Shows motivation to choose meaningful, realistic and demanding goals. Needs mentor's help to make best goal decisions. Often pursues "too many" goals at one time.	Shows motivation to choose goals that benefit self and community. Needs mentor's help to make these connections to community.	Shows motivation to break down goals into short-term steps. Needs mentor's help to identify short term steps and identify potential obstacles and solutions.	Shows motivation to choose goals that help in multiple ways and make meeting other goals easier. Needs mentor's help to choose these goals and identify the multiple ways or other goals that this particular goal will help.
2 Low initiative; low skill	Has no clear long-term goal. Shows low motivation and chooses goals when mentor presses, but does not choose his/her goals.	Goals that help the community are not yet a youth priority. Shows low motivation and chooses goals that benefit self and community only when mentor presses.	Short-term steps and identifying potential obstacles are not yet part of goal process. Shows low motivation and breaks down goals into short-term steps only when mentor presses.	Focused on goals in a particular part of life. Shows low motivation and chooses goals that help other goals or help in multiple ways only when mentor presses.
1 Lacks skill; pre-aware or disengaged	Doesn't yet choose meaningful, realistic and demanding goals or use goals to shape behavior and actions.	Doesn't yet choose goals that benefit self and community.	Doesn't yet work on breaking down long-term goals.	Doesn't yet choose goals that help other goals or help in multiple ways.

STEP-IT-UP-2-THRIVE

Thrive Foundation for Youth • www.stepitup2thrive.org
Creative Commons Attribution-Noncommercial-Share Alike 3.0 U.S. License
Last Updated: 2016/13

Fig. 1. An example of a rubric in Project GPS: Youth ages 14–18 self-scored Goal Selection.

activities with youth. Organizations may benefit in several ways. In an increasingly competitive funding market, organizations are often required to provide empirical evidence for their impact on the lives of their participants. Project GPS may provide such evidence, in terms of changes in ISR and PYD. The additional tools and activities, as well as the rubrics themselves, will be provided to organizations for free, potentially aiding organizations with restricted budgets that are looking for ways to improve PYD among the youth they serve.

Finally, the research community, looking to bridge the research-practice gap, may benefit in several ways. First, the Project GPS evaluation will provide insight into the variables that may influence positive mentoring; for instance, information will be provided about the ideal duration or "dosage" of a mentoring relationship in terms of ISR skill development, or about the differences in outcomes between individual- and group-based programs. Most germane to this chapter, Project GPS may offer insight into the development of ISR in adolescence, and the association between this development and different personal and contextual factors. In short, Project GPS, an applied project concerned with the *optimization* of adolescent development and based on the *descriptive* data from the 4-H Study, should contribute to the *explanation* of the development of ISR in adolescence, and in turn, of its relation to PYD.

VI. Intentional Self-Regulation in Adolescence: Limitations of Current Studies and Suggestions for Future Research

To promote future advances in the study of ISR in adolescence, and to examine how these important skills are linked to PYD, several steps should be taken. These steps address the limitations in current research and provide directions for subsequent research. For instance, several of these limitations, and these directions for future work, involve methodological issues.

It is important to note that the research examining the SOC–PYD relation is generally limited with respect to considering contextual influences (with the exception of studies noted earlier, i.e., Napolitano, 2010; Urban et al., 2010). However, some examples in the broader literature indicate that adolescents' ISR (or ISR-related) behaviors, and their relation to levels of PYD (or PYD-related) outcomes, can vary based on, for instance, their cultural (e.g., Grob, Little, Wanner, Wearing, & Euronet, 1996) or parenting contexts (e.g., Moilanen et al., 2010). Further, the action–theoretical foundations of SOC emphasize the importance of contextual influences on the effectiveness of one's ISR (Baltes et al., 2006).

Given these precedents, we suggest that future research on the ISR–PYD relation continue to include measures from the various levels of adolescents' contexts. As these relations between an individual's ISR skills, contextual factors, and positive development presumably also vary at the exosystemic level (Bronfenbrenner & Morris, 2006), we further suggest that future research includes cross-cultural samples as well.

The 4-H Study findings concerning the ISR–PYD relation may also be methodologically limited in terms of the statistical analyses used in many studies. With one exception (Zimmerman, Phelps, & Lerner, 2008), past studies have used variable-centered, rather than person-centered, analyses. A reliance on variable-centered approaches, which assess the various components of the ISR–PYD relation at the mean level, may obscure unique ways that some adolescents may achieve positive outcomes through specific ISR strategies. In addition, our operationalization of the ISR construct—which emphasized the individual's unique contribution to his or her own development through goal-related actions-in-context—further suggests that research questions involving the development of ISR in adolescence, and the relation of ISR to PYD during this period, may especially benefit from taking a person-centered approach. One example of the benefit such analyses could provide involves using Configural Frequency Analysis (CFA; Lienert & Krauth, 1975; von Eye, 2002). Using CFA on a longitudinal data set, researchers could ascertain, for example, which patterns of an individual's Selection scores across adolescence are associated with high levels of PYD, and how this association may vary for an adolescent in different family, school, or community contexts. These findings may identify subgroups of youth employing particular patterns of Selection skills in relation to developing high levels of PYD that may have been "hidden" using a variable-centered approach. Given that the explanation of the development of ISR in adolescence is in its early stages, we suggest that future research should involve both variable- and person-centered approaches to provide a multifaceted picture of this developmental process.

Another important methodological limitation that future work should address is the current reliance on self-report measures, usually collected about one year apart in most longitudinal datasets (e.g., Lerner et al., 2005; Phelps et al., 2009; see also Lerner, Schwartz, & Phelps, 2009), to assess the development of ISR in adolescence. While the SOC Questionnaire, for instance, has been shown to be a reliable and valid assessment of an individual's ISR across the life span (e.g., Freund & Baltes, 2002; Gestsdóttir et al., 2010), little is known about how an adolescent's self-assessed SOC scores vary on a daily or weekly basis, in different ecological settings, or at the behavioral level. Similarly, little is known about if (or how) an adolescent's SOC skills vary at the microanalytic level, that is, in relation to his or her shorter-term challenges, situations, and/or goals. Therefore, future work would benefit from, for example, both self-report and behavioral assessments of an adolescent's ISR (or SOC, specifically) that are characterized by careful consideration of the temporal design of data collection. Data collected from Project GPS should serve to partially address this concern.

There are also some important future steps of a more theoretical nature that will advance our understanding of the development of ISR in adolescence. As noted earlier, recent research indicated that, for older adolescents, high scores of optimization, compensation, and LBS—but not (elective) selection—were strongly associated with PYD (Gestsdóttir et al., 2009, 2010). As there are many paths toward PYD—including, for instance, making stable, long-term goal selections in early or, alternatively, in late adolescence—future research should investigate this differential relation by focusing on the development of these goal selection skills, and should seek to determine how certain individual or contextual factors may influence the relation between selection and PYD. In particular, one potentially fruitful research path may involve examining how the development of an adolescent's goal selection skills relate to his or her identity development, which, in the West, is often characterized by lengthy periods of long-term goal exploration (Côté, 2009).

Future research may also advance our understanding of ISR in adolescence by incorporating measures of the serendipitous life events that were noted earlier. Such events may require an individual's adjustment of his or her ISR strategies or his or her long-term goals. While a serendipitous event may initiate a life path for an adolescent once thought unattainable or simply never-though-of to begin with, such eventualities do not mean that the life path itself was random (Bandura, 1998). What may seem like pure chance is often the result of explorative ISR actions. "People can make chance happen," Bandura (1998) notes, "by pursuing an active life that increases the number of fortuitous encounters they are likely to experience" (p. 98). Incorporating measures of such events or encounters into future studies could allow researchers to determine which adolescents, from which contexts, use which types of ISR skills, choose to pursue or ignore which kinds of serendipitous opportunities, which lead to which developmental outcomes.

VII. Conclusions

We believe that future research aimed at understanding ISR in adolescence must consider the uniqueness and complexity of goal-related processes during the adolescent years, in part through utilizing research designs and/or research foci that address some limitations of the extant literature. By incorporating these suggestions, we believe as well that the field will continue to advance its understanding of the development of ISR in adolescence, and how these ISR skills relate to PYD during the second decade of life. Such research will uncover new knowledge about how adolescents may engage their contexts to promote their healthy and productive development.

Acknowledgment

This chapter was supported in part by grants from the National 4-H Council and the Thrive Foundation for Youth.

REFERENCES

Balsano, A. B., Phelps, E., Theokas, C., Lerner, J. V., & Lerner, R. M. (2009). Patterns of early adolescents' participation in youth development programs having positive youth development goals. *Journal of Research on Adolescence, 19*, 249–259.

Baltes, P. B. (1997). On the incomplete architecture of human ontology: Selection, optimization, and compensation as foundation of developmental theory. *The American Psychologist, 52*, 366–380.

Baltes, P. B., & Baltes, M. M. (1990). Psychological perspectives on successful aging: The model of selective optimization with compensation. In P. B. Baltes & M. M. Baltes (Eds.), *Successful aging: Perspectives from the behavioral sciences.* (pp. 1–34). New York, NY: Cambridge University Press.

Baltes, P. B., Lindenberger, U., & Staudinger, U. M. (2006). Life span theory in developmental psychology. In R. M. Lerner & W. Damon (Eds.), *Handbook of child psychology: Vol 1. Theoretical models of human development.* (6th ed., pp. 569–664). Hoboken, NJ: John Wiley & Sons Inc.

Bandura, A. (1982). The psychology of chance encounters and life paths. *The American Psychologist, 37*, 747–755.

Bandura, A. (1998). Exploration of fortuitous determinants of life paths. *Psychological Inquiry, 9*, 95–99.

Benson, P. L., Scales, P. C., Hamilton, S. F., & Sesma, J. A. (2006). Positive youth development: Theory, research and applications. In W. Damon & R. M. Lerner (Editors-in-chief) & R. M. Lerner (Ed.), *Theoretical models of human development. Handbook of child psychology* (6th ed., Vol. 1, pp. 894–941). Hoboken, NJ: Wiley.

Bowers, E. P., Li, Y., Kiely, M. K., Brittian, A., Lerner, J. V., & Lerner, R. M. (2010). The five Cs model of positive youth development: A longitudinal analysis of confirmatory factor structure and measurement invariance. *Journal of Youth and Adolescence, 39*(7), 720–735.

Brandtstädter, J. (1989). Personal self-regulation of development: Cross-sequential analyses of development-related control beliefs and emotions. *Developmental Psychology, 25*, 96–108.

Brandtstädter, J. (1998). Action perspectives on human development. In W. Damon (Editor-in-Chief) & R. M. Lerner (Vol. Ed.) *Handbook of child psychology: Vol. 1. Theoretical models of human development* (5th ed., pp. 807–863). New York: Wiley.

Brandtstädter, J. (2006). Action perspectives on human development. In R. Lerner & W. Damon (Eds.), *The handbook of child psychology: Vol. Theoretical models of human development.* (6th ed., pp. 516–568). New York: John Wily & Sons, Inc.

Bronfenbrenner, U., & Morris, P. A. (2006). The bioecological model of human development. In W. Damon & R. M. Lerner (Editors-in-chief) & R. M. Lerner (Ed.), *Theoretical models of human development Handbook of child psychology.* (6th ed., Vol. 1, pp. 793–828). Hoboken, NJ: Wiley.

Carver, C. S., & Scheier, M. F. (1981). *Attention and self-regulation: A control-theory approach to human behavior.* New York: Springer-Verlag.

Côté, J. E. (2009). Identity formation and self development in adolescence. In R. Lerner & L. Steinberg (Eds.), *Handbook of adolescent psychology.* (3rd ed., pp. 266–304). Hoboken, NJ: John Wiley & Sons.

Cunha, F., & Heckman, J. J. (2007). The technology of skill formation. *The American Economic Review, 97,* 31–34.

Cunha, F., Heckman, J. J., & Schennach, S. (2010). *Investing in our young people. NBER Working Paper Series* (Vol. w16201).

Diamond, L. M., & Savin-Williams, R. C. (2009). Adolescent sexuality. In R. Lerner & L. Steinberg (Eds.), *Handbook of adolescent psychology.* (3rd ed., pp. 479–523). Hoboken, NJ: John Wiley & Sons.

Ebner, N. C., Fruend, A. M., & Baltes, P. B. (2006). Developmental changes in personal goal orientation from young to late adulthood: From striving for gains to maintenance and prevention of losses. *Psychology and Aging, 21*(4), 664–678.

Eccles, J., & Gootman, J. A. (2002). *Community programs to promote youth development.* Washington, DC: Committee on Community-Level Programs for Youth Board on Children, Youth, and Families, Commission on Behavioral and Social Sciences Education, National Research Council and Institute of Medicine.

Eccles, J. S., & Roeser, R. W. (2009). Schools, academic motivation and stage-environment fit. In R. Lerner & L. Steinberg (Eds.), *Handbook of adolescent psychology.* (3rd ed., pp. 405–434). Hoboken, NJ: John Wiley & Sons.

Erikson, E. H. (1968). *Identity: Youth and crisis.* Oxford, England: Norton & Co.

Freud, A. (1969). Adolescence as a developmental disturbance. In G. Caplan & S. Lebovici (Eds.), *Adolescence.* (pp. 5–10). New York: Basic Books.

Freund, A. M., & Baltes, P. B. (1998). Selection, optimization, and compensation as strategies of life management: Correlations with subjective indicators of successful aging. *Psychology and Aging, 13,* 531–543.

Freund, A. M., & Baltes, P. B. (2002). Life-management strategies of selection, optimization and compensation: Measurement by self-report and construct validity. *Journal of Personality and Social Psychology, 82,* 642–662.

Gardner, M., & Steinberg, L. (2005). Peer influence on risk-taking, risk preference, and risky decision-making in adolescence and adulthood: An experimental study. *Developmental Psychology, 41,* 625–635.

Geldhof, G. J., Little, T. D., & Colombo, J. (2010). Self-regulation across the life span. In M. E. Lamb, A. M. Freud & R. M. Lerner (Eds.), *The handbook of life-span development: Vol. 2. Social and emotional development.* (pp. 116–157). Hoboken, NJ: John Wiley & Sons Inc.

Gestsdóttir, S., Bowers, E., von Eye, A., Napolitano, C. M., & Lerner, R. M. (2010). Intentional self-regulation in middle adolescence: The emerging role of loss-based selection in positive youth development. *Journal of Youth and Adolescence, 39*(7), 764–782.

Gestsdóttir, S., & Lerner, R. M. (2007). Intentional self-regulation and positive youth development in early adolescence: Findings from the 4-H Study of Positive Youth Development. *Developmental Psychology, 43,* 508–521.

Gestsdóttir, S., & Lerner, R. M. (2008). Positive development in adolescence: The development and role of intentional self-regulation. *Human Development, 51,* 202–224.

Gestsdóttir, S., Lewin-Bizan, S., von Eye, A., Lerner, J. V., & Lerner, R. M. (2009). The structure and function of selection, optimization, and compensation in middle adolescence: Theoretical and applied implications. *Journal of Applied Developmental Psychology, 30*(5), 585–600.

Grob, A., Little, T. D., Wanner, B., Wearing, A. J., & Euronet, (1996). Adolescents' well-being and perceived control across 14 sociocultural contexts. *Journal of Personality and Social Psychology, 71,* 785–795.

Hall, G. S. (1904). *Adolescence: Its psychology and its relations to physiology, anthropology, sociology, sex, crime, religion, and education* (Vols. 1 and 2), New York: Appleton.

Harter, S. (2006). The self. In R. M. Lerner & W. Damon (Eds.), *Handbook of child psychology: Vol 1. Theoretical models of human development.* (6th ed., pp. 505–570). Hoboken, NJ: John Wiley & Sons Inc.

Harter, S. (2011). *The construction of the self* (2nd ed.). New York: Guilford Press.

Heckhausen, J. (1997). Developmental regulation across adulthood: Primary and secondary control of age-related challenges. *Developmental Psychology, 33,* 176–187.

Heckhausen, J., & Schulz, R. (1995). A life-span theory of control. *Psychological Review, 102,* 284–304.

Hooker, K., & McAdams, D. P. (2003). Personality reconsidered: A new agenda for aging research. *Journal of Gerontology: Psychological Sciences, 58,* 296–304.

James, W. (1890). *The principles of psychology.* New York, NY: Holt.

Johnston, L. D., O'Malley, P. M., Bachman, J. G., & Schulenberg, J. E. (2009). *Monitoring the Future national results on adolescent drug use: Overview of key findings, 2008.* (NIH Publication No. 09-7401)Bethesda, MD: National Institute on Drug Abuse.

Jopp, D., & Smith, J. (2006). Resources and life-management strategies as determinants of successful aging: On the protective effect of selection, optimization, and compensation. *Psychology and Aging, 21*(2), 253–265.

Keating, D. P. (2004). Cognitive and brain development. In R. M. Lerner & L. Steinberg (Eds.), *Handbook of adolescent psychology.* (2nd ed., pp. 45–84). Hoboken, NJ: John Wiley & Sons Inc.

Kochanska, G., Murray, K., & Harlan, E. (2000). Effortful control in early childhood: Continuity and change, antecedents, and implications for social development. *Developmental Psychology, 36,* 220–232.

Krumboltz, J. D. (2009). The happenstance learning theory. *Journal of Career Assessment, 17,* 135–154.

Kuhn, D. (2009). Adolescent thinking. In R. M. Lerner & L. Steinberg (Eds.), *Handbook of adolescent psychology.* (3rd ed., pp. 152–186). New York: John Wiley & Sons.

Larson, R. W. (2000). Towards a psychology of positive youth development. *The American Psychologist, 55,* 170–183.

Lerner, R. M. (1982). Children and adolescents as producers of their own development. *Developmental Review, 2*(4), 342–370.

Lerner, R. M. (2002). *Concepts and theories of human development* Mahwah, NJ: Erlbaum.

Lerner, R. M. (2004). *Liberty: Thriving and civic engagement among American youth.* Thousand Oaks, CA: Sage Publications.

Lerner, R. M. (2006). Developmental science, developmental systems, and contemporary theories of human development. In W. Damon & R. M. Lerner (Editors-in-chief) & R. M. Lerner (Ed.), *Theoretical models of human development. Vol. 1. Handbook of child psychology.* (6th ed., pp. 1–17). Hoboken, NJ: Wiley.

Lerner, R. M. (2009). The positive youth development perspective: Theoretical and empirical bases of a strength-based approach to adolescent development. In C. R. Snyder & S. J. Lopez (Eds.), *Oxford handbook of positive psychology.* (2nd ed., pp. 149–163). Oxford, England: Oxford University Press.

Lerner, R. M. (2011). Structure and process in relational, developmental systems theories: A commentary on contemporary changes in the understanding of developmental change across the life span. *Human Development, 54,* 34–43.

Lerner, R. M., & Busch-Rossnagel, L. (1981). *Individuals as producers of their development: A life-span perspective.* New York, NY: Academic Press.

Lerner, R. M., Freund, A. M., De Stefanis, I., & Habermas, T. (2001). Understanding developmental regulation in adolescence: The use of the selection, optimization, and compensation model. *Human Development, 44,* 29–50.

Lerner, R. M., Lerner, J. V., Almerigi, J., Theokas, C., Phelps, E., Gestsdóttir, S., et al. (2005). Positive youth development, participation in community youth development programs, and community contributions of fifth Grade adolescents: Findings from the first wave of the 4-H Study of Positive Youth Development. *Journal of Early Adolescence, 25*(1), 17–71.

Lerner, J. V., Phelps, E., Forman, Y. E., & Bowers, E. (2009). Positive youth development. In R. M. Lerner & L. Steinberg (Eds.), *Handbook of adolescent psychology.* (3rd ed., pp. 524–558). Hoboken, NJ: Wiley.

Lerner, R. M., Schwartz, S. J., & Phelps, E. (2009). Problematics of time and timing in the longitudinal study of human development: Theoretical and methodological issues. *Human Development, 52*(1), 44–68.

Li, Y., Bebiroglu, N., Phelps, E., & Lerner, R. M. (2009). Out-of-school time activity participation, school engagement and positive youth development: Findings from the 4-H study of positive youth development. *Journal of Youth Development, 3*(3), doi: 080303FA00.

Lienert, G. A., & Krauth, J. (1975). Configural Frequency Analysis as a statistical tool for defining types. *Educational and Psychological Measurement, 35,* 231–238.

Mahoney, J. L., Larson, R. W., Eccles, J. S., & Lord, H. (2005). Organized activities as developmental contexts for children and adolescents. In J. Mahoney, R. Larson & J. S. Eccles (Eds.), *Organized activities as contexts of development: Extracurricular activities, after-school, and community programs* (pp. 3–22). Hillsdale, NJ: Erlbaum.

Mahoney, J. L., Vandell, D. L., Simkins, S., & Zarrett, N. (2009). Adolescent out-of-school activities. In R. M. Lerner & L. Steinberg (Eds.), *Handbook of adolescent psychology: Vol 2. Contextual influences on adolescent development.* (3rd ed., pp. 228–269). Hoboken, NJ: Wiley.

McClelland, M. M., Ponitz, C. C., Messersmith, E. E., & Tominey, S. (2010). Self-regulation: Integration of cognition and emotion. In W. F. Overton & R. M. Lerner (Eds.), *The handbook of life-span development: Vol. 1. Cognition, biology, and methods.* (pp. 509–553). Hoboken, NJ: John Wiley & Sons, Inc.

Mischel, W., Shoda, Y., & Rodriguez, M. L. (1989). Delay of gratification in children. *Science, 244,* 933–938.

Moilanen, K. L., Shaw, D. S., & Fitzpatrick, A. (2010). Self-regulation in early adolescence: Relations with mother-son relationship quality and maternal regulatory support and antagonism. *Journal of Youth and Adolescence, 39*(11), 1357–1367.

Napolitano, C. M. (2010). *Context and adolescent intentional self regulation: Testing the positive youth development model.* Medford, MA: Tufts University (Unpublished master's thesis).

Overton, W. F. (2010). Life-span development: Concepts and issues. In R. M. Lerner (Ed.), *The handbook of lifespan development* (Vol. 1, pp. 1–29). (pp. 1–29). Hoboken, NJ: Wiley.

Paus, T. (2009). Brain development. In R. Lerner & L. Steinberg (Eds.), *Handbook of adolescent psychology.* (3rd ed., pp. 95–115). Hoboken, NJ: John Wiley & Sons.

Perels, F., Dignath, C., & Schmitz, B. (2009). Is it possible to improve mathematical achievement by means of self-regulation strategies? Evaluation of an intervention in regular math classes. *European Journal of Psychology of Education, 24*(1), 17–31.

Phelps, E., Zimmerman, S., Warren, A. E. A., Jeličić, H., von Eye, A., & Lerner, R. M. (2009). The structure and developmental course of positive youth development (PYD) in early adolescence: Implications for theory and practice. *Journal of Applied Developmental Psychology, 30*(5), 628–644.

Rand, K. L., & Cheavens, J. S. (2009). Hope theory. In S. Lopez & C. Snyder (Eds.), *Oxford handbook of positive psychology* (pp. 323–333). New York: Oxford University Press.

Rhodes, J. E. (2002). *Stand by me: The risks and rewards of mentoring today's youth.* Cambridge, MA: Harvard University Press.

Rhodes, J. E., & DuBois, D. L. (2008). Mentoring relationships and programs for youth. *Current Directions in Psychological Science, 17*(4), 254–258.

Rhodes, J. E., & Lowe, S. R. (2009). Mentoring in adolescence. In R. M. Lerner & L. Steinberg (Eds.), *Handbook of adolescent psychology: Vol. 2. Contextual influences on adolescent development.* (2nd ed., pp. 152–190).

Roth, J. L., & Brooks-Gunn, J. (2003). What is a youth development program? Identification and defining principles. In R. M. Lerner, F. Jacobs, & D. Wertlieb (Series Eds.) & F. Jacobs, D. Wertlieb, & R. M. Lerner (Vol. Eds.), *Handbook of applied developmental science: Promoting positive child, adolescent, and family development through research, policies, and programs: Vol. 2. Enhancing the life chances of youth and families: Public service systems and public policy perspectives* (pp. 197–223). Thousand Oaks, CA: Sage Publications.

Shonkoff, J., & Phillips, D. (Eds.), (2000). *Neurons to neighborhoods: The science of early childhood development.* Washington, DC: National Academy Press.

Steinberg, L. (2011). *Adolescence* New York: McGraw-Hill.

Susman, E. J., & Dorn, L. D. (2009). Puberty: Its role in development. In R. Lerner & L. Steinberg (Eds.), *Handbook of adolescent psychology* (3rd ed., pp. 116–151). Hoboken, NJ: John Wiley & Sons.

Urban, J. B., Lewin-Bizan, S., & Lerner, R. M. (2010). The role of intentional self regulation, lower neighborhood ecological assets, and activity involvement in youth developmental outcomes. *Journal of Youth and Adolescence, 39*(7), 783–800.

von Eye, A. (2002). *Configural frequency analysis: Methods, models, and applications.* Mahwah, NJ: Lawrence Erlbaum Associates Publishers.

Werner, H. (1957). The concept of development from a comparative and organismic point of view. In D. B. Harris (Ed.), *The concept of development.* (pp. 125–148). Minneapolis, MN: University of Minnesota Press.

Wiese, B. S., Freund, A. M., & Baltes, P. B. (2002). Subjective career success and emotional well-being: Longitudinal predictive power of selection, optimization, and compensation. *Journal of Vocational Behavior, 60*, 321–335.

Zaff, J. F., Hart, D., Flanagan, C. A., Youniss, J., & Levine, P. (2010). Developing civic engagement within a civic context. In R. M. Lerner (Ed.), *The handbook of life-span development.* Hoboken, NJ: Wiley.

Zimmerman, S., Phelps, E., & Lerner, R. M. (2007). Intentional self-regulation in early adolescence: Assessing the structure of selection, optimization, and compensations processes. *European Journal of Developmental Science, 1*, 272–299.

Zimmerman, S., Phelps, E., & Lerner, R. M. (2008). Positive and negative developmental trajectories in U.S. adolescents: Where the PYD perspective meets the deficit model. *Research in Human Development, 5*(3), 153–165.

YOUTH PURPOSE AND POSITIVE YOUTH DEVELOPMENT

Jenni Menon Mariano and Julie Going

UNIVERSITY OF SOUTH FLORIDA S-M, SARASOTA, FLORIDA, USA

Abstract

This chapter reviews research and findings on youth purpose as it relates to positive youth development (PYD) and thriving. The authors note that purpose is defined in multiple ways in the youth development literature, including one-dimensional and multi-dimensional definitions, and those that combine purpose with other constructs, like meaning. Although research on youth purpose and thriving is in its early stages, however, multiple other purpose-like constructs appear in the positive youth development literature, such as life goals, contribution, and sparks, that can tell us about how purpose and PYD may interact. Recent research suggests that purpose aligns with several positive states during adolescence and young adulthood, like life -satisfaction, coping, generosity, optimism, humility, mature identity

Advances in Child Development and Behavior
Richard M. Lerner, Jacqueline V. Lerner and Janette B. Benson : Editors

status, and more global personality integration. Purpose may also be promoted through social support from people in young people's lives who are sensitive and responsive to their interests and concerns.

I. Introduction

Many might argue that adolescence, the period of life that initiates the transition to adulthood, is generally fraught with conflict, storm, and strife (i.e., see Arnett, 2000; Hall, 1904). However, recent research in the field of positive youth development (PYD) indicates that, although adolescents are undergoing rapid developmental and physiological changes, generally youth choose a life path that is more positive rather than negative (Berk, 2009). Instead of focusing on the problems, tribulations, and failures of young people, the PYD approach envisions young people as resources with observable potentialities (Damon, 2004; and see Mariano, 2011b).

In this chapter, we discuss research that shows that many young people develop their potentialities in conjunction with a positive purpose in life (PIL). Evidently, there is much research that points out how personal and social goals can lead to a range of outcomes that are typified by negative as well as positive behaviors—social movements, both historical and contemporary, that are directed toward destructive aims come to mind. Other strands of research are typically occupied with describing what happens to development in the absence of purpose. Individuals without a clear aim or purpose in their life might be thought of as "drifters" (Damon, Menon, & Bronk, 2003; Moran, 2009, p. 146), and there is plenty of evidence that such individuals are more likely to experience things like depression, addictions, aggression, lack of productivity, self-absorption, psychosomatic ailments, and a host of other unpleasant psychosocial problems (i.e., see Damon, 1995; Damon et al., 2003, Noblejas de la Flor, 1997; Padelford, 1974; Sappington & Kelly, 1995; Sayles, 1994; Schlesinger, Susman, & Koenigsberg, 1990; Waisberg & Porter, 1994).

In contrast to these bodies of work about purpose, our interest is in examining a more positive, agency-inclusive, and bidirectional person–context view of purpose that is frequently neglected in the youth development literature. Analogies are helpful to illustrate and differentiate subtle differences in views of novel concepts. A commonly invoked metaphor for purpose is a beacon, or a lighthouse, which acts as a guide for the young person. For many youngsters, it is indeed possible that purpose acts as a "lifeline" in a difficult world, and a way of adapting to threatening conditions (Damon et al., 2003). Theorists interested in youth resiliency in the face of crisis, stress, and challenge emphasize this defensive and healing role of purpose (i.e., see Benard, 1991; Erikson, 1968). Some argue, however, that this stance indicates an overly negative bias toward the capacities of young people and human nature in general (i.e., see Damon et al., 2003, pp. 123–124) and places less emphasis on the agentic and proactive nature of adolescents than is warranted.

A more appropriate metaphor sees purpose as a tool, or medium, by which adolescents can employ their distinct talents, gifts, interests, and strengths in a person–context relationship (Damon, 2004). The tool metaphor emphasizes the directed and prosocial stance on purpose represented in this chapter. To invoke a third metaphor, human capabilities might be seen as a sailboat. A sense of purpose is like the wind that animates the sails and directs the speed of its movement, while the valence and content of one's chosen purposes is the rudder that provides direction. This metaphor underscores the deeply internal nature of purpose emphasized by many thinkers while giving attention to the inextricable connection between the person and the resources and opportunities proffered by his or her environment. In fact, in describing how youth purpose arises and is sustained, a person–context emphasis is befitting, given recent theories in developmental science that focus on the dynamic and bidirectional nature of development generally from person to context or context to person, and back again (i.e., see Thelen & Smith, 2006), and of purpose more specifically (i.e., see Marken, 1990). We suspect that the same relationship applies to purpose and thriving.

In the following pages, we describe and analyze the current state of the field of youth purpose research and what it tells us about how young people do well. The study of what goes right in human development is often referred to with different terms (i.e., being competent, flourishing, having assets, adapting well, optimal functioning, etc., see e.g., Keyes, 2002; Masten & Coatsworth, 1998). Actually, when examined carefully, each of these terms is quite different. In spite of considerable advances over the past few years in discussing, naming, and measuring positive developmental experiences for young people, however (i.e., see Alberts et al., 2006; King et al., 2005; Lerner et al., 2005; Theokas et al., 2005), a consensus around the issue is still in the making (Benson & Scales, 2009, p. 86).

We utilize the terms PYD and youth thriving interchangeably throughout this chapter to refer broadly to being the best one can be and to optimal development during adolescence and emerging adulthood (Arnett, 2000). As far as we can see, both terms emphasize a sense of doing well in a comprehensive and nonsuperficial sense. In other words, they both signify more than "okay" development (Benson & Scales, 2009, p. 86). Further, there is considerable cross-dissemination of work among scholars who are interested in these two topics (i.e., see Alberts et al., 2006; King et al., 2005). Our discussion also requires us to enter the territory covered by positive psychologists—through references to positive states, experiences, emotions, and dispositions, for instance, that may not be completely incorporated into current models of PYD and youth thriving.

It is true that many individuals struggle with finding a sense of purpose even into adulthood (Warren, 2002). Here, we emphasize studies that focus on the period of youth, and for reasons that extend beyond the fact that youth is the focus of this volume. Theorists have long considered adolescence to be a formative period of self-discovery during which young people search for answers to pressing questions about life, relationships, and their role in society (i.e., see Erikson, 1968; Marcia, 1980). Historically, young people have grappled with, and frequently questioned, dominant worldviews offered by parents, teachers, counselors, peers, the media, and influential others. It is in adolescence that individuals—many for the first time in a serious manner—entertain meaning and future-orientated questions, such as, *for what purpose do I exist? Why does my life matter?* and *why am I here?* The degree to which youths successfully seek and find answers to these questions has important implications for youth thriving.

Given the bourgeoning nature of the youth purpose field, in the next section of the chapter we introduce conceptual links of purpose to PYD. To accomplish this, we first discuss studies of lay-person's views of purpose (as opposed to academics'), their views of thriving, and how the two fit together. We then discuss the concepts of purpose most frequently used in the research literature and what these concepts, by their very nature, suggest about the hypothesized relationship between purpose and youth thriving. The study of youth purpose is relatively new, and thus research on the purpose–PYD relation is scarce. For this reason, we find it necessary to include purpose-like constructs in our discussion (i.e., concepts that do not use the word "purpose" but are clearly about purpose). In the subsequent section of the chapter, we analyze a sample of some of the most recent and representative empirical findings on purpose and selected positive youth characteristics and outcomes. Finally, in a concluding section, we consider some directions that youth purpose research should take to furnish a better understanding of its connection with youth thriving.

II. PYD, Purpose, and Purpose-Like Constructs

Analogies help with a basic philosophical understanding of novel concepts like purpose, and its relation to other novel concepts, like thriving. Precise definitions are more useful for empirical measurement.

To facilitate such definitions, a common method is to invoke adolescents' and adults' views. Insights from recent work of this type on PYD and thriving indicators suggest that purpose can legitimately be considered, in different circumstances, as a thriving indicator and as a thriving outcome. The research here is relatively scarce, but the work that has been accomplished highlights the central role of purpose in PYD, as well as age differences in perspectives on the matter.

One case in point is the research conducted by King et al. (2005). They asked a diverse sample of 173 youth-serving practitioners, parents, and early and late adolescents to express their ideas about thriving through in-depth interviews. In addition, youth practitioners were asked to identify and discuss the attributes of one or more adolescents who manifested exemplary, positive development. Responses were reliably reduced to 77 thriving indicators, many of which referred to different aspects of purpose. "Future orientation" is the most frequently identification of these purpose-like constructs, followed by "contribution," "meaning and purpose," being "committed," and being "focused" (pp. 102–103).

Alberts et al. (2006) also examined the conceptions of youth and their parents about the nature of a thriving young person. They too identified a number of purpose-like and purpose-inclusive concepts that participants related to positive development, such as caring for others, professional and educational aspirations, and positive contribution to self, family, and community. Parents and youths, however, differed significantly in the weight they placed on the centrality of all three of these characteristics to positive development, with significantly higher proportions of youths endorsing all three as thriving attributes. Parents, however, placed greater emphasis on the thriving young person as a happy and competent individual. Additionally, when parents used terms typically linked to contribution, they were more likely to cite contribution to the self rather than to context (i.e., community or family) as indicative of and important for youth thriving.

Research on young people's conceptions of purpose support the general insights of King et al.'s (2005) and Alberts et al.'s (2006) observations about the views of youth. When adolescents are asked what a PIL means to them, they give a range of responses citing activities referring to varying levels of engagement and prosocial orientation (Mariano & Savage, 2009, p. 8). Indeed, adolescents hold multifaceted conceptions of purpose. They propose that purpose provides a foundation and direction for one's life, is about finding happiness, is about being prosocial, is related to religion and spirituality, and is about attaining occupational goals (Hill, Burrow, O'Dell, & Thornton, 2010). But many adolescents, including the majority of older adolescents, define purpose as something that makes an impact in the world (Hill et al., 2010; Moran & Damon, 2008).

Youths and adults clearly allocate difference weight to contribution as a necessary component of thriving. Generational differences in purpose may also exist. Evidence on this point comes from the work of Inhelder and Piaget's (1958) early studies of young people's diary entries. They discovered that adolescents express purpose differently than adults: youths often refer to their aspirations in more extreme and grandiose ways. Because purpose is a newly emerging skill during that period, adolescents may parade it more proudly than older individuals who have already had many years to master it (see Damon et al., 2003, p. 124).

Other understandings of purpose's relation to thriving come from theoretical studies. Benson and Scales (2009) cite a sense of purpose as a marker of youth thriving in their model. Additionally, young people's ability to name and describe personal talents and interests "that give them energy and purpose" is a thriving marker (p. 97). In other work, meaning and purpose is a core thriving indicator (King, 2004, cited in Benson & Scales, 2009).

Researchers also embrace multiple definitions of purpose, which in turn are reflected in how purpose is measured. In fact, given the exploratory nature of almost all youth purpose research to date, it is not unusual for single studies to utilize, and to measure multiple versions of the purpose construct (i.e., see Mariano & Savage, 2009). To simplify things, definitions can be seen as ranging from more specific to more general, and from primarily one-faceted to multidimensional; but these classification groupings are not mutually exclusive.

Which type of definition is best for understanding the purpose–thriving relation? Our stance is that for research purposes, any of the above articulations might be useful as long as they are specified. For the purposes of this review, however, and given the nascent state of both youth purpose and youth thriving research, it is pragmatic to describe findings from studies representing a range of views on the issue. Presently, the state of the purpose research as it relates to youth thriving is best conceptualized as a vast landscape, the mapping of which is in its earliest stages. At this juncture, theoretical insights on youth purpose legitimately connect to any of multiple bodies of more established research in youth development, such as motivation and goal theory, moral development, and competence, to name just a few. Thus, each set of purpose definitions is discussed below in respect to youth thriving.

A. SPECIFIC AND ONE-DIMENSIONAL DEFINITIONS

Specific and one-faceted approaches measure a general "sense" or feeling that one has found meaning or purpose in his or her life, or is searching for it (i.e., Frankl, 1959; Ryff & Singer, 1998; Steger, Frazier,

Oishi, & Kaler, 2006). An increasingly used measure of purpose called the Meaning in Life Questionnaire (MLQ), for example (Steger et al., 2006), takes this approach in part, including survey items about seeking and finding purpose, like "My life has a clear sense of purpose" and "I am seeking a purpose or mission for my life." Seminal approaches like part A of Crumbaugh and Maholick's (1969) PIL test also follow this method.

A key emphasis offered by measures of this sort is on purpose as an experience that is fundamentally internal in nature, though apparently still quite accessible to study. This coheres with renditions of youth purpose as young people's "ultimate concerns" (Emmons, 1999), as "inner strength" (Frankl, 1959, p. 76), as having an "inner hold" (p. 78) on one's core self, and as the ultimate motivator and reason for living (p. 88). From this point of view, purpose is implicated in thriving (and it is generally assumed that it is) to the degree that purpose achieves a central place in the individual's identity and psychological functioning. Most of these types of measures do not specify more external aspects of purpose, such as the content of purpose or the sources from which purpose is derived. Nor do they specify individual differences in these purpose contents and sources. This measurement tradition has yielded a number of reliable and valid instruments which, though not initially appropriate for adolescent populations, have increasingly been adapted to suit that age group.

B. SPECIFIC AND MULTIDIMENSIONAL DEFINITIONS

In comparison, specific and multidimensional purpose definitions emphasize the importance of separating purpose from broader constructs like meaning. They conceptualize purpose as a higher-order phenomenon that integrates in an orderly way various aspects of human functioning (i.e., see Damon et al., 2003; Moran, 2009). A frequently cited definition of this type is initially offered by Damon et al. (2003) in their critical review of the youth purpose literature and is only modified slightly in later works that invoke their definition. They conceive of purpose as "a stable and generalized intention to accomplish something that is at once meaningful to the self and of consequence to the world beyond the self" (p. 121).

In addition, purpose has three distinct characteristics that further define it from Damon et al.'s (2003) perspective. First, purpose involves a "stable" and far-reaching goal or goals that go beyond merely accomplishing everyday tasks such as showing up to work on time or deciding what one will have for dinner (p. 21). Second, purpose, though more specific than meaning, can certainly be a central part of one's personal search for meaning (p. 121). Purpose is internal but, unlike meaning, also has an external feature to it that includes a desire to contribute to the world in a meaningful way. Simply put, purpose extends beyond the fulfillment of self—it is an external quest to make the world a better place for human-kind and is intrinsically self-fulfilling as well as potentially prosocial. Finally, purpose is "always directed at an accomplishment toward which one can make progress" (p. 121). Being able to actually reach or attain a goal is not the essential attribute of purpose. Instead, it is the sense of direction that purpose provides toward fulfillment of that aim that is paramount.

Therefore, using Damon et al.'s (2003) definition, we can say that PIL is content specific to the degree that it extends beyond the simple fulfillment and motivation of basic human biological and physiological needs. Scholars who invoke the definition in their work usually point out that although it seeks to make a difference in the world beyond self, purpose need not always be prosocial. Yet most who follow its lead admit an inter-est in studying noble purposes.

Because multifaceted views of purpose require coordination of multiple skills that act in concert (Mariano & Savage, 2009, p. 18), attention is given to studying and comparing instances of more normally occurring youth purpose with more exemplary youth purpose. One trend is to identify qualitative forms of purpose that differ in the degree and extent to which they exhibit each skill. To date, the most frequently used method is qualitative analysis of in-depth interviews collected in normative studies of adolescents and emerging adults (i.e., see Malin et al., 2008), although factoring and clustering procedures with quantitative survey measures is also utilized to differentiate purpose forms. In brief, purpose forms fall across a continuum in which they are differentiated by prosocial versus primarily self-oriented rationales, and by the degree to which the young person reports long-term action and plans associated with those purposes. Reliability of these purpose forms, or slight variations thereof, has been achieved across studies (i.e., see Mariano, Going, Schrock, & Sweeting, 2011).

A second method employs in-depth qualitative case studies of young purpose exemplars, gleaned from nomination studies by experts. This work utilizes an *a priori* multifaceted definition of purpose, like the one noted above, to guide the selection of exemplars (i.e., see Bronk, 2005, 2008). The underlying assumption of this construction of purpose is that more complex forms of purpose—those that incorporate more dimensions of the construct—are more likely to align with PYD indicators and out-comes. Further, since purpose exemplars are diverse, an alternate approach examines cases of adolescents who are exemplary in other ways (i.e., gifted or talented adolescents), and then studies the nature of their purposes (i.e., Reilly, 2009).

An advantage offered by specific and multifaceted definitions over those that measure purpose purely as a sense is that they tell us something about the content and sources of adolescents' purposes. Researchers can code not only for purpose forms but also for categories of activity in the young person's life that fulfill all purpose criteria. Purposeful intentions and activities are thus differentiated from activities that are less central in the youngster's life.

Although the details need refinement through further research (i.e., see Reilly, 2009, for case descriptions that show how purpose forms are not always simply delineated), it is found that more complex and complete forms of youth purpose more positively relate to some thriving indicators than do less compete forms—a finding that we discuss in greater detail in the next section. The same has yet to be found in relation to content or domains of purpose sources when they are gleaned specifically from interview data. Other methods that use broad, or general definitions of purpose are somewhat more fruitful in investigating the significance of purpose source and content to positive development.

C. GENERAL DEFINITIONS THAT CONFLATE PURPOSE WITH OTHER CONSTRUCTS

On the farthest end of the classification of purpose definitions are broad understandings that use language that conflate purpose with constructs like meaning, mattering, importance, centrality, goals, and/or other positive characteristics (i.e., vitality, energy, life satisfaction, identity, empathizing, and caring) (see, e.g., Crumbaugh & Maholick, 1969; Hutzell, 1995; Hutzell & Finck, 1994; Reker & Peacock, 1981). A close examination reveals that some scales that measure a "sense" of purpose also fall within this grouping. For example, the PIL scale (Crumbaugh & Maholick, 1969; and not originally intended for youth) measures purposefulness in part by reports on a seven-point scale rating of how excited participants are about their life ("Life to me see always exciting" (7) versus "completely routine" (1)), how enthusiastic or bored they are, how novel each new day feels to them, and the degree to which they have progressed toward achieving their life goals.

Definitions and measurement do not always align in the clean and concise way that researchers would like them to. This is especially true when dealing with concepts like purpose that younger participants are not always familiar with, and with open-ended methodologies that probe for participants' deeper understanding. For example, the Youth Purpose Interview (Andrews et al., 2006) is repeatedly employed with adolescents to operationalize Damon et al.'s (2003) very specific purpose definition. Yet in its questioning procedure, it uses a myriad other concepts to invoke purpose and is thus more aligned with a broad approach. Interview questions relate to what is important to the adolescent, what the adolescent cares about, and what the adolescent's "ideal world" looks like. The word "purpose" is not used until the very end of the protocol. The interview's aim is quite pragmatic, however: it probes for a deeply residing phenomenon that is not always accessible through direct methods, in the same way that a prognosis is reached through assessment of the symptoms of a condition.

It is likely therefore that purpose links to a number of constructs (i.e., meaning, etc.) in important ways that could provide insights into the purpose–thriving relationship. For this reason, and for the sake of brevity, we next describe some of the most recent methodologies used to study youth meaning and life goals that were designed with the specific intention of learning about young people's purposes in life. When limited in this way, and to research with adolescents and young adults, a more condensed body of research emerges that imply connections to thriving. An analysis of a selection of such studies and their methods are thus discussed.

D. RESEARCH ON YOUTH MEANING

Methods that examine purpose via meaningful experiences and through life goals afford insights into the contents and sources of purpose and how they relate to thriving in ways not accomplished by other procedures. As noted above, several researchers use the terms meaning and purpose simultaneously. Meaning is alternately defined as "to have a purpose or intention in mind," while purpose is "something one intends to get or do; [an] intention; [or] aim" (Webster's New World Dictionary of American English, 1991, p. 839, 1092). In other conceptualizations, purpose is a component, or descriptor of meaning, often appearing alongside other psychological variables (Baumeister, 1991; Reker & Wong, 1988).

People of all ages tend to agree that meaning can be inspired by sources providing potentially prosocial content, such as building positive personal relationships, and the preservation of values and ideals (Prager, 1996, 1998). As with the specific study of purpose, studies of youth meaning are relatively rare. A set of studies dealing with young people's views on meaning sources are offered by De Vogler and Ebersole's (1980, 1983) research on categories of meaning in life. Using the Meaning Essay Document, participants were asked in two studies to write about and rank the most meaningful things in their lives and then report associated experiences to go along with them. In the first study (1980), college students cited eight meaningful life categories coded as relationships, service, growth, beliefs, existential-hedonistic, obtaining, expression, and understanding. Later (1983), 13- and 14-year-olds endorsed the same categories, but rarely mentioned beliefs. Not surprisingly, however, a replication of the 1983 research by Showalter and Wagener (2000) found that young adolescents attending a Christian summer camp find beliefs more meaningful than do less religious peers of their age. The young adolescents in De Vogler & Ebersole's (1983) study also cited three new categories of activities, school, and appearance. For the sake of comparison, it is notable that adults (1981) endorsed younger people's categories, but added health and life work.

Meaning categories are examined in other studies but measured by terms like importance, dedication, and commitment of time and energy. Two studies initially shaped by a more specific definition of youth purpose use such measures. In one case, 444 adolescents and emerging adults utilized a scale to endorse a list of 18 categories via the prompt, "We are interested in finding out the types of things you feel are most important to you, based on how much time you commit to them" (Damon, 2008, pp. 52–53; Mariano & Damon, 2008, p. 215; Menon, Bronk, & Damon, 2004). In another study, 500 college students endorsed six categories through the prompt, "*How important are the following to you?*" (Mariano, 2010). In each case, we find similar categories endorsed overall, but with some variation in category rankings, given the age of participants. In both studies, categories include relational things like family, friendship, and romance; moral and civic domains like community service, politics, religious faith, and personal values; and matters pertaining to personal welfare, like happiness, growth, and health (p. 215). There is some evidence that career is the meaning category that provides many college students with most opportunity to practice purpose, in the multidimensional sense of the word (i.e., to actively pursue career-related activities, form future plans around them, and to be moved by prosocial rationales for doing so). This is a logical conclusion for college-goers who are in the process of contemplating and trying out the work world. However, given the limitations of the sample, the evidence should be considered preliminary (Mariano, 2010).

These studies on meaning categories specific to youth populations do not investigate thriving *per se*, but the trends in what people find to be meaningful mirror age-specific understandings of what constitutes PYD in other research (Alberts et al., 2006; King et al., 2005). Clearly, age-related contexts shape views of the good life. We suspect that this trend affects the purpose–PYD relationship as well. The proposition is consistent with a lifespan perspective that articulates very different types of life tasks at different life stages.

Schnell (2009) and Schnell and Becker (2006) offer a more established measure of meaning sources. For their research, content analysis of in-depth qualitative interviews helped develop a scale measuring 26 meaning sources classified under self-transcendence, self-actualization, order, or well-being and relatedness (Schnell, 2009). They highlight personality differences in endorsement of meaning categories, with some categories being more predictive of personality dimensions that are classically evaluated as being positive (Grum & von Collani, 2007). For example, the self-transcendent category of "care" is positively predicted by the traits of openness and conscientiousness, and negatively predicted by disagreeableness (Schnell & Becker, 2006, p. 125). Openness and conscientiousness also predict personal growth, determination, and goal attainment (p. 121, 125), which are considered "self-actualization" sources by the authors but also clearly reflect purpose. A limit of the findings for our aims is their primary focus on adults, though some traditional-age college students are included in the sample.

E. RESEARCH ON LIFE GOALS

It is perhaps not coincidental that meaning in life is conceptually associated with life goals. Molcar and Stuempfig (1988), who separate purpose, meaning, and life goals, also tend to connect them. They suggest that PIL is composed of two factors: satisfaction with goals and meaning in life. Emmons too notes that goals that serve as a source of personal meaning can provide "unity and purpose" (p. 147).

Some research on life goals intentionally extends an understanding of purpose sources associated with characteristics discussed in the positive psychology literature. The Categories of Identified Purpose Scale (Bundick et al., 2006; and see Bronk & Finch, 2010) assesses young people's endorsement via a Likert scale of 17 categories gleaned from related research. In keeping with approaches that conflate purpose with other constructs, respondents are given the prompt: "In the following section, 'purpose' refers to the MOST IMPORTANT overall goal or goals for your life. The purpose of my life is to …," followed by the category listings. The resulting categories are condensed in different psychometrically valid ways across studies depending on the interpretation. In each case, category endorsement is related in meaningful ways to positive developmental characteristics. For example, one approach labeled participants as primarily endorsing one of four goal categories: creative, hedonistic, moral/spiritual, and social/practical (Mariano & Savage, 2009) goals. All goal categories aligned with reports of adolescents' experiences of empathy and gratitude, but with most frequent alignment with these positive states occurring with creative goals (i.e., items related to "beautifying and bettering the world," "creating and discovering new things," and "influencing the thinking of others") (p. 9). Another approach clustered participants in four groups based on the types of long-term aims suggested by their patterns of category endorsement (Bronk & Finch, 2010). Youths with other-oriented long-term aims (i.e., "purposeful" youth) were more likely to show the personality trait of openness. They were also more likely to report higher life satisfaction.

Roberts and Robins (2000) also constructed a life goals measure that is utilized in purpose research. Their definition of life goals is actually quite akin to the idea of purpose as "intentions" (Damon et al., 2003). In fact, they see life goals as "explicit, concrete intentions for future activities" (Roberts & Robins, 2000, p. 1294). For this scale measure, the prompt given to participants is, "How important are the following goals in your life?" followed by 20 statements that hang together in seven factors: economic goals, esthetic goals, social goals, relationship goals, political goals, hedonistic goals, and religious goals (p. 1289). These authors also conclude that, at least among college students, life goal types are predicted by personality dispositions. Highly extraverted and disagreeable individuals desire purposes involving economic and political status and find prosocial purposes less desirable. The same is true of narcissistic individuals. However, it is questionable whether narcissism is in itself a mediator of negative outcomes and never of positive ones. In some contexts, narcissistic illusions may promote well-being and contribute to positive outcomes (Roberts & Robins, 2000, p. 1294; Taylor & Brown, 1988).

Hill et al. (2010) constructed their own measure of life goals in order to assess purpose orientations in young and middle adulthood. They drew life goal items developed and refined by the Higher Education Research Institute (HERI) at UCLA, which administers a survey given to college students across the United States for several decades. Four purpose orientation factors are identified among their sample of undergraduate college seniors, including a prosocial orientation, a financial orientation, a creative orientation, and a personal recognition orientation. They then investigated the short- and long-term benefits of endorsing each goal orientation by examining follow-up surveys with participants in middle adulthood. Apparently, the orientations correlate somewhat, suggesting that people often endorse more than one type of purpose. All four orientations were also positively related to perceived personal development in college. Individuals' purpose orientation is quite stable between college and the mid-30s, but in the 30s, prosocial purpose is the only one of the orientations that positively predicts middle adulthood thriving variables (p. 177). The findings suggest that a variety of purposes work well for younger people's thriving, yet as individuals grow older, the value of purpose for development lies in its specificity. This point is supported by research that shows that seeking a purpose is related to life satisfaction in adolescence and emerging adulthood, but not in mid-life (Bronk, Hill, Lapsley, Talib, & Finch, 2009). Thus, the relation between purpose and thriving is altered according to life stage.

F. PURPOSE AS "SPARKS"

Two more constructs used in the PYD and youth thriving literatures are akin to purpose: "sparks" and "contribution." The "sparks" construct was originally developed by the Search Institute in the context of their research program on young people's developmental assets (see Benson, 2006). The best definition is drawn from their survey measure prompt used with teenagers, in which sparks are described as "interests or talents you have that you are really passionate about." Involvement with sparks is accompanied by "joy and energy." One might even "lose track of time" because of such involvement, and a spark is "a really important" part of one's life. Consequently, a spark by definition gives one "a sense of purpose or focus" (Scales, Roehlkepartain, & Benson, 2010, p. 25).

"Sparks" capture the spirit of what many researchers are trying to get at when utilizing other youth purpose definitions. To a degree, "sparks" encapsulates Damon et al.'s (2003) idea of purpose as an "intention" to accomplish something that is important to self, and possibly of consequence to the world beyond self. When measured in qualitative data, some researchers who endorse Damon, Menon, and Bronk's definition seem unable to avoid operationalizing purpose as passion and interests rather than just "intentions." In practice, purpose is really measured as intentions that are acted upon, because the accounts of purpose are less convincing in the absence of such reports (i.e., see Malin et al., 2008; Mariano & Savage, 2009; Mariano & Vaillant, 2011; Moran, 2009).

"Sparks" does differ from most definitions of purpose in placing foremost emphasis on a fulfilling sense of engagement. As with categories of purpose and meaning, sparks can encompass a wide range of things. In two surveys of American 15-year-olds, however, Scales et al. (2010) found that the most frequently reported primary sparks involve the creative arts, sports, and technology. Other categories mentioned were studying and learning, the outdoors, religion and spirituality, service and activism, construction and engineering, teaching, and entrepreneurship (p. 31). With some exceptions, these findings depart from category of meaning research. However, they could explain strong links in youth purpose research of creative types of purpose to positive experiences like empathy and gratitude: these purpose types involve getting one's hands dirty in creating new things and bettering the world through concrete measures (Mariano & Savage, 2009).

As with purpose research, depth of one's sparks is a concern for thriving. The Sparks Index measures teens' knowledge of their sparks (i.e., they can identify them), how important their spark is based on what the teen experiences when doing the spark and the time spent on it, and the initiative the teen takes to develop the spark (Scales, Benson, & Roehlkepartain, 2010, p. 27). Sparks relate positively to a general sense of purpose not only by definition: teens with higher ratings on the Sparks Index report a higher sense of purpose and hope for the future (p. 32). They also report higher ratings on other positive youth outcomes, like doing well in school.

G. PURPOSE AS "CONTRIBUTION"

The term "contribution" is introduced in work developed by Lerner and colleagues (e.g., Alberts et al., 2006; Bowers et al., 2010; King et al., 2005; Lerner et al., 2005) who include it in their model of PYD. PYD has five components, or "Cs" including competence, confidence, connection, character, and caring (or compassion). Contribution is a second-order latent construct which emerges in the young person's life when the five Cs are present and is thus considered a sixth "C." Its measurement reveals its meaning. To obtain a young person's contribution score, responses to two open-ended questions are gathered. The questions ask youth to describe themselves as they would like to be and as they actually are, in terms of "what they are like and the sorts of things they do" (Lerner et al., 2005, p. 54). Responses that reflect a desire to give something to the world are coded as "absent (0), present (1), or important (2)." The second measure has youth report on participation in activities that reflect active engagement in the world around self. Contribution thus combines equally weighted ideological and behavioral components, with an emphasis on doing something that helps others, such as being a group leader, a tutor or mentor, helping friends or neighbors, volunteering in the community, or participating in school government and religious groups. The emphasis is principally on civic types of contribution, but the construct aligns quite well with practical applications of Damon et al.'s (2003) and other multifaceted purpose definitions: it combines ideological and behavioral components and self-transcendence in engaging those components. One-dimensional purpose definitions are considered in the PYD model too, however. Having a PIL os considered an aspect of positive identity inherent in "confidence" and is measured by one scale item (Lerner et al., 2005, p. 4).

H. SPECIFIC RESEARCH STUDIES ON YOUTH PURPOSE AND PYD INDICATORS AND OUTCOMES

Up to this point, we have considered conceptual relations between PYD and purpose constructs. We now discuss research that supports empirical links between youth purpose and a variety of PYD variables, broadly conceived. First, we report findings about purpose and its relation to positive person-centered variables. Next, we report purpose's relation to context-centered variables. In Table I, key studies and how they contribute to explaining the purpose–thriving relation are listed.

I. POSITIVE PERSON-CENTERED VARIABLES

We distinguish positive person-centered variables from positive context-centered variables. Two sets of person-centered variables that illustrate the purpose–PYD relationship are those pertaining to positive states and experiences relating to identity development. Relevant context-centered variables pertain to the impact that purposeful adolescents have on the world, and include contribution, and gathering support from one's environment.

J. POSITIVE STATES

We use the term "positive states" to refer to a vast array of good experiences, including positive feelings, positive personality dispositions, and positive ways of being. It is probably a good thing that we do, as multiple studies measure the same constructs in different ways. In purpose research, we note that well-being, for example, is measured according to

Table I

Overview of Research on Youth Purpose and Positive Characteristics

Author(s)	Purpose construct (s) studied	Positive characteristic(s) pertaining to findings
Bronk (2008)	Exemplary purpose	Humility
Bronk (2005)	Exemplary purpose	Openness
		Focus
		Vitality and enthusiasm
		Humility
		Gratitude
		Integrity
		Mentor relationships
		Like-minded peer communities
Bronk and Finch (2010)	Seeking purpose	Hope
	Identifying purpose	Life satisfaction
	Meaning	Openness
	Long-term aims in life	
Bronk, Hill, Lapsley, Talib, and Finch (2009)	Seeking purpose	Hope
	Identifying purpose	Life satisfaction
Burrow et al. (2010)	Purpose exploration	Hope
	Purpose commitment	Positive affect
		Goal-directed thinking (hope)
Dawes and Larson (2011)	Pursuing purpose	Engagement
Hill, Burrow, Brandenberger, Lapsley, and Quaranto (2010)	Purpose orientations	Personal development
Lerner et al. (2005)	Contribution	Character
		Confidence
		Competence
		Positive social connections
		Caring and compassion
Mariano (2011a)	Finding purpose	Social supports and influences
		Informational social supports
Mariano (2010)	Sense of purpose	Vitality
		Hope
		Optimism
		Self-control
Mariano and Damon (2008)	Purpose	Spirituality

(Continued)

Table I (*Continued*)

Author(s)	Purpose construct (s) studied	Positive characteristic(s) pertaining to findings
Mariano et al. (2010)	Purpose forms	School and teacher supports
Mariano and Savage (2009)	Purpose forms	Coping styles
	Seeking purpose	Positive experiences
	Presence of purpose	Empathy
	Life goals	Gratitude
		Generosity
		Humor
Mariano and Vaillant (2011)	Purpose forms	Positive personality traits
		Psychological adjustment
		Positive childhood environment
		Educational attainment
Roberts and Robins (2000)	Life goals	Positive personality dispositions
Reilly (2009)	Goal orientations	Talent
Scales, Benson, and Roehlkepartain (2010)	Sparks	Prosocial outcomes
		Academic well-being
		Psychological well-being
		Social well-being
Scales, Roehlkepartain, and Benson (2010)	Sparks	Achievement in school
		Positive ethnic identity
		Learning outside school
		Community involvement
		Concern with social inequalities
		Hope
		Strong relationships
		Mentor relationships
Schnell and Becker (2006)	Meaning	Openness
	Goal attainment	Conscientiousness
Shek (1993)	Sense of purpose in life	Psychological well-being
Steger et al. (in press)	Search for meaning/ purpose	Life satisfaction
Tirri and Quinn (2010)	Religious/ spiritual purpose	Authenticity
Yeager and Bundick (2009)	Purposeful work goals	Meaning in life
		Meaning in schoolwork

its aspects, such as positive affect or mood, life satisfaction, or other constructs that authors might endorse as constituting the larger construct that is well-being. We use the term positive states to fairly encompass the wide range of positive person-centered developmental experiences that have been found to be associated with youth purpose, though we are aware that researchers might not use the same reference so loosely.

The research on the types of positive states that accompany purpose is not elaborate, but some patterns are distinguishable. There is evidence that having a PIL supports coping mechanisms in adolescence, such as focusing on positive events and future states in the face of psychological challenges (Mariano & Savage, 2009) and helping youths focus on the greater implications of their efforts (Bronk, 2005). Youths with more complete and exemplary forms of purpose report exercising and experiencing these skills in ways that less purposeful youths do not. In these ways, purpose could support transcendence.

Character strengths (i.e., see Park & Peterson, 2006) that require some degree of transcendence beyond self to focus on others are associated with youth purpose, such as generosity (Bronk, 2005; Mariano & Savage, 2009), empathy (Mariano & Savage, 2009), and gratitude (Bronk, 2008; Mariano & Savage, 2009). In one study, youths with more complete forms of purpose were considered as having more "humanistic" and "political" personality dispositions, suggesting a concern for activities related to civic engagement and social welfare (Mariano & Vaillant, 2011). A puzzling finding in one interview study is that more purposeful youths report less experiences of humor than their peers. Perhaps purposeful youths take themselves, and life, much more seriously than others. However, perhaps less purposeful youths use humor as a defense in these interviews to detract attention from the fact that they have little purpose (Mariano & Savage, 2009). The need for articulation is needed in further research whether the finding is due to type of measurement or some other contingency.

Moran (2009) describes purpose as a type of "giftedness" in intrapersonal intelligence. Indeed, purpose links to various forms of psychological cohesion in adolescence and young adulthood. This happens in ways applicable to both mental health and moral character. In one study, youths with more complete forms of purpose were more likely to be rated as having well-integrated personalities by mental health professionals (Mariano & Vaillant, 2011). Young purpose exemplars exhibit greater commitment to the core value of integrity than do other adolescents (Bronk, 2005). For emerging adults, greater PIL is positively associated with greater self-control (Mariano, 2010). Purpose provides balance in thought and behavior. Purposeful young people show greater vitality and energy than others their age (Bronk, 2005; Mariano, 2010), and they show openness to ideas (Bronk, 2005; Bronk & Finch, 2010). Yet, they balance openness with focus (Bronk, 2005). Young purpose exemplars show humility: as strength of temperance (Peterson & Seligman, 2004) humility means achieving a healthy understanding of one's strengths and limitations; it is thereby distinguished from narcissism or self-regard.

Some scholars point out that feeling good and "doing well" need not correlate with either thriving (Benson & Scales, 2009) or purpose (Damon et al., 2003). Many social movers throughout history were so moved not by their satisfaction with life but rather by their dissatisfaction with it (Colby & Damon, 1992). However, for many young people, purpose does feel good (Mariano & Savage, 2009). This occurs in a number of ways. First, purpose provides young people with a conciliatory view of their present and future, and in this way, may provide comfort. Connections of purpose with hope and optimism are more than theoretical or definitional: they correlate in research with young adults (Bronk & Finch, 2010; Mariano, 2010). All types of purpose, whether primarily prosocial or directed toward self-development, correlate with perceptions of personal development for college students (Hill et al., 2010). Adolescents with more purposeful work goals find more meaning in their lives and in their schoolwork (Yeager & Bundick, 2009). Searching for a life purpose is associated with greater life satisfaction for both adolescents and emerging adults (Bronk et al., 2009). The presence of meaning or PIL is more strongly related to life satisfaction for college students who are also searching for it (Steger, Oishi, & Kesibir, in press). Shek (1993) showed that psychological well-being is connected to Chinese college students' sense of purpose.

K. POSITIVE IDENTITY

Theoretically, purpose and identity share conceptual and behavioral territory as critical developmental tasks in adolescence (Yeager & Bundick, 2009). In research, youth purpose is measured in a variety of ways akin to identity's measurement. Purpose researchers define forms; identity researchers examine statuses. Purpose researchers talk about seeking or identifying one's PIL; identity researchers speak of identity moratorium and achievement. Individuals without purpose are drifting; individuals lacking direction are described as having diffused identities (Marcia, 1980). Exploration and commitment are distinguishing characteristics of both youth purpose and identity.

In any case, the research on identity statuses and positive youth outcomes is far more established than the research on youth purpose and thriving. Adolescent identity achievement and moratorium are clearly associated with positive outcomes, such as aspects of psychological well-being. Like purpose, identity formation plays a protective role. A secure ethnic identity especially among ethnic minority adolescents, for instance, is associated with better self-esteem, optimism, and a sense of mastery over one's environment (e.g., St. Louis & Liem, 2005; Umana-Taylor & Updegraff, 2007). Extended moratorium and diffusion, however, yield less positive outcomes (e.g., see Adams & Marshall, 1996; Berzonsky, 2003; Berzonsky & Kuk, 2000; Schwartz, Zamboanga, Weisskirch, & Rodriguez, 2009). It is no wonder therefore that purpose researchers are interested in associations between purpose and identity. If there is such an alignment, could what we already know about identity and thriving tell us something about purpose and thriving? The proposition seems viable.

We know that young people who have deeper "sparks" are more likely to have a positive sense of their own ethnic identity (Scales, Roehlkepartain, & Benson, 2010, p. 27). To date, however, only one study explicitly investigates identity status alignment with purpose in a way that could tell us something about positive development. The evidence is that purpose and identity align quite well, at least for certain subgroups of adolescents. In their sample of predominantly White 14- to 18-year-olds, Burrow, O'Dell, & Hill (2010) found it possible to classify adolescents into four profiles by levels of purpose exploration and commitment in ways that concur with theories on identity formation. Results indicate a high level of purpose commitment relative to exploration within their "achieved" and "foreclosed" groups, while the opposite pattern was depicted in their "uncommitted" profile. Their "diffused" profile was distinguished by comparatively lower scores on both purpose exploration and commitment.

The terms used by Burrow, O'Dell, and Hill (2010) do not concur exactly with some interpretations of classic identity profiles because they emphasize exploration (or "seeking") to a greater degree than do these profiles. Thus, their achieved purpose groups may be very different from "identity achieved" individuals who, according to at least one author (Berk, 2009, p. 465), are not necessarily distinguished by their levels of search. Similarly, the uncommitted purpose profile, which is low on commitment but highest of all profiles on exploration, aligns much better with an explanation of youths in identity moratorium (p. 465). The distinction is important for understanding purpose's relation to thriving variables. In the study, linkages with a number of positive attributes (hope, positive emotions, and goal-directed thinking) were most apparent among achieved and foreclosed purpose groups and least apparent among the uncommitted and diffused groups. In contrast, research on identity formation favors achieved and moratorium (like the uncommitted group in Burrow, O'Dell, & Hill's study) statuses when it comes to positive developmental indicators. Identity foreclosed (along with identity diffused) individuals tend to have more adjustment difficulties (Berk, 2009, p. 465). This research thus suggests that when it comes to PYD, identity and purpose may work in slightly different ways. As Burrow et al. (2010) note, there may be "a correspondence between stronger commitments to purpose and youths' sense of personal agency and well-being." Purpose might promote youth thriving to the degree that it engenders commitment to something good. The issue of purpose search may not be as important for positive development as it is in identity research.

L. POSITIVE CONTEXT-CENTERED VARIABLES

Context-centered variables refer to multiple things. Here, we use the term to refer to positive experiences or relationships associated with purpose that are located within the young person's environment. We also consider the young person's actions pertaining to purpose that are directed toward community in a positive way. How does having a purpose influence young people's contribution to others? How do the people within the young person's environment, in turn, support the emergence and inspiration of purpose? These are all questions addressed by a context-centered focus. The focus is in keeping with recognition of the bidirectional nature of person and context variables in considering how purpose connects to thriving. In theory, this perspective allows a more comprehensive approach to understanding the purpose–thriving relationship and provides a full picture of the young person's functioning. Benson (2006), for instance, identifies variables in both the person and environment considered to be positive developmental assets.

Recent studies indicate that the development of a positive purpose during adolescence results in long-term benefits not only to young people but also to society (Damon, 2008; Damon et al., 2003). In practice, we find that research on how youth purpose is impacted by, and impacts, positive context-centered variables is rare. Scales, Benson, and Roehlkepartain (2010) found that young people who have deeper sparks are more involved in community issues than other youths. A contrasting view is offered by an early study, in which Butler (1968) concluded that having a sense of PIL does not impact levels of social action in college students.

Measures used to study sparks and sense of purpose is clearly different, however, and may impact these results.

In one analysis, Lerner et al. (2005) found that their five "Cs" of positive development jointly contribute to adolescents' contribution behaviors. Confidence, character, and personal and social competence are the variables that relate most closely to contribution when other variables (i.e., income) are controlled for, however (p. 55). Thus, of the five Cs, social variables like achieving school engagement (one component of competence in the model) may align most with having a prosocial purpose.

Emerging research finds that for some groups of adolescents, reports of the presence of general social supports correlate positively and significantly with finding a PIL. Supports for purpose come from a variety of sources, including parents, teachers, classmates, friends, and the school environment, as well as other mentors and role models. Young purpose exemplars report more intense and long-term relationships with mentors than do adolescents with no discernible sense of purpose (Bronk, 2005). Receiving of general support from others are reported by almost all adolescents. Highly purposeful youths, however, report receiving support that both aligns with their personal interests and goals and that is informational in nature, providing new knowledge that the young person can utilize toward his or her chosen ends (Mariano, 2011a,b). School is clearly an important context for the development of youth purpose. However, in middle school, adolescents with only moderately complete forms of purpose report most support from their teachers and school. Highly purposeful youths, and youths with little purpose, report less support from these sources (Mariano, Going, Schrock, & Sweeting, 2010). These findings need to be borne out with more representative samples, however.

III. Discussion

Current research on purpose and its relationship to PYD requires elaboration in a number of directions. Future research should more extensively articulate how communities can promote youth purpose in a way that is beneficial for adolescents. Researchers need to consider ways that purpose can be taught and fostered, through formal education or otherwise, and in a way that will promote thriving. Evidence-based practices are needed. Current studies highlight environmental variables that may distinguish youths with high levels of purpose, such as higher quality role model and mentor relationships, good teachers, supportive schools, and support from individuals that is informative and directed at adolescents' interests (Bronk, 2005; Mariano, 2011a; Mariano, Going, Schrock, &

Sweeting, 2011; Scales et al., 2010). Further, pursuing a purpose is found to be one goal type that helps adolescents who are already involved in organized youth programs to stay involved and feel really engaged in them (Dawes & Larson, 2011). Given the limited nature of these studies, however, much still needs to be known about the ecologies that support purpose. Fortunately, applied research on instructing for purpose is underway as of the writing of this chapter. A body of research of this type might tell us something new about the purpose–PYD relationship.

We do not discuss in great detail how cultural and demographic differences affect the purpose–thriving relationship. Differences by gender, ethnicity, socioeconomic status, educational status, culture, or other variables certainly would not be surprising to find. At the moment, the findings are somewhat unclear. Purpose level differences are found by gender in some studies, but are absent in others (Damon et al., 2003, p. 125). Girls and boys do endorse sparks of a different nature, however: significantly more boys cite sports and technology, while more girls mention the arts (Scales et al., 2010, p. 31). Children whose parents have at least a college education have significantly greater sparks than children of parents with only some college (p. 30). Females have significantly higher contribution scores than males, yet there are no significant differences in contribution by race or ethnicity (Lerner et al., 2005, p. 55). These findings on purpose-related constructs could illumine demographic differences in the purpose–thriving relation, but they need to be compared with similar studies that utilize the purpose construct with more specification.

Cross-national and cultural differences in purpose and thriving seem like almost a given if one engages sociocultural perspectives that describe the content of purpose as culturally transmitted. One's life purpose and what it means to achieve it in hunter-gatherer societies will certainly differ from modern western cultural expectations, for instance (Bronk, Menon, & Damon, 2004). However, direct research in this area is still needed to accurately describe purpose–thriving variations by culture. To elaborate on this point, consider the idea that ultimate happiness, a rather elusive term, is frequently considered a parent's fundamental goal for their emerging young adult. In the context of a normative parent–adolescent relationship, this ideal is not thought to be misplaced or negatively construed in western society. Parents and others might argue that attention to self-development first is, or should be, the context from which purpose develops. But the tendency to separate self from others is a definitively western and middle class cultural view. In western perspectives, the self is made meaningful primarily in reference to a set of attributes that are internal to the bounded, separate self. In contrast, some other cultures adopt a more collective view of self. In Asian cultures, development is meaningful in reference to the social relations of which the self is a participating part (Kitayama, Markus, Matsumoto, & Norasakkunkit, 1997). So how do such opposite pathways to and from purpose manifest themselves in adolescents' lives? How does each pathway promote thriving? Do both pathways work well in promoting PYD? We are not the first to point out the need to settle these types of questions, ideally with waves of longitudinal data (Lerner et al., 2005, p. 62).

For the sake of providing boundaries in the discussion, this review neglects multiple purpose-related constructs. Our aim is to avoid the risk of giving only brief attention to constructs that really require extensive discussion. Some constructs represent cutting edge research pertaining to PYD. Lerner, Roeser, and Phelps (2008), for instance, astutely suggest that the sense of generosity derived from transcendence and noble purpose that allows the young person to contribute in important ways to his or her world is "the essence of spirituality" (2008, p. 3). We do not discuss spirituality, even though there is some work that investigates it in the context of youth purpose (e.g., Mariano & Damon, 2008; Tirri & Quinn, 2010). Fortunately, these topics are given proper attention elsewhere in this volume (e.g., see King's chapter on spirituality and PYD).

IV. Conclusions

We find that the work on youth purpose and PYD is still in its early stages. Although the research efforts are rare, the progress made thus far is quite promising. For one, it is remarkable that the fields of psychology and child development have evolved to such an extent that purpose — a topic that at one time might have been considered a rather soft, not to mention unmeasurable, aspect of human experience — is now at the forefront of inquiry. This fact is evident in the attention given to purpose in this volume. The research reviewed in this chapter shows that purpose is very measurable, and in a variety of ways. A second remarkable development is that purpose is now considered important for the positive development of young people and not just adults. People do not just develop meaning and purpose in response to a long life: purpose is a salient and emergent phenomenon in adolescence and is important for *youth* thriving in a number of ways. The charge now is for social scientists to explore even more extensively just how purpose supports PYD for all young people, everywhere.

REFERENCES

Adams, G. R., & Marshall, S. (1996). A developmental social psychology of identity: Understanding the person in context. *Journal of Adolescence, 19,* 429–442.

Alberts, A. E., Christiansen, E. D., Chase, P., Naudeau, S., Phelps, E., & Lerner, R. (2006). Qualitative and quantitative assessments of thriving and contribution in early adolescence: Findings from the 4-H study of positive youth development. *Journal of Youth Development, 1*(2).

Andrews, M., Bundick, M., Jones, A., Bronk, K. C., Mariano, J. M., & Damon, W. (2006). *Revised youth purpose interview.* Unpublished instrument. Stanford,CA: Stanford Center on Adolescence.

Arnett, J. (2000). Emerging adulthood: A theory of development from the late teens through the twenties. *The American Psychologist, 55,* 469–480.

Baumeister, R. F. (1991). *Meanings of life.* New York, NY: Guilford.

Benard, B. (1991). *Fostering resiliency in kids: Protective factors in the family, school and community.* San Francisco, CA: Western Regional Center for Drug Free Schools and Communities, Far West Laboratory.

Benson, P. L. (2006). *All kids are our kids: What communities must do to raise caring and responsible children and adolescents* San Francisco, CA: Jossey-Bass.

Benson, P. L., & Scales, P. C. (2009). The definition and preliminary measurement of thriving in adolescence. *The Journal of Positive Psychology, 4*(1), 85–104.

Berk, L. E. (2009). *Child development* Boston, MA: Pearson.

Berzonsky, M. D. (2003). Identity style and well-being: Does commitment matter? *Identity: An International Journal of Theory and Research, 3,* 131–142.

Berzonsky, M. D., & Kuk, L. S. (2000). Identity status, processing style, and the transition to university. *Journal of Adolescent Research, 15,* 81–98.

Bowers, E. P., Li, Y., Kiley, M., Brittian, A., Lerner, J. V., & Lerner, R. M. (2010). The five Cs model of positive you development: A longitudinal analysis of confirmatory factor structure and measurement invariance. *Journal of Youth and Adolescence, 39,* 720–735.

Bronk, K. C. (2005). *Portraits of purpose: A study examining the ways a sense of purpose contributes to positive youth development.* Available from ProQuest Dissertations and Theses database. (UMI No. 3187267).

Bronk, K. C. (2008). Humility among adolescent purpose exemplars. *The Journal of Research in Character Education, 6*(1), 35–51.

Bronk, K. C., & Finch, W. H. (2010). Adolescent characteristics by type of long-term aim in life. *Applied Developmental Science, 14*(1), 35–44.

Bronk, K. C., Hill, P., Lapsley, D., Talib, T., & Finch, H. (2009). Purpose, hope, and life satisfaction in three age groups. *The Journal of Positive Psychology, 4*(6), 500–510.

Bronk, K. C., Menon, J., & Damon, W. (2004). *Youth purpose: Conclusions from a working conference of leading scholars.* Stanford, CA: Stanford Center on Adolescence.

Bundick, M., Andrews, M., Jones, A., Mariano, J. M., Bronk, K. C., & Damon, W. (2006). *Revise youth purpose survey.* Unpublished instrumentStanford, CA: Stanford Center on Adolescence.

Burrow, A., O'Dell, A., & Hill, P. (2010). Profiles of a developmental asset: Youth purpose as a context for hope and well-being. *Journal of Youth and Adolescence, 39*(11), 1265–1273.

Butler, A. C. (1968). Purpose in life through social action. *The Journal of Social Psychology, 74*(2), 243–250.

Colby, A., & Damon, W. (1992). *Some do care: Contemporary lives of moral commitment.* New York, NY: Free Press.

Crumbaugh, J. C., & Maholick, L. T. (1969). *Manual of instruction for the Purpose-in-Life-Test.* Munster, IN: Psychometric Affiliates.

Damon, W. (2004). What is positive youth development? *The Annals of the American Academy of Political and Social Science, 591*, 13–23.

Damon, W. (2008). *The path to purpose: How young people find their calling in life.* New York, NY: The Free Press.

Damon, W. (1995). *Greater expectations: Overcoming the culture of indulgence in our homes and schools.* New York, NY: Free Press.

Damon, W., Menon, J., & Bronk, K. C. (2003). The development of purpose during adolescence. *Applied Developmental Science, 7*(3), 119–128.

Dawes, N. P., & Larson, R. (2011). How youth get engaged: Grounded-theory research on motivational development in organized youth programs. *Developmental Psychology, 47*(1), 259–269.

De Vogler, K. L., & Ebersole, P. (1980). Categorization of college students' meaning in life. *Psychological Reports, 46*, 387–390.

De Vogler, K. L., & Ebersole, P. (1983). Young adolescents' meaning in life. *Psychological Reports, 52*, 427–431.

Emmons, R. (1999). *The psychology of ultimate concerns: Motivation and spirituality in personality.* New York, NY: Guilford.

Erikson, E. H. (1968). *Identity: Youth and crisis.* New York, NY: Norton.

Frankl, V. E. (1959). *Man's search for meaning: An introduction to logotherapy.* Boston, MA: Beacon.

Grum, M., & von Collani, G. (2007). Measuring Big-Five personality dimensions with the implicit association test—Implicit personality traits or self-esteem? *Personality and Individual Differences, 43*, 2205–2217.

Hall, G. S. (1904). *Adolescence: Its psychology and its relations to physiology, anthropology, sociology, sex, crime, religion, and education* (Vols. 1 and 2), Englewood Cliffs, NJ: Prentice-Hall.

Hill, P. L., Burrow, A. L., Brandenberger, J., Lapsley, D., & Quaranto, J. C. (2010). Collegiate purpose orientations and well-being in early and middle adulthood. *Journal of Applied Developmental Psychology, 31*, 173–179.

Hill, P. L., Burrow, A. L., O'Dell, A. C., & Thornton, M. A. (2010). Classifying adolescents' conceptions of purpose in life. *The Journal of Positive Psychology, 5*(6), 466–473.

Hutzell, R. R. (1995). Life purpose questionnaire. In L. L. Jeffries (Ed.), *Adolescence and meaning in life.* (Doctoral dissertation, University of Houston, 1995). Dissertation Abstracts International, 56, O8B 4634.

Hutzell, R. R., & Finck, W. C. (1994). Adapting the life purpose questionnaire for use in adolescent populations. *The International Forum for Logotherapy, 17*, 42–46.

Inhelder, B., & Piaget, J. (1958). *The growth of logical thinking from childhood to adolescence.* New York, NY: Basic Books.

Keyes, C. L. M. (2002). The mental health continuum: From languishing to flourishing in life. *Journal of Health and Social Behavior, 43*, 207–222.

King, P. E. (2004). Towards a theory of thriving: A perspective on optimal development. Unpublished paper, Fuller Theological Seminary, Pasadena.

King, P. E., Dowling, E. M., Mueller, R., White, K., Schultz, W., Osborn, P., et al. (2005). Thriving in adolescence. The voices of youth-serving practitioners, parents, and early and late adolescents. *Journal of Early Adolescence, 25*(1), 94–112.

Kitayama, S., Markus, H. R., Matsumoto, H., & Norasakkunkit, V. (1997). Individual and collective processes in the construction of the self: Self-enhancement in the United States and self-criticism in Japan. *Personality and Social Psychology, 72*(6), 1245–1267.

Lerner, R. M., Lerner, J. V., Almerigi, J. B., Theokas, C., Phelps, E., Gestsdottir, S., et al. (2005). Positive youth development, participation in community youth development programs, and community contributions of fifth-grade adolescents: Findings from the first wave of the 4-H Study of Positive Youth Development. *Journal of Early Adolescence, 25*, 17–71.

Lerner, R. M., Roeser, R. W., & Phelps, E. (2008). Positive development, spirituality, and generosity in youth: An introduction to the issues. In R. M. Lerner, R. W. Roeser & E. Phelps (Eds.), *Positive youth development and spirituality: From theory to research* (pp. 3–22). West Conshohocken, PA: Templeton Foundation Press.

Malin, H., Reilly, T. S., Yeager, D., Moran, S., Andrews, M., Bundick, M., et al. (2008). *Interview coding process for forms of purpose determination.* Stanford, CA: Stanford Center on Adolescence.

Marcia, J. E. (1980). Identity in adolescence. In J. Adelson (Ed.), *Handbook of adolescent psychology* (pp. 159–187). New York, NY: Wiley.

Mariano, J. M. (2010). Three problems in the study of youth purpose for college student development. In *Poster presented at the 36th Annual Conference for the Association for Moral Education (AME), St. Louis, MO.*

Mariano, J. M. (2011a). The psychological requirements of inclusion: A positive youth development view. In P. Jones, J. Carr & J. Fauske (Eds.), *Leading for inclusion.* New York, NY: Teacher's College Press.

Mariano, J. M. (2011b). An examination of how formal and informal educational contexts support purpose in adolescent girls. Manuscript submitted for publication (copy on file with author).

Mariano, J. M., & Damon, W. (2008). The role of religious faith and spirituality in supporting purpose in adolescence. In R. M. Lerner, R. W. Roeser & E. Phelps (Eds.), *Positive youth development and spirituality: From theory to research.* (pp. 210–230). West Conshohocken, PA: Templeton Foundation Press.

Mariano, J. M., Going, J., Schrock, K., & Sweeting, K. (2011). *Youth purpose and the perception of social supports among African American girls.* Manuscript submitted for publication (copy on file with first author).

Mariano, J. M., & Savage, J. (2009). Exploring the language of youth purpose: References to positive states and coping styles by adolescents with different kinds of purpose. *The Journal of Research in Character Education, 7*(1), 1–24.

Mariano, J. M., & Vaillant, G. V. (2011). Youth purpose among the "Greatest Generation". Manuscript submitted for publication (copy on file with first author).

Mariano, J. M., Going, J., Schrock, K., & Sweeting, K. (2010). Youth purpose and perceived social supports among ethnic minority middle school girls. Manuscript submitted for publication (copy on file with first author).

Marken, R. S. (1990). A science of purpose. *The American Behavioral Scientist, 34*(1), 6–13.

Masten, A. S., & Coatsworth, J. D. (1998). The development of competence in favorable and unfavorable environments: Lessons from research on successful children. *The American Psychologist, 53*(2), 205–220.

Menon, J., Bronk, K. C., & Damon, W. (2004). *Youth purpose survey.* Unpublished instrument. Stanford,CA: Stanford Center on Adolescence.

Molcar, C. C., & Stuempfig, D. W. (1988). Effects of world view on purpose in life. *The Journal of Psychology, 122*, 337–365.

Moran, S. (2009). Purpose: Giftedness in intrapersonal Intelligence. *High Ability Studies, 20* (2), 143–159.

Moran, S., & Damon, W. (2008). Adolescents' emic understanding of purpose. In *Paper presented at the Annual Meeting of the American Psychological Association. Boston, MA.*

Noblejas de la Flor, M. A. (1997). Meaning levels and drug abuse therapy: An empirical study. *International Forum for Logotherapy, 20*(1), 46–51.

Padelford, B. L. (1974). Relationship between drug involvement and purpose in life. *Journal of Clinical Psychology, 30,* 303–305.

Park, N., & Peterson, C. (2006). Moral competence and character strengths among adolescents: The development and validation of the Values in Action Inventory of Strengths for youth. *Journal of Adolescence, 29,* 891–909.

Peterson, C., & Seligman, M. E. P. (2004). *Character strengths and virtues: A handbook and classification.* Oxford, UK: Oxford University Press.

Prager, E. (1996). Exploring personal meaning in an age-differentiated Australian sample: Another look at the sources of meaning profile (SOMP). *Journal of Aging Studies, 10* (2), 117–136.

Prager, E. (1998). Observations of personal meaning in sources for Israeli age cohorts. *Aging & Mental Health, 2*(2), 128–136.

Reilly, T. S. (2009). Talent, purpose, and goal orientation: Case studies of talented adolescents. *High Ability Studies, 20*(2), 161–172.

Reker, G. T., & Peacock, E. J. (1981). The life attitude profile (LAP): A multidimensional instrument for assessing attitudes toward life. *Canadian Journal of Behavioral Science, 13,* 64–73.

Reker, G. T., & Wong, P. T. P. (1988). Aging as an individual process: Toward a theory of personal meaning. In J. E. Birren & V. L. Bengston (Eds.), *Emergent theories of aging.* (pp. 214–246). New York, NY: Springer.

Roberts, B. W., & Robins, R. W. (2000). Broad dispositions, broad aspirations: The intersection of personality traits and major life goals. *Personality and Social Psychology Bulletin, 26,* 1284–1296.

Ryff, C. D., & Singer, B. (1998). Middle age and well-being. *Encyclopedia of Mental Health, 2,* 707–719.

Sappington, A. A., & Kelly, P. J. (1995). Self perceived anger problems in college students. *International Forum for Logotherapy, 18,* 74–82.

Sayles, M. L. (1994). Adolescents' purpose in life and engagement in risky behaviors: Differences by gender and ethnicity (Doctoral dissertation. University of North Carolina at Greensboro, 1994). *Dissertation Abstracts International, 55,* 09A 2727.

Scales, P. C., Benson, P. L., & Roehlkepartain, E. C. (2010). Adolescent thriving: The role of sparks, relationships, and empowerment. *Journal of Youth and Adolescence,* doi:10.1007/s10964-010-9578-6.

Scales, P. C., Roehlkepartain, E. C., & Benson, P. L. (2010). *Teen Voice 2010: Relationships that matter to America's teens.* Minneapolis and Richfield, MN: Search Institute and Best Buy Children's Foundation.

Schlesinger, S., Susman, M., & Koenigsberg, J. (1990). Self esteem and purpose in life: A comparative study of women alcoholics. *Journal of Alcohol and Drug Education, 36,* 127–141.

Schnell, T. (2009). The sources of meaning and meaning in life questionnaire (SOME): Relations to demographics and well-being. *The Journal of Positive Psychology, 4*(6), 483–499.

Schnell, T., & Becker, P. (2006). Personality and meaning in life. *Personality and Individual Differences, 41,* 117–129.

Schwartz, S. J., Zamboanga, B. L., Weisskirch, R. S., & Rodriguez, L. (2009). The relationships of personal and ethnic identity exploration to indices of adaptive and maladaptive psychosocial functioning. *International Journal of Behavioral Development, 33* (2), 131–144.

Shek, D. T. (1993). The Chinese purpose-in-life test and psychological well-being in Chinese college students. *International Forum for Logotherapy, 16*, 35–42.

Showalter, S. M., & Wagener, L. M. (2000). Adolescents' meaning in life: A replication of De Vogler and Ebersole (1983). *Psychological Reports, 87*, 115–126.

St. Louis, G. R., & Liem, J. H. (2005). Ego identity, ethnic identity, and the psycho-social well-being of ethnic minority and majority college students. *Identity, 5*, 227–246.

Steger, M. F., Frazier, P., Oishi, S., & Kaler, M. (2006). The meaning in life questionnaire: Assessing the presence of and search for meaning in life. *Journal of Counseling Psychology, 53*, 80–93.

Steger, M. F., Oishi, S., & Kesibir, S. (in press). Is a life without meaning satisfying? The moderating role of the search for meaning in satisfaction with life judgments. *Journal of Positive Psychology.*

Taylor, S. E., & Brown, J. D. (1988). Illusion and well-being: A social psychological perspective on mental health. *Psychological Bulletin, 103*, 193–210.

Thelen, E., & Smith, L. B. (2006). Dynamic systems theories. In R. M. Lerner (Ed.), *Handbook of child psychology: Vol. 1. Theoretical models of human development.* (6th ed., pp. 258–312). Hoboken, NJ: Wiley.

Theokas, C., Amerigi, J. B., Lerner, R. M., Dowling, E. M., Benson, P. L., Scales, P. C., et al. (2005). Conceptualizing and modeling individual and ecological asset components of thriving in early adolescence. *Journal of Early Adolescence, 25*(1), 113–143.

Tirri, K., & Quinn, B. (2010). Exploring the role of religion and spirituality in the development of purpose: Case studies of purposeful youth. *British Journal of Religious Education, 32*(3), 201–214.

Umana-Taylor, A. J., & Updegraff, K. A. (2007). Latino adolescents' mental health: Exploring the interrelations among discrimination, ethnic identity, cultural orientation, self-esteem, and depressive symptoms. *Journal of Adolescence, 30*, 549–567.

Waisberg, J. L., & Porter, J. E. (1994). Purpose in life and outcome treatment for alcohol dependence. *The British Journal of Clinical Psychology, 33*, 49–63.

Warren, R. (2002). *The purpose driven life.* Grand Rapids, MI: Zondervan.

Webster's New World Dictionary of American English. (1991). New York, NY: Simon & Shuster.

Yeager, D. S., & Bundick, M. J. (2009). The role of purposeful work goals in promoting meaning in life and in school work during adolescence. *Journal of Adolescent Research, 24*(4), 352–423.

POSITIVE PATHWAYS TO ADULTHOOD: THE ROLE OF HOPE IN ADOLESCENTS' CONSTRUCTIONS OF THEIR FUTURES

Kristina L. Schmid* and Shane J. Lopez[†]

* ELIOT-PEARSON DEPARTMENT OF CHILD DEVELOPMENT, TUFTS UNIVERSITY, MEDFORD, MASSACHUSETTS, USA
[†] GALLUP & CLIFTON STRENGTHS SCHOOL, OMAHA, NEBRASKA, USA

Abstract

Hope has been studied within various disciplines since at least the 1950s, as researchers have attempted to describe, explain, and predict the association between human functioning and this seemingly vital–yet often abstract–construct. Recent work by Snyder and colleagues identified future goal orientation as a necessary component of hope. For developmental scientists, understanding the associations between hope and intentional self regulation strategies that may help young people achieve their goals could provide insight into the positive development of youth. In this chapter, we present a developmental systems framework for elucidating the links between hope and adaptive developmental outcomes, and we discuss recent research that provides evidence for the relationship between hopeful future expectations and thriving in the adolescent period. Finally, we provide guidelines for taking the next steps in not only

Advances in Child Development and Behavior
Richard M. Lerner, Jacqueline V. Lerner and Janette B. Benson : Editors

assessing hope among diverse youth, but also in harnessing that hope for positive constructions of adolescents' pathways to adulthood.

Hope, as a psychological phenomenon, has been studied within various disciplines since at least the 1950s (Menninger, 1960), as researchers have attempted to describe, predict, and explain the association between human functioning and this seemingly vital—yet often abstract—construct. While hope has been defined within the context of different theories and models over the past half century, recent work places hope largely in clinical and educational contexts as a cognitive, emotional, and motivational psychological asset. For example, research points to the role of hope in coping with stress and regulating emotions (e.g., Irving et al., 2004) and in predicting academic achievement among youth (e.g., Ciarrochi, Heaven, & Davies, 2007). In addition, hope has received a lot of recent attention in the nursing literature in regard to its potential to improve the quality of life among young cancer patients (Hendricks-Ferguson, 2008; Herth, 2001).

Despite the various conceptualizations of hope that might exist across fields and research laboratories, a critical, organizing theme is the link between hope and future goal orientation. For developmental scientists, the associations between hope and the motivational or self-regulatory behaviors, emotions, and cognitions that may help youth achieve their goals are of particular importance. Noting the formative role of goal achievement in different scholars' ideas about hope, Snyder and colleagues (e.g., Rand & Cheavens, 2009; Snyder, Rand, & Sigmon, 2002) define hope as an individual's self-perceived ability to generate paths toward attaining desired goals. They also regard hope as a means for the person to motivate himself or herself to act to travel along goal-directed pathways. Thus, Snyder's hope theory links hope to intentional self-regulation processes, a focus of concern among scholars interested in the links between intentional self-regulation processes and the positive development of youth (e.g., Schmid et al., 2011).

In epitomizing the link between action along goal-directed pathways and self regulation, Snyder's hope theory (see Rand & Cheavens, 2009, Figure 30.1 on p. 326) specifies that a person's learning history includes both "hope thoughts" and beliefs about one's efficacy. Whereas hope thoughts refer to one's understanding of pathways, that is, time-ordered correlated events or causal relations, efficacy beliefs refer to the agency of the individual in establishing and managing pathways. Together, pathways and agency represent an iterative process that involves the role of the self as an efficacious actor within a causal sequence. Snyder specifies as well that hope thoughts are precursors of a set of emotions about valued outcomes and, in turn, of additional thoughts about pathways and agency, that motivate the person to engage in actions that are directed to attaining a goal (Snyder, Rand, et al., 2002).

Research derived from Snyder's hope theory uses the measure he and colleagues developed to index one's confidence and competence to set and achieve goals (Snyder et al., 1997). This research has demonstrated covariation between high levels of hope and physical health (e.g., involving knowledge about health-related issues and intentions to follow health-supported regimens), coping with disease and injury, and mental health and adjustment (see Rand & Cheavens, 2009 for a review). These findings suggest that there are impressive links between hope and positive physical and psychological functioning.

Despite a growing interest in hope as a variable of importance in basic and applied research, particularly in terms of its applicability for positive youth development (PYD; Schmid et al., 2011), little empirical or theoretical work has considered the role of hope from a relational, developmental systems perspective (Overton, 2010). Embedding hope in such a theoretical frame would enable scholars to specify the role of this construct in facilitating developmental trajectories involving mutually influential and beneficial exchanges between the developing individual and the multiple, interconnected levels of the ecology of human development. These levels involve family and peer relations and connections to school, community organizations, faith institutions, and the institutions of civil society.

Moreover, the role of hope for shaping the developmental processes involved in adolescents' constructions of their futures remains an understudied arena within developmental science. In addition, although Snyder's theory relates hope to goal motivation (Rand & Cheavens, 2009; Snyder, Rand, et al., 2002), Aspinwall and Leaf (2002) note that a critical element missing from Snyder's treatment of hope is an explicit focus on future orientation, that is, the content of one's future goals and beliefs regarding future prospects. Given that, during adolescence, the individual prototypically engages in self-defining (identity) processes oriented to future roles (e.g., Nurmi, 1991), hope, as a facet of intentional self-regulation processes linked to the attainment of sought-after roles, becomes a crucial variable to study in regard to the successful, positive development of youth. Therefore, the purpose of this chapter is threefold. First, we will present a developmental systems framework for understanding the links between hope and adaptive developmental outcomes. Second, we will discuss recent research that provides evidence for the links between adolescents' hopeful future expectations and positive outcomes. A final goal for this chapter is to provide researchers with guidelines for taking the next steps in not only assessing hope among diverse youth but also in harnessing that hope for positive constructions of adolescents' future roles.

I. Hope and Adolescents' Future Orientations

Currently, Snyder's conception of hope frames important research about the status of America's youth. For example, using Snyder's hope theory framework, the 2010 *Gallup Student Poll* proposes that hope is "the ideas and energy for the future," a cognitive and motivational construct oriented in a young person's meaningful goals (Lopez, Agrawal, & Calderon, 2010). Findings from the 2010 *Gallup Student Poll*, which surveyed over 240,000 youth in Grades 5 through 12, suggested that hope is positively and significantly correlated with a host of thriving indicators. Most notably, the student poll found that hope was very strongly correlated with measures of self-efficacy, intentional self regulation, and well-being. Lopez and colleagues found that hope is a malleable construct, supported by key players in the youth context, including parents, school, and the community (Lopez et al., 2010).

Clearly, the second decade of life has potential to be a wellspring of hope, owing to the physical, physiological, emotional, and cognitive changes that define the adolescent period. According to Erikson (1959), Côté (2009), and others (e.g., Schwartz, Luyckx, & Vignoles, in press), a key task of adolescence is to organize these changes into a new definition of the self, one that will help the young person prepare for a future adaptive role. Cognitive developments prototypical during adolescence help the young person imagine and plan for his or her future self (Nurmi, 2004). To the extent that cognitions and emotions associated with these plans are positive and energizing, an adolescent may be said to have hopeful expectations for the future.

A. THE ROLE OF HOPE IN CONSTRUCTING A POSITIVE FUTURE

Adolescents' thoughts about their futures are typically concerned with normative developmental outcomes, including educational and vocational achievements, having a family, or lifestyle or material desires (Nurmi, 1991). These goals for one's future may in fact reflect actual possibilities for youth, since developmental paths may be marked by multidirectionality, equipotentiality, and equifinality across individuals

(Lerner, 2002). That is, across adolescence, the individual may pursue different end states and may take any number of routes toward his or her goals. Although starting at different points, individuals may end up reaching similar ends. Of course, the reality is that the particular paths taken by youth are shaped by both individual characteristics—aspirations, hope, cognitive, and behavioral skills—and contextual influences (e.g., "developmental assets"; Benson, Scales, Hamilton, & Semsa, 2006; Benson, Scales, & Syvertsen, 2011) found in families, schools, peer groups, communities, and the vicissitudes of their historical era. Variables in these settings may serve as barriers or assets to achieving future expectations (Nurmi, 2004).

Within developmental science, a key goal is to identify features of the individual or the context that will help explain why certain adolescents are able to construct positive futures, while others follow developmental paths marked by problematic behaviors. Just as researchers and practitioners are energized by the aspiration (the "hope") to optimize youth development (in addition to describing and explaining it; Baltes, Reese, & Nesselroade, 1988), so too may hope be a motivating factor for youth to attain their goals. Hope reflects positively valenced expectations about the self, others, valued institutions, or desired events, and it encompasses both cognitions and emotions regarding the future. Later, we discuss some processes by which hope may influence the behaviors of adolescents toward achieving future goals. However, in order to better understand the role of hope in shaping adaptive outcomes for youth, it is important to first place hope within a developmental systems framework.

II. Understanding Hope from a Developmental Systems Perspective

A focus on the nature of the influence of individual and contextual characteristics on the attainment of developmental outcomes represents a defining feature of contemporary developmental science (e.g., Lerner, 2006). Historically, theoretical foundations for the study of human development were based on a Cartesian split conception that development could be reduced to direct influences of either the environment or biology. However, the contemporary study of human development is predicated on a relational scientific worldview which holds that all levels of organization within an individual's ecology, from the biological to the sociocultural and historical levels, are integrated, or fused (Lerner, 2002; Overton, 2010).

This relational paradigm is thus a meta-theory that rejects debates of "nature versus nurture" (and other split conceptions, such as continuity–discontinuity) of human development as inherently counterfactual. That is, relational meta-theory maintains that because the organism and its context are always mutually embedded and mutually influential, it is not useful to discuss relative influences of environment, on one hand, or genetics on the other (Overton, 2010).

Theories within this relational paradigm are often modeled through a developmental systems framework (e.g., Bronfenbrenner & Morris, 2006; Ford & Lerner, 1992; Magnusson & Stattin, 2006; Overton, 2010). Developmental systems theory holds that development—for example, involving the physiological, somatic, cognitive, emotional, behavioral, and social processes that comprise individual ontogeny—is the result of dynamic interaction of the individual and his or her context. That is, because of the integration of the levels of organization within the individual's ecology (e.g., the biological, psychological, and social levels), developmental systems theories emphasize that there are mutually influential relations between the individual and his or her context, represented as individual $\leftrightarrow$ contextual relations (Lerner, 2004; Overton, 2006). These relations regulate the course of development. Further, because of the ability of the individual to act on his or her environment, the agency of an adolescent (or any individual) in guiding his or her own development is a critical feature of this fused relationship. That is, individuals actively contribute to the developmental regulations in which they are involved, and such actions constitute a means through which adolescents construct pathways toward future adult roles (Lerner, 2006).

One example of this agency is that the adolescent must select behaviors that both serve his or her own development and contribute to his or her own context in order to achieve future goals. In other words, to function adaptively in the face of the myriad changes that characterize adolescence, youth must maintain or enhance the developmental assets that exist in their ecologies, by supporting the contexts that are supporting them (e.g., Lerner, Freund, De Stefanis, & Habermas, 2001; Nurmi, 1991). That is, *adaptive developmental regulation* occurs when the person–context relationship is mutually beneficial to both person and context (Brandstädter, 2006). Moreover, one's capacity for adaptive developmental regulation, that is, his or her ability to successfully align individual strengths with contextual resources, is an agentic process that is shaped by such individual characteristics as intentional self regulation (e.g., Baltes, Lindenberger, & Staudinger, 2006; Gestsdóttir & Lerner, 2008). Intentional self regulation may involve selecting goals (S), optimizing one's resources in order to achieve those goals (O), and compensating by adjusting when original goals are blocked or when strategies for optimization fail (C; Freund & Baltes, 2002). This formulation reflects the "SOC" model of Baltes and colleagues (Baltes, 1997; Baltes & Baltes, 1990; Freund & Baltes, 2002).

In addition to intentional self regulation, other psychological characteristics related to cognitive and emotional development have been found to be important influences on the shaping of future adult roles (e.g., Nurmi, 2004). Hope has been a particular focus among researchers interested in the cognitive and motivational constructs associated with positive developmental outcomes, including educational achievement (e.g., Curry, Snyder, Cook, Ruby, & Rehm, 1997; Snyder et al., 2002), psychological well-being (e.g., Arnau, Rosen, Finch, Rhudy, & Fortunato, 2007; Valle, Huebner, & Suldo, 2006), coping and resilience (e.g., among adolescents with cancer; Haase, 2004), and predictors of thriving among youth, for example, in the form of PYD (e.g., Schmid et al., 2011). Figure 1 presents this role of hope within the individual ↔ context relations characterizing the developmental system. As seen in the figure, hope is conceptualized as an individual strength of adolescents that is fused with ecological assets. Together, adaptive developmental regulations lead to PYD, which in turn is positively associated with youth contribution, and negatively associated with risk or problem behaviors. These positive and negative developmental outcomes provide feedback vis-à-vis changes to both the individual and the context, as well as to the individual ↔ context relations.

As emphasized in contemporary developmental systems theories (e.g., Lerner, 2006; Overton, 2010), and as displayed in Figure 1, neither individual attributes (such as hope) nor contexts alone, or an additive combination of these factors, determine the course of development. Rather, mutually influential *relations* (as indicated by the bidirectional arrow) between the developing individual and his or her context constitute the fundamental process of development. Clearly, it is important to ascertain key individual-level variables, such as hope, that fuse or coact with the well-documented contextual variables noted above to shape the developmental pathways across adolescence.

III. Prospections, Possibilities, and Purpose

Successful selection of behaviors that allow an adolescent to realize his or her future goals depends on the presence of specific cognitive and behavioral functions, such as the ability to plan for the future and to appropriately act to reach one's goals. According to Nurmi (2004), "In order to be active agents in the selection of their future developmental

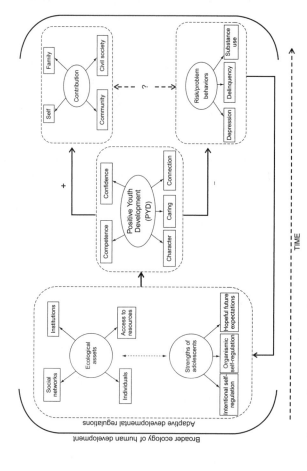

Fig. 1. A relational, developmental systems model of the role of hope in positive youth development.

trajectories, adolescents' personal goals need to be evidenced in their positive thinking about the future and belief in personal control" (p. 99). In other words, there may be an emotional component to behavioral selection that serves as an impetus in the process of achieving goals. Indeed, Synder's primary conclusion about hope, after extensive empirical, clinical, and ethnographic work (see Snyder, 1994), was that an individual's hope is rooted in his or her orientation toward specific goals. Positive motivation, in the form of hope, may be necessary to energize behavior in the direction of those goals.

Recent literature on the role of positive affect in how adolescents construct their future paths suggests that positive emotions with respect to one's future, such as hope or optimism, may be a crucial component in this process (e.g., Benson, 2009; Nurmi, 2004; Yowell, 2000). One line of research involves theories about the role of positive or optimistic future expectations in achieving developmental outcomes. For example, Markus and Nurius (1986) proposed that representations of one's future self may be thought of in terms of possible selves, which encompass one's expected, hoped for, and feared future self. According to Yowell (2000), "in facilitating meaning-making, incentives for behavior, and regulation, possible selves function to dynamically organize and energize behavior" (p. 251). In other words, behavioral outcomes in later adolescence are influenced by earlier prospections about the future through self-conceptions that determine how information is processed; in turn, these prospections serve to regulate an individual's behavior.

In studies of Latino adolescents' conceptions of their futures, Yowell (2000, 2002) found that while hoped-for selves did reflect the salient ideology of Latino adolescents, that is, to graduate from high school and to attend college, hoped-for selves did not predict students' academic performance. However, findings from these studies also suggested that participants had low procedural knowledge (e.g., optimization skills) about how to achieve their future goals, which may account for the lack of connection between hoped-for selves and academic achievement. In other words, a hopeful future may be a motivating factor in applying specific behavioral and cognitive skills to achieve one's future goals. However, without self-regulatory skills (i.e., without SOC skills), a hopeful future in and of itself may be insufficient. Although Yowell's findings are important for understanding variation in the connections between a hopeful future and academic achievement, they emphasize the necessity for further investigation into the mechanisms, or processes, through which a hopeful future might influence later developmental outcomes.

Given the associations between hope and future goals, research connecting future-oriented beliefs and intentional self regulation may be especially useful for understanding these mechanisms. For example, to account for the role of expectations in self-regulatory processes (particularly those related to academic achievement), Zimmerman (2002) proposed three cyclical phases of intentional self regulation. These are forethought, performance, and self-reflection. The forethought phase encompasses task analysis such as goal setting and planning. Also included in forethought are self-motivation beliefs, which refer to outcome expectations and learning goal orientation. According to Zimmerman (2002), students who are expert self-regulators "engage in high-quality forethought," compared to novices, who "instead attempt to self-regulate their learning reactively" (p. 69). Thus, the future goals activated in the forethought phase of intentional self regulation motivate the performance and self-reflection phases; in turn, students receive feedback from performance and self-reflection and adjust their goals and motivations accordingly. While expectations and hope clearly overlap with regard to adolescents' constructions of their futures, more research will need to be conducted on the nature of the relations between hope and intentional self regulation (e.g., Schmid et al., in press).

Finally, in addition to intentional self regulation, hope may represent an individual developmental asset by which youth engage meaningfully with their context (see Figure 1). For example, Damon, Menon, and Bronk (2003; see also Chapter 3) conceptualized hope with regard to the development of purpose; they define purpose as an "intention to accomplish something that is at once meaningful to the self and of consequence to the world beyond the self" (p. 121). An individual has purpose if he or she is able to set meaningful future goals that contribute to both the self and the larger context (e.g., society). Using this definition of purpose, Bronk, Hill, Lapsley, Talib, and Finch (2009) found that hope was correlated with both searching for one's purpose and having an identified purpose among adolescents and young adults. Moreover, findings from this study suggested that hope mediated the relationship between purpose and life satisfaction. Thus, hopefulness and purpose may be inextricably linked in driving action toward one's future goals. In other words, it may be that adolescents will not move forward on accomplishing a future goal—in fact, they may not ascribe meaning to that goal in the first place—if they do not first have some hope that such a goal can be achieved.

More broadly, the specific mechanisms by which hope for the future informs behavior in the present are at least related to, if not explicitly identified by, a broader domain of scholarship about expectations of self and context, and how such beliefs guide adaptive developmental regulations (see Eccles & Wigfield, 2002; Wigfield, Eccles, Schiefele, Roeser, & Davis-Kean, 2006 for reviews on motivational beliefs, values, and goals). For example, literatures informed by Bandura's (1997) self-efficacy theory, children and adolescents' development of self-concept (Harter, 1990), as well as theories related to locus of control (e.g., Skinner et al., 1998) are all pertinent for understanding the role of hope in how adolescents construct positive futures. Expectancy-value theories (e.g., Wigfield & Eccles, 1992) may be particularly useful for modeling the role of hope in motivation for academic achievement or school tasks. Further, work that focuses on optimism (e.g., Carver, Scheier, Miller, & Fulford, 2009) may provide insight into how the affective or emotional element of hope leads to positive future expectations, which in turn guide adolescents' behavioral selections.

These literatures are all key facets of the scholarship that points to the importance of a person's prospections in modulating one's trajectory through life. While hope exists in a positive manifold relationship with all of the constructs mentioned here, hope is distinct—at least insofar as the positive development of youth is concerned—in that, in the present conception, it provides the emotional fuel for intentional self regulations aimed at goal selection and optimization.

IV. Consequences of Hopelessness

What are the implications of an absence of hope among children and adolescents? Without hope, a person's goals for his or her future may more closely resemble the German concept of *Sehnsucht*, or life longings (Scheibe, Freund, & Baltes, 2007). Life longings are intense desires for optimal, even utopian, life states. However, unlike goals, which are theoretically specific and attainable, life longings are abstract and unattainable by definition. Further, whereas goals are future oriented, life longings take into account experiences and emotions from across ontogeny, that is, from a person's past, present, and future. Finally, emotions related to *Sehnsucht* may be both positive and negative, encompassing hope and excitement but also frustration or regret. Thus, the role of hope in relation to life longings is more ambivalent, or nostalgic. However, having a hopeful future may energize a person in the direction of his or her goals, preventing those future goals from becoming life longings.

Even more critical for adolescents is a sense of hopelessness about the future that may lead to engaging in risky behaviors in the present (Taylor, 1990, 1993). Bolland (2003) reported that, in a study of almost 2500 inner-city youth, about half of the males and 25% of the females felt hopeless about their futures. Youth who were hopeless endorsed survey questions such as, *All I see ahead of me are bad things, not good things*; and, *I don't expect to live a very long life.* Bolland (2003) and others (e.g., Stoddard, Henly, Sieving, & Bolland, 2011) have found that hopelessness is associated with violence, substance use, suicidal ideation, teen pregnancy, and other risk behaviors. Ethnographic research reveals similar trends. For example, interviews with female gang members conducted by Taylor (1993) revealed that young people participate in life-threatening behaviors because they have no hope that they will survive more than a few years into the future. However, as with the construct of hope, more research will need to be conducted to elucidate the relational, developmental processes by which hopelessness may lead to negative developmental outcomes.

V. Empirical Evidence for the Role of Hope in PYD

Informed by relational, developmental systems models of individual ↔ context relations (e.g., Overton, 2006, 2010), scholars have used the PYD perspective to study the bases and outcomes of thriving across the adolescent period. Researchers have sought to identify the strengths of young people that, when integrated with developmental resources in their ecology, provide foundations for trajectories of healthy, successful functioning (e.g., Lerner, Phelps, Forman, & Bowers, 2009). In this section, we describe evidence for the role of hope in constructing positive pathways to adulthood that has emerged from research framed by a developmental systems perspective (e.g., Schmid et al., 2011).

A. EVIDENCE FROM THE 4-H STUDY OF POSITIVE YOUTH DEVELOPMENT

Prior research testing processes involved in PYD have identified characteristics of intentional self regulation (e.g., SOC skills) as key individual strengths that, when aligned with developmental assets in families, schools, and communities, are linked to thriving, as operationalized by the Five Cs of PYD—Competence, Confidence, Character, Connection, and Caring (Gestsdóttir, Bowers, von Eye, Napolitano, & Lerner, 2010; Gestsdóttir & Lerner, 2007; Gestsdóttir, Lewin-Bizan, von Eye, Lerner, & Lerner, 2009; Urban, Lewin-Bizan, & Lerner, 2010; Zimmerman et al., 2007, 2008). Research conducted by Schmid and colleagues (e.g., Schmid et al., 2011, in press) sought to extend this literature by ascertaining whether a young person's hope for a positive future would add to, or interact with, characteristics of intentional self regulation in the prediction of thriving across the adolescent period. Based on the idea that a hopeful future constitutes both emotional and cognitive activation needed to make meaningful the use of intentional self-regulatory abilities (Benson, 2009; Damon, 2008; Damon et al., 2003), this work sought to expand understanding of the important individual attributes that may be necessary to find (or promote) in a young person in order to understand the presence and pathway of positive change across adolescence.

Analyses of data from Grades 7 to 9 of the 4-H Study of PYD (see Lerner et al., 2005, for a full description of this study) indicated that both intentional self regulation (as indexed by scores derived from the SOC measure developed by Freund & Baltes, 2002) and a hopeful future (as indexed by a measure developed from items present in the 4-H Study data set; Schmid et al., 2011) were associated in theoretically expected ways with trajectories of positive developmental outcomes (PYD and youth contribution), and of negative developmental outcomes (depressive symptoms and risk behaviors). That is, as expected, high scores for both intentional self regulation and hopeful future predicted membership in the highest instantiations of positive outcomes, as well as in the lowest problematic developmental trajectories. For example, participants with higher hopeful expectations for the future were significantly more likely to be in the group of youth who followed a path of high contribution scores across Grades 7 through 9, with contribution characterized by attitudes and actions about helping in one's community, school, and family. In addition, youth with higher hopeful future expectations were less likely to be among the group of participants characterized by high scores on risk behaviors (e.g., substance use, delinquency) across Grades 7 through 9.

Research has also explored the relations between hopeful future expectations and SOC in predicting PYD. Using data again from Grades 7 through 9 of the 4-H Study, Schmid et al. (in press) explored whether hopeful expectations for one's future would predict self-regulatory behaviors or if instead, the successful application of SOC skills would predict expectations for a hopeful future. The findings suggested that hopeful future expectations and intentional self regulation were reciprocal in their influences across Grades 7 and 8; however, the magnitude of the relationship indicated that earlier hopeful future expectations had greater influence on later SOC scores.

Given these findings from the 4-H Study, as well as the theoretical links between hopeful future, intentional self regulation, and positive developmental outcomes, we believe the hopeful future construct offers a rich new area for investigation into the variables involved in the relations between individuals and their context that are important for thriving across adolescence.

VI. Conclusions: The Future Study of Hope

Hope has long been regarded by scholars as an important facet of the human experience, although perhaps only within the past few decades have researchers begun to consider the role of hope in positive psychosocial functioning (Menninger, 1960). Attempts to understand the meaning of hope for developing youth are even more recent. Certainly, hope has important implications for adolescents' lives and represents a construct that can tell us much about the future expectations of diverse youth. Snyder's seminal work on hope theory (e.g., Snyder, 1994) provides a foundation for the understanding of hope as it relates to goal-directed processes. However, there remains a lack of developmental research. Furthermore, across the breadth of the literature that does exist, the construct of hope, or hopeful future expectations, lacks a cohesive definition.

Therefore, in this chapter, we explored the role of hope from a developmental systems perspective. We proposed that hope, much like intentional self-regulatory processes, represents a strength of adolescents that has potential to interact with features of their contexts, to produce adaptive developmental outcomes (Figure 1). Future research will be required to elucidate the nature of the relationship between intentional self regulation and hope (Schmid et al., in press).

We believe the theoretical and empirical findings presented here regarding the importance of hope for adolescents' well-being provide myriad implications for assessing hope in the future. Unfortunately, previous empirical research on hope has largely ignored the relational nature of the developmental system, in which hope is necessarily influenced by both individual-level variables, including self regulation and optimism, and contextual-level developmental assets, such as parental support. However, some research has already begun to delineate the relations among contextual assets and hope. For example, Dubow, Arnett, Smith, and Ippolito (2001) found that parental support, but not peer support, predicted increases in positive future expectations within a sample of disadvantaged, inner-city youth over a 9-month period. While such research provides a much-needed jumping off point for the study of the role of context in promoting hope, future investigations must further explore the ecological milieu that nourishes hope across childhood, adolescence, and early adulthood. Other contextual assets that may be important include a young person's social networks (e.g., peer networks or social resources within a neighborhood), access to resources, and institutions such as schools, youth development programs, and faith-based organizations (see Figure 1).

In turn, future research must consider the influence that hope may have on an individual's context. As previously noted, findings from the 4-H Study of PYD indicate that hopeful future expectations are associated across middle adolescence with both PYD and youth contribution (Schmid et al., 2011, in press). Damon and colleagues emphasize the mutual benefit of purpose and hopefulness for both the individual and context (Damon et al., 2003; see also Mariano & Going, 2011); thus, hopeful youth may be more likely to identify meaningful goals, or purposes, which actively engage with and contribute to their families, schools, and communities. Certainly, such work underscores the importance of a developmental systems framework for understanding the role of a hopeful future in achieving developmental outcomes in young people and their settings.

In recent years, the measurement of hope, particularly Snyder's Hope Scale (Snyder et al., 1997), has been criticized for the lack of evidence regarding its divergent validity with other measures, including measures of intentional self regulation, self-efficacy, and goal-theory (e.g., Aspinwall & Leaf, 2002). In addition, Aspinwall and Leaf (2002) note that emotional regulation and the social contexts that may be necessary to sustain hope are lacking from the theoretical discussion and empirical investigations of hope. Future research must attend to these validity concerns, both to identify the unique contribution of hope in promoting positive outcomes for individuals and, as well, to reconcile it with other commonly used measures, for example, the SOC assessment of intentional self regulation.

Finally, there are important gaps in the literature on the development of hope across the adolescent period. In fact, the literature has largely ignored variation in hope not only with respect to age but also in terms of other demographic markers (e.g., socioeconomic status) and with respect to diverse cultures and faith traditions. For instance, in the relatively small literature on adolescent spirituality, hope is equated to faith, especially where hope is institutionalized by a religious tradition (e.g., Erikson, 1968; Roehlkepartain, Benson, King, & Wagener, 2006). Nevertheless, little developmental analysis of, or culturally comparative research about, hope and religion/spirituality exists in regard to adolescence. Indeed, the interrelation of hope and other psychosocial or demographic marker variables has not been embedded thoroughly in either developmental or culturally comparative research.

Understanding the role of hope for diverse youth in constructing their positive futures will have important implications for applied youth development work. In fact, some researchers have begun to explore the usefulness of hope for enhancing psychosocial resilience in the context of youth development programs (e.g., Dubow et al., 2001; Wyman, Cowen, Work,

& Kerley, 1993). For example, among young urban adolescents exposed to highly stressful conditions, positive future expectations, such as being sure of having a happy life, may be associated with resilient developmental adaptations, including an internal locus of control (Wyman et al., 1993). However, as suggested by Yowell (2002), youth must be able to engage resources in their contexts if they are to realize their hopes for the future; therefore, simply building hopeful expectations may not be sufficient.

Nevertheless, given the previously noted relations between hope and intentional self regulation (Schmid et al., in press), hopeful expectations about one's future may be one indicator of the success of a program to build self-regulatory capacity in youth. Only a nuanced understanding of the implications of these constructs for diverse youth will provide researchers and practitioners with the tools for designing maximally beneficial programs to promote positive developmental outcomes and give youth a truly hopeful future.

REFERENCES

Arnau, R., Rosen, D., Finch, J., Rhudy, J., & Fortunato, V. (2007). Longitudinal effects of hope on depression and anxiety: A latent variable analysis. *Journal of Personality, 75*, 43–64.

Aspinwall, L. G., & Leaf, S. L. (2002). In search of the unique aspects of hope: Pinning out hopes on positive emotions, future-oriented thinking, hard times, and other people. *Psychological Inquiry, 13*(4), 276–288.

Baltes, P. B. (1997). On the incomplete architecture of human ontogeny: Selection, optimization, and compensation as foundation of developmental theory. *The American Psychologist, 52*, 366–380.

Baltes, P. B., & Baltes, M. M. (1990). Psychological perspectives on successful aging: The model of selective optimization with compensation. In P. B. Baltes & M. M. Baltes (Eds.), *Successful aging: Perspectives from the behavioral sciences.* (pp. 1–34). New York: Cambridge University Press.

Baltes, P. B., Lindenberger, U., & Staudinger, U. M. (2006). Life span theory in developmental psychology. In R. M. Lerner & W. Damon (Eds.), *Handbook of child psychology: Vol 1. Theoretical models of human development.* (6th ed., pp. 569–664). Hoboken, NJ: John Wiley & Sons Inc.

Baltes, P. B., Reese, H. W., & Nesselroade, J. R. (1988). *Life-span developmental psychology: Introduction to research methods.* Hillsdale, NJ: Erlbaum.

Bandura, A. (1997). *Self-efficacy: The exercise of control.* New York: Freeman.

Benson, P. L. (2009). *How parents can ignite the hidden strengths of your teenagers.* San Francisco: Jassey-Bass.

Benson, P. L., Scales, P. C., Hamilton, S. F., & Semsa, A. Jr., (2006). Positive youth development: Theory, research, and applications. In W. Damon & R. M. Lerner (Editors-in-chief) & R. M. Lerner (Ed.), *Theoretical models of human development. Volume 1 of handbook of child psychology.* Hoboken, NJ: Wiley.

Benson, P. L., Scales, P. C., & Syvertsen, A. K. (2011). The contribution of the developmental assets framework to positive youth development theory and practice. In R. M. Lerner, J. V. Lerner, & J. B. Benson (Eds.), *Advances in child development and behavior*. (pp. 125–228). Amsterdam, The Netherlands: Elsevier.

Bolland, J. M. (2003). Hopelessness and risk behaviour among adolescents living in high-poverty inner-city neighbourhoods. *Journal of Adolescence*, *26*, 145–158.

Brandstädter, J. (2006). Action perspectives on human development. In W. Damon (Series Ed.) & R. M. Lerner (Vol. Ed.), *Handbook of child psychology: Vol. 1. Theoretical models of human development* (6th ed., pp. 516–568). New York: Wiley.

Bronfenbrenner, U., & Morris, P. A. (2006). The bioecological model of human development. In W. Damon & R. M. Lerner (Eds.), & R.M. Lerner (Ed.). *Theoretical models of human development. Volume 1 of handbook of child psychology*. (6th ed., pp. 793–828). Hoboken, NJ: Wiley.

Bronk, K. C., Hill, P., Lapsley, D., Talib, N., & Finch, H. (2009). Purpose, hope, and life-satisfaction in three age groups. *The Journal of Positive Psychology*, *4*(6), 500–510.

Carver, C. S., Scheier, M. F., Miller, C. J., & Fulford, D. (2009). Optimism. In C. R. Snyder & S. J. Lopez (Eds.), *Handbook of positive psychology*. (pp. 303–311). New York: Oxford University Press.

Ciarrochi, J., Heaven, P. C. L., & Davies, F. (2007). The impact of hope, self-esteem, and attributional style on adolescents' school grades and emotional well-being: A longitudinal study. *Journal of Research in Personality*, *41*, 1161–1178.

Côté, J. E. (2009). Identity formation and self development in adolescence. In R. M. Lerner & L. Steinberg (Eds.), *Handbook of adolescent psychology*. (3rd ed., pp. 266–304). Hoboken, NJ: Wiley.

Curry, L. A., Snyder, C. R., Cook, D. L., Ruby, B. C., & Rehm, M. (1997). Role of hope in academic and sport achievement. *Journal of Personality and Social Psychology*, *73*, 1257–1267.

Damon, W. (2008). *The path to purpose. Helping our children find their calling in life*. New York: Free Press.

Damon, W., Menon, J., & Bronk, K. C. (2003). The development of purpose during adolescence. *Applied Developmental Science*, *7*(3), 119–128.

Dubow, E. F., Arnett, M., Smith, K., & Ippolito, M. F. (2001). Predictors of future expectations of inner-city children: A 9-month prospective study. *The Journal of Early Adolescence*, *21*(5), 5–28.

Eccles, J. S., & Wigfield, A. (2002). Motivational beliefs, values, and goals. *Annual Review of Psychology*, *53*, 109–132.

Erikson, E. H. (1959). Identity and the life-cycle. *Psychological Issues*, *1*, 18–164.

Erikson, E. H. (1968). *Identity: Youth and crisis*. New York: Norton.

Ford, D. H., & Lerner, R. M. (1992). *Developmental systems theory: An integrative approach*. Newbury Park, CA: Sage Publications.

Freund, A. M., & Baltes, P. B. (2002). Life-management strategies of selection, optimization and compensation: Measurement by self-report and construct validity. *Journal of Personality and Social Psychology*, *82*, 642–662.

Gestsdóttir, S., Bowers, E., von Eye, A., Napolitano, C. M., & Lerner, R. M. (2010). Intentional self-regulation in middle adolescence: The emerging role of loss-based selection in positive youth development. *Journal of Youth and Adolescence*, *39*(7), 764–782.

Gestsdóttir, S., & Lerner, R. M. (2007). Intentional self-regulation and positive youth development in early adolescence: Findings from the 4-H Study of Positive Youth Development. *Developmental Psychology*, *43*, 508–521.

Gestsdóttir, S., & Lerner, R. M. (2008). Positive development in adolescence: The development and role of intentional self-regulation. *Human Development, 51*, 202–224.

Gestsdóttir, S., Lewin-Bizan, S., von Eye, A., Lerner, J. V., & Lerner, R. M. (2009). The structure and function of selection, optimization, and compensation in middle adolescence: Theoretical and applied implications. *Journal of Applied Developmental Psychology, 30*(5), 585–600.

Haase, J. E. (2004). The adolescent resilience model as a guide to interventions. *Journal of Pediatric Oncology Nursing, 21*, 289–299.

Harter, S. (1990). Causes, correlates and the functional role of global self-worth: A life-span perspective. In J. Kolligian & R. Sternberg (Eds.), *Perceptions of competence and incompetence across the life-span.* (pp. 67–98). New Haven, CT: Yale University Press.

Hendricks-Ferguson, V. (2008). Hope and spiritual well-being in adolescents with cancer. *Western Journal of Nursing Research, 30*, 385–401.

Herth, K. A. (2001). Development and implementation of a hope intervention program. *Oncology Nursing Forum, 28*(6), 1009–1017.

Irving, L. M., Snyder, C. R., Gravel, L., Hanke, J., Hilberg, P., & Nelson, N. (2004). The relationship between hope and outcomes at the pretreatment, beginning, and later phases of psychotherapy. *Journal of Psychotherapy Integration, 14*(4), 419–443.

Lerner, R. M. (2002). *Concepts and theories of human development.* Mawah, NJ: Lawrence Erlbaum Associates.

Lerner, R. M. (2004). *Liberty: Thriving and civic engagement among American youth.* Thousand Oaks, CA: Sage.

Lerner, R. M. (2006). Developmental science, developmental systems, and contemporary theories of human development. In W. Damon (Series Ed.) & R. M. Lerner (Ed.), *Handbook of child psychology: Vol. 1. Theoretical models of human development* (6th ed., pp. 1–17). Hoboken, NJ: Wiley.

Lerner, R. M., Freund, A. M., De Stefanis, I., & Habermas, T. (2001). Understanding developmental regulation in adolescence: The use of the selection, optimization, and compensation model. *Human Development, 44*, 29–50.

Lerner, R. M., Lerner, J. V., Almerigi, J., Theokas, C., Phelps, E., Gestsdóttir, S., et al. (2005). Positive youth development, participation in community youth development programs, and community contributions of fifth grade adolescents: Findings from the first wave of the 4-H study of Positive Youth Development. *Journal of Early Adolescence, 25*(1), 17–71.

Lerner, J. V., Phelps, E., Forman, Y., & Bowers, E. P. (2009). Positive youth development. In R. M. Lerner & L. Steinberg (Eds.), *Handbook of adolescent psychology.* (3rd ed., pp. 524–558). Hoboken, NJ: Wiley.

Lopez, S. J., Agrawal, S., & Calderon, V. J. (2010). *The Gallup Student Poll technical report.* Washington, DC: Gallup.

Magnusson, D., & Stattin, H. (2006). The person in context: A holistic–interactionistic approach. In W. Damon & R. M. Lerner (Eds.), *Handbook of child psychology: Vol. 3. Social, emotional, and personality development.* (6th ed., pp. 400–464). New York: Wiley.

Mariano, J. M. & Going, J. (2011). Youth purpose and positive youth development. In R. M. Lerner, J. V. Lerner, & J. B. Benson (Eds.), *Advances in child development and behavior.* (pp. 37-66). Amsterdam, The Netherlands: Elsevier.

Markus, H., & Nurius, P. (1986). Possible selves. *The American Psychologist, 41*(9), 954–969.

Menninger, K. (1960). Hope. *Pastoral Psychology, 11*(3), 11–24.

Nurmi, J. E. (1991). How do adolescents see their future? A review of the development of future orientation and planning. *Developmental Review, 11*, 1–59.

Nurmi, J. E. (2004). Socialization and self-development: Channeling, selection, adjustment, and reflection. In R. M. Lerner & L. Steinberg (Eds.), *Handbook of adolescent psychology* (Vol. 2, pp. 85–124). Hoboken, NJ: Wiley.

Overton, W. F. (2006). Developmental psychology: Philosophy, concepts, methodology. In W. Damon (Series Ed.) & R. M. Lerner (Ed.), *Handbook of child psychology: Vol. 1. Theoretical models of human development* (6th ed., pp. 18–88). Hoboken, NJ: Wiley.

Overton, W. F. (2010). Life-span development: Concepts and issues. In R. M. Lerner (Ed.), *The handbook of lifespan development*. Hoboken, NJ: Wiley.

Rand, K. L., & Cheavens, J. S. (2009). Hope theory. In C. R. Snyder & S. J. Lopez (Eds.), *Handbook of positive psychology* (pp. 323–333). New York: Oxford University Press.

Roehlkepartain, E. C., Benson, P. L., King, P. E., & Wagener, L. (2006). Spiritual development in childhood and adolescence: Moving to the scientific mainstream. In E. C. Roehlkepartain, P. E. King, L. Wagener & P. L. Benson (Eds.), *The handbook of spiritual development in childhood and adolescence* (pp. 1–17). Thousand Oaks, CA: Sage.

Scheibe, S., Freund, A. M., & Baltes, P. B. (2007). Roward a developmental psychology of Sehnsucht (Life Longings): The optimal (utopian) life. *Developmental Psychology, 43* (3), 778–795.

Schmid, K. L., Phelps, E., Kiely Mueller, M., Napolitano, C. M., Boyd, M. J., & Lerner, R. M. (2011). The role of adolescents' hopeful futures in predicting positive and negative developmental trajectories: Findings from the 4-H Study of Positive Youth Development. *The Journal of Positive Psychology, 6*(1), 45–56.

Schmid, K. L., Phelps, E., & Lerner, R. M. (in press). Constructing positive futures: Modeling the relationship between adolescents' hopeful future expectations and intentional self-regulation in predicting positive youth development. *Journal of Adolescence.*

Schwartz, S. J., Luyckx, K., & Vignoles, V. L. (Eds.) (in press). *Handbook of identity theory and research*. New York: Springer.

Skinner, E. A., Zimmer-Gembeck, M. K., & Connell, J. P. (1998). Individual differences and development of perceived control. *Monographs of the Society for Research in Child Development, 63*(2–3, Serial No. 254).

Snyder, C. R. (1994). *The psychology of hope: You can get there from here.* New York: Free Press.

Snyder, C. R., Hoza, B., Pelham, W. E., Rapoff, M., Ware, L., Danovsky, M., et al. (1997). The development and validation of the Children's Hope Scale. *Journal of Pediatric Psychology, 22,* 399–421.

Snyder, C. R., Rand, K. L., & Sigmon, D. R. (2002a). Hope theory: A member of the positive psychology family. In C. R. Snyder & S. J. Lopez (Eds.), *Handbook of positive psychology.* (pp. 231–243). New York: Oxford University Press.

Snyder, C. R., Shorey, H., Cheavens, J., Pulvers, K. M., Adams, V., III,& Wiklund, C. (2002). Hope and academic success in college. *Journal of Educational Psychology, 94*(4), 820–826.

Stoddard, S. A., Henly, S. J., Sieving, R. E., & Bolland, J. (2011). Social connections, trajectories of hopelessness, and serious violence in impoverished urban youth. *Journal of Youth and Adolescence, 40,* 278–295.

Taylor, C. (1990). Gang Imperialism. In C. Ronald Huff (Ed.), *Gangs in America.* Newbury Park, CA: Sage.

Taylor, C. (1993). *Girls, gangs, women, and drugs.* East Lansing: Michigan State University Press.

Urban, J. B., Lewin-Bizan, S., & Lerner, R. M. (2010). The role of intentional self regulation, lower neighborhood ecological assets, and activity involvement in youth developmental outcomes. *Journal of Youth and Adolescence, 39*(7), 783–800.

Valle, M. F., Huebner, E. S., & Suldo, S. M. (2006). An analysis of hope as a psychological strength. *Journal of School Psychology, 44*, 393–406.

Wigfield, A., & Eccles, J. S. (1992). The development of achievement task values: A theoretical analysis. *Developmental Review, 12*, 265–310.

Wigfield, A., Eccles, J. S., Schiefele, U., Roeser, R., & Davis-Kean, P. (2006). Development of achievement motivation. In W. Damon & N. Eisenberg (Eds.), (6th ed., pp. 933–1002). *Handbook of child psychology* (6th ed., Vol. 3). New York: Wiley.

Wyman, P. A., Cowen, E. L., Work, W. C., & Kerley, J. H. (1993). The role of children's future expectations in self-system functioning and adjustment to life stress: A prospective study of urban at-risk children. *Development and Psychopathology, 5*, 649–661.

Yowell, C. M. (2000). Possible selves and future orientation: Exploring hopes and fears of Latino boys and girls. *Journal of Early Adolescence, 20*(3), 245–280.

Yowell, C. M. (2002). Dreams of the future: The pursuit of education and career possible selves among ninth grade Latino youth. *Applied Developmental Science, 6*(2), 62–72.

Zimmerman, B. J. (2002). Becoming a self-regulated learner: An overview. *Theory into Practice, 41*(2), 64–70.

Zimmerman, S., Phelps, E., & Lerner, R. M. (2007). Intentional self-regulation in early adolescence: Assessing the structure of selection, optimization, and compensations processes. *European Journal of Developmental Science, 1*(3), 272–299.

Zimmerman, S., Phelps, E., & Lerner, R. M. (2008). Positive and negative developmental trajectories in U.S. adolescents: Where the positive youth development perspective meets the deficit model. *Research in Human Development, 5*(3), 153–165.

INTRINSIC MOTIVATION AND POSITIVE DEVELOPMENT

Reed W. Larson* and Natalie Rusk[†]

* DEPARTMENT OF HUMAN AND COMMUNITY DEVELOPMENT, UNIVERSITY OF
ILLINOIS, URBANA, ILLINOIS, USA
[†] ELIOT-PEARSON DEPARTMENT OF CHILD DEVELOPMENT, TUFTS UNIVERSITY,
CAMBRIDGE, MASSACHUSETTS, USA

Advances in Child Development and Behavior
Richard M. Lerner, Jacqueline V. Lerner and Janette B. Benson : Editors

Abstract

Decades of scientific research shows that intrinsic motivation (IM) is a powerful "engine" of learning and positive development. This chapter synthesizes the research, first showing how the psychological state of IM is associated not only with enhanced engagement and perseverance in an activity, but also with greater use of meta-cognitive strategies and deeper processing of information. These features likely account for evidence that IM is related to greater and more effective learning. Second, we examine the determinants of this beneficial state. Evidence suggests that it results from the convergence of factors at multiple levels—from immediate conditions in the activity to longer-term personal goals, cultural values, and human dispositions. Drawing on these findings, we show that there is considerable potential for young people to develop their abilities to experience and regulate their IM within activities. In the third and final section, we then discuss how youth professionals can work with youth to help them cultivate the capacity for intrinsically motivated learning. We present ten guiding principles for cultivating IM derived from the research. We give particular attention to adolescence, because it is a period when youth become more able to engage in this deliberate cultivation – to be producers of their own development.

I. Introduction

"Perhaps no single phenomenon reflects the positive potential of human nature as much as intrinsic motivation."

Ryan & Deci (2000, p. 70)

Ron, a recent high-school dropout, is hunched over sound-mixing equipment in a state of intense absorption, a state his teachers would not have recognized. He is flipping switches and adjusting dials, working to enhance voice tracks from aspiring rappers by adding background music and beats. He explains how Midwestern rappers use fast lyrics with tongue twisters, while those from South use "curl rap." His challenge is to get just the right background tracks for each artist. Since he started using this equipment, Ron has wanted to learn everything he can about sound mixing, motivated by his "love of music." Although Sheri, a rural youth, is engaged in a much different activity—planning activities for young children—she experiences the same kind of deep absorption. She has learned how children of different ages and backgrounds like different activities. The challenge she and friends are working on is to plan games fit to Saturday's group of 5 to 7-year-olds. Similar to Ron, Sheri explains her motivation: "It's interesting, I love helping little kids."

Both youth experience a psychological state in which they are *highly motivated* and their *attention is deeply engaged* in the activity. Motivation drives their engagement; the engagement, in turn, creates experiences that reinforce their motivation. To be clear, this absorbed state is *not* what people experience watching a good movie. Ron and Sheri are not being passively entertained by a screenplay created by someone else. They are actively directing their own participation in the activity. They are motivated by the process of thinking through and addressing the challenges of getting the right sound mix and designing activities that 5- to 7-year-olds will enjoy.

Psychologists call this state of motivated engagement *intrinsic motivation* (IM). By "intrinsic," they mean the activity is—or has become—motivating in and itself. It is self-motivating. IM can be experienced in play, recreation, or work, any activity that is challenging (Csikszentmihalyi, 1990; Sansone & Harackiewicz, 2000). Psychologists contrast it with "extrinsic motivation" in which a person is driven, not by the activity, but by external rewards or threats.

Decades of research shows that IM is related to improved performance and learning within an activity. Controlling for other factors, individuals who are intrinsically motivated are likely to think more strategically, generate more creative solutions, persist through difficulties, and learn more from their experiences (Ryan & Deci, 2000). Because their attention and motivation (their "hearts and minds") are more fully engaged, their mental work is thought to be more efficient and effective. Increasing evidence suggests that IM is a basic human *psychological system* that mobilizes engagement in important but challenging activities, including learning (Izard & Ackerman, 2000; Ryan & Deci, 2008). Many scholars and educators have taken the next step and argued that this system has enormous—but often untapped—potential to energize young people's sustained engagement in learning and development (e.g., Bruner, 1966; Csikszentmihalyi, 1990; Dewey, 1913).

This chapter examines this potential. We present and evaluate the theory that IM can serve as a powerful engine of learning and development. Although we are proponents of this theory, we are also realists. Romantic images of eager teenagers rapturously engaged in a "natural" process of perpetual learning need to be viewed with a critical eye. Motivation is complex and is responsive to a myriad of factors. Sheri said she is most motivated when able to work unimpeded, thus she became de-energized when the adult supervising their next event vetoed her plans and forced them in an unwanted direction. In the real world, IM fluctuates as a function of a person's ongoing experiences in an activity, goals, expectations, and other factors that we will examine. Motivation also differs by person and activity. Although Ron's newfound passion for sound mixing later helped him earn his high-school degree, IM in one activity does not necessarily transfer to another.

The promise, however, is that the capacity for IM can itself develop. Like other basic psychological systems (such as those for attachment and for different emotions), we argue that the human IM system is designed to allow enormous developmental plasticity. It is what evolutionary biologist Ernst Mayr (2001) called an "open system," one that can be shaped by experience, culture, and deliberate cultivation. We give particular attention here to adolescence—because it is a period when youth become more able to engage in this deliberate cultivation—to be producers of their own development (Larson, 2011; Lerner, 2002). Adolescents gain potentials to acquire meta-cognitive understanding and executive skills for managing their psychological processes, including their motivation (Steinberg et al., 2006; Zimmerman, 2002).

In this chapter, we synthesize research from different conceptual paradigms (theories of interest, self-determination, flow, effectance motivation, mastery orientation) into a composite theory of IM as a *single* psychological system: a system that can mobilize positive development. (This composite, we acknowledge, overlooks some important debates in the motivation literature.) We begin by examining IM as a state: What are its subjective features and what is the evidence that this state facilitates learning and positive development? In the subsequent section, we examine the diverse factors that contribute to (as well as obstruct) a person's experience of this state. We also discuss how these factors can develop. In the final section, we then discuss the implications for professionals working with young people. What does the research suggest they can do to help youth experience and cultivate IM?

Many of the illustrations we use in the chapter, like those of Ron and Sheri, come from organized after-school youth programs. We believe they are a particularly good context to observe motivational development and positive development more generally (Larson, 2011). It should be noted that we focus on IM within a Western cultural context. We should also be clear that we do not see IM as the sole catalyst of positive development. Sometimes positive development stems from negative experiences, even horrific events that lead to personal reappraisal. Other psychological systems (e.g., for altruism) also contribute to development, separately or in tandem with IM.

II. Intrinsic Motivation as a Catalyst of Learning and Development

A. THE FUNCTION OF INTRINSIC MOTIVATION

IM can be seen as a missing piece in an important puzzle. Humans are designed as a species to be learners and doers. Although lacking in the sensory acuity, strength, speed, and built-in weapons of other creatures, we are distinguished by our enormous cerebral cortex—a massive central processing unit (about 20 billion neurons)—which allows us to pursue cognitively complex and challenging goals. A limitation is that a substantial portion of this massive processor arrives relatively "unprogrammed." But of course that is the beauty of the human brain. It allows us to learn and adapt to diverse physical, social, and, now, technological environments. In fact, humans have a longer childhood than any other species, presumably to allow us to begin loading all those neurons with experience, knowledge, and skills (Bjorklund & Ellis, 2005)—to practice and develop our human potential for learning and doing.

The missing piece is the motivation to do this—to learn and use this big brain for challenging activities. This is a major function that psychologists attribute to the IM system: to mobilize conscious and deliberate processes of learning and development (Csikszentmihalyi, 1990; Ryan & Deci, 2009). Just as it would make no evolutional sense to have sex organs without the motivation to use them, it would make no sense to have large, adaptable brains without a system to motivate us to develop them to address the challenges of diverse human environments. Although evidence on the neurological mechanisms of IM is very limited, it has been speculated that it represents an evolution of a basic "seeking system" from our evolutionary forbearers, a system for exploring and pursuing goals (Hidi, 2006; Panksepp, 1998).

In this section, we examine the proposition that IM mobilizes an *effective and efficient* psychological state for learning and development. The argument is that IM not only provides motivation to deal with challenges, but also it alters how the mind processes information to facilitate high quality attention to the task at hand. It allows humans to devote deep, sustained attention to episodes of work and learning. We first describe the subjectively experienced features of this state, and then, we examine evidence that it increases cognitive effectiveness and efficiency and helps sustain engagement.

B. FEATURES OF INTRINSICALLY MOTIVATED EXPERIENCES

Herbert Simon argued that a good place to start in trying to understand a conscious mental process is with accounts of people who experience it (Newell & Simon, 1972). Csikszentmihalyi and his students have given the most attention to this task for experiences of IM. Thus we draw on narrative reports from adults and adolescents they interviewed about episodes of IM. We summarize four central features of the experience of IM (which Csikszentmihalyi calls "flow") that suggest why this state creates favorable conditions for conscious learning and development (Csikszentmihalyi, 1975, 1990).

The first feature of IM experiences is *feeling challenged* by the activity. Like Ron and Cheri, the many people whom Csikszentmihalyi interviewed saw a problem or something difficult in the activity that they wanted to take on. From an early age, human's minds are attracted by curiosity toward things that are new (Lepper & Henderlong, 2000). As they get older, they are also attracted by longer-term future goals they want to accomplish, including goals that involve increasing complexity. At a yet more advanced stage, Csikszentmihalyi (1996) interviewed eminent scientists, authors, artists, and civic leaders who described experiencing deep IM in trying to solve complex challenges in their fields. Just because a task is difficult, however, does not mean someone will find it engaging. What one person finds challenging may be of no interest to someone else. We will discuss why this is in Section III, but for now it is important to recognize these individual differences.

A second feature of IM is experiencing a *sense of control* over the activity. People in the state of IM described a feeling of confidence that "I can do it" or "we can do it." This is similar to the experience of self- or collective efficacy that Bandura (1997) found to be important to motivation. Although one's confidence may be based on past experiences, what Csikszentmihalyi's respondents described was not just their actual control, but their perception that they could control what was ahead (i.e., "the *possibility* rather than the actuality, of control"; Csikszentmihalyi, 1990, p. 60). This requires keeping feelings of self-doubt and worry at bay—an attitude of optimism about one's abilities to address the challenges. For example, a 9th grader experiencing IM reported feeling "real strong and in control, like I could do anything" (Larson, 2000, p. 174). A dancer described the feeling of being able to "radiate an energy into the environment" (Csikszentmihalyi, 1975, p. 44). This sense of efficacy may help people think ahead, imagine emerging challenges, and decide how to deal with them (Bandura, 1997).

The third and fourth features, mentioned at the outset, are *deep attention* and the experience of *high motivation*. There is more to say about each. Csikszentmihalyi's (1975, 1990) respondents described their attention as totally focused on the task at hand, with their minds "cut off" from issues in their outside lives. Attention was fully engaged in the challenges of the activity. People experiencing IM report reduced self-consciousness and reduced awareness of passing time (afterwards they report that time went really slow, fast, or just disappeared). One youth reported, "You change, you forget everything around you" (Larson, 2000, p. 174). This deep attention is related to the other features of IM. Shernoff, Csikszentmihalyi, Schneider, and Shernoff (2003) found when high-school students experienced a classroom activity as challenging and within their control, they also rated their concentration and attention as greater.

Csikszentmihalyi (1990) argues that this focused attention helps a person use the finite capacity of the conscious mind most effectively. Research indicates that working memory—the central processor of human consciousness—can only hold 3–5 bits (or "chunks") of information at one moment. Studies show that even small distractions can severely compromise a person's ability to solve problems. The experience of deep, undisturbed attention in IM is theorized to allow optimal use of consciousness.

The fourth factor, high motivation, involves feeling energized by the activity. People report that the activity was enjoyable and self-rewarding. Csikszentmihalyi (1990) quotes a surgeon who said of her work, "It is so enjoyable that I would do it even if I didn't have to." (p. 67). Suzanne Hidi (2000) obtained similar descriptions from her research on the state of interest, and notes: "Although focusing attention and continuing cognitive engagement normally requires increased effort, when interest is high, these activities feel relatively effortless" (p. 311). Ryan and Deci (2000) emphasize that because challenge and attention are experienced as emergent from the self, people experience IM as self-determined: People are doing what they want to be doing. This enjoyment, effortlessness, and experience of volition are what make the activity self-sustaining: people report that these positive feelings encourage them to keep doing the activity and return to it in the future.

For Csikszentmihalyi (1990), a crucial point is that this motivation comes from engagement with "complexity"—with difficult and challenging problems. His research shows that the experience of flow is not confined to leisure activities. In fact, it is more frequent in people's jobs—when they are doing constructive work and creating order out of different forms of complexity. For adolescents, the experience of IM is most common in youth programs, a context in which youth are taking on complex, often unstructured challenges, for example, in creating a theater production or trying to improve their communities (Csikszentmihalyi, Rathunde, & Whalen, 1993; Larson, 2000). The psychological system of IM,

Csikszentmihalyi argues, is designed specifically to catalyze difficult work, including learning.

In sum, adults' and youth's accounts of their IM experiences suggest how this state provides conditions for effective, efficient, and self-sustained learning within an activity. IM is associated with the experience of control over the challenges of the activity, focused attention, and feelings of enjoyment and effortlessness in taking on these challenges. It is essential, however, to evaluate whether these benefits, identified from qualitative interviews, are verified by quantitative experimental and longitudinal studies. We first examine evidence on whether the state of IM changes immediate mental functioning in ways that facilitate learning. Then we ask whether repeated experiences of IM are associated with favorable long-term outcomes.

C. EVIDENCE ON THE IMMEDIATE EFFECTS OF INTRINSIC MOTIVATION

The first question is whether IM has immediate effects on how effectively people process information. A substantial number of studies provide evidence on this. These are largely single-session lab or classroom studies in which participants experiencing high versus low IM were compared on information processing tasks. In some studies, participants were subject to a manipulation that either increased or decreased their IM (e.g., by giving them interesting vs. boring tasks). In other studies, the high and low groups were identified based on their reports of enjoyment, interest, or engagement in a comparable task. This research has identified three differences in information processing related to IM.

1. More Strategy Use

First, IM predicts people's increased use of strategies, including metacognitive strategies, to guide their work (Hidi, 2001; Hidi & Harackiewicz, 2000; Krapp, 1999). In one example, 7th grade students who reported greater intrinsic interest in English and science tasks were more likely to employ self-regulatory and cognitive strategies (such as paraphrasing and planning) to improve their work in these tasks, regardless of prior achievement level (Pintrich & DeGroot, 1990). In another study, college students who expressed more interest in a course topic at mid-semester reported greater use of strategies such as critical thinking and elaboration to prepare for the final exam (Krapp, 1999). The strategies employed by IM students in these studies included those for more effective processing of information as well as those for enhancing their motivation and interest in the tasks (Sansone & Smith, 2000). Evidence for use of more advanced meta-cognitive strategies comes from studies with adolescents and college students. In sum, people who are intrinsically motivated appear to exercise more executive control to increase their learning effectiveness. Confirmation of this improved effectiveness and efficiency is provided by findings that college students who read interesting texts needed *less* time and were able to recall more (Shirey & Reynolds, 1988).

2. Deeper Processing of Material

Closely related, researchers have found that IM predicts greater cognitive activity and deeper cognitive processing of the task at hand. Studies that controlled for prior knowledge and intelligence found that youth experiencing greater IM engaged with more ideas, made more inferences, and were better able to answer complex questions about the material (Schiefele, 1999). In one study, Schiefele (1996) found that, whereas high-school students with low interest produced more verbatim representations of the text, those experiencing high interest were more likely to represent the text in propositional form and engage in more processing of the text's meaning. In another study, Schiefele (1991) found that college students who were more interested in a topic created more mental images, produced more thoughts and ideas about it, and made more connections to personal experience.

3. More Expansive and Integrative Reasoning

Laboratory research also suggests that IM predicts more open and creative processing of information. In random assignment studies, research subjects assigned to intrinsically motivating conditions (as compared to those in extrinsically motivating conditions) engaged in greater exploration, were more likely to break set, and were more likely to formulate original solutions to problems as evaluated by impartial judges (Amabile, 1983; Hennessey, 2000; Koestner, Ryan, Bernieri, & Holt, 1984). This finding is consistent with research showing that people experiencing positive emotional states are more likely to think expansively about possible actions and engage in creative problem solving (e.g., see reviews by Fredrickson, 2001; Isen, 2000).

Though subject to further testing, this research provides substantial evidence that IM influences how people process ideas and information. When intrinsically motivated, they are more likely to employ strategies including meta-cognitive strategies to regulate their thought processes and motivation. In addition, they are likely to engage in processing at deeper and more complex levels and do so in more original ways. Learning becomes more effective and efficient.

D. EVIDENCE ON THE CUMULATIVE OUTCOMES FROM INTRINSICALLY MOTIVATED EXPERIENCES

The most important test of the potential of IM as a catalyst of positive development is outcome research that evaluates whether repeated experiences of IM in a particular domain predict long-term differences in behavioral outcomes. Most studies that have addressed this have not directly measured repeated experiences of IM but rather examined whether youth reported enjoying, being motivated by, or having interest in an activity over a span of time. Our review focuses on the relationship between these variables and outcomes in three domains: learning, development, and motivation. Although we give most weight to longitudinal studies, we have included some cross-sectional research especially for outcomes where longitudinal findings are limited.

1. Learning and School Achievement

Studies in classroom settings have generally found a modest but positive predictive relationship between IM and learning (Lepper, Corpus, & Iyengar, 2005; Lepper, Sethi, Dialdin, & Drake, 1997; Ryan & Deci, 2009; Schiefele, Krapp, & Winteler, 1992). A few studies found that the relationship between interest and school performance becomes nonsignificant once other potential predictors were controlled (Köller, Baumert, & Schnabel, 2001). However, many other studies have shown more robust relationships. For example, a recent longitudinal study found that enjoyment mediated predictive relationships between subject matter goals and school achievement (Daniels et al., 2009). Although most of this research has only used general measures of learning (school grades or test scores), some studies have examined deeper cognitive processing. Consistent with the short-term studies we just reviewed, this research finds that students who report more IM in schoolwork show greater conceptual learning than other students, suggesting deeper processing of the material (e.g., Grolnick & Ryan, 1987; Vansteenkiste, Simons, Lens, Sheldon, & Deci, 2004). It should also be noted that several studies of interventions designed to increase students' interest in science have found evidence of improvements in the students' science achievement (e.g., Grolnick, Farkas, Sohmer, Michaels, & Valsiner, 2007; Hoffmann, 2002). In sum, most of the available evidence supports the postulate that the experience of IM enhances learning.

2. General Development

It is argued that IM can facilitate not just learning but more general development, including development of emotional maturity, identity, social skills, and other life skills (Csikszentmihalyi, 1990; Larson, 2000). This possibility is suggested by research showing that people who are self-motivated have higher vitality, self-esteem, and general well-being (Ryan & Deci, 2000, p. 69). We found only a few quantitative studies bearing directly on the relationship between IM and development. Most were conducted in after-school programs.

The findings, nonetheless, are consistent with the hypothesis that IM facilitates general development. In a longitudinal study, Mahoney, Parente, and Lord (2007) found that observational ratings of older children's engagement (paying attention, demonstrating interest) in the activities of nine after-school programs predicted significant increases in leader-rated social competence over a school year. In a cross-sectional study, Shernoff (2010) showed that middle school students' reports of psychological engagement during program activities mediated the relationship between program participation and measures of social competence. A third study was a survey of 1800 high-school juniors in which each reported on two activities, thus allowing use of within-person comparisons as well as other controls (Hansen & Larson, 2007). Multilevel analyses found that when students reported IM in an after-school activity, they reported more frequent developmental experiences related to identity work, developing initiative, emotional development, and acquiring teamwork and social skills.

3. Sustained Motivation in the Activity

One of the core hypotheses about IM is that it can lead to sustained motivation. In interest theory, initial experiences of IM (called *situational interest*) can grow into more enduring *dispositional interest*—the "love" Ron and Sheri described for their activities. The evidence on this question is quite robust. Findings confirm that experiences of IM are related to increased participation and interest. Reported experience of IM (or situational interest) consistently predicts a person's likelihood of subsequent participation in an activity or topic area (Harackiewicz, Barron, Tauer, Carter, & Elliot, 2000; Simpkins, Davis-Kean, & Eccles, 2006; Wigfield, Eccles, Schiefele, Roeser, & Davis-Kean, 2006). For example,

Lavigne and Vallerand (2010) found that high-school students who participated in science activities they enjoyed during the semester, later reported greater interest and intention to take further science classes and to pursue a career in science. Consistent with interest theory, the research shows that if initial experiences in an activity are positive, they can lead to dispositional interest and expanded long-term participation (Hidi & Renninger, 2006).

E. A CATALYST OF DEVELOPMENT?

Accumulating evidence, then, supports the existence of a psychological system that, when activated, mobilizes and enhances engagement including engagement in learning. Qualitative studies find that people in the state of IM experience control over challenging activities, as well as focused, efficient attention, and a feeling of enjoyment and reward that makes them want to continue participation in the activity. Quantitative research confirms influence on measurable behavior. Short-term studies indicate that IM is related to indicators of greater use of meta-cognitive strategies, deeper processing of information, and more expansive and integrative reasoning. Longer-term studies show that IM is associated with greater learning (though relationships to grades are modest) and sustained motivation.

Research on the postulate that IM facilitates general development is less advanced but is promising. The quantitative findings we reviewed are supportive but sparse, due to lack of research. Qualitative research, however, has documented processes in after-school programs through which youth's repeated episodes of deep motivated attention in projects led to significant developmental insights and the acquisition of self-management strategies. In our research and that of others, youth described how their engagement and grappling with psycho-social challenges in the activities was related to becoming more responsible (Wood, Larson, & Brown, 2009), developing skills to manage emotions (Larson & Brown, 2007), learning to regulate cognitive biases (Kirshner, Pozzoboni, & Jones, under review; Watkins, Larson, & Sullivan, 2007), and developing strategic skills for agency (Larson & Angus, 2011a). Kirchner and colleagues' study, for example, showed how youth leading a research project learned from struggling with the challenge of reconciling passionately held beliefs with data they obtained that contradicted these beliefs. We suggest that the IM experienced by youth in these after-school programs helped activate episodes of deeper, expansive, and integrative meta-cognitive reasoning that led to conscious developmental change. As Fredrickson (2001) argues, positive psychological states can help individuals "broaden and build" their cognitive resources.

It should be emphasized, however, that much further research is required on the IM system. More evidence is needed on the coherence of the different features of IM (how strongly do they co-occur?) and whether these features (singly or as a group) predict short- and long-term outcomes independently of possible confounds. Research across more diverse contexts is needed: the studies we reviewed come almost entirely from Western nations, and most focus on children or youth engaged in school tasks. Another concern is that our review combined evidence from different paradigms (most notably flow, interest, and self-determination theory [SDT]), yet there are cleavages in how these different frameworks conceptualize motivational processes.[1] Finally, more research on biological substrata of the IM system needs to be conducted. Some researchers have speculated on the specific neurological mechanisms associated with IM (e.g., Hidi, 2006), pointing to the possible role that the dopamine system plays in attention, intentional action, and the seeking of rewards or positive feedback (see reviews by Alcaro, Huber, & Panksepp, 2007; Seamans & Robbins, 2010). But rigorous tests have yet to be done.

Despite limitations of this research, there is enough evidence on the role of IM as catalyst of learning and development to ask the next question: What influences its occurrence? If it can mobilize deep, sustained, self-direct attention to learning and development, we need to know what activates it.

III. Factors that Shape the Experience of IM

A. THE URGENCY AND COMPLEXITY OF MOTIVATION

Motivation is an urgent issue for youth if they are to thrive in a complex global society. The quantity of information they must learn keeps increasing. The types of problems and opportunities they encounter as they come of age require that they are motivated to keep learning and problem solving (Larson, 2011). Yet as children move into the teen years, their daily experiences of intrinsic motivated learning typically decline—especially

---

[1]For example, in contrast to authors who posit general skills for IM (e.g., Csikszentmihalyi & Larson, 1984), Hidi and Renninger (2006) describe *interest* exclusively tied to a specific topic (e.g., birds or astronomy). Ryan and Deci (2000) reserve the concept of intrinsic motivation for experiences that are directly related to basic psychological needs.

in schoolwork—accompanied by decreased interest in taking on challenging tasks (Eccles & Roeser, 2009; Wigfield et al., 2006). They appear to have fewer episodes in daily life in which they benefit from the efficient, effective learning of IM. It is essential therefore to understand the mainsprings of the type of eager, sustained engagement in learning experienced by Ron and Sheri.

As with other human psychological systems, the determinants of IM are complex. IM is shaped by immediate ongoing factors within the activity, as well as longer-term factors and personal dispositions. Just as the reasons a person feels angry or in love are likely to entail more than what is happening in the moment, IM is influenced by an array of bio-psycho-ecological elements, including basic needs, personal values, goals, and cultural influences. Our goal in this section is to get a handle on how proximate and more global factors converge to activate IM. An underlying theme is that, although there are many obstacles to experiencing IM in real-world circumstances, research and theory suggest ways in which a person's capacities for IM can develop.

B. FACTORS IN THE ONGOING PERSON-ACTIVITY INTERACTION

What is happening in the immediate interaction is certainly crucial to whether a person experiences the motivated attention of IM. Csikszentmihalyi (1975, 1990) and others have identified a number of factors in a person's interaction with an activity that are associated with IM. Some are directly related to what we have already discussed: Is the person challenged? Do they experience a sense of control? Are there distractions that interfere with focused attention? IM also is more likely when activities include novelty (Berlyne, 1966) and are rich in sensory stimuli. Activities that engage the senses may engage the brain more deeply (Kandel, 2007). In addition, youth are more motivated when they are working on projects for an authentic audience and purpose (Lenhart, Arafeh, Smith, & Macgill, 2008; Magnifico, 2010). For example, in one study, students showed higher quality work when writing brochures for a local nature center than writing a similar assignment only to receive a grade (Purcell-Gates, Duke, & Martineau, 2007).

The *structure* of the interaction between person and activity also influences IM. Csikszentmihalyi found that IM is more frequent when the goals in the activity are clear and they possess clear models for action (i.e., techniques, guidelines, rules) to reach those goals. It is also important that people receive prompt and unambiguous feedback—that they have clear information on the effects of their actions. These factors help explain why games are enjoyable: they provide this type of clarity for players.

The factor that Csikszentmihalyi found to be particularly significant to IM was that the *difficulty of the challenges in the activity be matched to— or slightly above—a person's skill level*. When people perceive the challenges as much greater than their skills, they experience anxiety and often become demotivated. In after-school leadership programs we studied, youth reported anxiety (and demotivation) when they were trying to plan an activity without prior planning experience. Their motivation was restored, however, when staff members broke the tasks down into manageable pieces and gave them training that increased their skills. An opposite situation occurs when people perceive activities as too *easy* for their skills. This creates boredom and again IM can wane. In a consciousness-raising program, SisterHood, participating youth reported at midyear that their discussions, organized by the advisors, had become stale and boring. But the youth's motivation increased when the advisors turned the planning over to the youth, which demanded that they develop more advanced skills. The importance of this matching challenge to skills for fostering motivation, attention, and sense of control has been confirmed by experience sampling research (Massimini, Csikszentmihalyi, & Delle Fave, 1988; Moneta & Csikszentmihalyi, 1996). People are more likely to experience IM when they are grappling with challenges that fully demand but do not overwhelm their abilities.

A final factor, important to maintaining IM over time, is that the activity provides a *ladder of increasingly difficult challenges* (Csikszentmihalyi & Larson, 1984; Nakamura & Csikszentmihalyi, 2009). The reason for this is clear. If people keep addressing the same challenges over again, they will learn all they need to know and the activity will likely become boring. To continue to experience IM, people need to be able to move gradually toward more difficult challenges. This is another reason why many computer games are so alluring, because players can advance to harder yet manageable levels of challenge (Malone, 1980). At Sisterhood, this was achieved when youth progressed from providing suggestions on discussion topics to planning the discussions themselves. The optimal conditions for learning, then, occur when people can stay in what Csikszentmihalyi calls a "channel" of manageable challenges that increase as their skills develop.[2]

---

[2]This channel is similar to Vygotsky's notion of the "zone of proximal development"; but IM theory helps us understand that this zone or channel is important not only for learning processes but also for mobilizing and sustaining IM.

Csikszentmihalyi describes adults who were skilled at restructuring their activities to keep themselves in this channel. They had learned to extract meaningful feedback in situations that would be ambiguous to someone else. They were able to reframe their goals or break tasks down into manageable challenges in order to keep in the zone. If they got anxious or bored, they could read the cues and make adjustments. We discuss later how youth can develop these skills.

C. LONGER-TERM DISPOSITIONS AND FACTORS

IM, however, does not depend entirely on a person's *current* interaction with the activity. There are longer-term factors that also contribute. Researchers have identified different types of more enduring dispositions and factors that influence whether a person is engaged by the activity. These include psychological needs, dispositional interest, and connections between the activity and personal goals.

1. Psychological Needs

Self-determination theorists have identified three empirically supported human needs that contribute to IM. These basic needs—which they posit to be universal in the species—include needs for *connection, competence, and autonomy* (Ryan & Deci, 2000). The first two needs are not controversial. Over the past 50 years, psychologists have increasingly recognized the fundamental social nature of the human species—and a basic need for connection. Across ages, people function better and are more motivated when they have "secure attachments" and when they experience trusting and supportive relationships with people within an activity setting (Lerner, Phelps, Forman, & Bowers, 2009; Wentzel, 2009). A youth is much less likely to experience IM in a classroom or youth program if the social climate is hostile. The psychological need for competence is also strongly supported by research. The need to experience oneself as competent is recognized as a basic source of motivation, not only in SDT but also in achievement goal theory (Dweck & Leggett, 1988) and expectancy value theory (Eccles & Roeser, 2009), among others (White, 1959). People are most likely to be highly motivated in activity settings in which they have opportunities to experience competence.

The most controversial of the three needs is the need for autonomy. The controversy stems partly from the term "autonomy," which easily suggests Western notions of individualism. Ryan and Deci (2000) clarify, however, that, "Within SDT, autonomy refers not to being independent, detached, or selfish but rather to *the feelings of volition that can accompany any act, whether dependent or independent, collectivist or individualistic"* (p. 74, italics added). Their point is that humans have a need to experience volition (being an "origin" of one's actions), but it can be experienced as an individual or part of a group. In the example of SisterHood, youth's motivation stemmed from this experience of collective volition in planning their discussions (Larson, Jensen, Kang, Griffith, & Rompala in process). Research from multiple cultures confirms that this experience of volition is related to the features of IM (including greater engagement, better performance, and higher quality learning; Ryan & Deci, 2003).

Research also shows that these features of IM are increased when the adults in the setting provide "autonomy support"—when they promote youth's exercise of volition in the activity (Lavigne, Vallerand, & Miquelon, 2007; Pelletier, Séguin-Lévesque, & Legault, 2002; Soenens et al., 2007). Supporting youth's *perception* of volition, however, appears to be more important than maximizing their actual volition. When youth have responsibility for more than they can handle, this can create anxiety and undermine their IM (Larson & Dawes, in press). As youth become more experienced within a domain, they become capable of more autonomy and, indeed, may need it to maintain their experience of IM.

2. Dispositional Interest in the Activity

Another set of longer-term factors that influence IM is a person's development of dispositional interest in an activity or subject matter. We have already cited evidence showing that short-term positive experiences of "situational interest" can develop into enduring dispositional interest. As an example, Renninger (2010) describes how Jane Goodall's initial childhood interest in worms grew into a deep passion and a career as a world-renowned primatologist. Hidi and Renninger (2006) present a fuller research-based theory on how this development occurs, including a sequence of stages concluding with "well-developed" dispositional interest.

This development is driven by and depends on a person acquiring *knowledge, skills, and positive emotional associations* to the activity or subject. Acquisition of knowledge and skills provide a foundation for meaningful participation in the activity. As these grow, students become more able to generate their own curiosity, set challenges for themselves within the activity, and anticipate future steps in their work.

Development of interest also depends on a person experiencing positive emotions along with their acquisition of knowledge and skills (Hidi, 2006; Renninger, 2010). In the early stages, positive affect *during* the experience is important to the development of interest—memories of participation become associated with positive affect and meaning. In later stages, positive emotion may be generated by anticipation of the activity, ongoing curiosity about the topic, and enjoyment of gaining competence. These stored positive emotions fuel greater persistence when encountering obstacles and frustration. Memories of prior positive experiences help students sustain long-term constructive work, including persevering through frustrating obstacles in the work (Hidi & Renninger, 2006).

In principle, almost anything can become a topic of interest—worms, action figures, calculus proofs, no matter how obscure—as long as these processes occur. As suggested earlier, this flexibility is the "beauty of the human brain." Within educational settings, development of interest is more likely when students work in groups, work on projects, experience success, and interact with materials that are interesting (Ainley, Hidi, & Berndorff, 2002). Across stages, there appears to be a reciprocal relationship between success and growing dispositional interest: interest in a class predicts exam performance; exam performance predicts subsequent situational interest (Harackiewicz, Durik, Barron, Linnenbrink-Garcia, & Tauer, 2008).

3. Goals, Values, Purpose, and Personal Connection

The development of a positive disposition toward an activity, however, is not just a "bottom-up" process that emerges from immediate, ongoing experiences in the activity. There are also more general "top-down" processes that influence the meaning people attribute to that activity and, in turn, their propensity toward IM. Adolescence is a life stage when youth begin to work on identity issues: who am I, what do I care about, what do I want to do with my life? The values, goals, and life purposes they develop are another set of dispositions they bring to an activity that influence their participation, their investment in the challenges of an activity, and their experience of IM (Eccles, 2009; Nasir & Hand, 2008; Wortham, 2006). Damon (2008) describes how young people's development of purpose ("a stable and generalized intention to accomplish something that is at the same time meaningful to the self and consequential to the world beyond the self"; p. 121) can lead to passionate engagement in an activity (see Mariano & Going, this volume).

In many cases, these bottom-up and top-down processes and factors influence each other. Bottom-up experiences in activities feed development of knowledge, skills, and positive emotions in an activity. At the same time, people develop top-down life goals, values, and identities that feed investment and interest. We observed this reciprocal process among a group of adolescents who described marked increases in their IM in a youth program (Dawes & Larson, 2011; Pearce & Larson, 2007). Quite a number had joined for reasons that were not primarily related to the program's activities—they wanted to be with friends, parents had encouraged them to join, or participation fulfilled a high-school service requirement. They attributed their increased motivation to having formed a *personal connection* between the program activities and their values or emerging life goals. For youth in several activism programs, this connection, often shared with others, involved a process of coming to identify with the programs' social justice mission (e.g., to change their schools, to keep neighborhood youth out of gangs). Two youth in a theater program attributed their increased motivation to the program simultaneously helping them feel more certain about career goals (e.g., teaching, ministry) and seeing how skills they were learning would allow them to be competent in those professions.

This process of forming a personal connection closely resembles a process described by self-determination theorists through which an activity becomes integrated into the self (Ryan & Deci, 2000). Over many experiences, people may internalize and identify with the activity. As a result, they experience the motivation as coming from within as being self-determined.

4. Other Factors: Beliefs, Expectancies, and Culture

Eccles's (2005) comprehensive model of motivation identifies a host of additional dispositions that have been found to influence people's choices of activities, including beliefs, expectations of one's likelihood of achieving goals in the activity, perceptions of others' beliefs and expectations, gender roles, and cultural stereotypes. Research also shows that individuals who have a mastery goal orientation are more likely to experience IM and sustained effort (e.g., Cury, Elliot, Da Fonseca, & Moller, 2006; Dweck, 1999). Finally, research demonstrates how the beliefs, goals, social relationships, activities, and other factors that influence motivation are shaped by culture (Markus & Kitayama, 2003).

5. The Convergence of Factors

Psychology's understanding of the determinants of IM has advanced since an earlier era when, influenced by existentialism, a number of early IM theorists focused principally on immediate determinants. Recent research has led to a more multifactorial view of the springs of motivation. Diverse factors contribute from different levels of analysis: immediate and longer-term; individual and collective; setting characteristics and culture; basic psychological needs and a developing self. We suggest that it is the convergence of these multiple factors *as a whole* that shapes IM experiences.

We have given particular emphasis to the convergence of immediate and longer-term factors. Although immediate sensory-rich experiences may be a dominant source of IM in the first few years of life, as children develop, more distal, constructed, and enduring factors enter into how they experience interactions with the environment. Their prior experiences, knowledge, values, goals, goal orientation, and culture frameworks (among other things) play a larger role in how they experience an activity. These longer-term and more global factors engage attention, shape whether the activity is challenging, and form the basis of personal connections. This can happen in ways that are both conscious and nonconscious.

Of course, even in adulthood, one may still experience delight and IM in something completely new, and of course, people experience enjoyment of challenging leisure activities that are not directly related to their primary life values and goals. But as a working hypothesis, we suggest that the more different determinants are aligned to support IM—the more overdetermined IM is—the deeper and more sustained engagement is likely to be.

D. OBSTACLES TO INTRINSIC MOTIVATION IN YOUTH'S DAILY LIVES

But let us return to the situation of young people in the "real world" of a complex global society. To fully understand why IM in learning activities is not a prevalent part of many youth's lives—and what can be done about it—we need to consider the many obstacles to IM in the bio-psycho-social ecology of daily life.

To begin with, IM has a lot of competition from other psychological systems. Emotions (anger, anxiety), appetites (desire, pleasure), and the desire for extrinsic rewards (recognition, material resources) are all products of psychological systems that can compete with the IM system to influence behavior. These different systems were also shaped by evolution to direct attention to important individual needs, including some that are more urgent. Survival needs easily trump IM. Receiving extrinsic rewards for an activity can also undercut the experience of self-determination that is important to IM, especially when youth view them as part of someone's attempt to control their behavior (Deci, Koestner & Ryan, 1999). In a stimuli-saturated world, daily events can repeatedly trigger these systems, disrupting IM (Csikszentmihalyi et al., 1993; Ryan & Deci, 2000; Urdan, 2003).

Another obstacle is that many of youth's daily activities do not provide the convergence of ongoing conditions or personal connections that are necessary for IM. Many activities simply are not structured in ways that readily facilitate IM. They do not provide sufficient novelty, the challenges entail unstructured problems in which goals and feedback are ambiguous, or the challenges are not matched to youth's skills. Even if these ongoing conditions are present, the activity may not be sufficiently aligned with a youth's needs, interests, or goals for the challenges of the activity to be personally challenging. A significant problem is that many youth are disengaged from the goal of becoming adults in today's society (Arnett, 2000; Schneider & Stevenson, 1999), which makes it harder for them to form personal connections to activities related to preparation for adulthood.

As a whole, our complex global society offers youth many more options, particularly via the Internet, but also more opportunities to be overwhelmed and distracted. However, Piaget (1971) and many others scholars have shown how the human mind-brain is a biological organism built to learn and adapt to complexity. In Csikszentmihalyi's theory, challenges and complexity are precisely what drives the IM system.

E. DEVELOPMENT OF THE CAPACITY FOR INTRINSIC MOTIVATION

The beauty of the IM system is that it too can develop to adapt to enormously diverse environments. In contrast to species with fixed action patterns that dictate its members' responses to specific types of situations, IM in humans is designed to allow our big brains the opportunity to sculpt this "seeking system" to highly varied activities, subject matter, and goals. Just as developmental experiences help shape other psychological systems (i.e., to improve our working models of attachment and refine our emotional sensibilities), they can help us develop knowledge and skills that allow us to experience IM in highly varied task situations and within different culture contexts. We must view IM as an "epigenetic system" (Rutter, Moffitt, & Caspi, 2006), which allows humans to develop motivated engagement in diverse domains of expertise.

What develops in the development of IM includes competencies at multiple levels. The research we reviewed suggests that people can build domain specific skills that allow them to engage in an activity at higher degrees of challenge and complexity (Csikszentmihalyi, 1990). They can develop individual dispositional interests—enduring knowledge, skills, and emotional associations that support deeper, more stable engagement in an activity (Hidi & Renninger, 2006). They can also develop values, meanings, and personal or collective connections to an activity, which become integrated into the self and make the activity more congruent with one's goals and identity (Ryan & Deci, 2000). Development, then, can be a major determinant of IM.

Further, as young people move into adolescence, they have increased potential to control this development: to deliberately develop skills for regulation of the factors that shape IM (Lerner, 2002). As we said at the chapter outset, teens gain the potential to acquire meta-cognitive understanding and executive skills for controlling their psychological processes (Kuhn, 2009; Steinberg et al., 2006). But there is no guarantee a given youth will gain this control. Ordinary experience may not provide much impetus for developing these advanced levels of thinking. Klaczynski (2004) argues that in daily life, people do most of their thinking using expedient mental shortcuts and heuristics.

What is especially important about IM is that (as reviewed in Section II) it is a state in which adolescents are likely to activate these meta-cognitive and executive skills. They are more likely to process information at deeper levels: asking questions, processing meaning, engaging in more expansive, and integrative reasoning. We suggest then that IM is a state in which this deeper thinking is likely to include analysis and synthesis that helps them understand the determinants of their motivation and develop skills for regulating it.

Research suggests that this happens for many youth. Renninger (2010) observed that high-school students with well-developed interests were able to weigh and choose between competing goals, identify obstacles, and regulate their work to sustain engagement in their domain of interest. We suspect that adolescents are capable of learning to read the emotional cues of boredom and anxiety to adjust a task to keep themselves in a channel of IM. We also propose that adolescents have the potential to learn general skills for self-regulation of motivation that—with effort—can be transferred from one activity to another.

Of course, just because there is "potential" for these differing components of IM to develop in adolescence, it does not mean that they will. They can fail to develop or start to develop and be "snuffed out". This turns us to the urgency of our next topic.

IV. How Youth Professionals Can Support the Development of Intrinsic Motivation

A. PROMISE AND CHALLENGE

Many adults think of motivation as binary (Renninger, 2010): Either a young person is self-motivated or not—and, if not, may never be. The important message of the research just reviewed is that IM is not "all or nothing"; it can change and grow. It is influenced by a constellation of determinants, many of which can be cultivated. In our study of effective youth programs, 44 out of 100 youth reported marked increases in their motivation (Dawes & Larson, 2011). They grew to be more deeply engaged, including "loving" program activities in ways described by Ron and Sheri.

For youth professionals, however, dealing with young people who are unmotivated is by no means easy. Just as the determinants of IM is complex, so are the means to cultivating it. In fact, attempts to induce youth's motivation can have the opposite effect (Ryan & Deci, 2003). A dilemma for educators is that for youth to become intrinsically motivated (i.e., self-motivated), the change has to come at least partly from the youth themselves. Research cannot provide formulas for these and the many kinds of dilemmas encountered in youth practice (Larson & Walker, 2010). But what the research just reviewed does suggest are principles about what shapes youth's IM (see Table I) that can be applied across situations. In this section, we discuss how these principles can be adapted to the realities of practice.

Rather than starting with youth's immediate motivation (or lack thereof), we first examine what the research suggests about practitioners' roles in cultivating environments that provide conditions for IM to develop. Second, we discuss approaches to helping youth build interest in and personal connections to learning activities. With this background, we next examine how professionals can support youth's immediate, ongoing experiences of IM. At the end, we explore the question of helping youth develop skills for managing their *own* motivation.

B. CULTIVATING ENVIRONMENTS THAT INVITE AND MODEL ENGAGEMENT

When youth first walk into a program or classroom, the environment they encounter begins to influence their future motivation. The social climate, activity structures, and norms of the setting, among other elements, begin to create a foundation for youth's future engagement.

1. Motivating Environments

The *social environment* is critical. Research has shown that youth's motivation depends in part on whether their psychological need for connection is addressed (Principle 1). When a youth walks in the door, a

Table I

Principles for Cultivating Intrinsic Motivation Based on the Research

Practitioner goals	Principles from the research (Roman Numerals identify the section in the text in which each principle is discussed)
Cultivating environments that invite and model engagement	*Principle 1.* IM is more likely when youth experience relationships of trust and support. (IIIC)
	Principle 2. IM is more likely in environments that provide youth opportunities for experiencing competency and developing mastery. (IIIC)
	Principle 3. IM is more likely when youth experience volition in meaningful activities. (IIIC)
	Principle 4. IM is most likely to continue in activities in which youth can experience gradations of increasingly difficult challenges. (IIIB)
	Principle 5. IM is more frequent in settings in which youth experience clear goals and models of action (techniques, guidelines, rules) for reaching those goals. (IIIB)
Helping youth develop interest and make personal connections to an activity	*Principle 6.* IM develops as youth gain knowledge, skills, and positive emotional associations to the activity or content area. (IIIC)
	Principle 7. IM is greater when an activity is connected to youth's personal values, life goals, and identities. (IIIC)
Sustaining ongoing conditions for engaged attention	*Principle 8.* IM is greater when youth receive accurate and authentic feedback on product and process of work. (IIIB)
	Principle 9. To experience IM youth need to be engaged by challenges that are matched to their skills. (IIIB)
Facilitating development of skills for managing motivation	*Principle 10.* Educators can facilitate youth's development of skills for managing motivation by helping them gain conscious awareness of motivational processes, how their thoughts and actions influence these processes, and how skills for managing motivation can be transferred to other contexts. (IVE)

welcoming atmosphere influences whether he or she connects with the group and wants to return.[3] At a deeper level, a culture of interpersonal trust and support (both youth–youth and youth–staff) creates a foundation for youth's future development of collaborative working relationships (Rhodes, 2004) in which IM is experienced not just individually but collectively (Pearce & Larson, 2006).

The *task environment* is also critical. To facilitate IM, the setting needs to provide structures that support youth's work and learning. Research indicates that structures in the setting should provide opportunities for youth's ongoing experiences of competence and volition (Principles 2 and 3); this includes opportunities for experiencing competence in increasingly challenging activities (Principle 4). In addition, research suggests that IM is more frequent in settings in which the models for action include clear goals and models of action techniques (including techniques, guidelines, rules) for reaching those goals (Principle 5). Additional elements of motivating environments are summarized by Kaplan and Maehr (2007).

The difficult question, however, is how youth professionals can create social and task environments with these features. Part of the challenge is that a number of these features involve norms that are only meaningful if they are shared by all youth; and adults cannot just impose a normative order, especially on adolescents. Youth must buy in. Let us provide an example of how this was done successfully.

2. Cultivating a Motivating Environment: An Illustration

Several weeks before the Computer Clubhouse first officially opened, there was a "soft launch" that involved a smaller pilot group of youth. This after-school program was designed for 12–18-year-olds, and its aim is to engage youth's natural interest in art, animation, robotics, and other areas as a means for them to develop technical and broader skills (Rusk, Resnick, & Cooke, 2009). The pilot youth were asked to try out equipment in order to help staff figure out what types of projects might be interesting to create. For example, a couple of youth were asked to try out the image scanner and they experimented with digitizing their photos and drawings. Youth were given a lot of autonomy but were also playing a role in starting to develop the models for future youth in the program, including models of how youth and adults interact.

---

[3]For some older youth, caring may be less important than trust and respect. Halpern (2005) described how youth in apprenticeship programs were highly motivated in "matter of fact" professional relationships with an adult expert.

As a result, when the full set of youth joined on opening day, the space was already active. The pilot youth were eagerly collaborating at computer stations around the room: editing images, recording music, and designing computer games. These teens invited new youth to join projects, or helped them start new ones. New youth saw the pilot youth's art and technology projects on the walls—examples that suggested a range of activities youth could try. A shared culture came into life, one that supported positive relationships, competency, youth volition, and other ways of acting and thinking that facilitated IM.

3. The Role of Youth

Peer-to-peer influence is powerful (Brown, Bakken, Ameringer, & Mahon, 2008). This kind of "soft opening" is one way to involve youth in jumpstarting a shared culture that supports IM. The pilot youth passed on a welcoming, trusting social environment, as well as a task environment with models of action. In other programs, a similar process occurs when veteran youth, returning from prior years, pass on norms and share what happened and how things were done in the past (Polman & Miller, 2010).

It is important to recognize that this transfer between youth is not a process of rote imitation or conformity. In a controlled study, Kitsantas, Zimmerman, and Cleary (2000) found that girls (ages 14–16 years) who watched a person throw darts perfectly 15 times in a row were not as motivated as those who watched the person improve their skills over successive trials. The girls who had watched the person improve were more likely to attribute their successful shots to strategy (rather than ability), and this attribution led them to their experiencing greater self-efficacy and intrinsic interest. What is transferred that stimulates IM is not simply behaviors, it is the mental process of engaging with the challenges of an activity.

4. The Role of Staff

Although peers are important, youth professionals play vital roles as well. In interviews, youth describe how program staff positively influence their motivation by cultivating welcoming and trusting relationships within programs, including both youth–adult and youth–youth relationships (Larson & Dawes, in press). At the Computer Clubhouse, the staff spent months in advance thinking through the social and task environment they wanted to cultivate among youth and staff (Rusk et al., 2009). Effective youth professionals are intentional in cultivating core working principles (Walker, Marczak, Blyth, & Bordon, 2005). Staff can also play an important role through modeling. Adults' demonstration of how they approach work, their expectations, values, and beliefs can be transmitted to youth and facilitate their IM (Bakker, 2005; Basom & Frase, 2004; Halpern, 2009). As a general pattern, effective youth professionals cultivate favorable conditions for IM that are then passed on from youth to youth.

C. HELPING YOUTH DEVELOP INTEREST AND MAKE PERSONAL CONNECTIONS

But the environment, of course, is not enough to spark motivation in all youth. They need to have interest in the activities or subject matter. Some adolescents are chronically bored across activities in their lives (Larson & Richards, 1991). In after-school programs, some youth arrive unable to identify or articulate anything that motivates them. When asked what interests them, they shrug their shoulders and say they don't know.

Interest theory helps us think about how immediate experiences, over time, can lead to youth's development of dispositional interest. It suggests that IM is likely to grow as function of youth's acquisition of knowledge, skills, and positive emotional associations to the activity or subject (Principle 6).

Stina Cooke, one of the founders of the Computer Clubhouse, provides a valuable illustration of how to apply this and related principles to cultivating youth's interest. Chay, a shy and withdrawn youth, was reluctant to talk with either youth or staff in the program. Stina observed Chay collecting images from a Web site and began to notice a theme: many of these images contained airplanes. She unobtrusively helped him with the printer when needed, and eventually he was comfortable enough to speak with her.

Surprisingly, one of the first things Chay said to her was, "You don't hate me?" Stina replied by drawing him out, and he explained his fears about being scorned for his ethnic background and immigrant status. This is a useful example of how emotions—including those hidden from view—can interfere with youth's engagement in a setting. By getting Chay to talk about his anxieties and reassuring him, Stina was able to begin to build the kind of interpersonal trust we just discussed that provides a safe space for engagement and exploration.

As trust grew, Stina asked Chay about his experience with airplanes. He explained that the first (and only) time he was in an airplane was when his family flew to the United States after his family's release from a refugee camp. Seeing that this was a personal theme, Stina suggested projects he might want to work on involving airplanes, such as an animation, video, or 3D model. Chay dove into creating on a 3D model of an airplane. This attracted the interest of another boy. The two decided to work together on a project and began developing a collaborative friendship. As Chay's work continued, his knowledge grew and emotional connections to the topic of airplanes strengthened. He was developing dispositional interest, and this helped him persist in the face of obstacles he encountered with the 3D design software.

This example illustrates how different types of support may be needed at different phases. Hidi and Renninger (2006) describe how, at initial stages, learners' interest may require more external support, including support for exploring their own ideas. In this case, Chay initially browsed Web sites to find images, and Stina encouraged him to experiment in areas that attracted his attention. When his interest in airplanes became more apparent, Stina provided options for pursuing this interest. As Chay started working on creating a project based on his interest, his need for feedback and support shifted as well. He moved from depending on supports in the environment for attracting his attention to a more established ongoing interest, persisting in pursuing a project over time. At later stages, learners' development of interest can benefit from constructive feedback and input on how to most effectively reach their goals (Renninger, 2010).

In this example, Stina helped Chay develop his interest through his immediate experiences in the activity. Educators can also help youth increase their motivation by supporting connections between the activity and youth's values, identities, or life goals (Principle 7). In our findings on youth programs, this occurred when staff helped youth see links between what they enjoyed in an activity and possible career goals (Rickman, 2009) or connections between the activity and societal values and injustices (Pearce & Larson, 2007).

D. SUSTAINING ONGOING CONDITIONS FOR ENGAGED ATTENTION

The young artists at Art-First experienced the favorable conditions we discussed thus far. The program provided an inviting environment that was rich in models of action. Youth also had no lack of interest: they had a well-developed base of knowledge and positive emotions; and they were excited that each would be painting a mural to be mounted on the metro platform. But the murals were bigger than any paintings they had done, creating anxiety. They soon discovered, too, that the metro authority had numerous rules that restricted use of their individual artistic styles in the murals. Other problems emerged: time was short, some youth got bored, and later their murals were vandalized (Larson & Walker, 2006).

This is where the real world comes in. Although real-world activities can be highly motivating, they also generate threats and obstacles to youth's motivation. Practitioners face the challenge of trying to sustain conditions for IM (such as that in Table I) in the face of this real-world complexity: How do they enable youth to find a "zone"—to be in a channel or "sweet spot"—in which the conditions for IM are maintained?

Welcome to the world of practice. Youth professionals carry out their work on a "rough ground" in which the real world is a continuous part of the terrain (Larson, Rickman, Gibbons & Walker, 2009). Across professions, practice involves navigating complex unfolding events and situations. Stuff happens. Often practitioners must try to *balance* multiple competing goals (Schwandt, 2003; Sternberg et al., 2000). For youth professionals, supporting youth's motivation is only *one* of many competing goals they must balance, including curricular, organizational, community, ethical, and developmental goals (Larson & Walker, 2010). Even when they have the luxury of focusing solely on youth's motivation, we have identified numerous determinants of IM at different levels of analysis that need to be taken into account. Sternberg (1998) articulates how the "balancing" of practitioners can take many forms, including weighing, integrating, and reconciling divergent concerns.[4] The expertise of youth practitioners lies partly in their skills for this balancing and navigation of multiple considerations in complex contexts (Larson & Walker, 2010). Let us highlight a few of the balancing acts that leaders of youth programs navigate in helping sustain youth's IM;

1. Balancing Youth's Volition with Providing Them Needed Assistance

Youth's experience of volition is fundamental to their experience of IM (Principle 3). Yet insufficient adult supervision can compromise youth's learning of skills (Kirshner, 2008), leave youth floundering, or result in their work heading in directions that are inconsistent with youth professionals' obligations to keep youth safe, satisfy stakeholders, and maintain positive community relationships (Camino, 2005; Ozer et al., 2008). Leaders negotiate a balancing act of supporting youth's volition while

[4]Smetana, Crean, and Campione-Barr (2005) suggest that effective parenting requires delicate balancing, referred to as "precision parenting" (p. 43), in which just the right parental input is provided to fit a particular child and situation.

helping keep their work on track (Larson & Angus, 2011a,b). Even the simple process of providing input on youth's work can be experienced by youth as patronizing. Clear unadulterated feedback is important to IM (Principle 8)—as well as being vital to learning (Hattie & Timperley, 2007). Yet how do adults provide input (especially corrective feedback and process feedback) in ways that support rather than undercut youth's agency?

Effective youth professionals are skilled at this balancing act. We found that effective program leaders used "youth ownership" as a mantra—and youth reported that the freedom they experienced was an important factor in their motivation (Larson & Dawes, in press). Yet these leaders provided limited and judicious structure and input for youth's work in ways that sustained youth's experience of volition. They "led from behind." For example, rather than telling youth what to do, they would ask guiding questions—which kept responsibility for answering the questions with youth. At Art-First, they helped youth find ways to express themselves within the metro authority's constraints. We also found that youth valued leaders' input when they were stuck, needed help, or were headed in a wrong direction (Larson & Angus, 2011a,b). Rather than undercutting their volition, this help appeared to restore youth's sense of control. It helped restore conditions for IM and get them back in the zone of IM.

2. Helping Keep Challenges Matched to Youth's Skills

Another important balancing act of youth professionals is helping youth experience challenges matched to their skills (Principle 9). It is important to recognize that challenges come in heterogeneous forms. They involve not just subject matter content (as is typical in a school classes). In youth programs, they may involve unstructured problems, unfamiliar procedural steps, or managing complex interpersonal processes (e.g., group dynamics and emotions). Zeldin and Camino (1999) observed that inexperienced program leaders sometimes expect youth to handle tasks containing difficulties that even the leaders themselves could not handle.

We have already described several examples of advisors achieving this balance (e.g., by helping them break difficult tasks down into manageable pieces; or at SisterHood, responding to youth's boredom by helping youth take charge of group discussions). At Art-First, when youth felt panicked about the size and short timeline for their murals, the advisors helped them find shortcuts. When the match between challenges and skills was off, leaders helped youth get back into a zone (or "flow channel") that helped restore conditions for IM.

3. Additional Balancing Acts

Research suggests other motivational puzzles that skilled leaders navigate. One involves limited but *adroit use of extrinsic rewards*. Research shows that rewards can undermine IM, but in specific situations they can be helpful. These include to initiate the engagement of someone whose initial motivation is low and to get people through boring tasks (Covington, 2002). Another balancing act concerns *appropriate use of praise*. If excessive and indiscriminate, praise can be harmful to motivation; but it can be useful in situations where it provides recognition for effort (Mueller & Dweck, 1998) and when the rewards provide information and do not compromise a person's self-control of their actions (Deci et al., 1999). Youth also report that encouragement from leaders is helpful when they experience self-doubt and when the leaders help them envision where their work is headed. Another balancing act that youth said supported their motivation was the leaders' *balancing of serious work with fun* (Larson & Dawes, in press). Of course, for all of these, timing is critical: judging when youth need a particular type of input to bring them back into their zone of IM.

Because of their experience, youth professionals are in a position to see and balance diverse considerations that may influence youth's motivation. It is worth noting that balancing multiple competing considerations is something that adults generally do better than adolescents (Byrnes, Miller, & Reynolds, 1999).

E. FACILITATING YOUTH'S DEVELOPMENT OF SKILLS FOR MANAGING INTRINSIC MOTIVATION

Let us introduce one more practitioner balancing act that is important at more advanced stages of motivational development. The youth at Art-First were experienced painters with well-developed interest, but the goals of the program advisor, Rebecca, entailed more than just sustaining this passion; it including getting youth "out of their comfort zone." The aim was to move youth from the fun of painting for its own sake to learn about real-world experiences associated with careers in the arts. This included youth learning to manage challenges, such as the boredom, frustration, and anxiety that come with the territory. Rebecca did not want to entirely ignore youth's aversive experiences, and risk having them quit. But her goals were to *balance concern with sustaining their short-term motivation with creating conditions for them to learn to manage ups and downs in their motivation.*

Indeed the restrictions on the Art-First murals undercut youth's enthusiasm. So Rebecca kept reminding them that this is art in the real world. Given the youth's well-developed interest, they were perseverant and adapted to the restrictions: One reported, "Everyone realized we're here to do a job; it's not like summer camp or anything." Enthusiasm returned. A similar cycle of adaptation followed youth's devastating experience of having their completed murals vandalized. Rebecca responded by creating a class on art restoration in which youth not only repaired the murals but also reported learning a powerful lesson in resiliency (Larson & Walker, 2006). Youth were learning to regulate their motivational states. They were deploying their adolescent meta-cognitive potentials to develop executive skills for managing challenging real-world threats.

A valuable role of leaders in facilitating this learning is helping youth develop conscious awareness of strategies for managing their own motivation (Principle 10; Wolters, 2003). This can involve talking with youth as they plan their work, for example, interjecting questions about possible turns of events they might want to consider (Heath, 1999). It can also involve helping them stand back and reflect on their recent and past experiences (Priest & Gass, 1997).

Research suggests several topics of conversation that may be particularly useful in helping youth learn to manage their IM. First, the most important message for youth (as for practitioners) is that *motivation can change and develop over time*. Something you are not currently interested in may become more interesting later. And, one interest can lead to another.

A second important topic of talk with youth about motivation is *the process of goal setting*. A large body of research indicates that youth benefit when they learn to focus on improvement goals rather than comparison to others. Cultivating a mindset focused on the rewards of learning leads to more persistence after setbacks or failure (Blackwell, Trzesniewski, & Dweck, 2007). Research shows that people benefit from learning to set concrete attainable goals (rather than just "do your best") (Latham & Seijts, 1999). Research shows that even in long-term projects, youth should learn to focus on shorter-range goals, because they are more easy to control and, thus, more motivating (Bandura, 1997; Bandura & Schunk, 1981).

A third important topic of conversation involves *strategies for reaching goals in complex real-world contexts*. This includes helping youth anticipate potential obstacles (including motivational obstacles) and strategies for avoiding or problem solving when one encounters them. The effectiveness of this was demonstrated in an intervention in which high-school students planned for what they would do when they encountered obstacles to achieving their academic goals (Oyserman, Bybee, & Terry, 2006). Students were asked to draw future timelines for themselves that included possible forks in the road and obstacles. As described by the researchers, "The metamessage was 'everyone has difficulties, and failures and setbacks are a normal part of timelines'" (pp. 191). Youth should not interpret setbacks as a sign that they are not competent and should give up. Youth in this intervention showed declines in school absences and behavioral problems and improvements in academic initiatives, test scores, and grades—with effects sustained in a 2-year follow-up. In a separate study, Gollwitzer and Brandstätter (1997) found that students were three times more likely to reach difficult goals when they had thought about *how* and *when* they would implement their goals.

A fourth topic is helping youth reflect on how the strategies they learn about managing motivation can be *transferred to other contexts*. Research in learning science repeatedly shows that learners often fail to transfer new knowledge and skills across settings, but that educators can help by assisting them in thinking through how new knowledge and skills can be translated across diverse situations (Pugh & Bergin, 2006).

In concluding this section, we want to repeat our underlying themes that motivation is complex and that practice is more nuanced than researchers (including ourselves) and policy makers can do justice to. In fact, academics' theories can have negative effects if they are applied to practice without consideration to the real world of practice. Effective practice is an art. It entails balancing the consideration of numerous factors in a given context. Supporting youth's development of their capacity for IM—for deep engaged attention—requires both restraint and tenacity to adapt and persevere through the ups and downs of youth's experiences, as illustrated by Stina Cooke and the many other expert educators we have learned from. At a higher level, policy makers and administrators of youth serving organizations need to create institutional environments that support front-line staffs' development of skills and exercise of flexibility to adapt these principles to individual youth and ongoing motivational situations.

V. Conclusions: Combining Intrinsic Motivation and Positive Development

This chapter has focused on IM as a system that can catalyze learning and development but has said little about learning and development of what? The research indicates that IM mobilizes effective, efficient, and self-sustaining attention—also that given the plasticity of the human brain, the content toward which this attention is directed can vary widely across people as a function of their experiences. Much prior research has focused on IM and school learning, but at the end of Section II, we provided qualitative evidence on how IM can catalyze youth's engagement with psycho-social challenges that led to their development of emotional skills, responsibility, and insights on how to regulate their cognitive biases. Certainly, episodes of IM could also fuel development in the many other areas of positive development discussed in the volume. At the same time, theorists also caution that IM is not inherently oriented to learning only prosocial behavior: it is argued that, under certain conditions, malevolent activities can be intrinsically rewarding and IM can catalyze development of Machiavellian and criminal skill sets (e.g., Csikszentmihalyi, 1990).

Practitioners, researchers, and other adults, therefore, have common cause in cultivating IM around prosocial goals and life purposes. This leads to another set of balancing acts, for example, that of facilitating youth's experience of IM in computer activities, while discouraging pirating and malicious hacking, or supporting youth's personal connection to a just cause, yet helping them learn to manage the cognitive biases and insensitivity to other viewpoints that strong beliefs and passions can create (Kirshner et al., under review; Youniss, 2009). Although the goal of supporting IM is to help youth develop increased control over their motivation, this does not mean it should be encouraged in a vacuum. Positive development is most likely when it occurs in a context of positive relationships, institutions, communities, and value traditions (Benson, Scales, Hamilton, & Sesma, 2006; Youniss, 2009).

Acknowledgment

We would like to thank the William T. Grant Foundation for its support of this work.

REFERENCES

Ainley, M., Hidi, S., & Berndorff, D. (2002). Interest, learning and the psychological processes that mediate their relationship. *Journal of Educational Psychology, 94*, 545–561.

Alcaro, A., Huber, R., & Panksepp, J. (2007). Behavioral functions of the mesolimbic dopaminergic system: An affective neuroethological perspective. *Brain Research Reviews, 56*, 283–321.

Amabile, T. M. (1983). Social psychology of creativity: A componential conceptualization. *Journal of Personality and Social Psychology, 45*, 357–376.

Arnett, J. J. (2000). Emerging adulthood: A theory of development from the late teens through the twenties. *The American Psychologist, 55,* 469–480.

Bakker, A. B. (2005). Flow among music teachers and their students: The crossover of peak experiences. *Journal of Vocational Behavior, 66,* 26–44.

Bandura, A. (1997). *Self-efficacy: The exercise of control.* New York: Freeman.

Bandura, A., & Schunk, D. (1981). Cultivating competence, self-efficacy and intrinsic interest through proximal self-motivation. *Journal of Personality and Social Psychology, 41,* 586–598.

Basom, M. R., & Frase, L. (2004). Creating optimal work environments: Exploring teacher flow experiences. *Mentoring and Tutoring, 12,* 241–258.

Benson, P. L., Scales, P., Hamilton, S., & Sesma, A. (2006). Positive youth development: Theory, research and applications. In W. Damon & R. M. Lerner (Eds.), *Theoretical models of human development Vol. 1. Handbook of Child Psychology.* (6th ed., pp. 894–941). NJ: Wiley.

Berlyne, D. E. (1966). Curiosity and exploration. *Science, 153,* 25–33.

Bjorklund, D. F., & Ellis, B. J. (2005). Evolutionary psychology and child development: An emerging synthesis. In B. J. Ellis & D. F. Bjorklund (Eds.), *Origins of the social mind: Evolutionary psychology and child development.* (pp. 3–18). New York: Guilford.

Blackwell, L., Trzesniewski, K., & Dweck, C. S. (2007). Implicit theories of intelligence predict achievement across an adolescent transition: A longitudinal study and an intervention. *Child Development, 78,* 246–263.

Brown, B. B., Bakken, J. P., Ameringer, S. W., & Mahon, S. D. (2008). A comprehensive conceptualization of the peer influence process in adolescence. In M. J. Prinstein & K. Dodge (Eds.), *Peer influence processes among youth.* (pp. 17–44). New York: Guildford.

Bruner, J. S. (1966). *Toward a theory of instruction.* Cambridge, MA: Harvard University Press.

Byrnes, J. P., Miller, D. C., & Reynolds, M. (1999). Learning to make good decisions: A self-regulation perspective. *Child Development, 70,* 1121–1140.

Camino, L. (2005). Pitfalls and promising practices of youth-adult partnerships: An evaluator's reflections. *Journal of Community Psychology, 33,* 75–85.

Covington, M. V. (2002). Rewards and intrinsic motivation: A needs-based, developmental perspective. In F. Pajares & T. Urdan (Eds.), *Academic motivation of adolescents.* (pp. 169–192). Greenwich, CT: IAP.

Csikszentmihalyi, M. (1975). *Beyond boredom and anxiety.* San Francisco: Jossey-Bass.

Csikszentmihalyi, M. (1990). *Flow: The psychology of optimal experience.* New York: HarperPerennial.

Csikszentmihalyi, M. (1996). *Creativity: Flow and the psychology of discovery and invention.* New York: HarperCollins.

Csikszentmihalyi, M., & Larson, R. (1984). *Being adolescent.* New York: Basic Books.

Csikszentmihalyi, M., Rathunde, K., & Whalen, S. (1993). *Talented teenagers: The roots of success and failure.* New York: Cambridge University Press.

Cury, F., Elliot, A. J., Da Fonseca, D., & Moller, A. (2006). The social–cognitive model of achievement motivation and the 2 X 2 achievement goal framework. *Journal of Personality and Social Psychology, 90,* 666–679.

Damon, W. (2008). *Path to purpose: Helping our children find their calling in life.* NY: Free Press.

Daniels, L. M., Stupnisky, R. H., Pekrun, R., Haynes, T. L., Perry, R. P., & Newall, N. E. (2009). A longitudinal analysis of achievement goals: From affective antecedents to emotional effects and achievement outcomes. *Journal of Educational Psychology, 101,* 948–963.

Dawes, N. P. & Larson, R. W. (2011). How youth get engaged: Grounded-theory research on motivational development in organized youth programs. *Developmental Psychology, 47,* 259–269.

Deci, E. L., Koestner, R., & Ryan, R. M. (1999). A meta-analytic review of experiments examining the effects of extrinsic rewards on intrinsic motivation. *Psychological Bulletin, 125,* 627–668.

Dewey, J. (1913). *Interest and effort in education.* Carbondale, IL: Southern Illinois University Press.

Dweck, C. S. (1999). *Self-theories: Their role in motivation, personality, and development.* Philadelphia: Psychology Press.

Dweck, C. S., & Leggett, E. L. (1988). A social-cognitive approach to motivation and personality. *Psychological Review, 95,* 256–273.

Eccles, J. S. (2005). Studying gender and ethnic differences in participation in math, physical science, and information technology. *New Directions for Child and Adolescent Development, 110,* 7–14.

Eccles, J. S. (2009). Who am I and what am I going to do with my life? Personal and collective identities as motivators of action. *Educational Psychologist, 44,* 78–89.

Eccles, J. S., & Roeser, R. W. (2009). Schools, academic motivation, and stage-environment fit. In R. M. Lerner & L. Steinberg (Eds.). *Handbook of adolescent psychology* (3rd ed., Vol. 1, pp. 404–434). Hoboken, NJ: Wiley.

Fredrickson, B. L. (2001). The role of positive emotions in positive psychology: The broaden-and-build theory of positive emotions. *The American Psychologist, 56,* 218–226.

Gollwitzer, P. M., & Brandstätter, V. (1997). Implementation intentions and effective goal pursuit. *Journal of Personality and Social Psychology, 73,* 186–199.

Grolnick, W. S., Farkas, M. S., Sohmer, R., Michaels, S., & Valsiner, J. (2007). Facilitating motivation in young adolescents: Effects of an after-school program. *Journal of Applied Developmental Psychology, 28,* 332–334.

Grolnick, W. S., & Ryan, R. M. (1987). Autonomy in children's learning: An experimental and individual difference investigation. *Journal of Personality and Social Psychology, 52,* 890–898.

Halpern, R. (2005). Instrumental relationships: A potential relational model for inner-city youth programs. *Journal of Community Psychology, 33,* 11–20.

Halpern, R. (2009). *The means to grow up: Reinventing apprenticeship as a developmental support in adolescence.* Chicago: Routledge.

Hansen, D. M., & Larson, R. W. (2007). Amplifiers of developmental and negative experiences in organized activities: Dosage, motivation, lead roles, and adult-youth ratios. *Journal of Applied Developmental Psychology, 28,* 360–374.

Harackiewicz, J. M., Barron, K. E., Tauer, J. M., Carter, S. M., & Elliot, A. J. (2000). Short-term and long-term consequences of achievement: Predicting continued interest and performance over time. *Journal of Educational Psychology, 92,* 316–330.

Harackiewicz, J. M., Durik, A. M., Barron, K. E., Linnenbrink-Garcia, L., & Tauer, J. M. (2008). The role of achievement goals in the development of interest: Reciprocal relations between achievement goals, interest, and performance. *Journal of Educational Psychology, 100,* 105–122.

Hattie, J., & Timperley, H. (2007). The power of feedback. *Review of Educational Research, 77,* 81–112.

Heath, S. B. (1999). Dimensions of language development: Lessons from older children. In A. S. Masten (Ed.), *Cultural processes in child development: The Minnesota symposium on child psychology* (Vol. 29, pp. 59–75). Mahwah, NY: Erlbaum.

Hennessey, B. A. (2000). Rewards and creativity. In C. Sansone & J. Harackiewicz (Eds.), *Intrinsic and extrinsic motivation: The search for optimal motivation and performance* (pp. 55–78). New York: Academic Press.

Hidi, S. (2000). An interest researcher's perspective: The effects of extrinsic and intrinsic factors on motivation. In C. Sansone & J. Harackiewicz (Eds.), *Intrinsic and extrinsic motivation: The search for optimal motivation and performance.* (pp. 311–342). NY: Academic.

Hidi, S. (2001). Interest, reading and learning: Theoretical and practical considerations. *Educational Psychology Review, 13,* 191–210.

Hidi, S. (2006). Interest: A motivational variable with a difference. *Educational Research Review, 1,* 69–82.

Hidi, S., & Harackiewicz, J. (2000). Motivating the academically unmotivated: A critical issue for the 21st century. *Review of Educational Research, 70,* 151–179.

Hidi, S., & Renninger, A. (2006). The four-phase model of interest development. *Educational Psychologist, 41,* 111–127.

Hoffmann, L. (2002). Promoting girls' learning and achievement in physics classes for beginners. *Learning and Instruction, 12,* 447–465.

Isen, A. M. (2000). Positive affect and decision making. In M. Lewis & J. Haviland-Jones (Eds.), *Handbook of emotions.* (2nd ed., pp. 417–435). New York: Guilford.

Izard, C. E., & Ackerman, B. P. (2000). Motivational, organizational, and regulatory functions of discrete emotions. In M. Lewis & J. M. Haviland-Jones (Eds.), *Handbook of emotions.* (2nd ed., pp. 253–264). New York: Guilford.

Kandel, E. (2007). *In search of memory: The emergence of a new science of mind.* New York: Norton.

Kaplan, A., & Maehr, M. (2007). The contributions and prospects of goal orientation theory. *Educational Psychology Review, 19,* 141–184.

Kirshner, B. (2008). Guided participation in three youth activism organizations: Facilitation, apprenticeship, and joint work. *The Journal of the Learning Sciences, 17,* 60–101.

Kirshner, B., Pozzoboni, K., & Jones, H. (in press). Learning how to manage bias: A case study of youth participatory action research. *Applied Developmental Science.*

Kitsantas, A., Zimmerman, B., & Cleary, T. (2000). The role of observation and emulation in the development of athletic self-regulation. *Journal of Educational Psychology, 91,* 241–250.

Klaczynski, P. A. (2004). A dual-process model of adolescent development: Implications for decision making, reasoning, and identity. In R. V. Kail (Ed.), *Advances in child development and behavior* (Vol. 31, pp. 73–123). San Diego, CA: Academic Press.

Koestner, R., Ryan, R. M., Bernieri, F., & Holt, K. (1984). Setting limits on children's behavior: The differential effects of controlling versus informational styles on intrinsic motivation and creativity. *Journal of Personality, 52,* 233–248.

Köller, O., Baumert, J., & Schnabel, K. (2001). Does interest matter? The relationship between academic interest and achievement in mathematics. *Journal for Research in Mathematics Education, 32,* 448–470.

Krapp, A. (1999). Interest, motivation, and learning: An educational-psychological perspective. *Learning and Instruction, 14,* 23–40.

Kuhn, D. (2009). Adolescent thinking. In R. M. Lerner & L. Steinberg (Eds.), *Handbook of adolescent psychology* (3rd ed., Vol. 1, pp. 152–186). Hoboken, NJ: Wiley.

Larson, R. W. (2000). Toward a psychology of positive youth development. *The American Psychologist, 55,* 170–183.

Larson, R. W. (2011). Positive development in a disorderly world. *Journal of Research on Adolescence, 21,* 317–334.

Larson, R. W., & Angus, R. M. (2011a). Adolescents' development of skills for agency in youth programs: Learning to think strategically. *Child Development, 82*, 277–294.

Larson, R. W., & Angus, R. (2011b). Pursuing paradox: The role of adults in creating empowering settings for youth. In M. Aber, K. Maton & E. Seidman (Eds.), *Empowering settings and voices for social change* (pp. 65–93). New York: Oxford.

Larson, R. W., & Brown, J. R. (2007). Emotional development in adolescence: What can be learned from a high school theater program. *Child Development, 78*, 1083–1099.

Larson, R. W. & Dawes, N. P. (in press). Cultivating intrinsic motivation in American youth programs: Challenges and paradoxes navigated by youth professionals. In M. Csikszentmihalyi (Ed.), *Education and youth development in cross-cultural perspective: Contributions from positive psychology.* New York: Springer.

Larson, R. W., Jensen, L., Kang, H., Griffith, A., & Rompala, V. (in process). Peer groups as a crucible of positive value development in a global world. In G. Trommsdorff & X. Chen (Eds.), *Values, religion, and culture in adolescent development.* Cambridge: Cambridge Press.

Larson, R. W., & Richards, M. (1991). Boredom in the middle school years: Blaming schools versus blaming students. *American Journal of Education, 91*, 418–443.

Larson, R. W., Rickman, A. N., Gibbons, C. M., & Walker, K. C. (2009). Practitioner expertise: Creating quality within the daily tumble of events in youth settings. *New Directions for Youth Development, 121*, 71–88.

Larson, R. W., & Walker, K. (2006). Learning about the "real world" in an urban arts program. *Journal of Adolescent Research, 21*, 244–268.

Larson, R. W., & Walker, K. C. (2010). Dilemmas of practice: Challenges to program quality encountered by youth program leaders. *American Journal of Community Psychology, 45*, 338–349.

Latham, G. P., & Seijts, G. H. (1999). The effects of proximal and distal goals on performance on a moderately complex task. *Journal of Organizational Behavior, 20*, 421–429.

Lavigne, G. L., & Vallerand, R. J. (2010). The dynamic processes of influence between contextual and situational motivation: A test of the hierarchical model in a science education setting. *Journal of Applied School Psychology, 40*, 2343–2359.

Lavigne, G. L., Vallerand, R. J., & Miquelon, P. (2007). A motivational model of persistence in science education: A self-determination theory approach. *European Journal of Psychology of Education, 22*, 351–369.

Lenhart, A., Arafeh, S., Smith, A., & Macgill, A. (2008). Writing, technology, and teens. *PEW Internet and the American Life Project*—Retrieved from http://www.pewinternet.org/Reports/2008/Writing-Technology-and-Teens.aspx.

Lepper, M. R., Corpus, J. H., & Iyengar, S. S. (2005). Intrinsic and extrinsic motivational orientations in the classroom: Age differences and academic correlates. *Journal of Educational Psychology, 97*, 184–196.

Lepper, M., & Henderlong, J. (2000). Turning "play" into "work" and "work" into "play": 25 years of research into intrinsic vs. extrinsic motivation. In C. Sansone & J. M. Harackiewicz (Eds.), *Intrinsic and extrinsic motivation: The search for optimal motivation and performance* (pp. 257–307). New York: Academic.

Lepper, M. R., Sethi, S., Dialdin, D., & Drake, M. (1997). Intrinsic and extrinsic motivation: A developmental perspective. In S. S. Luthar, J. A. Burack, D. Cicchetti & J. R. Weisz (Eds.), *Developmental psychopathology: Perspectives on adjustment, risk, and disorder* (pp. 23–50). New York: Cambridge University Press.

Lerner, R. (2002). *Concepts and theories of human development* Mahwah, NJ: Erlbaum.

Lerner, J. V., Phelps, E., Forman, Y., & Bowers, E. (2009). Positive youth development. In R. M. Lerner & L. Steinberg (Eds.), *Handbook of adolescent psychology* (3rd ed., Vol. 1, pp. 524–558). Hoboken, NJ: Wiley.

Magnifico, A. M. (2010). Writing for whom? Cognition, motivation, and a writer. *Educational Psychologist, 45,* 167–184.

Mahoney, J. L., Parente, M. E., & Lord, H. (2007). Program-level differences in afterschool program engagement: Links to child competence, program quality and content. *The Elementary School Journal, 107,* 385–404.

Malone, T. W. (1980). What makes things fun to learn? Heuristics for designing instructional computer games. In *Proceedings of the 3rd ACM SIGSMALL Symposium and the First SIGPC Symposium on Small Systems* (pp. 162–169). Palo Alto, CA: ACM Press.

Mariano, J. M., & Going, J. (2011). Youth purpose and positive youth development. *Advances in Child Development and Behavior, 41,* 37–66.

Markus, H. R., & Kitayama, S. (2003). Models of agency: Sociocultural diversity in the construction of action. In *Nebraska Symposium on Motivation,* Lincoln, NB: Nebraska University Press.

Massimini, F., Csikszentmihalyi, M., & Delle Fave, A. (1988). Flow and biocultural evolution. In M. Csikszentmihalyi & I. S. Csikszentmihalyi (Eds.), *Optimal experience: Psychological studies of flow in consciousness.* (pp. 60–81). Cambridge: Cambridge Press.

Mayr, E. (2001). *What evolution is.* New York: Basic Books.

Moneta, G. B., & Csikszentmihalyi, M. (1996). The effect of perceived challenges and skills on the quality of subjective experience. *Journal of Personality, 64,* 275–331.

Mueller, C. M., & Dweck, C. S. (1998). Intelligence praise can undermine motivation and performance. *Journal of Personality and Social Psychology, 75,* 33–52.

Nakamura, J., & Csikszentmihalyi, M. (2009). Flow theory and research. In C. R. Snyder & S. J. Lopez (Eds.), *Handbook of positive psychology.* (2nd ed., pp. 195–206). New York: Oxford.

Nasir, N. S., & Hand, V. (2008). From the court to the classroom: Opportunities for engagement, learning and identity in basketball and classroom mathematics. *The Journal of the Learning Sciences, 17,* 143–180.

Newell, A., & Simon, H. (1972). *Human problem solving.* Englewood Cliffs, NJ: Prentice Hall.

Oyserman, D., Bybee, D., & Terry, K. (2006). Possible selves and academic outcomes: How and when possible selves impel action. *Journal of Personality and Social Psychology, 91,* 188–204.

Ozer, E. J., Cantor, J. P., Cruz, G. W., Fox, B., Hubbard, E., & Moret, L. (2008). The diffusion of youth-led participatory research in urban schools: The role of the prevention support system in implementation and sustainability. *American Journal of Community Psychology, 41,* 278–289.

Panksepp, J. (1998). *Affective neuroscience: The foundations of human and animal emotion.* New York: Oxford University Press.

Pearce, N., & Larson, R. (2006). The process of motivational change in a civic activism organization. *Applied Developmental Science, 10,* 121–131.

Pearce, N. J., & Larson, R. (2007). How youth become engaged in youth programs: The process of motivational change. *Applied Developmental Science, 10,* 121–131.

Pelletier, L. G., Séguin-Lévesque, C., & Legault, L. (2002). Pressure from above and pressure from below as determinants of teachers' motivation and teaching behaviors. *Journal of Educational Psychology, 94,* 186–196.

Piaget, J. (1971). *Biology and knowledge.* Chicago: University of Chicago Press.

Pintrich, P. R., & DeGroot, E. V. (1990). Motivational and self-regulated learning components of classroom academic performance. *Journal of Educational Psychology, 82*, 33–40.

Polman, J. L., & Miller, D. (2010). Changing stories: Trajectories of identification among African American youth in a science outreach apprenticeship. *American Educational Research Journal, 47*, 879–918.

Priest, S., & Gass, M. A. (1997). *Effective leadership in adventure programming.* Champaign, IL: Human Kinetics.

Pugh, K. J., & Bergin, D. A. (2006). Motivational influences on transfer. *Educational Researcher, 41*, 147–160.

Purcell-Gates, V., Duke, N. K., & Martineau, J. A. (2007). Learning to read and write genre-specific text: Roles of authentic experience and explicit teaching. *Reading Research Quarterly, 42*, 8–45.

Renninger, K. A. (2010). Working with and cultivating the development of interest, self-efficacy, and self-regulation. In D. D. Preiss & R. J. Sternberg (Eds.), *Innovations in educational psychology: Perspectives on learning, teaching, and human development* (pp. 107–138). New York: Springer.

Rhodes, J. E. (2004). The critical ingredient: Caring youth–staff relationships in after-school settings. *New directions in youth development: After-school worlds, 101*, 145–161.

Rickman, A. N. (2009). *A challenge to the notion of youth passivity: Adolescents' development of career direction through youth programs.* Unpublished Masters Equivalency, University of Illinois.

Rusk, N., Resnick, M., & Cooke, S. (2009). Origins and guiding principles of the Computer Clubhouse. In Y. Kafai, K. Peppler & R. Chapman (Eds.), *The Computer Clubhouse: Constructionism and creativity in youth communities* (pp. 17–25). New York: Teachers College Press.

Rutter, M., Moffitt, T., & Caspi, A. (2006). Gene-environment interplay and psychopathology: Multiple variables but real effects. *Journal of Child Psychology and Psychiatry, 47*, 226–261.

Ryan, R. M., & Deci, E. L. (2000). Self-determination theory and the facilitation of intrinsic motivation, social development, and well-being. *The American Psychologist, 55*, 68–78.

Ryan, R. M., & Deci, E. L. (2003). On assimilating identities to the self: A self-determination theory perspective on internalization and integrity within cultures. In M. R. Leary & J. P. Tangney (Eds.), *Handbook of self and identity* (pp. 255–273). New York: Guilford.

Ryan, R. M., & Deci, E. L. (2008). Self-determination theory and the role of basic psychological needs in personality and the organization of behavior. In O. P. John, R. W. Robbins & L. A. Pervin (Eds.), *Handbook of personality: Theory and research* (pp. 654–678). New York: Guilford.

Ryan, R. M., & Deci, E. L. (2009). Promoting self-determined school engagement: Motivation, learning, and well-being. In K. R. Wentzel & A. Wigfield (Eds.), *Handbook of motivation in school* (pp. 171–196). New York: Taylor Francis.

Sansone, C., & Harackiewicz, J. (Eds.), (2000). *Intrinsic and extrinsic motivation: The search for optimal motivation and performance.* New York: Academic Press.

Sansone, C., & Smith, J. L. (2000). Interest and self-regulation: The relation between having to and wanting to. In C. Sansone & J. M. Harackiewicz (Eds.), *Intrinsic and extrinsic motivation: The search for optimal motivation and performance* (pp. 341–372). New York: Academic.

Schiefele, U. (1991). Interest, learning, and motivation. *Educational Psychologist, 26*, 299–323.

Schiefele, U. (1996). Topic interest, text representation, and quality of experience. *Contemporary Educational Psychology, 21*, 3–18.

Schiefele, U. (1999). Interest and learning from text. *Scientific Studies of Reading, 3*, 257–280.

Schiefele, U., Krapp, A., & Winteler, A. (1992). Interest as a predictor of academic achievement: A meta-analysis of research. In K. A. Renninger, S. Hidi & A. Krapp (Eds.), *The role of interest in learning and development* (pp. 183–212). Hillsdale, NJ: Erlbaum.

Schneider, B., & Stevenson, H. (1999). *The ambitious generation: America's teenagers, motivated but directionless.* New Haven, CT: Yale University Press.

Schwandt, T. A. (2003). Back to the rough ground: Beyond theory to practice in evaluation. *Evaluation, 9*, 353–364.

Seamans, J. K., & Robbins, T. W. (2010). Dopamine modulation of the prefrontal cortex and cognitive function. In K. A. Neve (Ed.), *The dopamine receptors.* (2nd ed., pp. 373–398). New York: Humana Press.

Shernoff, D. (2010). Engagement in after-school programs as a predictor of social competence and academic performance. *American Journal of Community Psychology, 45*, 325–337.

Shernoff, D. J., Csikszentmihalyi, M., Schneider, B., & Shernoff, E. S. (2003). Student engagement in high school classrooms from the perspective of flow theory. *School Psychology Quarterly, 18*, 158–176.

Shirey, L. L., & Reynolds, R. E. (1988). Effect of interest on attention and learning. *Journal of Educational Psychology, 80*, 159–166.

Simpkins, S. D., Davis-Kean, P. E., & Eccles, J. S. (2006). Math and science motivation: A longitudinal examination of the links between choices and beliefs. *Developmental Psychology, 42*, 70–83.

Smetana, J. G., Crean, H. F., & Campione-Barr, N. (2005). Adolescents' and parents changing conceptions of parental authority. *New Directions for Child and Adolescent Development, 108*, 31–46.

Soenens, B., Vansteenkiste, M., Lens, W., Luyckx, K., Goossens, L., Beyers, W., et al. (2007). Conceptualizing adolescent perceptions of parental autonomy support: Adolescent perceptions of promoting independence versus promoting volitional functioning. *Developmental Psychology, 43*, 633–646.

Steinberg, L., Dahl, R., Keating, D., Kupfer, D. J., Masten, A. S., & Pine, D. S. (2006). The study of developmental psychopathology in adolescence: Integrating affective neuroscience with the study of context. In D. Cicchetti & D. Cohen (Eds.), *Developmental psychopathology* (2nd ed., Vol. 2, pp. 710–741). New York: Wiley.

Sternberg, R. J. (1998). A balance theory of wisdom. *Review of General Psychology, 2*, 347–365.

Sternberg, R. J., Forsythe, G. B., Hedlund, J., Horvath, J. A., Wagner, R. K., Williams, W. M., et al. (2000). *Practical intelligence in everyday life.* Cambridge: Cambridge, UK.

Urdan, T. (2003). Intrinsic motivation, extrinsic rewards, and divergent views of reality. *Educational Psychology Review, 15*, 311–325.

Vansteenkiste, M., Simons, J., Lens, W., Sheldon, K. M., & Deci, E. L. (2004). Motivating learning, performance, and persistence: The synergistic role of intrinsic goals and autonomy-support. *Journal of Personality and Social Psychology, 87*, 246–260.

Walker, J., Marczak, M., Blyth, D., & Bordon, L. (2005). Designing youth development programs: Toward a theory of developmental internationality. In J. Mahoney, R. Larson & J. Eccles (Eds.), *Organized activities as contexts of development: Extracurricular activities, after-school and community programs.* (pp. 399–418). Mahwah, NJ: Lawrence Erlbaum.

Watkins, N., Larson, R., & Sullivan, P. (2007). Learning to bridge difference: Community youth programs as contexts for developing multicultural competencies. *The American Behavioral Scientist, 51*, 380–402.

Wentzel, K. R. (2009). Students' relationships with teacher as a motivational context. In K. R. Wentzel & A. Wigfield (Eds.), *Handbook of motivation at school.* (pp. 301–322). New York: Guilford.

White, R. W. (1959). Motivation reconsidered: The concept of competence. *Psychological Review, 66,* 297–333.

Wigfield, A., Eccles, J., Schiefele, U., Roeser, R., & Davis-Kean, P. (2006). Development of achievement motivation. In W. Damon, & R. M. Lerner (Series Eds.) & N. Eisenberg (Vol. Ed.), *Handbook of child psychology: Social, emotional, and personality development* (Vol. 3, pp. 933–1002). New York: Wiley.

Wolters, C. A. (2003). Regulation of motivation: Evaluating an underemphasized aspect of self-regulated learning. *Educational Psychologist, 38,* 189–205.

Wood, D., Larson, R. W., & Brown, J. (2009). How adolescents come to see themselves as more responsible through participation in youth programs. *Child Development, 80,* 295–309.

Wortham, S. (2006). *Learning identity: The joint emergence of social identification and academic learning.* New York: Cambridge University Press.

Youniss, J. (2009). When morality meets politics in development. *Journal of Moral Education, 38,* 129–144.

Zeldin, S., & Camino, L. (1999). Youth leadership: Linking research and program theory to exemplary practice. *New Designs for Youth Development, 15,* 10–15.

Zimmerman, B. J. (2002). Becoming a self-regulated learner: An overview. *Theory into Practice, 41,* 64–70.

SCHOOL ENGAGEMENT: WHAT IT IS AND WHY IT IS IMPORTANT FOR POSITIVE YOUTH DEVELOPMENT

Yibing Li

EDUCATION, HUMAN DEVELOPMENT, AND THE WORKFORCE, AMERICAN INSTITUTES
FOR RESEARCH, WASHINGTON, DISTRICT OF COLUMBIA, USA

Advances in Child Development and Behavior
Richard M. Lerner, Jacqueline V. Lerner and Janette B. Benson : Editors

Abstract

The observation that too many students are disengaged from school has inspired interest in the concept of school engagement. However, the growing excitement about school engagement is tempered by numerous conceptual and measurement issues. In this chapter, I briefly reviewed the history of the study of school engagement, summarized some prominent theoretical perspectives in the school engagement literature, discussed why it is important to understand the mechanism through which school engagement promotes positive youth development, and made recommendations on future research directions for this topic. Specifically, I called for a better understanding of and the nuances within the school engagement construct, advocated for the development of school engagement measures with sound psychometric property, and encouraged methodological innovations that can be used to understand the development of school engagement and its implications to positive youth development.

In this chapter, I first describe why, from a developmental perspective, particularly one that pertains to adolescence, focusing on school engagement is important for understanding the person–context relations that are fundamental to human development (Lerner, 2002). Specifically, I highlight the importance of understanding school engagement from a positive youth development perspective. This discussion involves a brief summary of the history of the study of school engagement. This summary illustrates that there are several theoretical perspectives framing school engagement, one that have resulted in varying conceptualizations and definitions used in the literature. Next, I review some prominent theoretical perspectives used to frame school engagement, and I discuss the nature of, and problems associated with, different conceptualizations used in the literature. Based on the overview, I elaborate the reasons why it is important to fuse behavior, emotion, and cognition in conceptualizing school engagement and call for attention to the operationalization and measurement of the construct. Last, I propose promising directions for future study. In particular, I call for greater attention to the developmental process of school engagement in order to understand the mechanism through which school engagement is conducive to positive adolescent development. It is useful to begin this presentation with a brief specification of the nature of adolescence, one that will help naturalize the links between PYD and school engagement.

Adolescence is a biopsychosocial process in which biological growth, psychological development, and transitions in social contexts simultaneously occur. Adolescence is also a time when young people make many choices and engage in various behaviors likely to influence the rest of their lives. For example, adolescents pick which high-school courses to take, which after-school activities to participate in, and which peer groups to join. They begin to make future educational and occupational plans and to implement these plans through school course work and out-of-school time activity choices. In the same time, some experiment with quite problematic behaviors such as drug and alcohol consumption and unprotected sexual intercourse. Most youth do not suffer long-term consequences for this experimentation, although some do.

Until recently, parents, educators, researchers, and policy makers were pessimistic about the journey children make their way toward adult life. Parents are relieved when their teenagers do not show problematic or undesirable behaviors by the end of high school. Researchers were focused on documenting the prevalence of smoking, drinking, drug use, unsafe sex, teenage pregnancy, and violence among young people, highlighting how much danger young people may face, and advocating how much harder we should try to prevent these negative behaviors from happening. As pointed out by Benson (2003), "research and practice are steered to naming, counting, and reducing the incidence of environmental risks ... and health-compromising behaviors ..." (p. 24). A deficit model sees young people at best "good clients" and at worst "problems to be managed." Not enough attention has been given to the growing young men and women's own contribution to the creation of their developmental history (Brandtstädter, 2006).

I. PYD: A New Perspective on Young People and the Contexts of Their Life

Since the late years of the twentieth century, contemporary theorists began to recognize that young people play an active part in shaping their development. A prominent example is relational, developmental systems theories of human development (Overton, 2004), which emphasize the mutually beneficial relations between the developing young person and his or her context that promote normal, healthy, and successful development (Baltes et al., 2006; Jelicic, Bobek, Phelps, Lerner, & Lerner, 2007; Lerner, 2002). In relational, developmental systems models, the process of human development is relatively plastic (i.e., capable of systematic change), legitimizing an optimistic view of the potential of to-be-developed young people. Further, the active role of young people as agents of development is explicitly highlighted in the action perspective. Brandtstädter (2006) points out that the plans young people make, the projects they engage, and the actions they take by spending time and investing effort form their own development. Along with the advancement in developmental theories, a new vocabulary for depicting youth as "resources to be developed" has begun to emerge (King et al., 2005). Increasingly, indicators have become available to describe the healthy, desirable, and goal-driven behaviors of adolescents (Lerner, 2004).

Giving credit to young people in forming their own development does not downplay the importance of various developmental opportunities provided in youth's social and institutional environment. Quite the opposite, these theories highlight the essentiality of ecology in the promotion of positive developmental outcomes. School and family top the two most frequently mentioned contexts regardless of one's theoretical stance. Given that children spend more of their time in school than in any other non-home settings throughout their growing years, schools are considered not only a legislated place for development but also an institutionalized gateway to opportunities in adulthood (Gilligan, 1998). The other reason why school gains so much attention is that schools have or are supposed to have development-promoting features such as physical and emotional safety, appropriate supervision, clear structure, engaging activities, and skill-building opportunities, which all have been identified by scholars such as Eccles and Gootman (2002), Gambone and Connell (2004), and Theokas and Lerner (2006). Thus, the extent to which children are actively involved in and psychologically committed to their schooling and how much they are able to capitalize on what the school provides can more or less direct whether they will experience positive or negative development.

A. STUDENT DISENGAGEMENT: AN OLD PROBLEM

Unfortunately, scholars have noted that children's enthusiasm for learning deteriorate as they march through the school system, with striking losses during the transitions from elementary to middle school and from middle to high school (Skinner, Kindermann, Connell, & Wellborn, 2009; for a review, see Wigfield, Eccles, Schiefele, Roeser, & Davis-Kean, 2006). As a result, by high school, as many as half the student body in the United States becomes chronically and actively disengaged from school, not including those who have already left (Sedlak, Wheeler, Pullin, & Cusick, 1986; Steinberg, Brown, & Dornbush, 1996). Boys, young people of color, and children from disadvantaged backgrounds have a greater likelihood of being bored and alienated from school (Finn, 1993; McDermott, Mordell, & Stolzfus, 2001; Meece & Kurtz-Costes, 2001; Ogbu, 2003).

Given the prevalence of disengagement, even among college-bound students and students who stay out of trouble (Fredricks & Eccles, 2002), in what ways not being engaged matter for youth development is an important question. Empirical studies have found that disengagement from school has significant implications for concurrent psychological and behavioral well-being and for long-term development (Johnson, Crosnoe, & Elder, 2001). The liabilities of disengagement, at least for some students, may include adjustment problems such as delinquency and substance use (Li & Lerner, 2011). Conversely, the benefits of not being disengaged identified in the literature range from receiving better grades and having a greater likelihood of graduating from high school (Finn & Rock, 1997).

B. SCHOOL ENGAGEMENT AND PYD: AN UNCLEAR LINK

To circumvent student disengagement, researchers are increasingly interested in studying the development of school engagement because they think this construct is important to staying in high school and, as well, to many facets of adolescent development. However, the current literature is limited given that what we have learned most is how school engagement is associated with absence of problematic development (e.g., Li, Bebiroglu, Phelps, Lerner, & Lerner, 2008; Li & Lerner, 2011). As for relations between school engagement and positive aspects of youth development, ample evidence has been accumulated on the link between various forms of school engagement and academic performance (for a review, see Fredricks et al., 2004). For instance, Johnson, McGue, and Iacono (2006) found that behavioral engagement was directly associated with changes in academic achievement during adolescence, above and beyond background characteristics. Students' problematic behavioral engagement early on was associated with lower achievement and their eventual decision to drop out from high school (Alexander, Entwisle, & Horsey, 1997).

While the study of school engagement heavily and persistently focuses on the academic "consequences" of school engagement, the amount of attention allocated to an understanding of the role of school engagement in promoting healthy social and emotional development is far from enough. Nevertheless, there have been investigations of the associations between school engagement and problematic adjustment such as delinquency, substance use, and depression, although the volume is much smaller than the number of studies on the engagement–achievement link. Lack of engagement may be

considered a form of problematic behavior. It also could be considered a reason for problematic development. Taking externalizing behavior problems as
an example, these problems are frequently observed in schools among disengaged, low-achieving students, and their presence is predictive of long-term
maladjustment (Moffitt, Caspi, Dickson, Silva, & Stanton, 1996). Disengaged
students were found to be more likely to engage in substance use and delinquency and initiate such behaviors earlier than the more engaged students
(Li et al., in press; Li, & Lerner, 2011).

Observing the covariation between lack of or low school engagement
and problematic development, one may wonder how adequate (or high)
school engagement is related to positive development. As mentioned earlier, given the overwhelming concern about problematic behaviors, empirical studies that specifically focus on school engagement and the presence
of positive engagement are scarce. Even in studies focusing on school
engagement and positive aspects of adolescent development, relations
have been only speculated between school engagement and limited
outcomes, mostly academic. Future studies should address this gap so that
the construct of school engagement earns its credit not only in prevention
but also in promotion. Studies that can address developmental questions
such as how improvement in school engagement contributes to PYD
outcomes would extend the literature significantly.

II. School Engagement: History and Recent Developments

The observation that too many students are bored and uninvolved or, in
other words, disengaged from school has inspired interest in the concept
of school engagement (Appleton, Christenson, & Furlong, 2008; Skinner,
Kindermann, Connell, et al., 2009; Skinner, Kindermann, & Furrer, 2009).
Not surprisingly, "student disengagement" is one of the most frequently
used terms in any discussion of academic problems such as underachieve-
ment (Newmann, 1992), academic failure (Finn, 1989; Finn & Rock,
1997), and high dropout rates in urban schools (Rumberger, 1987, 2004).
In this sense, the study of school engagement emerged from the study of
its obverse.

A. A BRIEF HISTORY OF THE USE OF THE SCHOOL
ENGAGEMENT CONCEPT

Frequent use of the term "engagement" in educational research literature began in the mid-1980s, especially after two national centers on effective schools were established at Johns Hopkins University and the

University of Wisconsin-Madison, funded by the federal government. The term "(dis)engagement" arguably was first used by Natriello (1984). A year later, Mosher and McGowan (1985) used the term "student engagement" in a review of conceptions of, and assessments and instruments for indexing, secondary school students' engagement. "Pioneer" users of this term also included Meece, Blumenfeld, and Hoyle (1988), Finn (1989), Skinner, Wellborn, and Connell (1990), and Newmann, Wehlage, and Lamborn (1992). All of these authors switched between "engagement" and "disengagement." Consistent usage of the term "engagement" did not begin until the early 1990s.

Several seeds of confusion were planted early on. First, disengagement was often treated as the antithesis of engagement. However, the absence of obvious disengagement is not the same active engagement. As articulated by Newmann et al. (1992), a student who does not disrupt or skip classes, and who is compliant enough to attend class and complete assignments, may just be trying to get by with a minimal amount of effort. The focus on disengagement has resulted in over reliance on readily observable behavioral indicators in the early work on school engagement.

Second, definitions of engagement available during the first 10 years after the initial use of the term varied considerably. Although almost all the definitions included a behavioral component, authors did not agree about what else should be implied by the term engagement (Appleton et al., 2008; Fredricks et al., 2004). Some authors (Mergendeller & Mitman, 1985; Natriello, 1984) defined engagement as a unidimensional construct; others took a more expansive approach, including behavior and at least one other component (Finn, 1993; Marks, 2000; Newmann et al., 1992). For instance, Newmann et al.'s (1992) definition includes cognition (psychological investment, in their words) and behavior (effort). Finn's (1989) identification–participation model describes one of the first tripartite definitions of engagement in the literature. Thus, disagreement upon the exact number of dimensions has existed among investigators who consider school engagement multidimensional.

The term "school engagement" was first used by Pierson and Connell (1992). Finn also used this term in his 1993 book titled "School engagement and students at risk." Neither of these publications explicitly justified the reason for switching terminology to "school engagement" from "student disengagement." Nevertheless, the concept of school engagement has attracted burgeoning interest due, in part, to its potential usefulness in representing reciprocal relations between students and the school context (Fredricks et al., 2004). In addition, the term encompasses students' engagement in school beyond academics and outside of the regular classroom.

B. USE OF THE SCHOOL ENGAGEMENT CONCEPT: RECENT DEVELOPMENTS

Uses of the term "school engagement" have increased exponentially in recent years. Other than individual articles and dissertations, two special journal issues and one special journal section on school engagement have been published. These collections included several seminal reviews of the conceptual as well as the measurement issues involved in the study of school engagement. For instance, Appleton et al. (2008) partitioned the engagement literature into prominent motivation theories (see Kortering & Braziel, 2008). The review published by Fredricks et al. (2004) represents another important contribution to the development of the school engagement literature, by advocating for a multidimensional conceptualization. Since then, a multidimensional understanding of engagement emerged. However, various definitions and operationalizations continue to be used across the literature. Such lack of clarity has led to inconsistent use of terminology, cloudy evidence of relations, and poor measurement. This lack of clarity also is reflected by the different theories used to frame the study of school engagement.

III. Theoretical Perspectives on School Engagement

Several theoretical frameworks, from education, developmental and educational psychology, as well as criminology and sociology, offer theoretical perspectives for research on school engagement. These frameworks have guided the literature in the understanding of the predictors of engagement and the role of school engagement in predicting a variety of youth development outcomes. These frameworks include motivational models, the participation-identification model, the social control theory, and the attachment theory.

A. MOTIVATIONAL MODELS

Motivational models are one of the most important and arguably, a dominant framework in the school engagement literature. Many related terms, such as identification and school belonging, have a motivational origin. Motivational models posit that there are fundamental human needs and that optimal development happens in contexts where these needs are met (Eccles, Early, Fraser, Belansky, & McCarthy, 1997). For instance, the person and stage-environment fit theories of motivation (e.g., Eccles & Midgley, 1989; Eccles et al., 1993) focus on the "goodness-of-fit" between school characteristics and children's fundamental needs, including competence, autonomy, and relatedness (Connell, 1990; Deci & Ryan, 1985; Skinner, 1995). It is postulated that children enjoy better development in schools that provide structure for them to acquire competencies, that provide the opportunity for autonomous behavior, and that offer an emotional climate in which a strong sense of relatedness can be fostered (Connell & Wellborn, 1991; Eccles et al., 1993, 1997).

The motivational models of engagement are a modified version of more general motivation models. They are construed at the interface of the psychological and educational literatures. For instance, in the Eccles (2004) version of these motivational models, the construct of school engagement has been inserted into the original equation "academic outcomes $= \int($individual characteristics, motivation, social contexts)." This model posits that the extent to which children's fundamental needs are fulfilled in the school context determines their quality of motivation, which, in turn, determines their levels of engagement in, or disaffection with, school. The idea is that being motivated in school is not enough; students who are excited about specific learning activities may nevertheless not learn anything unless they are actively engaged in these activities. In this sense, school engagement is treated as an outward manifestation of increased or sustained motivation (Skinner, Kindermann, Connell et al., 2009; Skinner, Kindermann, & Furrer, 2009).

However, conceptual ambiguity exists about the relations between motivation and engagement. While motivation is regarded as only a facilitator of school engagement by some (e.g., Furlong & Christenson, 2008; Furlong et al., 2003), it is treated as a surrogate of school engagement in others' work. For instance, some researchers use engagement and motivation interchangeably (National Research Council and Institute of Medicine, 2004). However, motivation and school engagement are two distinct constructs. They should not be used as synonyms. Most importantly, motivation is an internal cognitive and emotional state that could trigger action but does not include behavior, while behavior is a key feature of school engagement.

B. PARTICIPATION–IDENTIFICATION MODEL

The participation–identification model, proposed by Finn (1989), represents another important theoretical framework for understanding school engagement. By emphasizing students' active participation and a concomitant feeling of identification with school, this model is arguably the first model that separates the behavioral and emotional dimensions of school engagement (termed as involvement in schooling). In integrating the management literature on job involvement and the social control theory from the sociological literatures, Finn emphasizes the importance of students' sense of identification with school in preventing problematic outcomes, such as dropping out and delinquency. Another salient feature of the participation–identification model is that it further differentiates two themes within the identification dimension. As articulated by Finn (1989), identification includes an internalized conception of belongingness, or identification with the place, and students' commitment to learning. This model is perhaps the genesis of the tripartite models that emerged in some of the more recent reviews (e.g., Fredricks et al., 2004; Jimmerson et al., 2003). Indeed, inspired by Finn's model, some scholars proposed tripartite models, in which belongingness and valuing schooling were classified as two distinct dimensions: emotional and cognitive.

Finn (1989) believes that participation in school activities enables students' sense of belonging and of valuing of education to be realized. Hence, in this model, participation precedes identification: withdrawal (disengagement from school) starts as an absence of participation (or nonparticipation), resulting in unsuccessful school outcomes; such outcomes, in turn, lead to emotional withdrawal. A key asset of the participation–identification model is its nuanced understanding of the behavioral component of school engagement. Using a four-part taxonomy, Finn distinguished four hierarchical levels of participation, with different intensity and quality. According to Finn (1989), participation could range from being prepared and responsive to teachers' directions or questions, initiating questions and displaying enthusiasm by spending extra time or doing more work than required, participating in the social and athletic aspects of school life, and participation in governance of the school. Thus, participation in the social, extracurricular, and athletic aspects of school life are considered part of behavioral engagement. Finn's conception of behavioral engagement also may have contributed to diverse ways of defining and measuring this component, and sometimes may have caused confusion, because of the long "laundry list" of behaviors the model encompasses.

C. SOCIAL CONTROL THEORY

Social control theory suggests that the establishment of a social bond is a psychological condition that buffers against risk factors in life (Hirschi, 1969). According to Hirschi (1969), attachment to a positive institution, commitment to conventional pathways of achievement, and beliefs in the legitimacy of societal order are key elements in establishing a social bond. An established social bond exerts effective control on deviant behavior (Catalano, Haggerty, Oesterle, Fleming, & Hawkins, 2004). However, weak social bonds may result in increased risk for delinquency or crime. Social control theory researchers often choose to study school bonding and school connectedness, which overlap with the emotional aspects of school engagement.

Hawkins and Weis (1985) defined school bonding as attachment to pro-social peers, commitment to academic and social activities at school, and belief in the established norms for school behavior (Simons-Morton, Crump, Haynie, & Saylor, 1999). Similarly, Resnick et al. (1997) focused on how school connectedness can protect adolescents from harm. As a possible protective force for youth, school connectedness may buffer against delinquency and deviant behavior, may act as a preventive force for school dropout, and may provide protection from negative influences.

Social control theory has been modified and developed into a slightly different theory—a social development model (e.g., Catalano & Hawkins, 1996; Hawkins, 1997; Hawkins & Lishner, 1987). Integrating social control and social learning theories, the social development model hypothesizes that strong bonds of attachment and commitment can only be formed when "reinforcements" from the environment for desired behaviors are available; these reinforcements are needed so that youth have positive experiences with interacting with other members of the social group (Hawkins & Weis, 1985). That is, social bonding or attachment is developed when behaviors that are consistent with conventional standards are rewarded consistently through a positive reinforcement process. The development of a strong social bonding further increases positive behaviors and prevents problematic behavior (Hawkins, Guo, Hill, Battin-Pearson, & Abbott, 2001).

D. ATTACHMENT THEORY

The attachment literature, focusing on the importance of forming a strong emotional tie to school and its personnel, offers another framework for research related to school engagement (Bretherton, 2005). Other than school engagement, related terms, for example, school belonging or bonding, derive, at least partially, from theories of attachment. In this tradition, interpersonal connections are regarded as internal working models of attachment figures (Bretherton & Munholland, 2008; Crittenden, 1990). Children's secure attachment to their caregivers and the corresponding internal representations provide a safe base from which children can explore and engage actively in activities and interactions with others (Baumrind, 1991). In this sense, the interpersonal connections between children and parents are extended to the positive relationships students have with teachers, school administrators, coaches, and other adult figures in the school (Cernkovich & Giordano, 1992). The school, as an actual institution, also is considered an attachment figure, by providing comfort, safety, and support.

In sum, several frameworks provide theoretical foundations for the study of school engagement. These theoretical frameworks allow investigators to conduct research from different angles. For instance, attachment models share notable similarities with motivational models in that these two lines of thinking both recognize that the extent to which children's fundamental needs are met and are supported by social partners determines their generalized beliefs about the nature of the self, which, in turn, influence how children react to their contextual reality (Baumrind, 1991). In addition, social control theory and attachment models share the notion that strong social attachment prevents the initiation of problematic behavior. However, the juxtaposition of various perspectives has led to inconsistency in the terminologies used in different studies. A plethora of labels for the same or similar behaviors/phenomena may be due to imprecision or to a lack of integration of constructs across different theoretical frameworks (Finn, 1989). Nevertheless, across these different theories, most scholars have come to endorse a multidimensional conceptualization of school engagement. Perhaps, a focus of the multidimensional nature of school engagement may provide a means to circumvent theoretically predicated differences and definitional confusion and to arrive at a more integrated conceptualization of this construct.

IV. School Engagement: Toward an Integrated Conceptualization

The various ways in which school engagement is defined have prevented the study of school engagement from capitalizing integratively on the potential of this construct as a multidimensional entity (Appleton et al., 2008; Fredricks et al., 2004). In the following section, I will present the confusions and challenges in the school engagement literature and then elaborate how a tripartite theoretical model, as exemplar of multidimensional conceptions of engagement, can fuse behavior, emotion, and cognition in representing students' relationships with the school.

A. CONFUSIONS AND CHALLENGES

Two major challenges prevent a comprehensive understanding of school engagement and the extent to which the construct is important for understanding various youth outcomes (Glanville & Wildhagen, 2007). The first challenge of conceptualizing and defining school engagement is that conceptualizations, definitions, and methods of measurement vary broadly from one study to the next, and no one scholar seems to be fully successful in persuading others to agree with his or her approach. As a result, there is no one preferred definition in the current school engagement literature. Even among users of "engagement," names vary—from student engagement, school engagement, student engagement in/with school, classroom engagement, academic engagement, and engagement in school/academic work.

The above-listed terms can be further classified into groups. Student engagement and school engagement may be two different abbreviated terms of "student engagement in/with school," whereas classroom engagement, academic engagement, and engagement in school work/academic work are more academic focused and context specific (i.e., within the classroom). That is, school engagement and student engagement usually tap students' experiences in academic and nonacademic activities within and beyond classrooms, whereas academic engagement focuses on the academic aspects of school experiences, and classroom engagement is specific for the classroom context.

Since the term "engagement" was first introduced to the literature, there are cases when an author used one term, say, school engagement, in the title of a paper but switched to student engagement in the body of the same article. For instance, Pierson and Connell (1992) used "school engagement" in the title of their paper, but never mentioned it again throughout the article. In this case, student engagement and school engagement are treated as if they have identical meanings. In addition, inconsistency, such as selecting different terms or providing different definitions for the same term in different publications by the same author, is not a rare occurrence; as well, there are definitional disparities among authors. Different terms may be used to represent the same concept, while the same term may mean something completely different. These somewhat arbitrary practices may blur the subtle difference among terms and complicate their operationalization. Studies that are based on inaccurate operationalization could generate meaningless findings. In this writing, I use the term school engagement over other terms in order to emphasize that engagement does not reside in students; instead, it is a joint product of the student and the school context. Choosing this term, however, does not mean that research findings produced through using other terms are excluded in the review.

The second major challenge in the conceptualization of school engagement lies in the juxtaposition of several related terms beyond "engagement," which may or may not share the same meaning, may or may not have the same number of dimensions, and may or may not be based on the same theoretical framework. Yet, such terms also have been used, either as synonyms of engagement or as "close relatives" of engagement. Jimerson, Campos, and Greif (2003) identified a myriad of constructs including connectedness, connection, belonging, bonding, identification, satisfaction, and attachment. Libbey (2004) reported a breadth of constructs similar to the summary presented by Jimerson et al. (2003). Libbey (2004) correctly pointed out, "the pre-eminence of one construct versus the others cannot be determined by current research" (p. 53). Indeed, the use of various terms may be purely due to researchers' theoretical perspectives or personal preferences. At times, different terms may be assessed with the same items (Jimerson et al., 2003). Studies based on such arbitrary choices of terminology and selections of items have resulted in inconsistent and sometimes contradictory findings. These findings, in turn, have been cited by school engagement researchers as if the evidence is directed to school engagement. Sorting out the similarities and differences among these terms is crucial to advancing understanding of school engagement.

Despite these inconsistencies, data pertinent to the coexistence of various definitions of engagement elucidate several trends across groups of researchers (Appleton et al., 2008). First, positive behaviors, such as participation in school-based activities or completing homework, have been included consistently as indicators of engagement (Jimerson et al., 2003). Indeed, engagement is traditionally investigated as a behavioral construct, regardless of the exact term used. Second, with a few exceptions, most researchers define school engagement in a general, broad sense, rather than as a task-specific construct (Appleton et al., 2008). In other words, the school engagement literature does not focus on a particular subject knowledge in which students are or should be engaged. Treating school engagement as a general, non-content-specific construct allows us to focus on students' various behaviors, thoughts, and feelings without limiting the discussion to a specific knowledge area. Such a general focus does not mean that the study of school engagement fails to account for fluctuations in students' levels of engagement from one class to another or over time. In fact, the malleability of school engagement is generally recognized in the literature (e.g., Appleton et al., 2008; Fredricks et al., 2004).

Regardless of the exact conceptualizations of engagement, theorists seem to agree that engagement goes beyond behavior. Although no agreement on the exact number and names of engagement dimensions has been reached, most researchers endorse the multidimensionality of the construct; for instance, scholars point to emotional or, at times, cognitive engagement (e.g., Fredricks et al., 2004; Jimerson et al., 2003). Even writings produced by investigators who focus on behavioral indicators of school engagement at times include the idea that positive emotions and cognitive process are involved when students are engaged in school. Researchers seem to agree that active participation is important but not sufficient to capture the quality of students' engagement in learning activities. How students feel about the activities and school as a community and their commitment to education should be considered as part of the construct.

B. A TRIPARTITE CONCEPTUALIZATION OF SCHOOL ENGAGEMENT

Over the past 10 years, the major shift in school engagement literature is the move away from unidimensional definitions (mostly behavioral ones) to more multidimensional notions of engagement (Yonezawa, Jones, & Joselowsky, 2009). Thanks to the advocacy efforts of Finn and Voelkl (1993), Fredricks et al. (2004), and Jimerson et al. (2003), most scholars have embraced the idea that school engagement should be conceptualized as a multidimensional construct so that students' behavioral, emotional, and cognitive experiences at school can be studied simultaneously, rather than separately.

While the exact number and names of elements may vary from one model to another, several recent reviews have endorsed a tripartite conceptualization. For instance, reviewing school engagement and related literatures, Jimerson et al. (2003) grouped a myriad of constructs that were identified in the literature and analyzed the main feature of each based on the definitions provided. They found that the extracted elements of most constructs can be classified depending upon whether they were behavioral, emotional, cognitive, or a combination of these three characteristics. The elements identified by Jimerson et al. (2003) are aligned to the three dimensions summarized by Fredricks et al. (2004). The only difference is that Jimerson et al. (2003) labeled one of the components as "affective," while Fredricks et al. named it as "emotional." Making a careful comparison between these two terms as they were used, I found no substantive difference. "Emotional" was chosen here over "affective" because it tends to be more inclusive. According to Damasio (1999), affect is the conscious emotional experience, while emotion could be both unconscious and conscious.

This tridimensional conceptualization of engagement has gained increasing popularity in the recent literature. To illustrate, the review conducted by Fredricks et al. has been cited more than 340 times since it was published in 2004, and it is also one of the most frequently cited articles in the school engagement literature.

Given the comprehensiveness of this conceptualization, here, I briefly introduce this tripartite theoretical structure. Developers and believers of this theoretical structure argue that behavioral characteristics, such as the amount of participation in academic work, including attendance, time spent on academic activities, or the intensity of effort, alone are inadequate indicators of engagement. At times they may be indicative of the extent students are willing to comply with school rules, rather than a representation of genuine commitment or actual investment to learning. Deep engagement entails concentration and effort as well as investment and commitment. Similarly, positive emotions, or simply liking school, do not guarantee that meaningful effort is exerted. In addition, commitment and motivation do not mean that someone is engaged, unless a student actively participates in the specific activities in school. Active participation, with great concentration and effort, positive emotions, or feeling of excitement and sense of connectedness, and cognitive processes such as commitment and values are all necessary ingredients for students' engagement with school.

There are other multidimensional models that include four engagement components, instead of three. For example, some investigators propose to include an additional element to reflect the amount of time students spend on academic learning (e.g., Appleton, Christenson, Kim, & Reschly 2006; Reschly & Christenson, 2006a; Sinclair, Christenson, & Thurlow, 2005). They argue that variables such as "time on task," credits earned toward graduation, and homework completion are indicators of academic engagement, while attendance, suspensions from classroom participation, and extracurricular participation are (positive or negative) indicators of behavioral engagement (Appleton et al., 2006). In addition, Skinner, Kindermann, Connell, et al. (2009) and Skinner, Kindermann, and Furrer (2009) attempted to conceptualize active engagement and active disengagement, in terms of both behavior and emotions, in the same model. Their rationale is that the opposite of engagement is not lack of engagement, but active disengagement, which may be characterized by disruptive noncompliance, frustration, anger, or other enervated emotions.

These two alternative models, although having some empirical support, face several challenges. The first four-component model suffers from splitting behaviors that are somewhat similar without providing a strong rationale. Academic engagement could be incorporated into the behavioral engagement component. Thus, adding a fourth element to the model creates unnecessary redundancy and complexity. The second four-dimensional model cannot readily explain how the "passive" form is developmentally different from the "disruptive" form of emotional engagement. This model also fails to include the thoughts and ideas students have regarding school and education. Overall, the behavior–emotion–cognition triangle offers a rich characterization of children as whole persons, without confusing the indicators and facilitators of engagement or involving unnecessary redundancy (e.g., including components that may in fact be the same thing).

Thus, within a multidimensional framework, school engagement is understood as the extent to which students are involved, attached, and committed to the academic and social activities provided in school. Such engagement is a state of being influenced by the ongoing interactions between students and the school context; it is not a personal trait of the student (Furlong & Christenson, 2008). That is, engagement is a relational, person–context construct and is thought to develop as a function of daily interactions between a developing adolescent and his or her experiences in various academic and social activities and with different individuals. These experiences occur in the changing school context, which may involve patterns of perceptions, behaviors, and emotions of others who happen to be in the context (Skinner, Kindermann, Connell, et al., 2009; Skinner, Kindermann, & Furrer, 2009).

V. The Operationalization and Measurement of School Engagement

As described in prior sections of this chapter, there is inconsistency in the ways school engagement has been conceptualized. This inconsistency is coupled with disparity in the ways they are measured (Jimerson et al., 2003). On the one hand, there are varying ways to measure the same types of engagement. On the other hand, there is duplication of items across the behavioral, emotional, and cognitive aspects of school engagement (Fredricks et al., 2004). The somewhat arbitrary choices of measures have left considerable room for measurement error. In this section, I discuss the prevalent measurement problems existing in the literature. I then elaborate why systematic psychometric analysis is needed.

A. PROBLEMS IN THE MEASUREMENT OF SCHOOL ENGAGEMENT

First, although the multidimensionality of school engagement is well recognized, its measurement does not always reflect this understanding. With only a few exceptions, prior research has either combined conceptually different engagement measures into a general index or only tested one or two of the three engagement components. For instance, Smerdon (2002) collapsed nine items from the NELS questionnaire that are designed to measure relationships with teachers, interest in classes, importance of education, and sense of belonging into a single measure of school engagement. When subjected to confirmatory factor analysis (CFA) using the same data set, Smerdon's (2002) measure fails to achieve an adequate fit based on the cutoffs of multiple goodness-of-fit statistics (Glanville & Wildhagen, 2007). Janosz, Archambault, Morizot, and Pagani (2008) also combined items measuring participation, enjoyment and interest, and willingness to learn into a global construct of school engagement.

The second prevalent problem is that studies at times leave out one or more components of school engagement. Given that components may be formed with items extracted from already existing larger national datasets, many studies were only able to measure one or two aspects of engagement, most typically behavioral and emotional (e.g., Finn & Rock, 1997; Reschly & Christenson, 2006b). For example, while endorsing a tripartite conception of school engagement, Ladd and Dinella (2009) only measured how much children like and avoid school, hence failing to provide any information about children's participation in school. Collapsing all items into a general measure or leaving out some important components affords an incomplete understanding of the school engagement construct. Such work cannot disentangle the unique contribution of each component of engagement for different youth development outcomes or understand the interrelations among these components.

Third, it is not rare that within the same study, school engagement is conceptualized one way but measured in another way. For instance, Garcia-Reid, Reid, and Peterson (2005) define school engagement as students' commitment to schooling, but they then measure the construct by using three items that asked whether students "find school fun and exciting." Similarly, Hughes, Luo, Kwok, and Loyd (2008) sought to measure school engagement by using items pertinent to the Big Five personality dimensions. Such mismatch between conceptualization and measurement may produce invalid measures that are nevertheless reliable. As noted earlier, this mismatch may be due to reliance on items drawn retroactively from existing studies that were designed to measure something else. What are needed to address these limitations are theoretically sound measures of school engagement that are proved to have good psychometric property.

In addition, many studies were conducted without establishing a strong theoretical framework (Appleton et al., 2006). As a result, even when working with the same data set, arbitrary choice of items and scales prevails. For instance, Glanville and Wildhagen (2007) examined four widely used measures with the NELS data set that were proposed by Finn and Rock (1997), Finn and Voelkl (1993), Lee and Smith (1993), and Smerdon (1999, 2002). Their assessment of these measures not only revealed considerable amounts of measurement error but also suggested that some of the measurement models fit poorly to the data, especially those that follow a unidimensional approach (Glanville & Wildhagen, 2007). A large part of these measurement problems arises from the fact that there are few measures devoted exclusively to school engagement. When the measurement of engagement is derived from items that are part of a larger matrix of constructs measuring related but different constructs, the actual items may not represent adequately conceptual definitions of school engagement.

An additional limitation of the current practice is that few investigations have been devoted to evaluating the psychometric properties of school engagement measures and examining whether they measure the construct the same way for all groups and ages of students. These omissions are unfortunate because point-in-time studies of school engagement and, especially, developmental analyses rest on such work to ascertain measurement equivalence. A major improvement would be the creation and validation of a measure exclusively of school engagement that had broad equivalence across multiple demographic variable markers.

B. A NEED FOR SYSTEMATIC PSYCHOMETRIC ANALYSIS

Traditionally, classic test theory has defined observed scores as composed of true and error values and has evaluated the quality of measures in terms of reliability and validity (Vandenberg & Lance, 2000). Researchers who apply classic test theory typically evaluate a measure's reliability (e.g., internal consistency and/or test–retest stability) and validity (e.g., convergent, discriminant, factorial, or predictive validity). For instance, in regard to internal consistency indices of reliability, Crobach's alphas, computed with a current sample and, compared to previously reported coefficients, if available, are used. In practice, reliability coefficients that reach conventional cutoff values, such as 0.70, have been treated as if measurement error may be ignored, that is, once this level of internal consistency is reached, few authors raise the issue of inaccurate measurement.

The issue of validity concerns whether an instrument actually measures a construct that it is designed to measure. The issue of divergent validity is of particular relevance when theoretical disputes exist. For instance, a question may be raised about whether emotional engagement and school connectedness are separate constructs, or whether one is actually measuring cognitive engagement and not motivation. Empirical evidence of validity may come from findings that the measure's hypothesized association with other constructs held true, or from results of factor analysis of the items indexing the construct.

In turn, results of factor analyses are used often to support the assumption that the items used are a valid operationalization of an underlying attribute. Based on this assumption, group assessments of change are made by comparing observed mean scores. These mean scores are believed to represent the true score for a particular group. However, as with the above-noted issues of measurement error being ignored when alpha values reach or exceed the "rule-of-thumb" threshold of acceptability (usually 0.7), means are compared here as if they provide a certain index of the construct identified by the factor loading pattern (despite "rules-of-thumb," such as the root of criterion or the 0.3 item loading pattern being used) and, as if, therefore no issues of measurement error need to be considered.

Of course, evidence of reliability and validity is important in that they indicate a measure's psychometric attributes. However, good reliability coefficients or strong validity data do not suffice for unambiguous interpretation of differences of, or changes in, observed scores. Such interpretation also requires that (1) the item set evokes the same conceptual frame of reference in each group subject to comparison or, in other words, each of the items should not mean one thing to one group and something else to other groups and (2) relations between the observed items and the underlying construct should not be different across groups or over time. For example, if a score of "4" out of 5 on a particular item may mean "extremely satisfactory" to one group, but only "satisfactory" to another group, this item functions nonequivalently. It is also reasonable to wonder whether time-related changes, for example, life events, maturation, or interventions, alter the conceptual frame of reference used by people to respond to a measure (Vandenberg & Lance, 2000).

A more general question is whether or not, under different conditions, there is measurement equivalence (Horn & McArdle, 1992). Therefore, one needs to ascertain if respondents of different age, gender, ethnic, or socioeconomic characteristics interpret an instrument in similar ways, and/or if the contents being measured remain the same, even in the face of manifest validity. The issue of measurement equivalence is particularly relevant for investigations into how youth of different ethnic and family backgrounds may be engaged in school differently. Unless we are able to ascertain that a measure of school engagement is valid and that it behaves the same way across these groups, discussions of gender, racial, or family background differences in school engagement are unwarranted. Likewise, unless it is proved that school engagement of students at different ages can be measured by the same scale the exact same way, inference should not be drawn with regard to the development of engagement.

Measurement equivalence is an important psychometric property that was neglected until advances in analytic techniques beyond classical test theory became relatively more accessible (Vandenberg & Lance, 2000). Interpretation of mean differences or change may be problematic unless we are certain that the underlying constructs are the same across populations and over time (Wu, Chen, & Tsai, 2009). Violation of measurement equivalence at least casts doubt or even makes interpretations of any between—group comparisons meaningless (Bollen, 1989; Vandenberg & Self, 1993). As pointed out by Horn and McArdle (1992), "if there is no evidence indicating presence or absence of measurement equivalence—the usual case—or there is evidence that such invariance does not obtain, then the basis for drawing scientific inference is severely lacking: Findings of differences between individuals and groups cannot be unambiguously interpreted" (p. 117).

Evaluation of measurement equivalence can be conducted in frameworks such as confirmatory factor analysis (CFA) and item response theory (IRT); both are measurement tools of estimating the relationships between measured variables and underlying constructs based on the relations among the observed variables. Under CFA, the relations between observed response and an underlying latent construct are linear (Meade & Lautenschlager, 2004). The IRT framework assumes a log-linear, rather than a linear, relationship between the observed item responses and the latent variable (Reise, Widaman, & Pugh, 1993). The CFA approach is advantageous with regard to its various well-developed fit indices and its applicability to multidimensional measurement (Reise et al., 1993). Thus, CFA is a statistical tool for testing whether the conceptualized structure is consistent with the observed data (Pitts, West, & Tein, 1996). Using maximum likelihood algorithms embedded in statistical programs such as LISREL (Jöreskog & Sörbom, 1996) or Mplus (Muthén & Muthén,

2004), CFAs are the most widely accepted procedures used for evaluating measurement equivalence (Vandenberg & Lance, 2000).

Summarizing discussions of procedures for testing measurement equivalence, Vandenberg and Lance (2000) recommend that researchers use multiple samples to test for measurement equivalence. In such cases, Jöreskog's (1971) recommendations for applying multigroup covariance structure analysis should be followed. In addition, there is a consensus that three levels of measurement equivalence need to be examined: configural, metric, and scalar. Invariance at the configural level requires the same items to be indicators of the same latent factor in different groups or across measurement occasions. That is, the factor structure, or in other words, the items assigned to measure each factor, and the specification of free and fixed patterns of factor loadings are equivalent (Horn, McArdle, & Mason, 1983; Widaman & Reise, 1997). Metric invariance means that the relations between each item of the measure and the underlying construct are invariant, that is, factor loadings of like items are invariant. Invariance at the scalar level indicates that the intercepts of like items' regressions on the latent construct are invariant (Meredith, 1993). Other than tests for the relations between the observed items and the underlying construct, tests concerning the relations of the underlying constructs themselves may be recommended as well (Byrne, Shavelson, & Muthén, 1989).

As pointed out by Vandenberg and Lance (2000), with some variations, there is a typical sequence of testing. Tests for configural invariance should precede tests for metric invariance, because configural invariance is a necessary condition for assessing further aspects of equivalence. In other words, configural invariance models usually are a baseline model (Pitts et al., 1996). It is considered weak evidence of measurement equivalence. Although not everyone agrees, tests for metric invariance are often recommended after configural invariance has been established (Bollen, 1989). Evidence of measurement equivalence at the metric level is considered strong. Metric invariance must be established for subsequent tests to be considered necessary and meaningful (Horn & McArdle, 1992). According to advocates for testing measurement equivalence, these tests should be conducted before applying any latent growth models or conducting cross-group comparisons (Vandenberg & Lance, 2000).

In addition to psychometric validation with empirical data, such as examining cross-group or longitudinal measurement equivalence or discriminant validity, it is important to ensure that at the item development step, the measure possesses good content validity and has strong and clear linkages with its theoretical foundations (Germain, 2006).

VI. Summary and Conclusions

The growing excitement about the construct of school engagement is tempered by the numerous measurement issues persisting with school engagement (Appleton et al., 2008). Perhaps the most pressing direction for future research is the development of measures of school engagement with proved validity and reliability and measurement equivalence. As pointed out by Appleton et al. (2008), work is to be done to identify and improve measurement across groupings of youth, whether the criteria of grouping are age, race/ethnicity, or socioeconomic status (SES) variations. Of course, any measure development work should be guided by careful definitions of the construct of interest. A measure can only be a good measure when it is designed to measure something that can be measured. Vagueness in conceptualizations not only causes a variety of measurement issues but also pollutes the field by producing contradictory research findings. In addition, grades, although very important, should not be seen as the only indicator of PYD. Future research should strive to comprehensively assess the relations between different aspects of school engagement with important social, emotional, and academic outcomes.

A. FUTURE DIRECTION 1: BETTER UNDERSTANDING OF, AND THE NUANCES WITHIN, THE SCHOOL ENGAGEMENT CONSTRUCT

There is insufficient information about how behavioral, emotional, and cognitive engagement influences each other (Ladd & Dinella, 2009). It is possible that these aspects of school engagement are influenced not only exogenously by outside forces but also internally, that is, by each other (e.g., Ladd & Dinella, 2009; Skinner, Furrer, Marchand, & Kindermann, 2008). However, no conclusion has been reached regarding the internal dynamics among these components of school engagement (Fredricks et al., 2004). One may argue that positive feelings may be complemented with at least basic effort and investment in school. However, the way students behave in school may not be consistent with how they feel about school. Students who come to school to hang out with friends who attend school may feel connected but may only try to get by with minimal effort. Similarly, students who perceive school and education as important and relevant may not always actively participate in academic activities for various reasons, such as low self-efficacy (Eccles & Roeser, 2009).

The question is what precedes what? Does active participation lead to increased positive feeling toward school? Or does positive affect toward school result in heightened commitment to education? What about the relations between behavioral and cognitive engagement? Unraveling this complexity is vital in helping us understand how differences in the association among students' behaviors, feelings, and thoughts within school may contribute to differences in their academic performance and, as well, other aspects of youth development.

B. FUTURE DIRECTION 2: INNOVATIVE METHODOLOGIES TO UNDERSTAND THE DEVELOPMENT OF SCHOOL ENGAGEMENT AND ITS IMPLICATIONS TO PYD

Researchers and educators are attracted to this concept because of its presumed malleability and responsiveness to contextual changes. Without deliberate interventions being implemented in schools, school engagement is usually postulated to lessen as children progress through high school. Unfortunately, the development of school engagement and its malleability remains a matter of speculation, in that most research has been conducted with cross-sectional designs (Fredricks et al., 2004). First, due to the scarcity of longitudinal studies on this topic, limited empirical information on the natural development of school engagement is available. Not knowing how school engagement changes in the ordinary school context is unfortunate, given that evaluation of the effectiveness of any interventions needs to be based on such "baseline" knowledge. Second, there has been little attempt to understand the interindividual variation with regard to changes in school engagement. Thus, we need to go beyond prediction analysis so that we can exploit the richness of longitudinal data sets to a fuller degree. Techniques that grant researchers capabilities to empirically examine the process in which different components of school engagement produce various adolescent outcomes are to be further developed.

Acknowledgments

This chapter is based in part on a dissertation submitted by the first author to Tufts University in partial fulfillment of the requirements for the doctoral degree. The author is grateful to Dr. Richard M. Lerner for his invaluable contribution to the research reported in this chapter.

REFERENCES

Alexander, K. L., Entwisle, D. R., & Horsey, C. S. (1997). From first grade forward: Early foundations of high school dropout. *Sociology of Education, 70,* 87–107.

Appleton, J. J., Christenson, S. L., & Furlong, M. J. (2008). Student engagement with school: Critical conceptual and methodological issues of the construct. *Psychology in the Schools, 45,* 369–386.

Appleton, J. J., Christenson, S. L., Kim, D., & Reschly, A. L. (2006). Measuring cognitive and psychological engagement: Validation of the student engagement instrument. *Journal of School Psychology, 44,* 427–445.

Baltes, P. B., Lindenberger, U., & Staudinger, U. M. (2006). Life span theory in developmental psychology. In W. Damon & R. M. Lerner (Eds.), *Handbook of child psychology: Vol. 1. Theoretical models of human development* (6th ed., pp. 569–664). New York: Wiley.

Baumrind, D. (1991). Effective parenting during the early adolescent transition. In P. E. Cowan & E. M. Hetherington (Eds.), *Advances in family research* (pp. 309–330). Hillsdale, NJ: Erlbaum.

Benson, P. L. (2003). Developmental assets and asset-building community: Conceptual and empirical foundations. In R. M. Lerner & P. L. Benson (Eds.), *Developmental assets and asset building communities: Implications for research, policy, and practice* (pp. 19–43). Norwell, MA: Kluwer.

Bollen, K. A. (1989). *Structural equations with latent variables.* New York: Wiley.

Brandtstädter, J. (2006). Action perspectives on human development. In W. Damon (Series Ed.) & R. M. Lerner (Ed.), *Handbook of child psychology: Vol. 1. Theoretical models of human development* (6th ed., pp. 516–568). Hoboken, NJ: Wiley.

Bretherton, I. (2005). In pursuit of the internal working construct and its relevance to attachment relationships. In K. E. Grossmann, K. Grossmann & E. Waters (Eds.), *Attachment from infancy to adulthood: The major longitudinal studies.* (pp. 13–47). New York: Guilford Press.

Bretherton, I., & Munholland, K. A. (2008). Internal working models in attachment relationships: Elaborating a central construct in attachment theory. In J. Cassidy & P. Shaver (Eds.), *Handbook of attachment: Theory, research and clinical application.* New York: Guilford.

Byrne, B. M., Shavelson, R. J., & Muthén, B. (1989). Testing for the equivalence of factor covariance and mean structures: The issue of partial measurement invariance. *Psychological Bulletin, 107,* 238–246.

Catalano, R. F., Haggerty, K. P., Oesterle, S., Fleming, C. B., & Hawkins, J. D. (2004). The importance of bonding to school for healthy development: Findings from the Social Development Research Group. *The Journal of School Health, 74,* 252–262.

Catalano, R. F., & Hawkins, J. D. (1996). The social development model: A theory of antisocial behavior. In J. D. Hawkins (Ed.), *Delinquency and crime: Current theories* (pp. 149–197). New York: Cambridge University Press.

Cernkovich, S. A., & Giordano, P. C. (1992). School bonding, race and delinquency. *Criminology, 30,* 261–291.

Connell, J. P. (1990). Context, self, and action: A motivational analysis of self-system processes across the life-span. In D. Cicchetti (Ed.), *The self in transition: Infancy to childhood* (pp. 61–97). Chicago: University of Chicago Press.

Connell, J. P., & Wellborn, J. G. (1991). Competence, autonomy and relatedness: A motivational analysis of self-system processes. In M. Gunnar & L. A. Sroufe (Eds.), *Minnesota symposium on child psychology: Vol. 23. Self processes in development* (pp. 43–77). Chicago: University of Chicago Press.

Crittenden, P. M. (1990). Internal representational models of attachment relationships. *Infant Mental Health Journal, 11*, 259–277.

Damasio, A. (1999). *The feeling of what happens: Body, emotion and the making of consciousness.* London: Random House.

Deci, E. L., & Ryan, R. M. (1985). *Intrinsic motivation and self-determination in human behavior.* New York: Plenum.

Eccles, J. (2004). Schools, academic motivation, and stage-environment fit. In R. Lerner & L. Steinberg (Eds.), *Handbook of adolescent psychology.* (pp. 125–152). New York: Wiley.

Eccles, J. S., Early, D., Fraser, K., Belansky, E., & McCarthy, K. (1997). The relation of connection, regulation, and support for autonomy to adolescents' functioning. *Journal of Adolescent Research, 12*, 263–286.

Eccles, J., & Gootman, J. A. (Eds.), (2002). *Community programs to promote youth development.* Washington, DC: National Academies Press.

Eccles, J. S., & Midgley, C. (1989). Stage/environment fit: Developmentally appropriate classrooms for early adolescents. In R. Ames & C. Ames (Eds.), *Research on motivation in education* (Vol. 3, pp. 139–181). New York: Academic Press.

Eccles, J. S., Midgley, C., Wigfield, A., Buchanan, C. M., Reuman, D., Flanagan, C., et al. (1993). Development during adolescence: The impact of stage-environment fit on young adolescents' experiences in schools and families. *The American Psychologist, 48*, 90–101.

Eccles, J. S., & Roeser, R. W. (2009). Schools, academic motivation, and stage-environment fit. In R. M. Lerner & L. Steinberg (Eds.), *Handbook of adolescent psychology* (3rd ed., pp. 404–434). Hoboken, NJ: John Wiley & Sons.

Finn, J. D. (1989). Withdrawing from school. *Review of Educational Research, 59*, 117–142.

Finn, J. D. (1993). *School engagement and students at risk.* (No. NCES-93-470)Washington, DC: National Center for Educational Statistics.

Finn, J. D., & Rock, D. A. (1997). Academic success among students at risk for school failure. *The Journal of Applied Psychology, 82*, 221–234.

Finn, J. D., & Voelkl, K. E. (1993). School characteristics related to school engagement. *The Journal of Negro Education, 62*, 249–268.

Furlong, M. J., & Christenson, S. L. (2008). Engaging students at school and with learning: A relevant construct for all students. *Psychology in the Schools, 45*, 365–368.

Furlong, M. J., Whipple, A. D., Jean, G. S., Simental, J., Soliz, A., & Punthuna, S. (2003). Multiple contexts of school engagement: Moving toward a unifying framework for educational research and practice. *The California School Psychologist, 8*, 99–113.

Fredericks, J. A., Blumenfeld, P. C., & Paris, A. H. (2004). School engagement: Potential of the concept, state of the evidence. *Review of Educational Research, 74*, 59–109.

Fredricks, J. A., & Eccles, J. S. (2002). Children's competence and value beliefs from childhood to adolescence: Growth trajectories in two "male-typed" domains. *Developmental Psychology, 38*, 519–533.

Gambone, M., & Connell, J. (2004). The community action framework for youth development. *The Prevention Researcher, 11*, 17–20.

Garcia-Reid, P., Reid, R. J., & Peterson, N. A. (2005). School engagement among Latino youth in an urban middle school context, valuing the role of social support. *Education and Urban Society, 37*, 257–275.

Germain, M.L. (2006). Stages of psychometric measure development: The example of the generalized expertise measure (GEM), in F. Nafukho (Ed.), *Academy of Human Resource Development 2006 Conference Proceedings.*

Gilligan, R. (1998). The importance of schools and teachers in child welfare. *Child and Family Social Work, 3*, 13–25.

Glanville, J. L., & Wildhagen, T. (2007). The measurement of school engagement: Assessing dimensionality and measurement invariance across race and ethnicity. *Educational and Psychological Measurement, 67*, 1019–1041.

Hawkins, J. D. (1997). Academic performance and school success: Sources and consequences. In R. P. Weissberg, T. P. Gullotta, R. L. Hampton, B. A. Ryan & G. R. Adams (Eds.), *Healthy children 2010: Enhancing children's wellness. Issues in children's and families' lives* (Vol. 8, pp. 278–305). Thousand Oaks, CA: Sage Publications.

Hawkins, J. D., Guo, J., Hill, K. G., Battin-Pearson, S., & Abbott, R. D. (2001). Long-term effects of the Seattle Social Development intervention on school bonding trajectories. *Applied Developmental Science, 5*, 225–236.

Hawkins, J. D., & Lishner, D. (1987). Etiology and prevention of antisocial behavior in children and adolescents. In A. S. Bellack, & M. Hersen (Series Eds.) & D. H. Crowell, I. M. Evans, & C. R. O'Donnel (Eds.), *Applied clinical psychology. Childhood aggression and violence: Sources of influence, prevention, and control* (pp. 263–282). New York: Plenum.

Hawkins, J. D., & Weis, J. G. (1985). The social development model: an integrated approach to delinquency prevention. *Journal of Primary Prevention, 6*, 73–97.

Hirschi, T. (1969). *Causes of delinquency.* Berkeley, CA: University of California Press.

Horn, J. L., & McArdle, J. J. (1992). A practical and theoretical guide to measurement invariance in aging research. *Experimental Aging Research, 18*, 117–144.

Horn, J. L., McArdle, J. J., & Mason, R. (1983). When is invariance not invariant: A practical scientist's view of the ethereal concept of factorial invariance. *The Southern Psychologist, 1*, 179–188.

Hughes, J. N., Luo, W., Kwok, O., & Loyd, L. K. (2008). Teacher-student support, effortful engagement, and achievement: A 3-year longitudinal study. *Journal of Educational Psychology, 100*, 1–14.

Janosz, M., Archambault, I., Morizot, J., & Pagani, L. S. (2008). School engagement trajectories and their differential predictive relations to dropout. *The Journal of Social Issues, 64*, 21–40.

Jelicic, H., Bobek, D., Phelps, E. D., Lerner, J. V., & Lerner, R. M. (2007). Using positive youth development to predict contribution and risk behaviors in early adolescence: Findings from the first two waves of the 4-H Study of Positive Youth Development. *International Journal of Behavioral Development, 31*, 263–273.

Jimerson, S. R., Campos, E., & Greif, J. L. (2003). Toward an understanding of definitions and measures of school engagement and related terms. *The California School Psychologist, 8*, 7–27.

Johnson, M. K., Crosnoe, R., & Elder, G. H., Jr., (2001). Students' attachment and academic engagement: The role of race and ethnicity. *Sociology of Education, 74*, 318–340.

Johnson, W., McGue, M., & Iacono, W. G. (2006). Genetic and environmental influences on academic achievement trajectories during adolescence. *Developmental Psychology, 42*, 514–532.

Jöreskog, K. G. (1971). Simultaneous factor analysis in several populations. *Psychometrika, 36*, 409–426.

Jöreskog, K. G., & Sörbom, D. (1996). *LISREL 8: Structural equation modeling with the SIMPLIS command language.* Chicago: Scientific Software International.

King, P. E., Dowling, E. M., Mueller, R. A., White, K., Schultz, R. M., Osborn, P., Dickerson, E., Bobek, D. L., Lerner, R. M., Benson, P. L., & Scales, P. C. (2005). Thriving in adolescence: The voices of youth-serving practitioners, parents, and early and late adolescents. *Journal of Early Adolescence, 25*, 94–143.

Kortering, L., & Braziel, P. (2008). Age appropriate transition assessment: A look at what students say. *Journal of At Risk Youth, 17*, 27–35.

Ladd, G. W., & Dinella, L. M. (2009). Continuity and change in early school engagement: Predictive of children's achievement trajectories from first to eighth grade? *Journal of Educational Psychology, 101*, 190–206.

Lee, V. E., & Smith, J. (1993). Effects of school restructuring on the achievement and engagement of middle-grades students. *Sociology of Education, 66*, 164–187.

Lerner, R. M. (2002). *Concepts and theories of human development* Mahwah, NJ: Lawrence Erlbaum.

Lerner, R. M. (2004). *Liberty: Thriving and civic engagement among America's youth.* Thousand Oaks, CA: Sage Publications.

Li, Y., Bebiroglu, N., Phelps, E., Lerner, J. V., & Lerner, R. M. (2008). Out-of-school activity participation, school engagement and positive youth development: Findings from the 4-H Study of Positive Youth Development. *Journal of Youth Development, 3*, 9–23. DOI: 080303FA001.

Li, Y., & Lerner, R. M. (2011). Developmental trajectories of school engagement across adolescence: Implications for academic achievement, substance use, depression, and delinquency. *Developmental Psychology, 47*, 233–247.

Li, Y., Lerner, J. V., & Lerner, R. M. (2010). Personal and ecological assets and adolescent academic competence: The mediating role of school engagement. *Journal of Youth and Adolescence, 39*, 801–815.

Li, Y., Zhang, W., Liu, J., Arbeit, M., Schwartz, S., Bowers, E. P., et al. (in press). The role of school engagement in preventing adolescent delinquency and substance use: A longitudinal analysis. *Journal of Adolescence.*

Libbey, H. P. (2004). Measuring student relationships to school: Attachment, bonding, connectedness, and engagement. *The Journal of School Health, 74*, 274–283.

Marks, H. M. (2000). Student engagement in instructional activity: Patterns in the elementary, middle, and high school years. *American Educational Research Journal, 37*, 153–184.

McDermott, P. A., Mordell, M., & Stolzfus, J. C. (2001). The organization of student performance in American schools: Discipline, motivation, verbal and non-verbal learning. *Journal of Educational Psychology, 93*, 65–76.

Meade, A. W., & Lautenschlager, G. J. (2004). A comparison of IRT and CFA methodologies for establishing measurement equivalence. *Organizational Research Methods, 7*, 361–388.

Meece, J. L., Blumenfeld, P. C., & Hoyle, R. (1988). Student's goal orientations and cognitive engagement in classroom activities. *Journal of Educational Psychology, 80*, 514–523.

Meece, J. L., & Kurtz-Costes, B. (2001). Introduction: The schooling of ethnic minority children and youth. *Educational Psychologist, 36*, 1–7.

Meredith, W. (1993). Measurement invariance, factor analysis and factorial invariance. *Psychometrika, 58*, 525–543.

Mergendeller, J. R., & Mitman, A. L. (1985). The relationship of middle school program features, instructional strategy, instructional performance, and student engagement. *The Journal of Early Adolescence, 5*, 183–196.

Moffitt, T. E., Caspi, A., Dickson, N., Silva, P. A., & Stanton, W. (1996). Childhood-onset versus adolescent-onset antisocial conduct in males: Natural history from age 3 to 18. *Development and Psychopathology, 8*, 399–424.

Mosher, R., & McGowan, B. (1985). *Assessing student engagement in secondary schools: Alternative conceptions, strategies of assessing, and instruments.* University of Wisconsin, Research and Development Center (ERIC Document Reproduction Service No. ED 272812).

Muthén, L. K., & Muthén, B. O. (2004). *Mplus user's guide.* Los Angeles: Muthén & Muthén.

National Research Council and Institute of Medicine, (2004). *Engaging schools: Fostering high school students' motivation to learn.* Washington, DC: The National Academies Press.

Natriello, G. (1984). Problems in the evaluation of students and student from secondary schools. *Journal of Research and Development in Education, 17,* 14–24.

Newmann, F. (1992). Higher-order thinking and prospects for classroom thoughtfulness. In F. Newmann (Ed.), *Student engagement and achievement in American secondary schools* (pp. 62–91). New York: Teachers College Press.

Newmann, F. M., Wehlage, G. G., & Lamborn, S. D. (1992). The significance and sources of student engagement. In F. M. Newmann (Ed.), *Student engagement and achievement in American secondary schools* (pp. 11–30). New York: Teachers College Press.

Ogbu, J. U. (2003). *Black American students in an affluent suburb: A study of academic disengagement.* Mahwah, NJ: Lawrence Erlbaum.

Overton, W. F. (2004). Embodied development: Ending the nativism-empiricism debate. In C. Garcia Coll, E. Bearer & R. M. Lerner (Eds.), *Nature and nurture: The complex interplay of genetic and environmental influences on human behavior and development.* (pp. 201–223). Lawrence Erlbaum Associates: Mahwah, NJ.

Pierson, L. H., & Connell, J. P. (1992). Effect of grade retention on self-system processes, school engagement, and academic performance. *Journal of Educational Psychology, 84,* 300–307.

Pitts, S., West, S., & Tein, J. (1996). Longitudinal measurement models in evaluation research: Examining stability and change. *Evaluation and Program Planning, 19,* 333–350.

Reise, S. P., Widaman, K. F., & Pugh, R. H. (1993). Confirmatory factor analysis and item response theory: Two approaches for exploring measurement invariance. *Psychological Bulletin, 114,* 552–566.

Reschly, A., & Christenson, S. L. (2006a). Promoting successful school completion. In G. Bear & K. Minke (Eds.), *Children's needs—III: Development, prevention, and intervention* (pp. 103–113). Bethesda, MD: National Association of School Psychologists.

Reschly, A., & Christenson, S. L. (2006b). Research leading to a predictive model of dropout and completion among students with mild disabilities and the role of student engagement. *Remedial and Special Education, 27,* 276–292.

Resnick, M. D., Bearman, P. S., Blum, R. W., Bauman, K. E., Harris, K. M., Jones, J., et al. (1997). Protecting adolescents from harm: Findings from the National Longitudinal Study on Adolescent Health. *Journal of the American Medical Association, 278,* 823–832.

Rumberger, R. W. (1987). High school dropouts: A review of issues and evidence. *Review of Educational Research, 57,* 101–121.

Rumberger, R. W. (2004). Why students drop out of school. In G. Orfield (Ed.), *Dropouts in America: Confronting the graduation rate crisis* (pp. 131–155). Cambridge, MA: Harvard Education Press.

Sedlak, M. W., Wheeler, C. W., Pullin, D. C., & Cusick, P. A. (1986). *Selling students short: Classroom bargains and academic reform in the American high school.* New York: Teacher's College Press.

Simons-Morton, B. G., Crump, A. D., Haynie, D. L., & Saylor, K. E. (1999). Student–school bonding and adolescent problem behavior. *Health Education Research, 14,* 99–107.

Sinclair, M. F., Christenson, S. L., & Thurlow, M. L. (2005). Promoting school completion of urban secondary youth with emotional or behavioral disabilities. *Exceptional Children, 71,* 465–482.

Skinner, E. A. (1995). *Perceived control, motivation, and coping.* Newbury Park, CA: Sage Publications.

Skinner, E. A., Furrer, C., Marchand, G., & Kindermann, T. (2008). Engagement and disaffection in the classroom: Part of a larger motivational dynamic? *Journal of Educational Psychology*, *100*, 765–781.

Skinner, E. A., Kindermann, T. A., Connell, J. P., & Wellborn, J. G. (2009a). Engagement as an organizational construct in the dynamics of motivational development. In K. Wentzel & A. Wigfield (Eds.), *Handbook of motivation in school*. Mahwah, NJ: Lawrence Erlbaum.

Skinner, E. A., Kindermann, T. A., & Furrer, C. J. (2009b). A motivational perspective on engagement and disaffection: Conceptualization and assessment of children's behavioral and emotional participation in academic activities in the classroom. *Educational and Psychological Measurement*, *69*, 493–525.

Skinner, E. A., Wellborn, J. G., & Connell, J. P. (1990). What it takes to do well in school and whether I've got it: The role of perceived control in children's engagement and school achievement. *Journal of Educational Psychology*, *82*, 22–32.

Smerdon, B. A. (1999). Engagement and achievement: Differences between African-American and White high school students. *Research in Sociology of Education and Socialization*, *12*, 103–134.

Smerdon, B. A. (2002). Students' perceptions of membership in their high schools. *Sociology of Education*, *75*, 287–305.

Steinberg, L., Brown, B. B., & Dornbush, S. M. (1996). *Beyond the classroom: Why school reform has failed and what parents need to do*. New York: Simon and Schuster.

Theokas, C., & Lerner, R. M. (2006). Promoting positive development in adolescence: The role of ecological assets in families, schools, and neighborhoods. *Applied Developmental Science*, *10*, 61–74.

Vandenberg, R. J., & Lance, C. E. (2000). A review and synthesis of the measurement invariance literature: Suggestions, practices, and recommendations for organizational research. *Organizational Research Methods*, *3*, 4–69.

Vandenberg, R. J., & Self, R. M. (1993). Assessing newcomers' changing commitment to the organization during the first 6 months of work. *The Journal of Applied Psychology*, *78*, 557–568.

Widaman, K. F., & Reise, S. P. (1997). Exploring the measurement invariance of psychological instruments: Applications in the substance use domain. In K. J. Bryant, M. Windle & S. G. West (Eds.), *The science of prevention: Methodological advances from alcohol and substance abuse research* (pp. 281–324). Washington, DC: American Psychological Association.

Wigfield, A., Eccles, J. S., Schiefele, U., Roeser, R., & Davis-Kean, P. (2006). Development of achievement motivation. In W. Damon (Series Ed.) & N. Eisenberg (Vol. Ed.), *Handbook of child psychology, Vol. 3. Social, emotional, and personality development* (6th ed., pp. 933–1002). New York: Wiley.

Wu, C., Chen, L., & Tsai, Y. (2009). Longitudinal invariance analysis of the satisfaction with life scale. *Personality and Individual Differences*, *46*, 396–401.

Yonezawa, S., Jones, M., & Joselowsky, F. (2009). Youth engagement in high schools: Developing a multidimensional, critical approach to improving engagement for all students. *Journal of Educational Change*, *10*, 191–209.

RELIGION, SPIRITUALITY, POSITIVE YOUTH DEVELOPMENT, AND THRIVING

Pamela Ebstyne King, Drew Carr, and Ciprian Boitor

SCHOOL OF PSYCHOLOGY, FULLER THEOLOGICAL SEMINARY,
PASADENA, CALIFORNIA, USA

Abstract

Issues of spirituality and thriving are pertinent to the period of adolescence given the marked changes in body, mind, and relationships. In order to provide an overview of the relationship between religion, spirituality, and positive youth development, this chapter offers a developmental systems perspective and proposes a relational spirituality as a framework for understanding adolescent religious and spiritual development. In

Advances in Child Development and Behavior
Richard M. Lerner, Jacqueline V. Lerner and Janette B. Benson : Editors

addition, the chapter examines various psychological mechanisms through which religion and spirituality may promote positive youth development. Existing empirical research on the relationships between adolescent religion, spirituality, thriving, and specific indicators of positive youth development is reviewed. Finally, future directions for continuing to build the field of study are discussed.

> "Spirituality affects the way we live. Spirituality means helping others."
> Sikh boy, India
> "I'm really, really passionate about justice. And I think when people look at me that's the one thing they see: I've just got loads of passion about sort of eradicating poverty ... That's motivated me. I think God's given me that passion."
> Christian girl, England
> "My spirituality motivates me to provide impassioned service, from a religion of compassion not of compulsion. I take all that is a part of who I am and put it into a life of service work. I am interested in finding the internal compassion that is the 'god' of every major religion. All religions have some concept of God and that he will always love you. I try to add to that internal compassion with my daily life."
> Humanist boy, USA
> "Spirituality means how well, to me, you can follow a set of morals that everyone pretty much has in common, and how well you can live up to I guess good standards for moral settings. So that would be a kind of spirituality. And how well you can connect with God."
> Hindu boy, USA[1]

These quotations reflect important aspects of adolescent development — spirituality and thriving. They suggest that young people search for meaning, ask questions about ultimate concerns in life, seek morals, embed themselves in religious narratives, live with passion, and endeavor to make a contribution to the greater good. They reflect an intentional pursuit of transcendence, conviction of beliefs, and making an effort to serve and give back.

Consistent with these quotations, in the past two decades, the field of developmental psychology has attempted to deepen an understanding of these domains of development. Although these distinct fields have come into their own, this chapter marks the timely and important investigation of the interrelations of religion, spirituality, and thriving (Benson, Roehlkepartain, & Scales, 2010; King & Benson, 2006; Lerner, Alberts, Anderson, & Dowling, 2006). As such, the chapter explores conceptual and theoretical distinctions and connections between spirituality and thriving, reviews existing empirical findings about the relationships between them, and points to future directions for scholarly inquiry and practice.

---

[1]These quotations originate from a study on adolescent spiritual exemplars (King, Clardy, & Ramos, 2010).

Issues of spirituality and thriving are particularly pertinent to the period of adolescence, given the marked changes in body, mind, and relationships, especially as youth endeavor to establish self-definition and belonging (King, Ramos, & Clardy, in press; Lerner, Roeser, & Phelps, 2008). As youth seek to form a meaningful identity and as they are exposed to a variety of beliefs, values, and roles, they ask existential questions and search for purpose (Damon, Menon, & Bronk, 2003; Markstrom, 1999). Additionally, adolescents not only ask the question "Who am I," but they also seek to understand to whom and where they belong (Erikson, 1950). Adaptive adolescents embark on such spiritual tasks and commit to ideals that ensure a meaningful self-concept and social connectedness.

Simultaneous to the pursuit of meaning, belonging, and identity, recent research reveals that the adolescent brain has its own formation process that may contribute to spiritual growth. During adolescence, the frontal and prefrontal cortex develop and neural connections increase (Paus, 2009). Brain development increases capacity for cognitive processes such as reflection, abstract reasoning, decision making, and processing speed. These processes are hypothesized to enable adolescents to cognitively engage with abstract narratives, meaning systems, and moral codes (Lerner et al., 2008). With growing cognitive abilities, adolescents are able to more meaningfully engage less concrete concepts such as God, an ideology, or a group of people. Thus, adolescent brain maturation may be an impetus for increased spiritual engagement.

In order to elucidate the relationship between religion, spirituality, positive youth development (PYD), and thriving, the chapter provides a survey of demographic trends of adolescent religiousness and spirituality. We delineate our understanding of important terms related to youth development, religion, and spirituality. Then, we affirm a developmental systems perspective and propose a *relational spirituality* as a framework for understanding adolescent religious and spiritual development within contemporary youth development research and discuss the connections and distinctions between PYD and spirituality. Further, the chapter examines various psychological mechanisms through which religion and spirituality may promote PYD. Then the chapter reviews the empirical research on the relationships between adolescent religion, spirituality, thriving, and specific indicators of PYD. In order to maintain a realistic and full understanding of the relationship between these domains, we will also address the potentially negative aspects of religion and spirituality during adolescence. Finally, future directions for continuing to build the field of study are discussed.

I. Demographics of Adolescent Religiousness and Spirituality

Current demographic research confirms young people's interest and participation in religion and spirituality. Although statistics varied by country, one trend suggested by the World Values Survey indicates that young adults aged 18–24 surveyed across 41 countries reported higher levels of belief in God compared to levels of importance of religion in their lives (see Lippman & Keith, 2006). Religious attendance is another indicator of adolescent religiousness and spirituality. An international study of 14-year-olds across 28 countries showed that average youth attendance is 42% in America, 14% in Western Europe, 28% in Southern Europe, 20% in Asia/Pacific regions, 13% in Northern Europe, and 10% in Eastern Europe (see Lippman & Keith, 2006).

From among the industrialized nations, the United States reported the highest rates of adolescent religion and spirituality. Two landmark nationally representative studies found that 84–87% of U.S. adolescents are affiliated with a specific religious group (Smith & Denton, 2005; Wallace, Forman, Caldwell, & Willis, 2003). Although a significant portion of U.S. youth report being engaged and valuing being religious, this is clearly not the case for all adolescents. Smith and Denton (2005) highlight that "the other half of U.S. teenagers express weak or no subjective attachment to religion and have fewer or no religious experiences" (p. 68). Among respondents, 54% of the NYSR said "very true" or "somewhat true" when asked if they considered themselves "spiritual but not religious." In short, although still relatively religious when compared to other industrialized nations, North American youth show a high degree of religious diversity and a growing number who self-identify as spiritual but not religious.

Existing statistics illustrate the complexity of religious and spiritual engagement in adolescents around the world. Although there is no set trend, it is clear that many young people across the globe are engaged in various forms of religion and spirituality. The next section provides an overview of concepts related to adolescent religiousness, spirituality, and thriving.

II. Definitions of Key Concepts

In order to provide clarity for the sake of discussion of this chapter and to encourage further study of spiritual development and thriving, this section presents our use of key terms.

A. PYD AND THRIVING

PYD is a broad interdisciplinary movement that includes both the study and practice of optimal development in young people. Thriving may be understood then as PYD's optimal developmental trajectory. Bundick, Yeager, King, and Damon (2010) defined thriving as "a dynamic and purposeful process of individual ↔ context interactions over time, through which the person and his/her environment are mutually enhanced" (p. 891). These concepts overlap in the literature and are used interchangeably in this chapter. By them, we infer four concepts foundational to PYD: an optimistic view of the child, the importance of context, a developmental and holistic perspective, and an emphasis on positive developmental outcomes (Benson, Scales, Hamilton, & Sesma, 2006; Bundick et al., 2010; Damon, 2004; Lerner, 2004, 2006).

1. Optimistic View of Child

PYD emphasizes youths' potential to grow as well as to change (Benson & Scales, 2009; Benson et al., 2006; Damon, 2004; Lerner, 2004, 2006). By emphasizing a youth's natural malleability, the potential of the child becomes a focus of study and interventions. Following, PYD is a strength-based approach in which youth develop by identifying and honing skills, competencies, and interests in a way that helps them reach their full potential. PYD also emphasizes that youth themselves play an active role in their development. Often, youth engendered development begins with the personal pursuit of a self-identified passion, or spark (Benson & Scales, 2009). As youth pursue their passion, they continue to refine their abilities to achieve their potential and experience satisfaction. From a PYD perspective, a standard of health is not merely "problem-free" nor merely competent, but emphasizes the extent to which a young person experiences optimal development.

2. Context

In addition to the positive nature of child, understanding the role of context is seminal to PYD. As such, thriving emphasizes that development occurs as a young person interacts with his or her many contexts. Positive development occurs when these interactions between person and context are mutually beneficial, maintaining healthy and positive functioning of the young person and the systems in which he or she lives. Developmental contexts (e.g., locations, relationships, community, and structures) offer youth a place to engage new roles and values through a safe environment. At their best, these contexts provide supports (e.g., relationships, opportunities, and resources) so that youth may have the tools and abilities necessary for adult life. Consequently, central to PYD is the emphasis on positive values and contribution to the greater good. Thriving emphasizes the well-being not only of the individual but also of the society (Benson et al., 2006; Bundick et al., 2010; Damon, 2004; Lerner, 2004, 2006).

3. Developmental and Holistic

PYD and thriving are developmental concepts that emphasize that the whole child is on a pathway to a hopeful future. While there is no fixed or ideal trajectory toward purposeful, relational, and healthy adulthood (Larson, 2000), thriving involves a generally stable upward trajectory across time (Bundick et al., 2010). When youth are adequately supported and scaffolded, obstacles and challenges provide opportunities for increased initiative, flexibility, and secure identity (Damon, 2004; Erikson, 1968). Recognizing the complexity of development and of the whole child, PYD entails thriving in all aspects of life and living with balance.

4. Positive Outcomes

The standard of health from a PYD perspective is more than the absence of pathology and risk behaviors; it also entails the presence of indicators of positive individual development and social contribution. Consequently, individual outcomes associated with PYD include the absence or reduction of mental illness, violence, delinquency, sexual abuse, and substance abuse as well as the presence or increase of health, life satisfaction, academic achievement, meaning, purpose, identity, altruism, and civic engagement. As such, a thriving young person is said to have personal satisfaction, a sense of purpose, and give back to the greater good of society. One helpful way to conceptualize thriving is the "Six Cs." Lerner (2004) indicated that an individual who develops Competence, Confidence, Connection, Character, and Caring over time manifests indicators of positive development. Lerner et al. (2006) research has demonstrated that the first five "Cs" predict the sixth "C," Contribution. From this perspective, the first five "Cs" as indicators of PYD promote thriving as indicated by an additional presence of the sixth "C."

B. RELIGION AND SPIRITUALITY

The meanings of religion, spirituality, and related terms also need to be addressed. As is often the case with an emerging field of study, at the time of publication of this volume, the literature on adolescent religiousness and spirituality lacked conceptual clarity. This should not be seen as a problem or weakness, but simply evidence of growth in this field. Given the interdisciplinary nature of these constructs, scholars from many disciplines have contributed to the literature in order to forge a more coherent understanding of the relationship of religion and spirituality and being human. Scholars have endeavored to understand religious and spiritual engagement, participation, and experience; the meaning of being religious and/or spiritual; the ontogeny of religious and spiritual development; spirituality as a human trait or quality; and the impact of religiousness and spirituality on human development, functioning, and coping. Given the diversity of voices participating in the scholarly dialogue, it is not surprising that ambiguity exists. Further, the multiplicity present in the literature is potentially an accurate reflection of the complexity and richness of religion and spirituality. Although it is not the aim of this chapter to provide one definitive definition, the chapter proposes an overarching framework relevant to the field of youth development.

Although a thorough review of the history of the study of adolescent religious and spiritual development is beyond the scope of this chapter on religion, spirituality, and thriving, it is important to summarize a concise overview of some of the varied and more prominent approaches to understanding the ontogeny of these transcendent domains in the lives of young people. As summarized in King & Roeser (2009; see also Oser, Scarlett, & Bucher, 2006; Scarlett & Warren, 2010), religious and spiritual development has been discussed in terms of (a) a relational system affording security and anxiety reduction (i.e., Freud, Rizzuto, Attachment Theory); (b) a meaning system addressing existential issues (i.e., Bering, Pargament, Mahoney); (c) the development of cognitive schemas indexing conceptions of religious phenomena such as prayer and God (i.e., Barrett, Bloom, Johnson); (d) the development of faith as an identity-motivation system organized around particular religious and spiritual goals, values, and ultimate concerns (i.e., Fowler); (e) social-cognitive-affective self-schemas or representations (i.e., Eccles, Roeser, Templeton); (f) states and stages of awareness that transcend ego-consciousness (i.e., Wilbur); and (g) a dynamic developmental systems perspective in which religious and spiritual development is seen in relation to multiple contexts, people, symbol systems, and opportunities and risks that foster or frustrate such development across the life span (i.e., Benson et al., 2010; King et al., in press; Lerner et al., 2006).

Despite the varied conceptual approaches, scholarship about adolescent religiousness and spirituality is not all theoretically framed. The field of psychology of religion and spirituality has proposed several definitions of religion and spirituality in order to distinguish the boundaries between the meanings of these key terms (Pargament, in press; Paloutzian & Park, 2005). Initially, the terms *religion* and *spirituality* were generally subsumed under the construct of religion (Spilka, Hood, Hunsberger, & Gorsuch, 2003). However, as the field evolved, the concepts of religion and spirituality began to diverge, both in the culture as well as in the sciences (Koenig, McCullough, & Larson, 2001; Zinnbauer & Pargament, 2005).

For example, research suggests that for the majority of the United States, there is a shift in meanings of religion and spirituality. As noted previously, research by Smith and Denton (2005) found that most American youth describe themselves as religious. However, 8% of their sample responded "very true" when asked if they considered themselves as "spiritual but not religious" and 46% said "somewhat true." It is important to note that, even though the number of people who describe themselves as "spiritual only" may be growing, a majority of the Americans continue to label themselves as both religious and spiritual (Marler & Hadaway, 2002). Although the public may not experience a tension between these two constructs, a growing distinction has emerged within the social science literature.

One prominent approach to distinguishing between religion and spirituality that has emerged in the literature is to conceptualize religion at the level of an organized sociocultural-historical system, and spirituality at the level of individuals' personal quests for meaning, satisfaction, and wisdom. For instance, a well-accepted definition refers to religion as

> ... an organized system of beliefs, practices, rituals, and symbols that serve to (a) to facilitate individuals' closeness to the sacred or transcendent other (i.e., God, higher power, ultimate truth) and (b) to bring about an understanding of an individual's relationship and responsibility to others living together in community. (Koenig et al., 2001, p.18)

From this perspective, religiousness or religiosity refers to the extent to which an individual has a relationship with a particular institutionalized doctrine about ultimate reality. This relationship occurs through affiliation with an organized religion, participation in its prescribed rituals and practices, and ascent to its espoused beliefs (Benson & Roehlkepartain, 2008).

In contrast, spirituality is defined as "a personal quest for understanding answers to ultimate questions about life, about meaning, and about relationship to the sacred or transcendent, which may (or may not) lead to or arise from the development of religious rituals and the formation of community" (Koenig et al., 2001, p. 18). This aligns with Pargament's (2007) view of personal religiousness or spirituality as a "search for the sacred" in which *the sacred* is defined in terms of individuals' concepts of God, the divine and transcendent reality, as well as other aspects of life that take on divine character or are imbued with divine-like qualities such as transcendence, immanence, boundlessness, and ultimacy (Pargament, 2007; Pargament et al., in press). It is also consistent with the frequently cited definition put forth by Benson et al. (2003):

> Spiritual development is the process of growing the intrinsic human capacity for self-transcendence, in which the self is embedded in something greater than the self, including the sacred. It is the developmental "engine" that propels the search for connectedness, meaning, purpose and contribution. It is shaped both within and outside of religious traditions, beliefs and practices. (p. 205–206)

Although the emphasis of the personal and institutional level may be helpful at pointing to potential distinctions between religion and spirituality, to overemphasize this point and dichotomize the constructs over this issue is shortsighted. Pargament et al. (in press) discuss how this limits an understanding of the complexity of both religion and spirituality. For example, when religion is viewed as purely institutional, such individual-level experiences and processes of selecting, interpreting, and constructing religious worldviews are missed. In addition, when spirituality is treated as a strictly individual phenomena, the rich and varied ways that spirituality expresses itself in intimate relationships, marriages, families, congregations, organizations, and cultures are potentially overlooked. Personal spiritual expressions are often embedded in larger religious, social, and cultural contexts. Religion and spirituality are multidimensional constructs that are made up of diverse cognitions, feelings, behaviors, experiences, and relationships and they must be considered multilevel from both theoretical and methodological perspectives.

Although, within the literature, there is growing consensus that spirituality and spiritual development involve meaningful transcendence through connection to something beyond oneself, this does not preclude these endeavors from religion or religiousness. Koenig et al. (2001) indicated that spirituality maybe either "moored" or "unmoored" to an established religious tradition. For the vast majority, the spiritual life is moored or tied to a religious tradition. Nonetheless, some individuals search for meaning to ultimate questions through unmoored sources of spirituality such as humanism and vocation in which the focal concerns center on humanity as a whole, universal ethics, and the cultivation of human potential rather than around a transcendent God.

Although these definitions bring conceptual clarity to the literature, within the field of youth development, they do not shed sufficient light onto the nature and dynamics of religious and spiritual development whether moored or unmoored to a religion. For that we turn to developmental systems theories (DST) to propose a *relational spirituality* that emphasizes the transcendence, fidelity, and behaviors that result from the relations between person and context.

III. A Developmental Systems Perspective on Religious and Spiritual Development

Given the emergent nature of the field, providing a theoretical footing is timely and, further, necessary for the field to move forward. To provide a theoretically based understanding of adolescent religious and spiritual development, we propose a developmental systems perspective as a helpful framework for understanding religious and spiritual development among diverse young people.

Foundational to DST is the significance of the relations between *person* and *context*. From this perspective, development occurs through the mutual interactions between individuals and the contexts in which they live. Thus, it is important to consider both the uniqueness of the individual or person and their larger systems or contexts. From a DST perspective, religious and spiritual development occurs through ongoing transactions between individuals and their multiple embedded sociocultural contexts of development (Lerner et al., 2006). DST is useful when considering adolescent religious and spiritual development because it presents a lens through which to observe the complex relations between individuals, their families, their cultures, and their religious traditions.

As such, religious development refers to the systematic changes in how one understands and participates in the doctrines, practices, and rituals of a religious institution. Spiritual development also occurs through a young person's interactions with the contexts in which he or she lives over time. However, given the general nature of spiritual development, it is not necessarily tied to the beliefs, relationships, or practices that are rooted in established religious traditions. Spiritual development refers to a broader domain of development that is experienced by all youth, regardless of whether they are a part of a religious tradition or not.

From a developmental systems perspective, spiritual development occurs in the ongoing transactions between people and their multiple embedded contexts. It is through these interactions that young people experience something of significance beyond themselves and gain a growing sense of transcendence. They may become aware of and feel connected to God or a divine entity, a sense of all of humanity, a specific religious community, peers, or perhaps even to nature. Lerner et al. (2008) described this as shifting a young person's cognitive and emotional orientation from the self to a transcendent other. Such experiences are spiritual when they are imbued with meaning that goes beyond provincialism or materialism and expresses authentic concerns about the world (Reich, 1998). As such, spiritual transcendence provides meaning and serves to motivate contribution to the well-being of the world beyond themselves. From this perspective, the interaction between the self and some form of other that informs one's beliefs and commitments and propels the young person to live in a manner mindful of others is seminal to spiritual development.

Erikson (1965, 1968) described this phenomenon as fidelity. He argued that youth who successfully resolve the identity crisis gain the virtue of fidelity, which is a sense of loyalty to an ideology that engages younger people in the world beyond themselves (King & Roeser, 2009; Lerner et al., 2006, 2008). Spirituality is more than a feeling of transcendence, but a growing sense of identity or awareness, that motivates or propels young people to care for themselves and to contribute to the greater good. As such, spiritual development involves transcendence, fidelity, and generative actions.

It is important to note that as discussed previously, spiritual development is not limited to religious contexts, but may occur in other contexts such as political groups, social group, or nature. It is when these experiences, activities, or affiliations take on larger meaning and enable youth to move beyond their daily concerns and connect with something bigger than themselves in a meaningful way that simultaneously promotes optimal individual development and commitment to the common good that they become spiritual enterprises. Such engagements may promote transcendent experiences that lead to spirituality development and thriving.

IV. Intersection of Spirituality and Thriving

Relational spirituality emphasizes that spiritual development occurs in the ongoing relations between people and their multiple embedded contexts. From this perspective, the heart of spiritual development lies in the interaction between the self and another that informs one's beliefs and commitments and motivates the young person to live in a manner mindful of others. Given that defining features of PYD also include social connections, positive values, and giving back to society (Benson et al., 2006; Bundick et al., 2010; Damon, 2004; Lerner, 2006), it is useful to examine the differences between spirituality and PYD. From a DST perspective, positive development can be observed within the mutually beneficial relationships between a young person and the many contexts in which he or she lives and is marked by a thriving individual and community.

Spiritual development specifically involves growing in transcendence, fidelity, and prosocial behaviors. Spiritual development refers to experiences of transcendence that shapes a young person's beliefs and behaviors. As such, spirituality may serve as the fuel that propels an individual's commitments to contribution, markers of PYD, and thriving. A thriving young person is on the pathway to a hopeful future, living up to his or her potential and experiencing life satisfaction, and contributes to the greater good. Spirituality is both a cognitive and emotional orientation that directs and motivates behaviors that are indicative of thriving. If thriving is the process of being and becoming a person who contributes to both self and society, spirituality provides the impetus to make and sustain such commitments by growing in the meaningful connections to something beyond the self that inspires devotion not only to a worldview but also to action consistent with one beliefs and values.

What then distinguishes these constructs? Is all adaptive developmental regulation spiritual development? Clearly, the conceptualizations presented in this chapter suggest shared pathways of spiritual and positive development. They both involve a convergence of cognitive, affective, and behavioral qualities (Spiewak & Sherrod, 2010). Perhaps, their uniqueness lies in the meaning of the transaction between individual and context. Specifically, spiritual development involves transactions with "something beyond the self," which maybe ideological, social, or supernatural (King, 2008). Although this does not need to be an expression of the divine to instigate spiritual development, it is imbued with divine-like qualities, such as transcendence, immanence, boundlessness, and ultimacy (Pargament et al., in press), and provides meaning beyond the mundane and material and has ultimate value. Consequently, spiritual development does not stem from any positive interactions between a person and their context, but rather it is those transactions marked by transcendence that bring about meaning and beliefs that motivate and sustain a commitment to contributing to self and other. As such, spirituality provides the direction and motivation to thrive and flourish.

V. The Influence of Religion and Spirituality on Positive Development

Although there are differences between the constructs, from a developmental systems perspective, religion and spirituality are closely aligned with PYD. The following section summarizes existing conceptual explanations for why religion and spirituality may be important developmental contexts for young people. In addition to discussing the important role of the ideological and social resources potentially embedded within religion and spirituality, which are more typically addressed in the literature, we also explore the transcendent resources that may offer unique benefits to youth.

A. IDEOLOGICAL CONTEXT

Young people strive to make sense of the world and to assert their place in it. The beliefs, worldviews, and values of religious traditions and spiritualities provide an ideological context in which a young person can generate a sense of meaning, order, and place in the world that is crucial to adolescent development (King, 2008). Erikson (1965) pointed to religion as an important aspect of the sociohistorical matrix in which identity takes shape. He argued that religion is the oldest and most lasting institution that promotes fidelity. Religion intentionally offers beliefs, moral codes, and values from which a young person can build a personal belief system (Smith, 2003b). Spiritual development entails the intentional identification and integration of beliefs, narrative, and values in the processes of identity formation, making meaning, and seeking purpose—all foundational to PYD.

Studies of individuals nominated for moral excellence suggest the importance of religious beliefs and moral directions formative among many nominees. Colby and Damon (1999) found that most of the moral exemplars in their study claimed that faith commitments played a significant role in their moral lives. The authors suggested that religion acts as a unifying construct in the lives of those with a salient moral identity, promoting the integration of personal goals and moral concerns. Hart and Fegley (1995) made a similar observation noting the positive role of religion in the lives of youth recognized for their remarkable commitment to caring and contributions to others. In addition, Larson, Hansen, and Moneta (2006) found that youth involved in faith-based youth programs were significantly more likely to be engaged in higher rates of identity work than youth not engaged in faith-based programs. Further, they found that 75% of youth in faith-based programs reported that "We discussed morals and values," compared with 24% of youth involved in other types of organized youth programs. In addition, King and Furrow (2004) found that adolescent religiousness was associated with having significantly more shared beliefs, values, and expectations with parents, friends, and adults. Further, another study on pupils at Dutch Christian secondary schools found that the students' religiously grounded education was associated with a commitment to a certainty of one's worldview (Bertram-Troost, de Roos, & Miedema, 2009).

B. SOCIAL CONTEXT

Religion and spirituality not only provide a transcendent worldview, but also a context in which community members more or less embody these ideological norms in a community setting and thereby act as role models for youth (Erikson, 1968). Although religion and spirituality do not exclusively offer these social resources, research documents that they may be particularly effective in offering social capital, helpful networks, social support, and mentors.

Social capital models posit that religion's constructive influence on young people may be accounted for by the nature and number of relationships—and the benefits associated with them. For instance, through religious involvement, young people have access to intergenerational relationships that are recognized as rich sources of social capital (King & Furrow, 2004; Putnam, 2000; Smith, 2003a). Few other social institutions afford the opportunity to build trustworthy cross-generational relationships and link youth to sources of helpful information, resources, and opportunities. King and Furrow (2004) found that religiously engaged youth reported significantly higher levels of social capital resources than less active youth. In addition, secondary analysis of the Survey of Youth and Parents yielded results substantiating that congregations promote *network closure*, providing dense social networks within which youth are embedded, offering oversight of and information about youth to their parents (Smith, 2003b). This approach suggests that the social support available through religion is particularly effective for promoting thriving.

Religious institutional involvement may also involve social channeling, the conscious process on the part of adults to steer their children toward particular individuals positioned to discourage negative behaviors and promote positive life practices among young people (Smith, 2003b). Research shows that social channeling in congregations has been helpful to promote both spiritual development and general positive development (Martin, White, & Perlman, 2003). For example, Regnerus and Elder (2003) found that for youth in urban, low-income neighborhoods, church attendance is especially important because it channels youth into relationships with those who support academics and who help them build "a transferable skill set of commitments and routines" (p. 646). Similarly, a recent study found that religious involvement served as a protective factor by encouraging less contact with deviant peers and more contact with parents and school officials (Schreck, Burek, & Clark-Miller, 2007).

Religious institutions and the relationships they afford also provide forms of social support that are particularly important to adolescent coping, resilience, and well-being. Two studies of adolescents showed that social support of religious community members was the strongest negative predictor of depressive symptoms (Miller & Gur, 2002; Pearce, Little, & Perez, 2003). Findings showed that expectations of social support from congregations in times of need were associated with less depressive symptoms, but that expectations that congregations were critical of teenagers was associated with increased depressive symptoms. Thus, religious communities can be sources of social support or socioemotional distress based on the ways adults in those communities perceive and relate to youth.

Spiritual modeling and mentorship are two other ways theorists have discussed how adults socialize young people's religious and spiritual identities in the direction of the beliefs, norms, and expectations of a particular religious group. Spiritual modeling refers to emulating another in order to grow spiritually (Oman, Flinders, & Thoresen, 2008). This occurs through observing and imitating the life or conduct of a spiritual example or model who may be a living or historic example of religious or spiritual ideology and values. Spiritual modeling is based on social modeling and observational learning in the acquisition and maintaining of human behaviors (Bandura, 2003). Foundational to this approach is the notion that the people with whom we regularly associate shape the behavioral patterns that will be repeatedly observed and learned most thoroughly.

Religious and spiritual contexts are often intentional about mentoring its younger members (Schwartz, Bukowski, & Aoki, 2006). For example, the Hindu tradition has gurus, the Jewish tradition sages, and the Christian tradition elders. Through these intentional relationships, adults connect youth to a larger whole, enabling them to identify with a community beyond himself or herself (Schwartz, 2006). King and Furrow (2004) found that religious youth reported higher levels of trust, social interaction, and shared values with adults outside the family than their less religious peers. Larson et al. (2006) found that youth involved in faith-based youth programs were significantly more likely to be engaged in positive relationships and in adult networks than youth not engaged in faith-based programs. A study on Somali refugees found that youth went to religious figures and school personnel for support when troubled versus accessing mental health services (Ellis et al., 2010).

The developmental asset framework also provides a helpful way to conceptualize the potential resources available to youth through religious and spiritual involvement. Through secondary analyses, Search Institute looked at the developmental resources or *assets* (see Chapter 8) embedded within a congregation that may contribute to positive outcomes in young people. Wagener, Furrow, King, Leffert, and Benson (2003) found that the positive benefits of adolescent religiousness were partially mediated through developmental assets available to these youth. Although the study found that religious variables have some independent effect on risk behaviors, the study showed that the positive benefits of religion were significantly mediated by these assets.

C. TRANSCENDENT CONTEXT

Religion and spirituality not only provide important ideological resources and social relationships that nurture positive development, but they also provide opportunities for transcendent experiences. Transcendence, connecting with something beyond the self in such a way that brings about deeper awareness of one's self and others, is generally intentionally nurtured in religious and spiritual communities. Although the literature available is small, it suggests that transcendence has a positive association with beneficial outcomes. The following studies are not all youth samples, but nonetheless provide insight into the potential relationship between adolescence and transcendence.

Yates and Youniss (1996) found that participating in community service within a religious context was associated with increased levels of transcendence, in which participants moved from an increased awareness of their similarity to those whom they served, to a more abstract awareness of systemic issues such as poverty, justice, and social inequality. Li (2008) explored the moderating effects of self-transcendent meaning for college students in Beijing from Buddhist backgrounds. Outcomes moderated by self-transcendence were negative associations with mental health problems and a positive association with self-esteem. One study by Bean and Wagner (2006) of adult patients with liver cancer found that self-transcendence was associated with increased quality of life, perceived distress due to illness, and self-reported health status. These studies suggest that experiences of transcendence serve to promote positive outcomes and coping.

These preliminary studies suggest a correlation between transcendence and positive outcomes and coping; however, they do not shed much light on the mechanisms behind the relationship. Recent exploratory research examining the nature of spiritual development suggests that being aware of and connected to something larger than the self is an important part of spirituality. Transcendence may affirm one's own sense of identity and self-worth through a profound sense of connection to a divine or ultimate other. In a recent qualitative study on spiritually exemplary youth, a boy nominated for living with profound spirituality in Kenya described this sentiment, "Knowing that I'm actually a child of the Most High God, I find that I'm actually a bit special" (King et al., 2010). In an affiliated international quantitative study of youth, initial findings suggest that awareness of one's inherent value and strength is a common aspect of spirituality among youth from eight different countries (Benson et al., 2010).

In addition, youth may experience transcendence through connection to specific others. For example, as young people participate in religious congregations, they may locate themselves as members of a historic tradition. An American exemplar explained, "Well, we're [the Jews] a people who suffer. That's who we are and what we do. I get my social consciousness, my beliefs, my view of humanity from my Jewish traditions" (King et al., 2010). Similarly, Benson et al. (2010) found that having a sense that life is interconnected and interdependent is a factor of adolescent spirituality.

Not limited to religious traditions are experiences of transcendence that occur in nature. Encountering the majesty of creation or being sensually aroused through the esthetics of nature may offer experiences of boundlessness and ultimacy (Pargament et al., in press) that may inspire perspective on one's sense of self or one's life. Spiritual experiences in nature may promote positive development by nurturing identity formation, a sense of purpose, and/or well-being. In the study on youth spiritual exemplars, a Catholic boy from India described his general connection to God in the out of doors, "Just being in this world, just in that place where there are trees and the beaches, I just feel the presence of God in those places." Benson, Scales and Roehlepartain (2010) also identify this sense of awareness of the world as one of the four factors of spirituality.

Spirituality promotes transcendence through ritual, whether through worship, spiritual practices, or rites of passage. Ongoing worship rituals may promote one's awareness of divine or human other as well as confirm one's place in a community. In the exemplar study, a Hindu boy from India talked about rituals in this way: "It's because of the ceremonies, which are held, and it makes people come together... and then sometimes you get a connection with God, a special time with God" (King et al., 2010). A qualitative study of the experience of nine Jewish boys indicates that the Bar Mitzvah may strengthen the individual's sense of worth and his confidence in performing new roles and serve as way to encourage important relationships with mentors outside the family (Zegans & Zegans, 1979). Such rites of passage are unique events that intentionally celebrate and affirm a young person's sense of identity as a believer as well as recognize their place within their faith community potentially contributing to both personal development and a commitment to something beyond themselves.

Spiritual practices or disciplines also promote experiences of transcendence. Smith and Denton (2005) found that 10% of all youth reported practicing religious or spiritual meditation, during the prior year. The practice of meditation promotes the realization of higher states of awareness and unity with others (Roeser, 2005). A growing body of research reflects potential benefits of spiritual practices. One qualitative study with families from the Latter Day Saints found that daily Bible study and prayer had specific perceived benefits for the members of these families: increased spiritual growth, stronger familial relationships, greater family cohesiveness, better communication, and better parenting (Loser, Hill, & Klein, 2009).

These experiences of transcendence may promote key facets of positive development. This moving beyond the self provides the opportunity for the search for meaning and belonging that is central to PYD (Damon et al., 2003). Awareness that stems from this search provides ultimate answers and perspective in the larger issues of life that are crucial to the resolution of the adolescent identity crisis (Erikson, 1965). Devotion, responsibility, and commitment inspired by transcendence may play an important role in both motivating and sustaining an altruistic or generative life style. Spirituality provides opportunities to experience a profound sense of connectedness with either supernatural or human other that invokes a sense of awareness of self in relation to other. This heightened consciousness of others often triggers an understanding of self and sense of fidelity that is intertwined and responsible to the other. This attentiveness usually promotes a manner of living that is carried out with the highest regard to the life of self, others, and/or the divine. As the Fetzer Institute (1999) wrote, "Spirituality can call us beyond self to concern and compassion for others" (p. 2). Consequently, the transcendent quality of spirituality is especially pertinent to shaping a commitment to contributing to the common good within young people and thriving.

The various environments in which youth live will foster positive development insofar as they offer clear ideology, social resources, and transcendent experiences. Whether secular or faith based, settings can promote spiritual development by enabling young people on the quest for self-awareness, meaning, purpose—shaping their core identity and their place in their families, communities, and the larger world. Perhaps, the most unique aspect of spirituality is the potential for transcendence. Many youth programs and organizations offer ideological and rich social environments, but few intentionally promote experiences of transcendence, where a young person acutely experiences an entity beyond themselves in such a way that transforms their ideological commitments, inspires devotion, and shapes generative behavior. That said, relationships, programs, and institutions that provide clear beliefs, moral directives, and values; peer and adult relationships that model and reinforce these prosocial norms; and experiences that move young people beyond their daily concerns and connect them with something beyond themselves, are apt to nurture youth on such a quest. Such influences may therefore enhance adolescent development more generally.

VI. Correlates of Religion, Spirituality and PYD

A growing body of literature documents the role of religious and spiritual factors associated with various elements of PYD and thriving. Generally, this research establishes a dual role of religion and spirituality as a protective factor inhibiting risk-taking behavior as well as a factor that promotes positive developmental outcomes, including prosocial behavior and academic achievement. Several syntheses of this literature have been published (Bridges & Moore, 2002; King & Benson, 2006; King & Roeser, 2009). The following section overviews existing literature on associations between adolescent religiousness and spirituality and various indicators related to thriving.

A. THRIVING AND PYD

Currently, religion and spirituality are rarely distinguished as unique variables, making it difficult to discern the unique effects of these different factors. Religious variables dominate the current literature. An exception is work by Dowling et al. (2004), where adolescent spirituality and religiosity were distinctly operationalized. They found that spirituality and religiousness are both associated with thriving. Secondary analysis of Search Institute's Youth and Their Parents dataset found that spirituality and religion both had direct effects on thriving. In this case, spirituality was defined as experiencing transcendence, defining self in relationship to others, and having genuine concern for others, and religion was defined as institutional affiliation and participation with a religious tradition and doctrine. In addition, religion mediated the effects of spirituality on thriving. These findings suggest that spirituality and religiousness may both play unique roles in the development of thriving.

1. Health

A number of studies suggest that religion and spirituality may promote overall adolescent physical health. Church attendance has been found to be a key factor in promoting health-enhancing behaviors, such as exercise, diet, dental hygiene, and seat belt use (Jessor, Turbin, & Costa, 1998). Using a large nationally representative sample of high school seniors, another study demonstrated that religious youth are more likely to take care of themselves through proper nutrition, exercise, and rest, and less likely to engage in health-compromising behaviors (Wallace & Forman, 1998). In one study that emphasized looking at spiritual practices over religious variables, Barnes, Johnson, and Treiber (2004) found that the practice of mediation was associated with reduced ambulatory blood pressure among African American adolescents.

2. Mental Health and Coping

The literature suggests that religion provides adolescents with important coping strategies in dealing with their problems (Mahoney, Pendleton, & Ihrke, 2006). Those adolescents who valued church attendance and religion in general experienced fewer feelings of depression, loneliness, and hopelessness (Pearce, Little, et al., 2003; Schapman & Inderbitzen-Nolan, 2002; Sinha, Cnaan, & Gelles, 2007; Smith & Denton, 2005; Wright & Frost, 1993). For example, one study of Jewish adolescents found that they used three distinct religious coping strategies. They tended to reframe their difficulties from a spiritual perspective, draw on their Jewish cultural relationships, and pray to God (Dubow, Pargament, Boxer, & Tarakeshwar, 2000). In a similar study, African American students who were more religious were less likely to appropriate derogatory societal messages regarding the African American community (Brega & Coleman, 1999).

Besides protective qualities, religiosity and spirituality may promote positive mental health. For example, adolescent religiousness and spirituality have been shown to be correlated with life satisfaction (Kelley & Miller, 2007; Varon & Riley, 1999) and happiness (Abdel-Khalek, 2007). Several studies spanning Spain, the United States, and Germany found a positive correlation between church attendance, reported salience of religion, and self-esteem (Donahue, 1995; Smith, Weigert, & Thomas, 1979). Besides improved self-esteem, adolescents that reported spiritual aspirations reported more positive emotions including vitality and zest (Leak, DeNeve, & Greteman, 2007).

3. Academic Achievement

Several studies have added to the body of literature on the relationship between religious and spiritual development and school performance. Several studies demonstrated that religious attendance and salience have a modest positive association with academic performance (Benson, Scales, Sesma, & Roehlkepartain, 2005; Muller & Ellison, 2001; Regnerus, 2000). Religiosity also seems to predict likelihood of higher education. A longitudinal study found that religiousness in high school adolescents was associated with completion of a bachelor's degree even when locus of control, self-concept, parental involvement, and prior academic achievement were controlled for (Lee, Puig, & Clark, 2007).

4. Civic Engagement and Moral Development

Central to PYD is youth contribution to the greater good. Several studies indicate that various attitudes and behaviors related to generative action, such as community service and altruism, are positively related to religion and spirituality (Kerestes, Youniss, & Metz, 2004; Youniss, McLellan, & Yates, 1999). For example, several studies showed that more religious youth were significantly more likely to be involved in various forms of civic engagement than their less religious peers (Crystal & DeBell, 2002; Serow & Dreyden, 1990). King and Furrow (2004) found that religious salience and religious attendance were correlated with altruism and empathy; structural equation models revealed that social capital resources mediated the effects of religion on these moral outcomes. Another study demonstrated that religious identity was positively associated with personal meaning and a prosocial concern for others (Furrow, King, & White, 2004). As noted earlier, studies of individuals nominated for moral excellence also report religion as an important influence on their moral commitments of caring and justice (Colby & Damon 1999; Hart & Fegley, 1995). In an effort to understand what aspects of religion influence adherents to participate in volunteer service, a study of college undergraduates revealed that the best predictor of intention to repeat volunteer service was intrinsic motivation to volunteer which was associated with prayer styles and a personal relationship with God (Ozorak, 2003).

5. Identity

As discussed in the previous section, religion and spirituality contribute to thriving by directly influencing identity development. Several studies provide support for the argument that religion can function as a resource in positive identity development among youth. Youniss et al. (1999) demonstrated that community service conducted in religious contexts nourished identity development. Related to identity, Tzuriel (1984) found that religiously involved youth reported higher levels of commitment when compared to less religiously engaged youth. Fulton (1997) noted that intrinsic forms of religiousness were more likely linked to identity achievement than extrinsic or utilitarian forms of religiousness. Several studies explored the relationship between various aspects of religiousness and Marcia's (1966) categories of identity commitments. Although these studies demonstrate the complexity of religion's influence throughout adolescence, overall the studies suggest that religion is correlated with identity (Hunsberger, Pratt, & Pancer, 2001; Kiesling, Sorell, Montgomery, & Colwell, 2008; Markstrom, 1999; Markstrom-Adams & Smith, 1996; Markstrom-Adams, Hofstra, & Dougher, 1994).

6. Meaning and Purpose

Development along religious and spiritual dimensions seems to shape adolescents' search for and construction of a sense of purpose, meaning, and fidelity to certain beliefs (Chamberlain & Zika, 1992; Francis, 2000; Roeser, Issac, Abo-Zena, Brittian, & Peck, 2008; Tzuriel, 1984). In a study on spiritual strivings and psychological health, findings suggest that strivings that transcend the self were positively associated with intentional growth toward a sense of purpose (Leak et al., 2007). Several studies found that youth who participated in religious communities tended to report awareness of a sense of purpose (Hart & Fegley, 1995; Markstrom, 1999). Similarly, another study found that religion was an important source of construction of meaning for adolescents participating in a Christian summer camp (Showalter & Wagener, 2000). A qualitative study found that spirituality and religiosity appeared to serve as a guide for some adolescents toward development of specific intents such as character development, service, and a general life purpose (Mariano & Damon, 2008).

B. RISK-TAKING BEHAVIORS

A significant body of research demonstrates that religion and spirituality may buffer against risk-taking behavior such as delinquency, substance abuse, sexual activity, substance use, and suicide. The youth are still likely to engage in such behavior but to a lesser degree than their nonreligiously oriented peers.

1. Delinquency

The inverse relationship between religiosity and delinquent behavior among adolescents has also been well established (Baier & Wright, 2001). Adolescent religiosity has also been linked to lower delinquent and violent problem behavior (Johnson, Jang, Larson, & De Li, 2001; Regnerus & Elder, 2003). For instance, a national probability sample found that youth aged 13–18 who considered religion to be influential in their lives and attended church frequently were 50% less likely to engage in serious fighting than their nonreligious peers (Sloane & Potvin, 1986). Johnson et al. (2001) found that adolescent religiosity was negatively correlated with adolescents' attitudes toward delinquent behaviors, their association with delinquent peers, and their engagement in delinquent behaviors after controlling for their socio-demographic backgrounds. Pearce, Jones, Schwab-Stone, and Ruchkin (2003) found that frequent exposure to religious content (e.g., reading, watching, or hearing religious information) decreased the likelihood of antisocial practices, witnessing violence, or being the victim of violence. In a nationally representative sample of youth in grades 7–12, Regnerus and Elder (2003) found evidence for a cyclical trend in the relationship between adolescent religiosity and delinquency. In this sample, religiosity was related to a slight decrease in delinquent behaviors in early adolescence, disappeared as a predictor of delinquent behaviors during middle adolescence, and emerged as a stronger negative predictor in late adolescence.

2. Substance Use

Youth who were religious were less likely than their nonreligious peers to drink in excess, smoke cigarettes daily, drink alcohol weekly, or smoke marijuana (Sinha et al., 2007). A caveat to this finding was that there was a sexual orientation effect in which religiosity did not seem to buffer against substance use for gay, lesbian, and transgendered youth as it did for heterosexual youth (Rostosky, Danner, & Riggle, 2007). A nationally representative longitudinal study demonstrated that importance of religion was more predictive of abstinence from marijuana use than social control or involvement in religious institutions (Longest & Vaisey, 2008). In comparing private religiosity and public religiosity, Nonnemaker, McNeely, and Blum (2006) found that private religiosity was a stronger protector against substance use. There may be a developmental component to how youth interact with the protective effects of religion and spirituality. Religion also seemed to reinforce cultural prohibitions against alcohol use and smoking tobacco for adolescents in Asian (specifically Punjabi) cultures when compared to non-Asians (Bradby & Williams, 2006).

3. Sexual Activity

Those adolescents who attend church regularly and value religion are more likely to assent to the importance of sexual abstinence until marriage than nonreligious peers, even though their beliefs may not be congruent with their actions (Smith & Denton, 2005). Despite the higher prevalence of the belief in the importance of sexual abstinence, religious youth are still likely to be sexually active but to a lesser degree than peers for whom religion is not salient (Donahue & Benson, 1995; Lammers, Ireland, Resnick, & Blum, 2000) For example, adolescent identification with religion at the age of 15 seemed to be a predictor of delayed sexual activity, in a longitudinal study measuring sexual activity at the age of 15 and then 21 (Rostosky, Regnerus, & Wright, 2003). The positive outcomes of lesser degree of sexual experience and assent to conservative attitudes regarding sexual activity held true across various cultures including Latin American, African American, European American, and Caucasian participants (Bridges & Moore, 2002; Edwards, Fehring, Jarrett, & Haglund, 2008).

4. Suicide Risk

Adolescents can be at risk for suicide when they struggle with feelings of worthlessness. Multiple studies have noted the correlation between religious affiliation and lower rates of suicide (Baker & Gorsuch, 1982; Gartner, Larson, & Allen, 1991; Sturgeon & Hamley, 1979; Trovato, 1992). Church attendance, importance of religion, and spiritual practices correlate with decreased suicidal ideations and attempts (Donahue & Benson, 1995; Jamieson & Romer, 2008; Nonnemaker et al., 2006). Religious and spiritual development appears to provide a crucial buffer against the risk of suicide.

In sum, the current literature paints a clear picture of the positive relationship between adolescent religious and spiritual development and indictors of thriving and reduced levels of various risk behaviors. Participating in various forms of religion and spirituality is clearly linked to higher levels of positive outcomes and lower levels of dangerous activities among young people. In order to maintain a realistic and full understanding, we turn to addressing the potentially negative aspects of religion and spirituality during adolescence.

VII. Negative Aspects of Religion and Spirituality

While there is ample evidence to support religion and spirituality as a resource for PYD, it is important to recognize that they are multivalent constructs that do not always promote thriving (Pargament et al., in press). Central to thriving is optimal development of both the individual and the contexts in which they live. Thus, if religion or spirituality causes detriment to either individual or societal well-being, then such expressions of religion and/or spirituality are deleterious. Both religion and spirituality have been documented to be a source of both significant personal and social distress (Oser et al., 2006; Wagener & Malony, 2006).

Many of the assertions of this chapter are predicated on the assumption that experiences of transcendence are positive and nurture a positive self-concept and prosocial values. Religious or spiritual experiences that inhibit personal growth or that inculcate a negative sense of personal identity are not conducive to thriving. Extreme religious groups that may elevate the identity and the needs of the group while devaluing the individual can hinder adolescent development. Religious environments that do not allow for adequate exploration, such as questioning and expressing religious doubt, during adolescence may also thwart optimal development. In addition, negative worldviews and perceptions of God can cause significant personal distress (Mahoney et al., 2006).

Thriving is also dependent on a prosocial ideology that nurtures a sense of moral and civic identity (Lerner et al., 2006). If the sources of transcendence do not engender a commitment to contribution to the greater good, they are negative spiritual influences. For example, religious or spiritual environments that use religion to encourage violence through ideology and example do not promote thriving. Religious expressions that encourage an "in-group" and promote suspicion or hostilities to others also run counter to PYD and are a detriment to society (Templeton & Eccles, 2008). Specifically, prejudice has been identified as a value that some religions endorse (Hunsberger et al., 2001). Studies also have linked religious fundamentalism and right-wing authoritarianism to ethnocentrism and prejudice (Hunsberger & Jackson, 2005).

The developmental systems perspective of religious and spiritual development proposed in this chapter provides a lens through which to understand when religion and spirituality may be deleterious. Specifically, we propose a relational spirituality that emphasizes the reciprocating relationship between an individual and the many contexts in which they live. When these relations between religious and spiritual contexts and the young person are not mutually beneficial, they are not conducive to thriving.

VIII. Future Directions

This volume, dedicated to the science of youth development, makes evident the prominence to which the study of thriving and PYD has arrived. The inclusion of this chapter also affirms the legitimacy of the study of adolescent religious and spiritual development as a salient aspect of human ontogeny. Although these distinct fields have come into their own, this chapter marks the timely and important investigation of the interrelations of religion, spirituality, and thriving (Benson et al., 2010; King & Benson, 2006; Lerner et al., 2008). Although religion and spirituality are multivalent constructs, contemporary approaches to youth development emphasize that religion and spirituality are potentially rich and fertile sources of positive development and thriving.

In order to continue to move the field forward, there are important conceptual and methodological tasks ahead. Although the literature reflects increased conceptual clarity, there is still much ambiguity in terms related to religion and spirituality. More nuanced knowledge is required to better elucidate the precise individual and contextual relations that account for adolescent religious and spiritual development and the positive outcomes associated with it. Currently, the literature most aptly addresses the social context of religion and spirituality and their potential for positive development through approaches such as social capital and developmental assets. The existing research is less clear on how ideology factors into both religious and spiritual development and thriving. How exactly do the worldviews, values, and moral order available through religion and spirituality help young people navigate through the waters of adolescence? What are the effects of ideologies that are not consistent or in conflict with family or ethnic culture?

Even less clear are conceptualizations and attempts to operationalize transcendence. Although there is growing consensus on the connection and awareness of something beyond the self and the meaning and motivation that ensues from it, the nature of the "something" is still largely debated (Benson et al., 2010; Lerner et al., 2006; Pargament, 2007). Concepts like "boundless" and "ultimate" are often used, but it is important to explore whether there is a threshold to what makes an engagement, pursuit, or relationship qualify as transcendent. As argued in this chapter, not all relations between a person and an element of their context are deemed spiritual, but those that give ultimate value and meaning are. Research needs to explore if there are varying degrees of transcendence? In other words, does the extent to which something is boundless, ultimate, or transcendent have the potential for more influence—for good or for bad? Does the perception of a relation involving a construct at the philosophical versus the supernatural level make a difference? Or is it the value of the relationship, rather than the entity being related to make a more significant difference?

In order to answer these questions, adequate measures are greatly needed. In addition to being theoretically grounded, measures need to assess the most salient dimensions of adolescent religiousness and spirituality. Current measures emphasize religious factors (i.e., religious salience, attendance, beliefs) and theistic traditions, while spiritual dimensions have been less frequently pursued in youth. That said, there are new measures and approaches being explored and developed (Benson et al., 2010; King, 2011; Lerner et al., 2011; Underwood & Teresi, 2002). These endeavors not only take on broader conceptualizations of spirituality that include transcendence, but they also explore these concepts among diverse populations.

Much of the existing research focuses on Judeo-Christian European American youth from the United States. Much less is known scientifically about spiritual or religious development in other cultures and traditions (Mattis, Ahluwalia, Cowie, & Kirkland-Harris, 2006). This emphasis on Western expressions of theistic religions does not capture the breadth and depth of religious and spiritual expressions found in other contexts such as more communal cultures, in nontheistic spiritualities, and specifically Easter traditions. Given that religion and spirituality are key facets of ethnicity, race, and culture (Mattis et al., 2006), a key direction for future research concerns the intersection among young people's developing ethnic/racial, cultural, and religious and spiritual identities in shaping patterns of positive or problematic youth development. New research in this area would enhance our understanding of the roles that religion and spirituality can play in the positive development of ethnically, racially, and culturally diverse youth.

There is also a great need for longitudinal research in this area. Understanding the developmental precursors and sequelae of religious and spiritual development will be critical for untangling patterns of influence and pathways of continuity and change in this aspect of human development. Some of the most comprehensive studies to date remain cross-sectional in design (e.g., Benson et al., 2005; Lerner et al., 2008; Smith & Denton, 2005). A focus on particular subgroups of interest such as those who are particularly spiritually precocious, those who undergo conversion experiences, or those who leave religion and decide they are atheists may be one way that such studies may advance understanding of not only normative but diverse patterns of religious and spiritual development across adolescence.

IX. Conclusions

Hopefully, the not too distant future will see the rise of creative and rigorous methodologies that will begin to answer some of the questions raised in this chapter regarding the relationship between religion, spirituality, and PYD. As the field continues to explore this dynamic relationship, we affirm a developmental systems perspective and propose a *relational spirituality* that emphasizes the richness of the interactions between a young person and their contexts. For it is in these relations that youth experience something beyond themselves that gives meaning and motivates a life of contribution. The ideological, social, and transcendent resources available through religion and spirituality elucidate how spirituality promotes a fertile ground for PYD. At their best, religion and spirituality provides an environment where youth can experience the self-embedded within a larger context that simultaneously validates the inherent value of the self as well as promotes a sense of belonging and connectedness beyond the self. When ideological, social, and transcendent contexts are activated, religion and spirituality serve as a potent aspect of the developmental system, where young people can thrive and flourish as individuals and sustain commitments to the common good.

REFERENCES

Abdel-Khalek, A. M. (2007). Religiosity, happiness, health, and psychopathology in a probability sample of Muslim adolescents. *Mental Health, Religion & Culture, 10*, 571–583. doi:10.1080/13674670601034547.

Baier, C. J., & Wright, B. R. E. (2001). If you love me keep my commandments: A meta-analysis of the effect of religon on crime. *Journal of Research in Crime and Delinquency, 38*, 3–21.

Baker, M., & Gorsuch, R. (1982). Trait anxiety and intrinsic-extrinsic religiousness. *Journal for the Scientific Study of Religion, 21*, 119.

Bandura, A. (2003). On the psychosocial impact and mechanisms of spiritual modeling. *The International Journal for the Psychology of Religion, 13*, 167–173.

Barnes, V., Johnson, M., & Treiber, F. (2004). Temporal stability of twenty-four-hour ambulatory hemodynamic bioimpedance measures in African American adolescents. *Blood Pressure Monitoring, 9*, 173–177.

Bean, K. B., & Wagner, K. (2006). Self-transcendence, illness, distress, and quality of life among liver transplant recipients. *The Journal of Theory Construction and Testing, 10*, 47–53.

Benson, P. L., & Roehlkepartain, E. C. (2008). Spiritual development: A mission priority in youth development. In P. L. Benson, E. C. Roehlkepartain & K. L. Hong (Eds.), *New directions for youth development: Special issue on spiritual development.* San Francisco, CA: Jossey-Bas, *118*, 13–28.

Benson, P. L., Roehlkepartain, E. C., & Rude, S. P. (2003). Spiritual development in childhood and adolescence: Toward a field of inquiry. *Applied Developmental Science, 7*, 204–212.

Benson, P. L., Roehlkepartain, E. C., & Scales, P. C. (2010). Spirituality and positive youth development. In L. Miller (Ed.), *The Oxford handbook of psychology of spirituality and consciousness.* New York, NY: Oxford University Press.

Benson, P. L., & Scales, P. C. (2009). The definition and preliminary measurement of thriving in adolescence. *The Journal of Positive Psychology, 4*, 85–104.

Benson, P. L., Scales, P. C., Hamilton, S. F., & Sesma, A. (2006). Positive youth development: Theory, research, and applications. In W. Damon & R. M. Lerner (Eds.), *Handbook of child psychology, Theoretical models of human development* (6th ed., Vol. I, pp. 894–941). Hoboken, NJ: John Wiley & Sons.

Benson, P. L., Scales, P. C., Sesma, A. J., & Roehlkepartain, E. C. (2005). Adolescent spirituality. In K. A. Moore & L. H. Lippman (Eds.), *What do children need to flourish?* (pp. 25–40). New York, NY: Springer.

Bertram-Troost, G., de Roos, S., & Miedema, S. (2009). The relationship between religious education and religious commitments and explorations of adolescents on religious identity development in Dutch Christian Secondary Schools. *Journal of Beliefs and Values, 30,* 17–27.

Bradby, H., & Williams, R. (2006). Is religion or culture the key feature in changes in substance use after leaving school? Young Punjabis and a comparison group in Glasgow. *Ethnicity & Health, 11,* 307–324. doi:10.1080/13557850600628372.

Brega, A., & Coleman, L. (1999). Effects of religiosity and racial socialization on subjective stigmatization in African-American adolescents. *Journal of Adolescence, 22,* 223–242.

Bridges, L. J., & Moore, K. A. (2002). Religious involvement and children's well-being: What research tells us (and what it doesn't). *Child Trends Research Brief,* 1–8.

Bundick, M. J., Yeager, D. S., King, P. E., & Damon, W. (2010). Thriving across the life span. In W. F. Overton (Ed.), *Handbook of life span development: Methods, biology, neuroscience, & cognitive development* (3rd ed., Vol. 1, pp. 882–923). Hoboken, NJ: John Wiley & Sons.

Chamberlain, K., & Zika, S. (1992). Religiosity, meaning in life, and psychological well-being. In J. F. Schumaker (Ed.), *Religion and mental health* (pp. 138–148). New York: Oxford University Press.

Colby, A., & Damon, W. (1999). The development of extraordinary moral commitment. In M. Killen & D. Hart (Eds.), *Morality in everyday life: Developmental perspectives* (pp. 342–370). New York, NY: Cambridge University Press.

Crystal, D. S., & DeBell, M. (2002). Sources of civic orientation among American youth: Trust, religious valuation, and attributions of responsibility. *Political Psychology, 23,* 113–132. doi:10.1111/0162-895x.00273.

Damon, W. (2004). What is positive youth development? *The Annals of the American Academy of Political and Social Science, 591,* 13–24.

Damon, W., Menon, J., & Bronk, K. (2003). The development of purpose during adolescence. *Applied Developmental Sciences, 7,* 119–127.

Donahue, M. J. (1995). Religion and the well-being of adolescents. *Journal of Social Issues, 51,* 145–160.

Donahue, M. J., & Benson, P. L. (1995). Religion and the well-being of adolescents. *Journal of Social Issues, 51,* 145–160.

Dowling, E. M., Gestsdottir, S., Anderson, P. M., von Eye, A., Almerigi, J., & Lerner, R. M. (2004). Structural relations among spirituality, religiosity, and thriving in adolescence. *Applied Developmental Science, 8,* 7–16.

Dubow, E. F., Pargament, K. I., Boxer, P., & Tarakeshwar, N. (2000). Initial investigation of Jewish early adolescents' ethnic identity, stress and coping. *Journal of Early Adolescence, 20,* 418.

Edwards, L. M., Fehring, R. J., Jarrett, K. M., & Haglund, K. A. (2008). The influence of religiosity, gender, and language preference acculturation on sexual activity among Latino/a adolescents. *Hispanic Journal of Behavioral Sciences, 30,* 447–462. doi:10.1177/0739986308322912.

Ellis, B. H., Lincoln, A. K., Charney, M. E., Ford-Paz, R., Benson, M., & Strunin, L. (2010). Mental health service utilization of Somali adolescents: Religion, community, and school as gateways to healing. *Transcultural Psychiatry, 47,* 789–811. doi:10.1177/ 1363461510379933.

Erikson, E. H. (1950). *Childhood and society.* New York, NY: Norton & Co.

Erikson, E. H. (1965). Youth: Fidelity and diversity. In E. H. Erikson (Ed.), *The challenges of youth* (pp. 1–28). Garden City, NY: Anchor Books.

Erikson, E. H. (1968). *Identity, youth, and crisis* (1st ed.). New York, NY: W.W. Norton.

Fetzer Institute. (1999). *Multidimensional measurement of religiousness/spirituality for use in health research.* Kalamazoo, MI: Fetzer Institute Publication.

Francis, L. J. (2000). The relationship between bible reading and purpose in life among 13-15 year olds. *Mental Health, Religion & Culture, 3,* 27–36.

Fulton, A. S. (1997). Identity status, religious orientation, and prejudice. *Journal of Youth and Adolescence, 26,* 1–11.

Furrow, J. L., King, P. E., & White, K. (2004). Religion and positive youth development: Identity, meaning, and prosocial concerns. *Applied Developmental Science, 8,* 17–26.

Gartner, J., Larson, D. B., & Allen, G. D. (1991). Religious commitment and mental health: A review of the empirical literature. *Journal of Psychology and Theology, 19,* 6–25.

Hart, D., & Fegley, S. (1995). Prosocial behavior and caring in adolescence: Relations to self-understanding and social judgment. *Child Development, 66,* 1346–1359.

Hunsberger, B., & Jackson, L. M. (2005). Religion, meaning, and prejudice. *Journal of Social Issues, 61,* 807–826.

Hunsberger, B., Pratt, M., & Pancer, S. M. (2001). Adolescent identity formation: Religious exploration and commitment. *Identity: An International Journal of Theory and Research, 1*(4), 365–386.

Jamieson, P. E., & Romer, D. (2008). Unrealistic fatalism in U.S. youth ages 14 to 22: Prevalence and characteristics. *The Journal of Adolescent Health, 42*(2), 154–160.

Jessor, R., Turbin, M. S., & Costa, F. M. (1998). Risk and protection in successful outcomes among disadvantaged adolescents. *Applied Developmental Science, 2*(4), 194.

Johnson, B. R., Jang, S. J., Larson, D. B., & De Li, S. (2001). Does adolescent religious commitment matter? A reexamination of the effects of religiosity on delinquency. *Journal of Research in Crime and Delinquency, 38,* 22–44.

Kelley, B. S., & Miller, L. (2007). Life satisfaction and spirituality in adolescents. *Research in the Social Scientific Study of Religion, 18,* 233–261.

Kerestes, M., Youniss, J., & Metz, E. (2004). Longitudinal patterns of religious perspective and civic integration. *Applied Developmental Sciences, 8,* 39–46.

Kiesling, C., Sorell, G. T., Montgomery, M. J., & Colwell, R. K. (2008). Identity and spirituality: A psychosocial exploration of the sense of spiritual self. *Psychology of Religion and Spirituality, 1,* 50–62.

King, P. E. (2008). Spirituality as fertile ground for positive youth development. In R. M. Lerner, R. Roeser & E. Phelps (Eds.), *Positive youth development and spirituality: From theory to research.* (pp. 55–73). West Conshohocken, PA: Templeton Foundation Press.

King, P. E., & Benson, P. L. (2006). Spiritual development and adolescent well-being and thriving and well-being. In E. C. Roehlkepartain, P. E. King, L. M. Wagener & P. L. Benson (Eds.), *The handbook of spiritual development in childhood and adolescence.* (pp. 384–398). Newbury Park, CA: Sage Publications.

King, P. E., Clardy, C. E., & Ramos, J. S. (2010). *Spiritual exemplars from around the world: An exploratory study of spiritual development in adolescents.* Paper presented at the Biennial Meeting of the Society for Research on Adolescence, Philadelphia, PA.

King, P. E., Clardy, C. E., Sung, K., Furrow, J. L., & Benitez, O. (2011). *Measuring adolescent spirituality: A factor analysis among Mexican youth.* Montreal, Canada: Paper presented at a symposium at the Biennial Meeting of the Society for Research on Child Development.

King, P. E., & Furrow, J. L. (2004). Religion as a resource for positive youth development: Religion, social capital, and moral outcomes. *Developmental Psychology, 40,* 703–713.

King, P. E., & Roeser, R. W. (2009). Religion and spirituality in adolescent development. In R. M. Lerner & L. Steinberg (Eds.), *Handbook of adolescent psychology, Vol 1: Individual bases of adolescent development* (3rd ed., pp. 435–478). Hoboken, NJ: John Wiley & Sons Inc.

King, P. E., Ramos, J. S., & Clardy, C. E. (in press). Searching for the sacred: Religious and spiritual development among adolescents. In K. I. Pargament, J. Exline, & J. Jones, E. Shafranski (Eds.), *APA handbook of psychology, religion and spirituality.* Washington, DC: American Psychological Association.

Koenig, H. G., McCullough, M. E., & Larson, D. B. (2001). *Handbook of religion and health.* New York, NY: Oxford University Press.

Lammers, C., Ireland, M., Resnick, M., & Blum, R. (2000). Influences on adolescents' decision to postpone onset of sexual intercourse: A survival analysis of virginity among youths aged 13 to 18 years. *The Journal of Adolescent Health: Official Publication of the Society for Adolescent Medicine, 26,* 42–48.

Larson, R. M. (2000). Towards a psychology of positive youth development. *The American Psychologist, 55,* 170–183.

Larson, R. W., Hansen, D. M., & Moneta, G. (2006). Differing profiles of developmental experiences across types of organized youth activities. *Developmental Psychology, 42,* 849–863. doi:10.1037/0012-1649.42.5.849.

Leak, G. K., DeNeve, K. M., & Greteman, A. J. (2007). The relationship between spirituality, assessed through self-transcendent goal strivings, and positive psychological attributes. *Research in the Social Scientific Study of Religion, 18,* 263–279. doi:10.1163/ej.9789004158511.i-301.102.

Lee, S. M., Puig, A., & Clark, M. A. (2007). The role of religiosity on postsecondary degree attainment. *Counseling & Values, 52,* 25–39.

Lerner, R. M. (2004). Diversity in individual context relations as the basis for positive development across the life span: A developmental systems perspective for theory, research, and application. *Research in Human Development, 1,* 327–346. doi:10.1207/s15427617rhd0104_5.

Lerner, R. M. (2006). Developmental science, developmental systems, and contemporary theories of human development. In R. M. Lerner & W. Damon (Eds.), *Handbook of child psychology: Theoretical models of human development* (6th ed., Vol. 1, pp. 1–17). Hoboken, NJ: John Wiley & Sons Inc.

Lerner, R. M., Alberts, A. E., Anderson, P. M., & Dowling, E. M. (2006). On making humans human: Spirituality and the promotion of positive youth development. In E. C. Roehlkepartain, P. E. King, L. M. Wagener & P. L. Benson (Eds.), *The handbook of spiritual development in childhood and adolescence.* (pp. 60–72). Newbury Park, CA: Sage Publications.

Lerner, R. M., Roeser, R. W., & Phelps, E. (Eds.), (2008). *Positive youth development and spirituality: From theory to research.* West Conshohocken, PA: Templeton Foundation Press.

Lerner, R. M., Warren, A., & Phelps, E. (Eds.), (2011). *Thriving and Spirituality among Youth: Research Perspectives and Future Possibilities.* Hoboken, NJ: John Wiley & Sons.

Li, H. (2008). College stress and psychological well-being: Self-transcendence meaning of life as a moderator. *College Student Journal, 42,* 531–541.

Lippman, L. H., & Keith, J. D. (2006). The demographics of spirituality among youth: International perspectives. In E. C. Roehlkepartain, P. E. King, L. Wagener & P. L. Benson (Eds.), *Handbook of spiritual development in childhood and adolescence.* (pp. 109–123). Thousand Oaks, CA: Sage Publications.

Longest, K. C., & Vaisey, S. (2008). Control or conviction: Religion and adolescent initiation of marijuana use. *Journal of Drug Issues, 38,* 689–715.

Loser, R. W., Hill, J. E., & Klein, S. R. (2009). Perceived benefits of religious rituals in the Latter-Day Saints home. *Review of Religious Research, 50,* 345–362.

Mahoney, A., Pendleton, S., & Ihrke, H. (2006). Religious coping by children and adolescents: Unexplored territory in the realm of spiritual development. In E. C. Roehlkepartain, P. E. King, L. M. Wagener & P. L. Benson (Eds.), *The handbook of spiritual development in childhood and adolescence.* (pp. 341–354). Newbury Park, CA: Sage Publications.

Marcia, J. E. (1966). Development and validation of ego-identity status. *Journal of Personality and Social Psychology, 3,* 551–558.

Mariano, J. M., & Damon, W. (2008). The role of spirituality and religious faith in supporting purpose in adolescence. In R. M. Lerner, R. W. Roeser & E. Phelps (Eds.), *Positive youth development and spirituality: From theory to research* (pp. 210–230). West Conshohocken, PA: Templeton Foundation Press.

Markstrom, C. A. (1999). Religious involvement and adolescent psychosocial development. *Journal of Adolescence, 22,* 205–221.

Markstrom-Adams, C., Hofstra, G., & Dougher, K. (1994). The ego-virtue of fidelity: A case for the study of religion and identity formation in adolescence. *Journal of Youth and Adolescence, 23,* 453–469. doi:10.1007/BF01538039.

Markstrom-Adams, C., & Smith, M. (1996). Identity formation and religious orientation among high school students from the United States. *Journal of Adolescence, 19,* 247.

Marler, P. L., & Hadaway, C. K. (2002). "Being religious" or "being spiritual" in America: A zero-sum proposition? *Journal for the Scientific Study of Religion, 41,* 289–300. doi:10.1111/1468-5906.00117.

Martin, T. F., White, J. M., & Perlman, D. (2003). Religious socialization: A test of the channeling hypothesis of parental influence on adolescent faith maturity. *Journal of Adolescent Research, 18,* 169.

Mattis, J. S., Ahluwalia, M. K., Cowie, S. E., & Kirkland-Harris, A. M. (2006). Ethnicity, culture, and spiritual development. In E. C. Roehlkepartain, P. E. King, L. Wagner & P. L. Benson (Eds.), *The handbook of spiritual development in childhood and adolescence* (pp. 283–296). Thousand Oaks, CA: Sage Publications.

Miller, L., & Gur, M. (2002). Religiousness and sexual responsibility in adolescent girls. *The Journal of Adolescent Health, 31,* 401–406.

Muller, C., & Ellison, C. G. (2001). *Religious involvement, social capital, and adolescents' academic progress: Evidence from the national education longitudinal study of 1988.* Cincinnati, OH: University of Cincinnati.

Nonnemaker, J., McNeely, C. A., & Blum, R. W. (2006). Public and private domains of religiosity and adolescent smoking transitions. *Social Science & Medicine, 62,* 3084–3095. doi:10.1016/j.socscimed.2005.11.052.

Oman, D., Flinders, T., & Thoresen, C. E. (2008). Integrating spiritual modeling into education: A college course for stress management and spiritual growth. *The International Journal for the Psychology of Religion, 18,* 79–107. doi:10.1080/10508610701879316.

Oser, F. K., Scarlett, W. G., & Bucher, A. (2006). Religious and spiritual development throughout the lifespan. In R. M. L. W. Damon (Ed.), *Handbook of child psychology:*

Theoretical models of human development (Vol. 1, pp. 942–998). Hoboker, NJ: John Wiley & Sons.

Ozorak, E. W. (2003). Love of god and neighbor: Religion and volunteer service among college students. *Review of Religious Research, 44*, 285–299.

Paloutzian, R. F., & Park, C. L. (2005). *Handbook of the psychology of religion and spirituality.* New York, NY: Guilford Press.

Pargament, K. I. (2007). *Spiritually integrated psychotherapy: Understanding and addressing the sacred.* New York, NY: Guilford.

Pargament, K. I., Mahoney, A., Exline, J., Jones, J., & Shafranskei, E. (in press). Envisioning an integrative paradigm for the psychology of religion and spirituality. In K. Pargament, J. Exline, & J. Jones (Eds.), *APA handbook of psychology, religion, and spirituality* (Vol. 1). Washington, DC: APA Press.

Paus, T. (2009). Brain development. In R. M. Lerner & L. Steinberg (Eds.), *Handbook of adolescent psychology: Individual bases of adolescent development* (3rd ed., Vol. 1, pp. 95–115). Hoboken, NJ: John Wiley & Sons Inc.

Pearce, M. J., Jones, S. M., Schwab-Stone, M. E., & Ruchkin, V. (2003). The protective effects of religiousness and parent involvement on the development of conduct problems among youth exposed to violence. *Child Development, 74*, 1682–1696. doi:10.1046/j.1467-8624.2003.00631.x.

Pearce, M. J., Little, T. D., & Perez, J. E. (2003). Religiousness and depressive symptoms among adolescents. *Journal of Clinical Child and Adolescent Psychology, 32*, 267.

Putnam, R. D. (2000). *Bowling alone: The collapse and revival of American community.* New York, NY: Simon & Schuster.

Regnerus, M. D. (2000). Shaping schooling success: Religious socialization and educational outcomes in metropolitan public schools. *Journal for the Scientific Study of Religion, 39*, 363.

Regnerus, M. D., & Elder, G. H. (2003). Staying on track in school: Religious influences in high- and low-risk settings. *Journal for the Scientific Study of Religion, 42*, 633–649. doi:10.1046/j.1468-5906.2003.00208.x.

Reich, K. H. (1998). Psychology of religion: What one needs to know. *Zygon: Journal of Religion and Science, 33*, 113–120.

Roeser, R. (2005). An introduction to Hindu India's contemplative psychological perspectives on human motivation, self, and development. In M. L. Maehr & S. Karabenick (Eds.), *Advances in motivation and achievement* (Vol. 14, pp. 297–345). New York, NY: Elsevier.

Roeser, R. W., Issac, S. S., Abo-Zena, M., Brittian, A., & Peck, S. C. (2008). Self and identity processes in spirituality and positive youth development. In R. M. Lerner, R. W. Roeser & E. Phelps (Eds.), *Positive youth development and spirituality: From theory to research* (pp. 74–105). West Conshohocken, PA: Templeton Foundation Press.

Rostosky, S. S., Danner, F., & Riggle, E. D. B. (2007). Is religiosity a protective factor against substance use in young adulthood? Only if you're straight!. *The Journal of Adolescent Health, 40*, 440–447. doi:10.1016/j.jadohealth.2006.11.144.

Rostosky, S. S., Regnerus, M. D., & Wright, M. L. (2003). Coital debut: The role of religiosity and sex attitudes in the add health survey. *Journal of Sex Research, 40*, 358–367.

Scarlett, W. G., & Warren, A. E. A. (2010). Religious and spiritual development across the life span: A behavioral and social science perspective. In M. E. Lamb, & A. M. Freund (Vol. Eds.), R. M. Lerner (Editor-in-Chief), *Social and emotional development. The handbook of life-span development* (Vol. 2, pp. 631–682). Hoboken, NJ: Wiley.

Schapman, A. M., & Inderbitzen-Nolan, H. M. (2002). The role of religious behaviour in adolescent depressive and anxious symptomatology. *Journal of Adolescence, 25,* 631. doi:10.1006/jado.2002.0510.

Schreck, C. J., Burek, M. W., & Clark-Miller, J. (2007). He sends rain upon the wicked: A panel study of the influence of religiosity on violent victimization. *Journal of Interpersonal Violence, 22*(7), 872–893. doi:10.1177/0886260507301233.

Schwartz, K. D. (2006). Transformations in parent and friend faith support predicting adolescents' religious faith. *The International Journal for the Psychology of Religion, 16,* 311–326. doi:10.1207/s15327582ijpr1604_5.

Schwartz, K. D., Bukowski, W. M., & Aoki, W. T. (2006). Mentors, friends, and gurus: Peer and nonparent influences on spiritual development. In E. C. Roehlkepartain, P. E. King, L. M. Wagener & P. L. Benson (Eds.), *The handbook of spiritual development in childhood and adolescence* (pp. 310–323). Newbury Park, CA: Sage Publications.

Serow, R. C., & Dreyden, J. I. (1990). Community service among college and university students: Individual and institutional relationships. *Adolescence, 99,* 553.

Showalter, S. M., & Wagener, L. M. (2000). Adolescents' meaning in life: A replication of DeVogler and Ebersole (1983). *Psychological Reports, 87,* 115–126. doi:10.2466/pr0.87.5.115-126.

Sinha, J. W., Cnaan, R. A., & Gelles, R. J. (2007). Adolescent risk behaviors and religion: Findings from a national study. *Journal of Adolescence, 30,* 231–249.

Sloane, D. M., & Potvin, R. H. (1986). Religion and delinquency: Cutting through the maze. *Social Forces, 65,* 87.

Smith, C. (2003a). Religious participation and network closure among american adolescents. *Journal for the Scientific Study of Religion, 42,* 259–267. doi:10.1111/1468-5906.00177.

Smith, C. (2003b). Theorizing religious effects among American adolescents. *Journal for the Scientific Study of Religion, 42,* 17–30.

Smith, C., & Denton, M. (2005). *Soul searching: The religious and spiritual lives of American teenagers.* New York, NY: Oxford University Press.

Smith, C. B., Weigert, A. J., & Thomas, D. L. (1979). Self-esteem and religiosity: An analysis of Catholic adolescents from five cultures. *Journal for the Scientific Study of Religion, 18,* 51–60.

Spiewak, G. S., & Sherrod, L. R. (2010). The shared pathways of religious/spiritual engagement and positive youth development. In A. E. Warren, R. M. Lerner & E. Phelps (Eds.), *Thriving and spirituality among youth: Research perspectives and future possibilities.* Hoboken, NJ: Wiley.

Spilka, B., Hood, R., Hunsberger, B., & Gorsuch, R. (2003). *The psychology of religion: An empirical approach* (3rd ed.). New York, NY: Guilford Press.

Sturgeon, R. S., & Hamley, R. W. (1979). Religiosity and anxiety. *The Journal of Social Psychology, 108,* 137–138.

Templeton, J. L., & Eccles, J. S. (2008). Spirituality, "expanding circle morality", and positive youth development. In R. M. Lerner, R. W. Roeser & E. Phelps (Eds.), *Positive youth development and spirituality: From theory to research* (pp. 197–209). West Conshohocken, PA: Templeton Foundation Press.

Trovato, F. (1992). A Durkheimian analysis of youth suicide: Canada, 1971 and 1981. *Suicide & Life-Threatening Behavior, 22,* 413–427.

Tzuriel, D. (1984). Sex role typing and ego identity in Israeli, Oriental, and Western adolesecents. *Journal of Personality and Social Psychology, 46,* 440–457. doi:10.1037/0022-3514.46.2.440.

Underwood, L. G., & Teresi, J. A. (2002). The daily spiritual experience scale: Development, theoretical description, reliability, exploratory factor analysis, and preliminary construct validity using health-related data. *Annals of Behavior Medicine, 24,* 22–33.

Varon, S. R., & Riley, A. W. (1999). Relationship between maternal church attendance and adolescent mental health and social functioning. *Psychiatric Services, 50,* 799–805.

Wagener, L. M., Furrow, J. L., King, P. F., Leffert, N., & Benson, P. (2003). Religious involvement and developmental resources in youth. *Review of Religious Research, 44,* 271–284.

Wagener, L. M., & Malony, H. N. (2006). Spiritual and religious pathology in childhood and adolescence. In E. C. Roehlkepartain, P. E. King, L. M. Wagener & P. L. Benson (Eds.), *The handbook of spiritual development in childhood and adolescence* (pp. 137–149). Newbury Park, CA: Sage Publications.

Wallace, J. M., & Forman, T. A. (1998). Religion's role in promoting health and reducing risk among American youth. *Health Education & Behavior, 25,* 721–741.

Wallace, J. M., Jr., Forman, T. A., Caldwell, C. H., & Willis, D. S. (2003). Religion and U.S. secondary school students: Current patterns, recent trends, and sociodemographic correlates. *Youth & Society, 35,* 98–125.

Wright, L. S., & Frost, C. J. (1993). Church attendance, meaningfulness of religion, and depressive symptomatology among adolescents. *Journal of Youth and Adolescence, 22,* 559.

Yates, M., & Youniss, J. (1996). Community service and political-moral identity in adolescents. *Journal of Research on Adolescents, 6,* 271–284.

Youniss, J., McLellan, J. A., & Yates, M. (1999). Religion, community service, and identity in American youth. *Journal of Adolescence, 22,* 243–253.

Zegans, S., & Zegans, L. S. (1979). Bar mitzvah: A rite for a transitional age. *Psychoanalytic Review, 66,* 115–132.

Zinnbauer, B. J., & Pargament, K. I. (2005). Religiousness and spirituality. In R. P. C. Parks (Ed.), *Handbook of psychology and religion* (pp. 21–42). New York, NY: Guilford Press.

THE CONTRIBUTION OF THE DEVELOPMENTAL ASSETS FRAMEWORK TO POSITIVE YOUTH DEVELOPMENT THEORY AND PRACTICE

Peter L. Benson, Peter C. Scales, and Amy K. Syvertsen

SEARCH INSTITUTE, MINNEAPOLIS, MINNESOTA, USA

Abstract

The framework of developmental assets posits a theoretically-based and research-grounded set of opportunities, experiences, and supports that are related to promoting school success, reducing risk behaviors, and increasing socially-valued outcomes including prosocial behavior, leadership, and resilience. A considerable body of literature on developmental assets has emerged in the last two decades, informing research and practice in education, social work, youth development, counseling, prevention, and community psychology. In addition to synthesizing this literature, this chapter

Advances in Child Development and Behavior

Richard M. Lerner, Jacqueline V. Lerner and Janette B. Benson : Editors

discusses: the recent development of the Developmental Asset Profile, an instrument designed, in part, to assess change-over-time; the utilization of asset measures in international research; the expansion of the assets framework to early childhood and young adults; and new research using latent class analysis (LCA) to identify classes or subgroups of youth.

I. Introduction

The framework of developmental assets, first posited in 1990 (Benson, 1990) and refined in 1995 (Benson, 1997, 2006), was explicitly designed to provide greater attention to the positive developmental nutrients that young people need for successful development, not simply to avoid high-risk behaviors, and to accent the role that community plays in adolescent well-being. As described in a series of publications (Benson, 2002, 2003; Benson, Leffert, Scales, & Blyth, 1998; Leffert et al., 1998; Scales & Leffert, 1999, 2004; Scales, Benson, Leffert, & Blyth, 2000), the framework establishes a set of developmental experiences and supports hypothesized to have import for all young people during the second decade of life. Recent work is taking a broader lifespan perspective, positing that developmental assets reflect developmental processes that have age-related parallels in infancy, childhood, and young adulthood (Leffert, Benson, & Roehlkepartain, 1997; Mannes, Benson, Kretzmann, & Norris, 2003; Scales, Roehlkepartain, & Benson, in press; Scales, Sesma, & Bolstrom, 2004a; VanderVen, 2008). This work will be addressed later in this chapter.

The framework synthesizes research in a number of fields with the goal of selecting for inclusion those developmental nutrients that (a) have been demonstrated to prevent high-risk behavior (e.g., substance use, violence, dropping out of school), enhance thriving, or strengthen resilience; (b) have evidence of generalizability across social location; (c) contribute balance to the overall framework (i.e., of ecological- and individual-level factors); (d) are within the capacity of communities to effect their acquisition; and (e) are within the capacity of youth to proactively procure (Benson & Scales, in press; Benson, Scales, Hamilton, & Sesma, 2006).

Because the developmental assets framework for adolescents ages 12–18 was designed not only to inform theory and research but also to have practical significance for the mobilization of communities, the 40 assets included in the model (Benson et al., 2006) are placed in categories that have conceptual integrity and can be described easily to the residents of a community. As seen in Table I, the assets are grouped into 20 external assets (i.e., environmental, contextual, and relational features of

Table I

The Framework of 40 Developmental Assets® for Adolescents

Search Institute has identified the following building blocks of healthy development that help young people grow up healthy, caring, and responsible.

External Assets

Support

1. *Family support*—Family life provides high levels of love and support.
2. *Positive family communication*—Young person and her or his parent(s) communicate positively, and young person is willing to seek advice and counsel from parent(s).
3. *Other adult relationships*—Young person receives support from three or more nonparent adults.
4. *Caring neighborhood*—Young person experiences caring neighbors.
5. *Caring school climate*—School provides a caring, encouraging environment.
6. *Parent involvement in schooling*—Parent(s) is actively involved in helping young person succeed in school.

Empowerment

7. *Community values youth*—Young person perceives that adults in the community value youth.
8. *Youth as resources*—Young people are given useful roles in the community.
9. *Service to others*—Young person serves in the community 1 h or more per week.
10. *Safety*—Young person feels safe at home, at school, and in the neighborhood.

Boundaries and expectations

11. *Family boundaries*—Family has clear rules and consequences and monitors the young person's whereabouts.
12. *School boundaries*—School provides clear rules and consequences.
13. *Neighborhood boundaries*—Neighbors take responsibility for monitoring young people's behavior.
14. *Adult role models*—Parent(s) and other adults model positive, responsible behavior.
15. *Positive peer influence*—Young person's best friends model responsible behavior.
16. *High expectations*—Both parent(s) and teachers encourage the young person to do well.

Constructive use of time

17. *Creative activities*—Young person spends three or more hours per week in lessons or practice in music, theater, or other arts.
18. *Youth programs*—Young person spends three or more hours per week in sports, clubs, or organizations at school and/or in the community.
19. *Religious community*—Young person spends one or more hours per week in activities in a religious institution.
20. *Time at home*—Young person is out with friends "with nothing special to do" two or fewer nights per week.

Internal Assets

Commitment to learning

21. *Achievement motivation*—Young person is motivated to do well in school.
22. *School engagement*—Young person is actively engaged in learning.
23. *Homework*—Young person reports doing at least 1 h of homework every school day.
24. *Bonding to school*—Young person cares about her or his school.
25. *Reading for pleasure*—Young person reads for pleasure three or more hours per week.

(Continued)

Table I

(*Continued*)

Positive values

26. *Caring*—Young person places high value on helping other people.
27. *Equality and social justice*—Young person places high value on promoting equality and reducing hunger and poverty.
28. *Integrity*—Young person acts on convictions and stands up for her or his beliefs.
29. *Honesty*—Young person "tells the truth even when it is not easy."
30. Responsibility—Young person accepts and takes personal responsibility.
31. *Restraint*—Young person believes it is important not to be sexually active or to use alcohol or other drugs.

Social competencies

32. *Planning and decision making*—Young person knows how to plan ahead and make choices.
33. *Interpersonal competence*—Young person has empathy, sensitivity, and friendship skills.
34. *Cultural competence*—Young person has knowledge of and comfort with people of different cultural/racial/ethnic backgrounds.
35. *Resistance skills*—Young person can resist negative peer pressure and dangerous situations.
36. *Peaceful conflict resolution*—Young person seeks to resolve conflict nonviolently.

Positive identity

37. *Personal Power*—Young person feels he or she has control over "things that happen to me."
38. *Self-Esteem*—Young person reports having a high self-esteem.
39. *Sense of Purpose*—Young person reports that "my life has a purpose."
40. *Positive View of Personal Future*—Young person is optimistic about her or his personal future.

Note. The 40 Developmental Assets® for Adolescents may be reproduced for educational, noncommercial uses only. Copyright 2005 by Search Institute®, Minneapolis, MN; 800-888-7828; www.search-institute.org. All Rights Reserved.

socializing systems) and 20 internal assets (i.e., skills, competencies, and values). The external assets comprise four categories: (a) support, (b) empowerment, (c) boundaries and expectations, and (d) constructive use of time. The internal assets are also placed into four categories: (a) commitment to learning, (b) positive values, (c) social competencies, and (d) positive identity. The scientific foundations for the eight categories and each of the 40 assets are described in more detail in Scales and Leffert (1999, 2004). An exploratory factor analysis conducted with 150,000 6th–12th grade students showed that 14 scales emerged for middle school students and 16 for high-school students, all conceptually reflecting the eight *a priori* asset categories; in addition, a second-order factor analyses identified two major superordinate scales, labeled individual assets and ecological assets, that mirrored the *a priori* designation of assets into internal and external classes (Theokas et al., 2005).

The developmental assets approach has become acknowledged as one of the most widespread and influential frameworks for understanding and strengthening positive youth development (PYD; Eccles & Gootman, 2002; Small & Memmo, 2004). Google Scholar shows that the developmental assets approach and/or Search Institute have been referenced in more than 17,000 peer-reviewed journal articles and other academic/professional publications since 1999. In addition to the assets framework, some of the most well-known approaches to PYD include the social development model and Communities That Care (promulgated by the University of Washington's Social Development Research Group), the 5Cs of PYD, and the 5 Promises of the America's Promise Alliance. A search in December 2010 of three major citation sources, Google Scholar, Academic Search Premier, and Psychinfo, showed that citations of the developmental assets approach and/or Search Institute far outstripped all the others in the 5 years from 2005 to 2010, with developmental assets/Search Institute being named 12,567 times, the social development model/Communities That Care cited 2182 times, the 5 Promises named 149 times, and the 5Cs cited 97 times. Google Scholar does not distinguish peer-review mentions from others, but in the Academic Search Premier and Psychinfo listings, developmental assets/Search Institute had a total of 1618 citations, compared with the closest other PYD approach, the social development model/Communities That Care, with 324 peer-reviewed mentions.

In addition to its predominance in the literature, the developmental assets framework has become a central organizing feature of youth programming in major national systems, such as the Y (formerly the YMCA of the USA) and Y Canada, Boys and Girls Clubs of America, Girl Scouts of the USA, the American Camp Association, the Salvation Army, major national religious denominations spanning the conservative to progressive spectrum, thousands of service-learning programs in schools, congregations, and youth organizations (through the National Youth Leadership Council and the support of the Corporation for National and Community Service), and more than 600 formal community coalitions trying to strengthen their communities as environments for young people, by focusing on initiatives for building the assets. In 2009 alone, more than 10,000 schools and youth programs were using Search Institute resources, and in the last 15 years, more than 20 million of the Institute's books and other resources have been disseminated worldwide. In the past decade, more than 300,000 leaders in education, health, social services, religion, youth development, and other fields have been trained in the assets framework, and more than 5 million people from over 180 countries have visited the Institute's Web site (www. search-institute.org). Scholars, educators, religious leaders, and youth work practitioners in more than 60 countries across the globe are using the asset approach in programs and data collection.

The national and international spread of the research on and practice of developmental assets is rooted in five strategies, each of which has fueled interest and action in the framework. First, the extensive research on the asset framework has, as noted earlier, created considerable attention within a number of fields of inquiry, including developmental psychology, community psychology, education, social work, and clinical/counseling psychology. This multidisciplinary exposure not only has fueled research by scholars and graduate students but has also activated practitioners in these fields to apply the research in countless communities and programs. Second, a long-term effort at the diffusion of the developmental asset research and its implications has brought the work, via Search Institute's training, public speaking, consulting, media communications, and conferences, to scholars and practitioners in every state and multiple nations. Third, the asset framework names developmental nutrients that are—in the words of many practitioners—both practical and actionable. Accordingly, thousands of professionals and citizens bring the work to local agencies and communities as an approach that helps deepen the impact of a wide range of other initiatives, including mentoring, service learning, youth leadership development, after-school programming, and parent education. Fourth, the asset framework, with its broad ecological approach, empowers many sectors—family, school, neighborhood, after-school programs, faith communities—to take action. Fifth, and perhaps most importantly, the asset framework (as shown by the research that undergirds it) can be positioned in a city or state or nation as a set of nutrients that matters, developmentally and behaviorally, for all youth regardless of race, ethnicity, family composition, gender, parental education, or geographic location. Hence, the asset model has the potential to create the kind of shared vision that can lessen fractured and siloed approaches that inhibit cooperation and collaboration.

II. Developmental Assets: Overview of Research

The foundational appeal of the assets framework is that it is rooted in and anchored by a vast scientific literature in child and adolescent development. The assets framework was originally conceived in 1990, with a review of the prevention, youth program evaluation, and resilience literatures yielding an initial framework of 30 developmental assets arrayed across six broad developmental categories that seemed rather consistently to be linked to a variety of indicators of youth well-being

(Benson, 1990). After several years of utilizing the framework in both research studies and community mobilization efforts, Search Institute solicited feedback from educators, youth workers, and others which led to the refinement of the framework into a final list of 40 assets that comprised the current eight categories (Benson et al., 1998).

Simultaneous with the revising of the framework on the basis of practitioner wisdom, a new and more comprehensive review of the empirical literature on adolescent development was conducted, with more than 1000 largely quantitative studies reviewed, and ultimately, more than 800 meeting criteria around sample size and design being cited in a wide-ranging synthesis that documented both the correlational and causational findings linking asset-like constructs (whether called protective factors, resilience factors, strengths, or assets) to PYD (Scales & Leffert, 1999, revised and updated further in Scales & Leffert, 2004). Subsequently, a similar literature review focusing on middle childhood yielded a comparably comprehensive synthesis of the assets literature–PYD association for younger children in middle childhood, listing and discussing more than 600 empirical citations (Scales et al., 2004a). Collectively, this demonstration of the rootedness of the assets framework in more than 1400 studies of child and adolescent development and its infusion with both empirical findings and practitioner insights provided considerable support for the construct, convergent, and predictive validity of the developmental assets approach.

Search Institute's own research with surveys that specifically defined the 40 developmental assets consistently has produced results that have fed the growing theoretical and applied utility of the framework. Major research findings are addressed in the following three sections: the accumulation hypothesis, the diversity hypothesis, and the differentiation hypothesis.

A. THE ACCUMULATION HYPOTHESIS

One of the central hypotheses in the developmental asset model is that assets are additive or cumulative. The consequence of this additive function is the reverse of that found in the research on risk factors. A risk factor "is an agent or characteristic of the individual or environment that is related to the increased probability of a negative outcome" (Campos, 2004, p. 264). Risks include a wide range of individual and community factors, including family conflict, neighborhood violence, poverty, physical and/or sexual abuse, and underperforming schools. A significant research literature has empirically established the cumulative impact of risk factors (Rutter, 1987a, 1987b). As the number of risks increase, the health and well-being of adolescents decline (Friedman & Chase-Lansdale, 2002).

As Campos (2004) succinctly puts it, "negative outcomes increase additively or exponentially as the number of risk factors increases" (p. 265).

Playing off the definition of risk given above, a developmental asset is an agent or characteristic of the individual or his/her developmental ecologies (e.g., family, peer group, neighborhood, school, community) that is related to the increased probability of *positive* outcomes. Like the risk model, but in reverse, positive outcomes (e.g., school success, social and emotional health, contribution, caring, and the absence of health-compromising behaviors such as alcohol use, drug use, violence, antisocial behavior) increase additively or exponentially as the number of developmental assets increases. This hypothesis is described in more detail in a recent systematic review of PYD theory and research (Benson et al., 2006). It should be noted here that the reduction of risk factors and the promotion of developmental assets are complementary approaches to promoting adolescent health (Scales, 1999).

Multiple studies confirm the additive developmental asset hypothesis, showing that the more developmental assets young people experience, the better off they tend to be, across a range of academic, psychological, social–emotional, and behavioral indicators of well-being. Search Institute has administered more than 3 million of its assets surveys to 4th–12th graders in the United States, involving more than 2000 communities large and small, urban, suburban, and rural in nature, and characterized by significant racial/ethnic and socioeconomic diversity. Four large aggregate samples ranging in size from roughly 50,000 to 215,000 students have been studied in 1990, 1995–1996, 1999–2000, and 2003 (a new aggregate sample of roughly 60,000 students is being constructed from 2010 surveys but was not available for analysis at the time of this writing).

In each of those large studies, assets have been scored on a binary basis (a youth has or does not have the asset), yielding a total number of assets experienced. Each of the samples was divided into quartiles based on this total number of assets, and the quartiles compared on their mean scores on 10 risk behavior patterns (e.g., problem alcohol use, engaging in violent behavior) and eight indicators of thriving (e.g., high GPA at school, persistence in the face of adversity). Across those differing samples spanning two decades, the same patterns relating assets to developmental outcomes have been observed: For nearly every outcome, every increase in the quartile level of assets experienced (e.g., going from 0–10 assets to 11–20, or from 21–30 assets to having 31–40) is associated with a significant increase in mean outcome scores. Because the very large sample sizes can be expected to render even small differences statistically significant, we look both at effect sizes and at the differences in the proportion of youth experiencing outcomes, as a function of their asset levels.

For example, Table II displays the standardized means and effect sizes for the quartile differences in means on problem alcohol use and engaging in violence (examples of the risk behaviors), and high grades in school and feeling physically healthy (examples of thriving indicators). "Asset-rich" youth, those with 31–40 of the 40 assets, are used as the reference group. The effect sizes for the difference between asset-rich and asset-poor youth are all equal to or greater than 1.0, a level well beyond what is traditionally considered a "large" effect. Even the differences between asset-rich youth and those with the next-highest level of assets, 21–30 or above-average, still are great enough to yield effect sizes in excess of .25. Although Cohen (1988) heuristically described that level as a "small" effect, the U.S. Department of Education's What Works Clearinghouse has established .25 as the level that signifies a "substantively important" effect (p. 20). These results show most of the effect sizes to be well above that substantively important criterion.

B. THE DIVERSITY HYPOTHESIS

A critical concern about any framework for preventing youth problems and promoting PYD is whether the approach works equally well for different groups of students, and if not, to understand better how to adapt the approach as needed to strengthen its efficacy for different youth populations. Throughout the varied studies Search Institute has conducted over the past 20 years, the most consistent finding in this regard is that the asset framework appears to have comparable validity across young people's gender, race/ethnicity, geographic residence, and socioeconomic background. Although absolute levels of assets sometimes do vary in these demographic comparisons, the effect sizes of those differences usually are quite small (Benson, Scales, Leffert, & Roehlkepartain, 1999). More importantly, the patterns noted above, of higher levels of assets being associated with lower levels of risk and higher levels of thriving, are consistently replicated across those demographic groups (Roehlkepartain, Benson, & Sesma, 2003; Scales et al., 2005). Girls generally have a higher average number of assets than boys (e.g., Scales & Leffert, 2004), but each gender shows the same patterns of correlation between higher levels of assets and both lower levels of risk behaviors and higher levels of thriving indicators. In one study more closely looking at the developmental asset of service to others, the asset was found to

Table II

Relation of Asset Quartiles to Selected Developmental Outcomes: Standardized Means and Effect Sizes

	Total number of assets												
	Asset poor			Average			Above average			Asset rich			
	0–10 Assets			11–20 Assets			21–30 Assets			31–40 Assets			
	M	Pooled SD	Effect sizes	M	Pooled SD	Effect sizes	M	Pooled SD	Effect sizes	M	Pooled SD	Effect sizes	F Statistic
Problem alcohol use	.45	.42	1.0	.26	.41	.56	.11	.28	.29	.01	–	–	$F_{(3,131612)} =$ 4854.84***
Engaging in violence	.61	.42	1.31	.37	.43	.69	.17	.36	.31	.06	–	–	$F_{(3,131612)} =$ 6536.19***
High grades in school	.08	.27	1.70	.19	.37	.95	.35	.44	.43	.54	–	–	$F_{(3,131612)} =$ 4339.47***
Feel physically happy	.27	.41	1.49	.47	.35	1.17	.69	.44	.43	.88	–	–	$F_{(3,131612)} =$ 6701.91***

Notes: *** $p \leq .0001$. All variables standardized to mean of 0 and standard deviation of 1. Cohen's d was used to calculate effect sizes, using youth with 31–40 assets as the reference group (M_1), using the formula ($M_1 - M_2$/Pooled SD). Pooled SD $= \sqrt{(n_1-1)SD_1^2 + (n_2-1)SD_2^2/(n_1+n_2-2)}$, calculated for each pair of 31–40 asset group with the other three quartile groups.

have a compensatory influence over socioeconomic status (SES). Poor students who reported engaging in community service had scores on school success measures that were much more like affluent students' scores, whereas their poor peers who did not engage in service had significantly worse scores on those school success measures (Scales, Roehlkepartain, Neal, Kielsmeier, & Benson, 2006).

C. THE DIFFERENTIATION HYPOTHESIS

The sheer number of developmental assets youth experience clearly has considerable implications for their health and well-being, regardless of the target outcome. But it would also strain credulity to imagine that every outcome is affected similarly by exactly the same assets. Rather, in addition to the accumulation hypothesis, we have also hypothesized and found through both stepwise and logistic regression analyses, that particular clusters of assets are especially influential predictors of various outcomes, both concurrently and longitudinally.

For example, in predicting GPA, youth who experienced in middle school a cluster of assets that, for the most part, thematically suggests community involvement (participation in after-school youth programs, religious community involvement, service to others, engaging in creative activities, and reading for pleasure) were three times more likely to have B+ or higher GPAs 3 years later in high school than youth who did not experience that cluster of assets as younger adolescents (Scales, Benson, Roehlkepartain, Sesma, & van Dulmen, 2006). Similarly, students who experienced a cluster of assets thematically suggesting adherence to norms of responsibility (positive peer influence, the value of restraint, spending time at home, peaceful conflict resolution, and school engagement) were twice as likely as other students to have high GPAs later in high school. Likewise, several assets including positive peer influence, school engagement, and the social skill of peaceful conflict resolution have been identified in both our cross-sectional and longitudinal studies as the best predictors of lower levels of antisocial behavior (e.g., stealing, vandalism) and violence (e.g., physical fighting, threatening to hurt others; Benson & Scales, 2009). Similar results have been found for other risk behavior patterns (Leffert et al., 1998) and indicators of thriving (Scales et al., 2000), that is, that several specific assets best predict concurrent and longitudinal (Roehlkepartain et al., 2003) outcomes, with the assets varying depending on the outcome in question.

III. Application of the Asset Framework to Policies and Programs

The research base suggests the likely efficacy of a dual-pronged applied policy and program strategy, of both attempting to build all 40 assets throughout young people's ecologies and especially targeting the promotion of specific clusters of assets that will vary depending upon the PYD goals of a program, organization, neighborhood, or community, for example, whether they are promoting school success (Starkman, Scales, & Roberts, 2006) or preventing substance abuse (Scales & Fisher, 2010).

One applied result of this research has found particular recent relevance in the arena of school reform, an application that is likely to grow in importance, given the high public policy priority given to the nonstellar performance of U.S. students in relation to the rest of the world's economic powers. Across various Search Institute studies, nine of the assets have been found in both bivariate and multivariate analyses to be the ones most consistently linked to indicators of school success that have included attendance, academic self-confidence, effort, sense of belonging to school, grades, and test scores (Roberts & Scales, 2005; Scales & Benson, 2007; Starkman et al., 2006). These assets—the "internal" assets of achievement motivation, school engagement, bonding to school, reading for pleasure, and the "external" or ecological assets of a caring school climate, parent involvement in schooling, service to others, high expectations, and participation in high quality after-school youth programs—increasingly are being used as both targets and measures to assess the effectiveness of school reform efforts.

In a series of pilot studies Search Institute conducted in Hawai'i with Kamehameha Schools (Scales & Tibbetts, in preparation), existing measures of those nine assets were strengthened to be both more internally consistent and more sensitive to detecting change-over-time, making them appropriate to use for tracking purposes. For example, the Dallas Independent School District will be surveying 50,000 middle- and high-school students, from 2011 on, for at least the next 4 years, with both a global measure of assets (Search Institute's *Developmental Assets Profile* (DAP), described more fully below), and specific measures of several of the nine "school success" assets, and tracking the relation of levels of and changes in those assets with more ultimate measures of school success such as grades and test scores, and other indicators of college and career readiness. Search Institute also was awarded in 2010 one of just 49 (out of 1700 applicants) highly competitive Investing In Innovation grants by the U.S. Department of Education to replicate and expand over 4 years a successful student intervention program based on the assets framework—Building Assets Reducing Risk (BARR)—in school districts in California, Maine, and Minnesota, with the goals of reducing disciplinary problems, school failure, and substance use, in part through promoting assets. As in the Dallas ISD, a global measure of developmental assets is paired with the specific school success asset measures, and other measures of school climate and success, as part of the evaluation of the BARR program.

Another major application illustrates the use of asset-building as a PYD strategy, in this case for achieving prevention goals. The RAND Corporation is leading a consortium including Search Institute and the Collaboration for Children and Youth in Maine (the latter spearheaded by the Governor's Children's Cabinet) in a landmark 5-year National Institute of Drug Abuse effort to use asset-building to reduce substance use and other risk-taking behaviors among Maine youth. A principal strategy is to train and provide technical assistance to educators, youth workers, and others in using a 10-step, research-based logic model called assets getting to outcomes (AGTO; Fisher, Imm, Chinman, & Wandersman, 2006) as a means of systematically building the capacity of community coalitions to promote assets in the service of reaching those prevention goals. The research design includes six community coalitions receiving the technical assistance on developmental assets and the AGTO model, and six control coalitions not receiving that intervention. A variety of measures are being used to assess changes in coalitions' PYD-promotion capacity over time, and one of the institute's surveys, the DAP, is used to measure related changes in youth's experience of developmental assets (Chinman et al., in press). In addition, a set of DAP implementation items was created that ask youth how much the program undertook activities to try to increase particular assets. Thus, for the first time, researchers will be able to directly link observations of change in youth assets with youth reports of explicit program efforts to promote that change, thereby helping scholars and practitioners alike to better understand *how* to build these developmental strengths.

IV. Research from New Measures of Developmental Assets

The Search Institute *Attitudes and Behaviors: Profiles of Student Life* (A&B) survey is a 160-item instrument that includes measures of the 40 individual assets, numerous risk-taking behaviors, and several indicators of positive behavior. It is the most widely used assets survey, accounting for more than 80% of the more than 3 million assets surveys the institute has administered over the past two decades. Its great strength lies in the clarity and simplicity of its accompanying data reports, with the two primary metrics being the mean total number of assets youth report experiencing, and the percentage of youth who experience asset-poor (0–10 assets), average (11–20), above-average (21–30), or asset-rich (31–40 assets) lives. Such ease of communicating results has fueled the survey's use as a mobilizing tool for communities. More than 3000 communities have used the A&B results to organize and strengthen initiatives to improve young people's developmental experiences. As discussed above, numerous research studies, using both cross-sectional and longitudinal designs, have shown that the accumulation of developmental assets as measured by the A&B survey (i.e., experiencing a relatively more asset-rich life) is strongly linked to better youth developmental outcomes, from lower substance use and violence to more volunteering and school success (Benson & Scales, 2009; Benson et al., 1998, 2006; Leffert et al., 1998; Scales & Leffert, 2004; Scales, Benson, et al., 2006; Scales et al., 2000, 2004a). Along with these strengths, the survey has some limitations. The measures of the 40 individual developmental assets reflect a mixture of psychometrically stronger and weaker measures. A number of them are measured with single items, for example, and a number of others have internal consistency reliabilities below the standard of .70 for an acceptable measure, and .60 for a promising one. Stability reliability is unknown for most of the asset measures, making it impossible to assess their appropriateness for change-over-time applications. Thus, although the survey is highly recommended for mobilization and communication purposes, it is a lengthy survey, has uneven psychometric quality, and it is not appropriate for the tracking, longitudinal, or program evaluation purposes that increasing numbers of potential users wish to pursue.

To provide an alternative asset measure, Search Institute created the DAP, a 58-item instrument that measures the eight *categories* of developmental assets originally identified by Search Institute scholars: support, empowerment, boundaries and expectations, constructive use of time ("external" relationships and opportunities provided by others for youth), and commitment to learning, positive values, social competencies, and positive identity ("internal" values, skills, and self-perceptions youth develop on their gradual path to self-regulation). The survey provides subscale scores for each of those eight asset categories and, by regrouping the items, subscale scores that suggest how asset-rich young people's asset experience is in various life *contexts*: Personal, Social, Family, School, and Community. Developed in 2005, the DAP was designed to be completed in 10–15 min, to be usable in both group administration and individualized clinical settings, and to be sensitive to change-over-time. It is the only assets survey that is an appropriate instrument for use in pre–post program evaluation applications. Each of the eight asset category subscales, five context view subscales, internal assets scale, external assets scale, and the overall DAP as a total scale have been found to have acceptable internal consistency reliabilities (per Cronbach's alpha) and stability or test–retest reliabilities, and there is considerable evidence for the DAP's construct, convergent, discriminant, and predictive validity (MGS Consulting, 2008; Search Institute, 2005; Wilson, O'Brien, & Sesma, 2009). The singular drawback of utilizing the DAP is that it measures assets at the level of the eight asset categories, whereas many provocative research questions and applied youth development programs focus on one or more of the 40 individual assets. Thus, since the DAP and A&B offer different strengths and limitations, users are able to choose either to serve as their primary data collection source on developmental assets, depending upon their specific data needs.

Because of its brevity and psychometric quality as a PYD instrument, in the past several years, scholars and practitioners around the globe have requested to adapt and translate the DAP for use in their cultural contexts. As a result, the DAP has now been used in more than a dozen countries, including Albania, Armenia, Azerbaijan, Bangladesh, Bolivia, Brazil, China, Colombia, the Dominican Republic, Egypt, Gaza, Iraq, Japan, Jordan, Lebanon, Mexico, Morocco, Nepal, the Philippines, Rwanda, and Yemen. A detailed secondary analysis of data from five of those countries with sufficiently sizeable datasets (Albania, Bangladesh, Japan, Lebanon, and the Philippines), including comparative U.S. data, concluded that most of the scales have acceptable reliability in other languages than English and cultural settings other than the United States, some of the scales have acceptable stability reliability, and there is evidence of the DAP having comparable validity in those countries as with U.S. samples (Scales, 2011).

Table III displays the percentages of youth in those five countries (and the United States) that report experiencing various levels of developmental assets.

V. Tracking Change in Developmental Assets Over Time

Because the DAP was designed for pre–post applications (so long as survey administrations are at least 3 months apart), it is rapidly becoming an instrument of choice to include in youth program evaluations and assessments. It already is a principal instrument in a major quasi-experimental study of community coalitions' impact on PYD (the AGTO project in Maine, described above); a large school district's long-term strategic data collection to assess its progress on College and Career Readiness for all

Table III

Percentage of Youth, by Country, in Quartile Levels of Developmental Assets
Profile (DAP) Scores

					Bangladesh		Philippines	
	United States	Japan	Lebanon	Albania	T_1	T_2	T_1	T_2
Overall DAP score quartiles								
Poor	14	2	11	5	31	3	16	8
Fair	38	33	47	44	58	35	61	46
Good	34	50	37	48	10	55	20	31
Excellent	15	15	5	3	1	8	3	14
Support								
Poor	16	28	15	7	37	2	15	9
Fair	28	31	25	19	43	25	44	31
Good	31	26	41	43	16	56	33	43
Excellent	25	15	18	31	2	17	9	17
Empowerment								
Poor	8	20	12	49	45	1	19	14
Fair	31	43	41	41	44	48	51	36
Good	33	27	34	8	8	37	24	34
Excellent	28	10	13	2	3	15	6	15
Boundaries and expectations								
Poor	16	26	13	5	30	4	15	8
Fair	29	34	31	17	41	23	39	28
Good	34	28	38	43	23	39	35	39
Excellent	22	12	17	34	5	33	11	25
Constructive use of time								
Poor	26	43	42	18	42	6	39	24
Fair	38	41	36	47	51	49	44	40
Good	22	12	15	27	7	30	13	24
Excellent	14	4	7	8	5	16	5	13
Commitment to learning								
Poor	19	34	23	4	18	6	11	8
Fair	30	35	33	17	34	18	42	31
Good	34	24	32	49	36	44	37	40
Excellent	18	7	11	31	11	31	10	22
Positive values								
Poor	15	39	7	9	29	1	21	12
Fair	39	44	34	39	57	41	56	47
Good	29	14	42	39	14	45	20	26
Excellent	17	3	17	13	1	13	3	15

(Continued)

Table III

(*Continued*)

	United States	Japan	Lebanon	Albania	Bangladesh T_1	Bangladesh T_2	Philippines T_1	Philippines T_2
Social competencies								
Poor	10	20	7	7	40	13	25	12
Fair	32	44	30	31	46	40	45	37
Good	35	28	41	42	10	38	23	31
Excellent	24	9	22	20	4	9	8	19
Positive identity								
Poor	16	46	21	14	39	20	29	20
Fair	38	37	40	37	44	41	48	35
Good	28	14	26	35	13	28	18	27
Excellent	18	4	13	14	5	12	5	17
Personal								
Poor	1	35	10	6	28	3	21	13
Fair	40	46	40	36	52	36	55	43
Good	30	16	39	46	16	48	20	27
Excellent	15	4	11	12	4	13	4	18
Social								
Poor	12	21	7	7	48	17	24	12
Fair	34	44	37	39	41	44	54	42
Good	31	26	38	43	9	31	18	29
Excellent	23	9	18	10	2	8	5	17
Family								
Poor	11	25	8	5	9	1	11	9
Fair	23	34	19	16	40	3	39	27
Good	28	26	33	47	38	34	36	35
Excellent	38	16	40	32	13	62	14	30
School								
Poor	17	25	17	4	22	5	10	6
Fair	33	38	32	20	37	13	37	29
Good	30	25	31	42	33	40	37	35
Excellent	21	12	21	35	8	42	17	31
Community								
Poor	19	50	33	24	68	16	35	22
Fair	42	37	44	51	28	54	51	43
Good	27	10	18	22	4	22	12	23
Excellent	13	2	5	4	0	8	2	12
N=	1312	13,946	1138	259	498		703	

Note: This table was adapted from Scales (2011).

students (Dallas ISD, described above); a new effort by the Salvation Army to infuse PYD and asset-building to all of its youth programming across the country; the replication and expansion in California, Maine, and Minnesota of the Building Assets Reducing Risk program for promoting school success, and the evaluation of that potentially landmark effort; and the measurement of youth development programs worldwide.

Regarding its use globally, the DAP was a primary data collection instrument in two youth development initiatives in Bangladesh and the Philippines. The Bangladesh effort focused on providing basic educational and social competence skills to young girls—an especially vulnerable population in that country—and the Philippines effort was a program to provide education and livelihood skills to out of school youth in a region that had suffered considerable conflicts and religious tension, as a way of connecting those youth more to mainstream institutions of school and work, and lessening their attractiveness as recruits for extremists. In both countries, youth participated in the PYD programs for 6–9 months, and the DAP was administered at the beginning and end of the programs. In Bangladesh, there also was a control group of girls included in the research design, with girls randomly assigned to intervention or control conditions. In each country, considerable gains in youths' assets were seen from pre- to posttest, 12% in the Philippines and 30% in Bangladesh. Even after statistically accounting for contamination and control group effects, the net gain in Bangladesh was 24%, as displayed in Figure 1.

The mean increase in asset level was from a "fair" experience of assets to a "good" one, a change that, in U.S. samples, has been linked to significant differences in well-being outcomes, such as a 53% drop in youth engagement in violence and a 79% increase in youth getting high grades in school (Scales, 2011). Those results demonstrated both the potential of PYD programs to significantly affect youths' developmental assets, and the ability of the DAP to detect such change, in non-U.S. settings.

A. EXPANSION OF THE ASSETS FRAMEWORK TO YOUNGER CHILDREN AND YOUNG ADULTS

The assets framework originally was developed out of a review of the literature on adolescent development, but conceptually it has apparent relevance for younger and older age groups as well. A considerable body of research has been synthesized to demonstrate the framework's theoretical utility for research and program development during early childhood (VanderVen, 2008) and middle childhood (Scales et al., 2004a). Although essentially the same 40 assets have been elaborated throughout the first

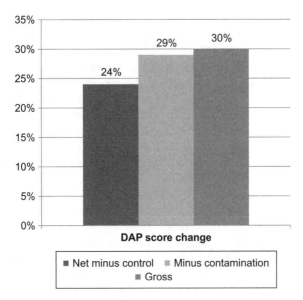

Fig. 1. Bangladesh net DAP score change, T$_1$–T$_2$ (6–9 months).

two decades of life, distinct accents and points of emphasis have also been described so that the assets have unique developmental integrity at each of the different age ranges of 3–5, 5–9, 9–12, and 12–18. More recently, similar although not yet as comprehensive synthesis work has been conducted to develop a revised framework of developmental assets for the period of young or emerging adulthood (Scales et al., in press). The research reviewed for this effort amply demonstrates that although the transition to new roles characterizes the essence of young adulthood, the social and psychological processes at work are much the same as in the first two decades of life. Other efforts have addressed pathways to successful young adult development, and defined what successful young adulthood entails (Schorr & Marchand, 2007), but are essentially about what *adolescents* need subsequently to have a successful young adulthood. The new assets framework *for* young adulthood, however, describes what *young adults* need *during* those years from 18 to 25 in order to enjoy current well-being and successful transition to later life.

A survey has been developed to measure the 40 individual assets in 4th–6th graders—Search Institute's *Me and My World* survey (Scales, Sesma, & Bolstrom, 2004b)—that shows generally acceptable evidence of reliability and validity across the asset measures. In addition, a *Developmental Assets Profile* for preteens (DAP-P), measuring assets at the level of the eight categories of assets, is in pilot testing in several sites in

2010–2011, with versions for children in grades 3–5 and parents of children in grades K-3 being tested. A new survey measuring the 40 individual assets for young adults ages 18–25 has also been developed—the Search Institute *Young Adult Developmental Assets Survey*—and is undergoing pilot testing at several universities in 2010–2011. At the conclusion of the various survey tests, by early 2012, it is anticipated that there will be a fleet of conceptually and theoretically sequenced, and psychometrically strong, measurement tools available for assessing the developmental assets experience of children, youth, and young adults from Kindergarten to age 25.

Me and My World: A Search Institute Survey of Developmental Assets for Grades 4 Through 6 (*MMW*) (Scales et al., 2004b) is the first survey for 4th–6th graders specifically focused on measuring Developmental Assets™. Through *MMW*, 4th–6th graders can report on their experience of the 40 developmental assets identified by Search Institute that have been shown to contribute to lessened risky behavior and greater thriving and resilience in the face of challenge. The *MMW* survey is conceptually based on the survey Search Institute has used for two decades to study the developmental assets of 6th–12th graders—the *Search Institute* A&B survey—and assesses positive experiences that research shows are particularly important for the developmental well-being of upper-elementary children (Scales et al., 2004a). The survey was piloted among 191, 4th–5th graders in New Brighton, Minnesota; 402, 4th–6th graders in Norman, Oklahoma; and 411, 4th–6th graders in Oklahoma City, Oklahoma. The pilot tests suggested extensive revisions, which were incorporated into a new version that was field-tested in 2003 with nearly 1300 4th–6th graders in California, Nevada, and New York. After field-testing, several additional revisions were made to improve the survey.

A relatively large dataset of completed *MMW* surveys was created by aggregating surveys from 6927 4th–6th grade students from 23 U.S. communities in 10 states, who were administered the survey in calendar 2008. The sample was evenly divided between boys and girls, and included 46% in the 4th grade, 33% in the 5th grade, and 21% in the 6th grade. The sample was racially/ethnically diverse, with 61% being white, 12% Hispanic/Latino, 9% multiracial, 8% African-American, 2% each Native American and Asian, less than 1% Hawai'ian, and 5% other.

Consistently, the accumulation of multiple assets is strongly related to better developmental outcomes among 6th–12th graders, with youth reporting each successively higher quartile of the assets (0–10, 11–20, 21–30, and 31–40) almost always reporting significantly better outcomes. The 2008 aggregate sample data show that the same patterns hold for 4th–6th graders, as displayed in Table IV.

Table IV

The Relationship Between Asset Levels and Thriving and Risk Indicators Among 4th–6th Grade Students

	Total number of assets				
	Asset poor	Average	Above average	Asset rich	
	0–10 Assets	11–20 Assets	21–30 Assets	31–40 Assets	F Statistic
High grades	.49^d	.66^c	.77^b	.88^a	$F(3,5808)=$ 116.53***
Helps others	.27^d	.54^c	.73^b	.91^a	$F(3,5877)=$ 320.01***
Values diversity	.50^d	.71^c	.83^b	.94^a	$F(3,5900)=$ 175.17***
Delays gratification	.16^d	.33^c	.50^b	.74^a	$F(3,5899)=$ 273.52***
Shares in self-regulation with parents	.71^c	.79^b	.82^{a,b}	.87^a	$F(3,5894)=$ 23.41***
Has coping skills	.14^d	.25^c	.44^b	.71^a	$F(3,5854)=$ 310.17***
Has life satisfaction	.43^d	.61^c	.82^b	.94^a	$F(5867)=$ 290.29***
Uses alcohol	.15^c	.09^b	.03^a	.03^a	$F(3,5836)=$ 46.40***
Smokes cigarettes	.08^c	.04^b	.01^a	.01^a	$F(3,5837)=$ 38.91***
Uses marijuana	.08^b	.03^a	.01^a	.01^a	$F(3,5824)=$ 26.07***
Engages in vandalism	.20^c	.09^b	.03^a	.01^a	$F(3,5838)=$ 91.33***
Commits aggressive or violent acts	.40^d	.27^c	.16^b	.08^a	$F(3,5826)=$ 110.87***
Is often sad	.48^b	.43^b	.43^b	.36^a	$F(35,834)=$ 17.46***
N=	283	1321	2387	1877	

Notes. *** $p \leq .0001$. All variables standardized to mean of 0 and standard deviation of 1. Standardized means in the same row, with differing superscripts, are significantly different from each other.

On six of the seven positive behavior outcome variables (86%), every level of increase in the assets students report experiencing is associated with a significantly better outcome, and on the seventh outcome, coregulation, students with the two highest levels of assets do better than students with only average levels of assets, who, in turn, do better than the students with the lowest levels of assets. The risk behaviors do not show as dramatic a linear association between assets and outcomes, simply because so few of these younger students in upper-elementary grades, relatively speaking, report engaging in those negative behaviors. Even here, however, lower levels of assets are linked to poorer scores on the outcomes, that is, a higher likelihood of experiencing risky behaviors. For most of the risk indicators, students in the top two levels of assets have about same outcome scores, but for aggression/ violence and sadness, the asset-rich students are better off than *all* other students.

Overall, the *MMW* measures of the school success assets for 4th–6th graders show the same kinds of patterns by demographics, and the same kinds of links to developmental outcomes, as seen for asset measures developed for older youth. Girls and younger students tend to have more of the assets (Scales et al., 2004a), and the more of these assets upper-elementary students have, the fewer high-risk behaviors they engage in, and the more they report engaging in positive behaviors. These results suggest a good base of construct validity for the 4th–6th grades asset measures. A majority of the 4th–6th grade measures also showed acceptable to good internal consistency reliability (Scales et al., 2004b).

VI. Developmental Asset Profiles

To date, nearly all the research on developmental assets has been variable centered. For this chapter, we also undertook a person-centered approach, using latent class analysis (LCA) to identify classes or subgroups of youth, differentiated on the basis of their respective patterns of reported assets. Variable-centered analysis is useful in understanding the typical or average experiences of young people but leaves unexplored the interindividual variability and complexity that is a hallmark of human growth. A person-centered approach, by naming patterns of asset combinations that seem to characterize young people, also offers additional applied lessons for program responsiveness and organizational change to better the developmental opportunities youth experience. For example, differing PYD strategies may be implicated for young people (and the adults around them) who seem to be lacking in social competencies, and yet somehow seem to experience considerable social support, and those who are lacking in both social competencies and social support. We briefly present here the highlights of the LCA. Additional methodological details may be found in a forthcoming paper (Syvertsen, Scales, & Benson, in preparation).

A. METHOD AND MODEL INDICATORS

The eight asset categories—for example, support, constructive use of time, positive values, social competencies, described in Table II—were used to fit the developmental asset profiles. To focus our analyses on those asset categories present in youths' lives, a score of "1" was assigned to youth who had 50% or more of the assets in a given category, while a score of "0" was assigned to those with less than 50% of the assets. The frequencies of youth having 50% or more of the assets in a category ranged from 36% (social competencies) to 66% (positive values), with about half of youth having 50% or more for each asset category.

B. LATENT CLASS DESCRIPTIONS AND MEMBERSHIP

Statistical fit indices were used to identify the best fitting model. Four subgroups of adolescents with distinct constellations of developmental assets emerged: *Supported–Competent–Confident, Supported Social Marginal, Unsupported Engaged*, and the *Unsupported–Unengaged–Unconfident*. These labels were assigned based on the pattern of item–response probabilities for each class. The item–response probabilities summarized in Table V represent the probability of having $\geq 50\%$ of the assets in a category conditional on membership in a specific latent class.

The *Supported–Competent–Confident* class is defined by high probabilities of having half or more of the assets in *all* eight asset categories. More than a quarter (27%) of participants displayed this rich constellation of external and internal assets. These analyses reveal that one out of every four adolescents in this dataset reported having 50% or more of the support, empowerment, boundaries, and expectations, constructive use of time, commitment to learning, positive values, social competencies, *and* positive identity assets. In stark contrast, the *Unsupported–Unengaged–Unconfident* class—best representing 29% of adolescents in this sample—is characterized by low probabilities of having *any* of the eight asset categories. The prominence of this response pattern in the data gives us cause for concern as it suggests that nearly one-third of adolescents are unlikely to experience at least half of the assets in each category.

The *Supported Social Marginal* and *Unsupported Engaged* classes are defined by more nuanced response patterns. Adolescents estimated to fit in the *Supported Social Marginal* class have moderate probabilities of having 50% or more of all four external asset categories as well as a high probability of embracing a positive self-identity. These adolescents are likely to feel supported by the contexts that structure

Table V
Probabilities of Having 50% of the Assets in an Asset Category and Prevalence of Latent Class Membership

		Latent classes							
		Supported–Competent–Confident		Supported Social Marginal		Unsupported Engaged		Unsupported–Unengaged–Unconfident	
Parameter		Γ	SE	Γ	SE	Γ	SE	Γ	SE
Class Membership Prevalence	Full sample	.27	.002	.20	.004	.24	.004	.29	.003
	Random subsample range	.24–.30	–	.16–.27	–	.17–.28	–	.24–.33	–
Item–Response Probabilities		P	SE	P	SE	P	SE	P	SE
External asset categories									
Support	Full sample	**.92**	.003	**.61**	.008	.24	.006	.05	.002
	Random subsample range	.89–.94	–	.51–.67	–	.16–.30	–	.02–.07	–
Empowerment	Full sample	**.81**	.003	**.58**	.006	.25	.005	.15	.003
	Random subsample range	.78–.84	–	.50–.67	–	.23–.32	–	.12–.18	–
Boundaries and expectations	Full sample	**.94**	.002	**.59**	.006	**.59**	.005	.17	.003
	Random subsample range	.92–.96	–	.49–.64	–	.54–.62	–	.14–.20	–
Constructive use of time	Full sample	**.84**	.002	**.63**	.005	**.67**	.004	.38	.003
	Random subsample range	.82–.85	–	.59–.67	–	.62–.71	–	.22–.42	–
Internal asset categories									
Commitment to learning	Full sample	**.89**	.002	.41	.006	**.65**	.005	.13	.003
	Random subsample range	.88–.91	–	.35–.45	–	.59–.69	–	.11–.15	–

Positive values	Full sample	**.97**	.002	.54	.007	**.87**	.004	.28	.003
	Random subsample range	.95–.98	–	.45–.58	–	.83–.94	–	.24–.32	–
Social competencies	Full sample	**.79**	.004	.11	.006	.48	.006	.04	.002
	Random subsample range	.73–.83	–	.06–.16	–	.41–.59	–	.02–.05	–
Positive identity	Full sample	**.92**	.002	**.79**	.005	.53	.005	.36	.003
	Random subsample range	.91–.94	–	.72–.85	–	.51–.59	–	.31–.38	–

Notes. The probabilities of having ≥50% of the assets in an asset category are reported. The full sample was 155,927 participants. To assess model fit, 10 random subsamples of $n = 5000$ were drawn. To demonstrate the similarity between the 4-class model in the full sample and in the random subsamples, the range of item–response probabilities (rho estimates) for these 10 subsamples are also reported. Bold typeface was used to highlight those item–response probabilities in the moderate to high range (.55–1.0).

their daily lives and cared for at home, at school, and by their communities. Moreover, these adolescents feel good about themselves and their future. Yet, they are unlikely to possess a strong commitment to school and learning, positive values, and the skills to competently handle social situations. Thus, while these adolescents may feel supported by others and confident about themselves, they are likely to be at the margins of social situations. One in five adolescents (20%) displayed this asset profile. The *Unsupported Engaged* class is best characterized by moderate probabilities of having half or more of the boundaries and expectations, constructive use of time, and commitment to learning asset categories and a high probability of having positive values. Despite feeling unsupported and unempowered at home, school, and in the community, the 24% of adolescents estimated to fit in this class feel bound by others' expectations, find themselves constructively engaged in school and community activities, and are likely to espouse a prosocial orientation toward values like caring, responsibility, restraint, integrity, and a commitment to equality and social justice.

C. MULTIGROUP ANALYSES

Gender, school level, race/ethnicity, and mothers' education were added, separately, to the 4-class LCA model as grouping variables to identify differences, if any, in adolescents' item–response probabilities and latent class membership (Collins & Lanza, 2010). The 4-class LCA model with the item–response probabilities held invariant across each of the groups was selected.

Table VI displays the prevalence of adolescents, broken down by grouping characteristics, in each latent class. Females were more likely than their male peers to be fit in the *Supported–Competent–Confident* and *Unsupported Engaged* classes, while males were more likely than females to be in the *Supported Social Marginal* and *Unsupported–Unengaged–Unconfident* classes. Comparisons of middle- and high-school-aged adolescents revealed an interesting, although unsurprising, developmental pattern. While middle- and high-school students shared similar probabilities of being fit into the *Supported Social Marginal* and *Unsupported Engaged* classes, younger adolescents were more likely to be in the *Supported–Competent–Confident* class, while older students were more likely to be in the *Unsupported–Unengaged–Unconfident* class. These LCA findings reflecting a better asset profile for younger adolescents and girls quite neatly mirror variable-centered analyses that repeatedly have found the same patterns (e.g., Benson et al., 1998; Scales & Leffert, 2004).

Table VI

Prevalence of Latent Classes by Gender, School-Level, Race, and Family SES

Class membership prevalence		Full sample	Latent classes							
			Supported–Competent–Confident		Supported Social Marginal		Unsupported Engaged		Unsupported–Unengaged–Unconfident	
		%	Γ	SE	Γ	SE	Γ	SE	Γ	SE
Gender	Males	49	.19	.003	.34	.004	.11	.003	.36	.004
	Females	51	.33	.003	.09	.003	.37	.004	.21	.003
School level	6th–8th Grade	43	.35	.003	.20	.005	.22	.005	.23	.003
	9th–12th Grade	57	.20	.002	.19	.005	.26	.005	.34	.003
Race/ethnicity	American Indian	2	.21	.009	.26	.013	.18	.012	.35	.013
	Asian	3	.22	.008	.04	.007	.47	.011	.26	.007
	Black	7	.21	.006	.33	.010	.23	.009	.22	.010
	Hispanic	6	.18	.005	.15	.007	.30	.008	.37	.007
	White	76	.28	.003	.21	.004	.22	.004	.29	.004
	Multiracial	7	.22	.005	.19	.007	.27	.008	.32	.007
Mothers' education	More than HS	64	.32	.003	.24	.003	.23	.005	.24	.003
	HS or less	36	.19	.003	.37	.004	.25	.005	.37	.004

Notes. All comparisons were tested in separate multigroup LCA analyses. In each analysis, item–response probabilities were constrained to be equal across groups. With the exception of Family SES, participants self-identified group membership.

Unsupported–Unengaged–Unconfident was the most prevalent class for American Indian (35%), Hispanic (37%), and Multiracial (32%) adolescents (and also included a large proportion—29%—of White youth), while nearly half of Asian adolescents (47%) fit into the *Unsupported Engaged* class and one-third of Black adolescents (33%) fit into the *Supported Social Marginal* class (a class that was nearly devoid of Asian adolescents). Compared to adolescents of different races and ethnicities, White adolescents were the most likely to be in the *Supported–Competent–Confident* class. Adolescents whose mothers had a high-school education or less were disproportionately fit into the *Supported Social Marginal* and *Unsupported–Unengaged–Unconfident* classes, as compared to those whose mothers had obtained some postsecondary training. Using mothers' education as a rough proxy for familial SES, these data suggest that adolescents from high SES families are more likely than their peers from low SES families to experience an adequate and diverse array of developmental assets.

D. THRIVING AND RISK BEHAVIOR

To further understand the correlates of being estimated to fit in any given latent class, we tested the association between latent class membership and two behavioral indices: thriving (e.g., school grades, help-giving behavior) and risk (e.g., substance use, fighting) behavior. The effects of the thriving and risk behavior covariates were both highly significant. Consistent with our expectations and previous variable-centered analyses (Scales et al., 2000), we found that a one standard deviation *increase* in thriving is associated with increased odds of being in the *Supported–Competent–Confident* (OR = 40.83), *Supported Social Marginal* (OR = 4.94), and *Unsupported Engaged* (OR = 8.71) as compared to the *Unsupported–Unengaged–Unconfident* class. Similarly, the odds of membership in the *Supported–Competent–Confident* (Inverse OR = 125), *Supported Social Marginal* (Inverse OR = 1.84), and *Unsupported Engaged* (Inverse OR = 5.56) classes, relative to the *Unsupported–Unengaged–Unconfident* class, increased with a standard deviation *decrease* in risk behavior, a result also in line with previous variable-centered analysis (Leffert et al., 1998) and person-centered (Syvertsen, Cleveland, Gayles, Tibbits, & Faulk, 2010) analyses.

In other words, compared to their peers fit in the *Unsupported–Unengaged–Unconfident* class, youth in the asset-rich *Support–Competent–Confident* class had much greater odds of engaging in thriving and refraining from risk behaviors. While this also held true for youth in the *Supported Social Marginal* and *Unsupported Engaged* classes as well, the odds of thriving and decreased risk (when expressed as inverse odds ratios) were substantially lower. The pattern of these findings suggests that youth estimated to fit in the *Supported Social Marginal* class are only slightly better off than their peers in the *Unsupported–Unengaged–Unconfident* class.

VII. Next Steps in Research and Practice

The growing research on developmental assets supports many of the hypotheses central to the theory of PYD (Benson et al., 2006). Among these are

- developmental nutrients such as assets are cumulative for enhancing thriving and reducing risk behaviors;
- developmental ecologies (e.g., schools, after-school programs) can be intentionally altered to enhance developmental assets;
- ecologies are also cumulative, in the sense that youth gain strength when multiple ecologies support and nourish assets;
- persons (in this case, youth) and contexts are in dynamic relationship to each other such that contexts inform assets and youth, by their actions, can change contexts; and
- particular clusters or "packages" of developmental strengths are influential predictors of various outcomes, both concurrently and longitudinally.

This said, we would argue that the research underpinnings for PYD can and should be strengthened, as well as critical applied implications. Five key challenges and opportunities are the lack of longitudinal research in this arena, the possibilities and pitfalls of growing international interest in the developmental assets approach, the maturation of the applied science of turning ecologies into asset-building contexts, the activation of all sectors as asset-building forces, and the stimulating of widespread social change that turns asset-building into a national movement.

A particularly glaring "hole" in the literature has to do with longitudinal research. Although as a collective the studies on developmental assets have been quite consistent in their findings, the great majority have been cross-sectional and correlational. Thus, we continue to lack the kinds of focused studies that help clarify the role of asset-building interventions in a wide range of critical issues, including successful transitions into middle school and high school, the prevention of risk behaviors, the enhancement of thriving, and the successful launch of youth into adulthood. All these foci require longitudinal designs to more validly link change in the experience of developmental assets to particular future developmental outcomes.

The spread of the asset model to many other nations presents some important opportunities for both knowledge and practice. A global system of research and consulting needs to be developed to both better ensure responsible applications, and to discover how well the model addresses and promotes healthy development in emerging and transitional as well as developed nations. A particularly challenging issue is to ensure the cultural equivalence of developmental assets surveys in a manner that allows rapid adaptation and, therefore, more widespread use of those measurement tools.

One of most surprising lacunae in the understanding of developmental assets is how to build more asset-building environments for young people. Central to the idea of PYD is that developmental contexts (e.g., schools, families, neighborhoods, programs) matter for promoting the developmental nutrients youth need to succeed in life. Given this obvious truth, one would think that there is a robust science on how to change less asset-building ecologies into more vibrant asset-building ones. Other than the more narrowly focused prevention programs that have traditionally dominated the youth development field, there are at best, however, only episodic and sporadic efforts to (a) develop a science-based approach to ecological change, (b) orchestrate that change, (c) measure change in the intended context, and (d) assess how context changes actually inform individual-level development. Until this science develops and matures, the promise of PYD for changing outcomes will be limited.

A fourth issue is broadening the participation of various sectors in asset-building. PYD principles embodied in the developmental asset model have moved quickly into some areas of practice. Schools, after-school programs, and community-building initiatives are among the formal settings that have embraced this approach. The model of asset-building, however, explicitly and intentionally, requires the activation of two sectors that are both more difficult to reach and essential for raising asset-rich youth. The first is family; however, it is constituted. Family adults, we would hypothesize, have disproportionate power for promoting assets. Simultaneously, parents and guardians serve as gatekeepers for how youth access quality, asset-building community resources. If we are to strengthen the asset infrastructure for young people, a major national initiative to reach and equip families is necessary.

The second sector that is critical but underutilized is the general public. Awakening public engagement requires a shift in national consciousness toward the idea that "all kids are our kids." This idea is not a central organizing principle in the United States (Benson, 2006; Scales et al.,

2003). Changing the public mindset may seem a Herculean task, but until this shift happens, much of the best energy for asset-building lays dormant.

Finally, there is the issue of social change and its role in elevating the asset profile of a nation's youth. As we have noted earlier, a considerable volume of research on developmental assets (and aligned frameworks like the 5 Promises of America's Promise Alliance—Scales et al., 2008) documents that many and perhaps most middle- and high-school youth in the United States experience low rather than high levels of critical developmental nutrients. Youth policy and funding in the United States is largely shaped around specific outcomes like school graduation rates/test scores or substance abuse prevention and rarely around the kinds of developmental building blocks/nutrients/assets that are so critical for the production of those and numerous other outcomes. Orchestrating national efforts around enhancing critical "inputs" for success is long overdue. In this regard, there may be something to be learned from the role of comparative studies in motivating action. In the first decade of the twenty-first century, for example, much has been made of international studies of math and science test scores and high school and college graduation rates. As the United States slides down the international rankings of developed nations on these kinds of measures, policy and funding is rallied around these issues. To mobilize a similar kind of wake-up call around developmental "inputs," an international comparison of youth developmental assets just might provide both a sobering national portrait and the spark that fuels a national call to action.

The irony in such national "calls," of course, is that these actions to improve the lives of *individuals* invariably improve *national* well-being. This relationship demonstrates at a grand scale the enduring validity of a staple principle of developmental systems theories, namely, that truly adaptive development enhances *both* the individual and the context. In this sense, thriving civil society and thriving young people go hand in hand (Benson & Scales, 2009; Lerner, 2004; Lerner, Brentano, Dowling, & Anderson, 2002; Scales, Benson, & Roehlkepartain, 2010). Thus, the stakes for both scholars and practitioners to better understand and more widely apply the framework of developmental assets and the science of PYD could not be higher.

REFERENCES

Benson, P. L. (1990). *The troubled journey: A portrait of 6th–12th grade youth.* Minneapolis, MN: Search Institute.

Benson, P. L. (1997). *All kids are our kids: What communities must do to raise caring and responsible children and adolescents.* San Francisco: Jossey-Bass.

Benson, P. L. (2002). Adolescent development in social and community context: A program of research. *New Directions for Youth Development, 95,* 123–147.

Benson, P. L. (2003). Developmental assets and asset building communities: Conceptual and empirical foundations. In R. M. Lerner & P. L. Benson (Eds.), *Developmental assets and asset-building communities: Implications for research, policy, and practice* (pp. 19–43). Norwell, MA: Kluwer Academic.

Benson, P. L. (2006). *All kids are our kids: What communities must do to raise caring and responsible children and adolescents* San Francisco: Jossey-Bass.

Benson, P. L., Leffert, N., Scales, P. C., & Blyth, D. A. (1998). Beyond the 'village' rhetoric: Creating healthy communities for children and adolescents. *Applied Developmental Science, 2*(3), 138–159.

Benson, P. L., & Scales, P. C. (2009). Positive youth development and the prevention of youth aggression and violence. *European Journal of Developmental Science, 3,* 218–234.

Benson, P. L., & Scales, P. C. (in press). Developmental assets. In R. J. R. Levesque (Ed.), *Encyclopedia of adolescence.* New York: Springer.

Benson, P. L., Scales, P. C., Hamilton, S. F., & Sesma, A. (2006). Positive youth development: Theory, research, and applications. In W. Damon & R. M. Lerner (Eds.), *Handbook of child psychology.* (6th ed., pp. 894–941). New York: John Wiley.

Benson, P. L., Scales, P. C., Leffert, N., & Roehlkepartain, E. C. (1999). *A fragile foundation: The state of developmental assets among American youth.* Minneapolis, MN: Search Institute.

Campos, B. E. (2004). Processes of risk and resilience during adolescence: Linking contexts and individuals. In R. M. Lerner & L. Steinberg (Eds.), *Handbook of adolescent psychology.* Hoboken, NJ: John Wiley & Sons.

Chinman, M., Acosta, J., Burkhart, Q., Clifford, M., Duffy, T., Ebener, P., et al. (in press). Establishing and evaluating the key functions of an Interactive Systems Framework based on assets-getting to outcomes. *American Journal of Community Psychology.*

Cohen, J. (1988). *Statistical power analysis for the behavioral sciences* Hillsdale, NJ: Erlbaum.

Collins, L. M., & Lanza, S. T. (2010). *Latent class and latent transition analysis: With applications in the social, behavioral, and health sciences.* Hoboken, NJ: John Wiley & Sons.

Eccles, J. S., & Gootman, J. A. (2002). *Community programs to promote youth development.* Washington, DC: National Academy Press.

Fisher, D., Imm, P., Chinman, M., & Wandersman, A. (2006). *Getting to outcomes with developmental assets: Ten steps to measuring success in youth programs and communities.* Minneapolis, MN: Search Institute.

Friedman, R. J., & Chase-Lansdale, P. L. (2002). Chronic adversities. In M. Rutter & E. Taylor (Eds.), *Child and adolescent psychiatry.* (4th ed., pp. 261–276). Oxford, UK: Blackwell Science.

Leffert, N., Benson, P. L., & Roehlkepartain, J. L. (1997). *Starting out right: Developmental assets for children.* Minneapolis, MN: Search Institute.

Leffert, N., Benson, P. L., Scales, P. C., Sharma, A. R., Drake, D. R., & Blyth, D. A. (1998). Developmental assets: Measurement and prediction of risk behaviors among adolescents. *Applied Developmental Science, 2*(4), 209–230.

Lerner, R. M. (2004). *Liberty: Thriving and civic engagement among America's youth.* Thousand Oaks, CA: Sage.

Lerner, R. M., Brentano, C., Dowling, E. M., & Anderson, P. M. (2002). Positive youth developmnt: Thriving as the basis of personhood and civil society. *New Directinos for Youth Development, 95,* 11–33.

Mannes, M., Benson, P. L., Kretzmann, J., & Norris, T. (2003). The American tradition of community development: Implications for guiding community engagement in youth development. In R. M. Lerner, F. Jacobs & D. Wertlieb (Eds.), *Handbook of applied developmental science: Promoting positive child, adolescent, and family development through research, policies and programs; Vol. 1, Applying developmental science for youth and families: Historical and theoretical foundations.* (pp. 469–499). Thousand Oaks, CA: Sage.

MGS Consulting. (2008). *Community access to technology program evaluation report—Year 3.* Seattle, WA: Author.

Roberts, C., & Scales, P. C. (2005). *Developmental assets and academic achievement. Miniplenary session presented at annual healthy communities, healthy youth conference, Dallas, TX* November 2005, Available throughwww.search-institute.org.

Roehlkepartain, E. C., Benson, P. L., & Sesma, A. (2003). *Signs of progress in putting children first: Developmental assets among youth in St. Louis Park, 1997–2001.* Minneapolis, MN: Unpublished report prepared by Search Institute for St. Louis Park's Children First Initiative.

Rutter, M. (1987a). Psychosocial resilience and protective mechanisms. *The American Journal of Orthopsychiatry, 57*(3), 316–331.

Rutter, M. (1987b). Psychosocial resilience and protective mechanisms. In J. Rolf, A. Masten, D. Cichetti, K. Nuechterlein & S. Weintraub (Eds.), *Risk and protective factors in the development of psychopathology.* (pp. 181–214). New York: Cambridge University Press.

Scales, P. C. (1999). Reducing risks and building developmental assets: Essential actions for promoting adolescent health. *The Journal of School Health, 69,* 113–119.

Scales, P. C. (2011). Youth developmental assets in global perspective: Results from international adaptations of the Developmental Assets Profile. Child Indicators Research, doi:10.1007/s12187-011-9112-8 Advance online publication.

Scales, P. C., & Benson, P. L. (2007). Building developmental assets to encourage students' school success. *Instructional Leader (Texas Elementary Principals and Supervisors Association), 20*(3), 1–3, 8–10, 12.

Scales, P. C., Benson, P. L., Leffert, N., & Blyth, D. A. (2000). Contribution of developmental assets to the prediction of thriving among adolescents. *Applied Developmental Science, 4*(1), 27–46.

Scales, P. C., Benson, P. L., Mannes, M., Hintz, N. R., Roehlkepartain, E. C., & Sullivan, T. K. (2003). *Other people's kids: Social expectations and American adults' involvement with children and adolescents.* New York: Kluwer Academic/Plenum.

Scales, P. C., Benson, P. L., Moore, K. A., Lippman, L., Brown, B., & Zaff, J. F. (2008). Promoting equal developmental opportunity and outcomes among America's children and youth: Results from the National Promises Study. *The Journal of Primary Prevention, 29,* 121–144.

Scales, P. C., Benson, P. L., & Roehlkepartain, E. C. (2010). Adolescent thriving: The role of sparks, relationships, and empowerment. *Journal of Youth and Adolescence, 40*(3), 263–277.

Scales, P. C., Benson, P. L., Roehlkepartain, E. C., Sesma, A., & van Dulmen, M. (2006). The role of developmental assets in predicting academic achievement: A longitudinal study. *Journal of Adolescence, 29,* 691–708.

Scales, P. C., & Fisher, D. (2010). *Tips for building the developmental assets most linked to common positive youth development program outcomes.* Retrieved January 26, 2011 from http://www.search-institute.org/system/files/PrevPrograms.pdf.

Scales, P. C., Foster, K. C., Mannes, M., Horst, M. A., Pinto, K. C., & Rutherford, A. (2005). School-business partnerships, developmental Assets, and positive developmental outcomes among urban high school students: A mixed-methods study. *Urban Education*, *40*, 144–189.

Scales, P. C., & Leffert, N. (1999). *Developmental assets: A synthesis of the scientific research on adolescent development*. Minneapolis, MN: Search Institute.

Scales, P. C., & Leffert, N. (2004). *Developmental assets: A synthesis of the scientific research on adolescent development* Minneapolis, MN: Search Institute.

Scales, P. C., Roehlkepartain, E. C., Neal, M., Kielsmeier, J. C., & Benson, P. L. (2006). Reducing academic achievement gaps: The role of community service and service-learning. *Journal of Experiential Education*, *29*(1), 38–60.

Scales, P. C., Sesma, A., & Bolstrom, B. (2004a). *Coming into their own: How developmental assets promote positive growth in middle childhood*. Minneapolis, MN: Search Institute.

Scales, P. C., Sesma, A., & Bolstrom, B. (2004b). *Me and my world: Technical manual*. Minneapolis, MN: Search Institute.

Scales, P. C., & Tibbetts, K. (in preparation). *The connection of school-relevant developmental assets and cultural competence to psychological and social well-being among Hawaiian youth: Initial results from the 'Opio Youth Development & Assets Survey*. Minneapolis: Search Institute.

Scales, P. C., Roehlkepartain, E. C., & Benson, P. L. (in press). Beyond adolescence: A framework of developmental assets for young adulthood. *Search Institute Insights & Evidence*.

Schorr, L., & Marchand, V. (2007). *Pathway to successful young adulthood. (Pathways Mapping Initiative)*. Washington, DC: Center for the Study of Social Policy. Retrieved January 19, 2010 from *http://www.cssp.org/uploadFiles/Youth%20Pathway%20PDF% 209-07.pdf*.

Search Institute. (2005). *Developmental assets profile: User manual*. Minneapolis, MN: Search Institute.

Small, S., & Memmo, M. (2004). Contemporary models of youth development and problem prevention: Toward an integration of terms, concepts, and models. *Family Relations*, *53*, 3–11.

Starkman, N. A., Scales, P. C., & Roberts, C. R. (2006). *Great places to learn: How asset-building schools help students succeed* Minneapolis: Search Institute.

Syvertsen, A. K., Cleveland, M. J., Gayles, J. G., Tibbits, M. K., & Faulk, M. T. (2010). Profiles of protection from substance use among adolescents. *Prevention Science*, *11*, 185–196.

Syvertsen, A. K., Scales, P. C., & Benson, P. C. (in preparation). *Patterns of developmental opportunity: A person-centered approach to exploring U.S. adolescents' experience of developmental assets*. Minneapolis: Search Institute.

Theokas, C., Almerigi, J. B., Lerner, R. M., Dowling, E. M., Benson, P. L., Scales, P. C., et al. (2005). Conceptualizing and modeling individual components of thriving in early adolescence. *Journal of Early Adolescence*, *25*(1), 113–143.

VanderVen, K. (2008). *Promoting positive development in early childhood: Building blocks for a successful start*. New York: Springer Science + Media.

Wilson, D. S., O'Brien, D. T., & Sesma, A. (2009). Human prosociality from an evolutionary perspective: Variation and correlations at a city-wide scale. *Evolution and Human Behavior*, *30*, 190–200.

YOUTH ACTIVITY INVOLVEMENT AND POSITIVE YOUTH DEVELOPMENT

Megan Kiely Mueller,* Selva Lewin-Bizan,* and Jennifer Brown Urban[†]

* TUFTS UNIVERSITY, MEDFORD, MASSACHUSETTS, USA
[†] MONTCLAIR STATE UNIVERSITY, MONTCLAIR, NEW JERSEY, USA

Abstract

Participation in high quality out-of-school-time activities constitutes a significant portion of the time that many youth spend away from their families or school settings, and current theory and research suggests that activity participation can be an influential contextual asset for promoting adaptive outcomes for youth. Therefore, the purpose of this chapter is to highlight how the relational developmental-systems-based positive youth development perspective is a useful framework for examining how and why high quality activity participation may be associated with positive developmental outcomes. As an example of research within this framework, we present findings from the 4-H Study of Positive Youth Development in order to illustrate how activity participation is an important facet of aligning individual youth strengths with resources within the environment. Finally, we discuss how to synthesize the research that exists on activity participation, and what the current research suggests for future empirical and applied steps in the field.

Advances in Child Development and Behavior
Richard M. Lerner, Jacqueline V. Lerner and Janette B. Benson : Editors

Both theory and research suggest that participation in high-quality out-of-school-time (OST) activities is an influential contextual asset for promoting positive outcomes in the lives of youth (Eccles & Gootman, 2002; Mahoney, Larson, & Eccles, 2005; Mahoney, Vandell, Simkins, & Zarrett, 2009). Eccles and Gootman (2002) synthesized existing data on community programs for youth and reported that positive experiences within these programs are important "developmental assets," that is, resources promoting the positive development of youth (Benson, Scales, Hamilton, & Sesma, 2006; Benson, Scales, & Syvertsen, 2011). Mahoney, Larson, Eccles and Lord (2005) have pointed to the features of organized activity participation that may provide these positive, growth-supportive experiences and, as such, promote healthy and adaptive development; these program features include appropriate structure, supportive relationships, and positive social norms (see Lerner, Phelps, Forman, & Bowers, 2009 and Mahoney et al., 2009 for further discussion).

OST activity participation constitutes a significant portion of the time that many youth spend away from their families or school settings. From the early elementary school years through high school, adolescent participants in extant longitudinal research have been found to engage in multiple OST activities (e.g., Larson, Hansen, & Moneta, 2006); in fact, the National Institute of Out-of-School Time (2003) reports that two-thirds of American adolescents participate in at least two OST activities during the school year.

However, such findings may be limited by the nature of the samples involved in this research. For example, some studies with younger participants found that children from low-income families are less likely to participate in OST activities (Dearing et al., 2009). As well, practitioners have noted that youth who live in low-resource environments (e.g., with a lack of financial resources to support or provide access to and engagement in such OST programs) are not, in fact, able to participate in OST activities (A. Roberts, personal communication, January 18, 2011). Do or can OST activities constitute developmental assets for youth across the range of demographic variables (involving socioeconomic status, race, ethnicity, rural–urban–suburban living status, etc.) characterizing contemporary American adolescents? Simply, current research is not comprehensive enough to afford a certain answer to this question, a point that will be discussed again in the final section of this chapter.

Nevertheless, given the potential importance of OST activity participation in shaping the lives of youth, the purpose of this chapter is threefold. First, we will highlight how the developmental systems-based positive youth development (PYD) perspective (Lerner, Lerner, & Benson, 2011) is a useful frame for exploring how and why high-quality activity participation is associated with adaptive developmental outcomes. Next, we use research from the 4-H Study of PYD to illustrate how activity participation is an important facet of aligning individual youth strengths with resources within the environment. Finally, we discuss how to synthesize the research that exists on activity participation, and what the current research suggests as future steps in the field. In particular, if OST participation is a vital developmental asset for youth, what are the barriers that exist for many youth in preventing them from participating in such programs? How can practitioners and policy makers use the extant research on youth programming to inform their programmatic and policy decisions? How can we better use OST activities to promote positive development among the diverse youth of America?

I. Adolescent Development and the PYD Perspective

Traditionally, adolescence has been considered a time of "storm and stress," with purported universal, biologically based changes believed to inevitably drive adolescents to a period of emotional and physical conflict and stress (e.g., Hall, 1904). This approach to adolescent research was based on a biological reductionism fostering the view that adolescents were simply "problems to be managed" (Roth & Brooks-Gunn, 2003) and that, in regard to empirical foci, research should consider how to prevent or ameliorate the inevitable biologically (e.g., genetically) predetermined negative consequences of the adolescent period (e.g., Erikson, 1968).

However, contemporary research in human development is framed by relational, developmental systems models (Overton, 2010). These models stress that the fundamental process of human development involves mutually influential relations between the developing individual and the multiple levels of the ecology of human development, represented as individual ↔ context relations. This relational, developmental systems framework rejects the reductionist notion of genetically predetermined outcomes.

As such, developmental systems theory provides a broader and more optimistic theoretical frame for studying adolescent development in particular. That is, developmental systems theory indicates that youth should be studied not in isolation but, instead, as the product of the bidirectional relationships between the individual and his or her environment. As well, because the theory emphasizes that there is plasticity (the potential for systematic change across the life span; Lerner, 1984) in these individual ↔ context relations, there are multiple directions of change (e.g., from problematic to positive) that can derive from variation in an adolescent's history of his or her relations within the context. If there is the potential for systematic change, then we can be optimistic that research can identify combinations of individual and contextual variables that can positively alter the course of development. Accordingly, in attempts to optimize development across the human life span, we can align the plasticity of youth with developmental assets in the changing context in order to enhance the course of human development. Therefore, relational, developmental systems theory is both different from and an advance beyond its theoretical predecessors. Many past developmental theories about adolescence have taken reductionist, split conceptions of development that separate nature and nurture variables (e.g., Plomin, 1986; Rowe, 1994) and do not allow for the optimism inherent in relational, developmental systems theories.

When the conceptual and empirical work predicated on a developmental systems theory model of individual ↔ context relations has been linked to the study of adolescent development, it has afforded the elaboration of a strength-based view of this age period, that is, the PYD perspective. The PYD perspective stresses that the plasticity of the individual ↔ context relations represents the strengths of individuals and the developmental assets of their ecologies, respectively; when these strengths and assets are aligned systematically over the course of the adolescent period, thriving is promoted. Current developmental research has been shaped by the innovations brought about by this (PYD) perspective (Lerner et al., 2009). As such, researchers have considered the integrated role of multiple contexts of adolescent development, such as the family, peers, schools, and neighborhoods, in providing a basis for, and outcomes of, the actions of people developing across this period of life (e.g., Lerner et al., 2005; Theokas & Lerner, 2006; Urban, Lewin-Bizan, & Lerner, 2009).

A. YOUTH ACTIVITY INVOLVEMENT AND PYD

Given the importance that the developmental systems-framed PYD perspective places on the relationship between an individual and his or her context, what, then, are the important contextual variables, that, when aligned with individual strengths, promote PYD? We have noted that one important contextual asset to consider is the role of community-based, youth-serving organizations, and how they may have resources that promote positive development (Li, Bebiroglu, Phelps, & Lerner, 2009). As designed facets of the ecology, programmatic experiences intended to foster positive development among youth are a potentially powerful basis of support of PYD (Mahoney et al., 2009).

In fact, an extensive body of research has shown that high-quality, structured OST programs promote a host of positive outcomes across many domains. One such asset afforded by many OST programs is the development of initiative skills (Hansen, Larson, & Dworkin, 2003; see also Larson & Rusk, 2011). Larson (2000) defines initiative as "... the ability to be motivated from within to direct attention and effort toward a challenging goal" (p. 170). Initiative also includes overcoming setbacks, and reevaluating and adjusting goal–achievement strategies (Larson, 2000). In addition to being associated with motivation and initiative skills, participating in OST activities has also been associated with setting goals, managing time, developing agency, taking leadership of their own development (Dworkin, Larson, & Hansen, 2003), and having personal responsibility (Wood, Larson, & Brown, 2009).

As adolescence is a significant period for identity formation, it is also important to note that youth activity participation choices have an impact on identity development in terms of expectations for success and self-beliefs about ability (Barber, Stone, Hunt, & Eccles, 2005). Activity participation has also been linked with youth self-concept of ability in the domain of the activity, which in turn predicts future continuation of participation in activities in the same domain (Simpkins, Vest, & Becnel, 2010).

In addition to promoting positive initiative and self-concept-related outcomes, OST participation has also been linked to civic engagement (Sherrod & Lauckhardt, 2009; Stoneman, 2002), interpersonal skills such as emotional regulation (Larson & Brown, 2007; Larson et al., 2006), and structuring positive and prosocial peer relations (Barber et al., 2005; Mahoney et al., 2009).

Participation in OST activities can also have an impact on youth achievement within the school setting (Zaff, Moore, Papillo, & Williams, 2003). Fredricks and Eccles (2005) found that in the high-school years, participation in a variety of extracurricular activities is linked to higher school engagement, lower risk behaviors, positive academic adjustment outcomes, and having more friends within the school setting. Similarly, Mahoney and colleagues found that youth participating in after-school programs reported higher academic performance and motivational attributes as compared to those who had parent, self, or sibling care during after-school hours (Mahoney, Lord, & Carryl, 2005).

Further, there is support for the notion that school-based extracurricular activities may be a mediator in promoting educational attainment. Participation in such activities is associated with adaptive goal skills (which are related to initiative). Such skills are a critical aspect of promoting both interpersonal competence (maintaining positive relationships, avoiding conflicts) and increased educational aspirations, which, in turn, are excellent predictors of educational attainment (Mahoney, Cairns, & Farmer, 2003). This relationship between consistent participation and educational success is especially strong for youth who start out with low interpersonal skills.

In addition to the host of domain-specific positive developmental outcomes associated with OST activity participation, involvement in a high-quality activity has also been linked to overall PYD (Lerner et al., 2009; Zarrett et al., 2009). Therefore, it is clear from the extant research that participation in structured OST activities is a developmental asset critical to promoting PYD (Lerner, 2005). Given the importance of OST activity participation as an ecological asset in promoting positive developmental outcomes in adolescence, it is important to understand the facets of activity participation, that, when aligned with individual strengths, are important in facilitating these positive outcomes.

B. FEATURES OF ACTIVITY PARTICIPATION

Given that OST programs are often structured with activities that are of interest to youth participants, they can provide a context with intrinsically appealing and motivating experiences, therefore enhancing the potential for promoting positive developmental outcomes (see Larson & Rusk, 2011). Hansen and Larson (2007) found that participants who were motivated by their organized activity participation experienced more positive developmental experiences within the activity context. Further, theories of motivation suggest that interest and intrinsic motivation are linked to positive achievement and motivational outcomes (Wigfield, Eccles, Schiefele, Roeser, & Davis-Kean, 2006; see also Larson & Rusk, 2011). The value of the activity is an important aspect of youth maintaining a sense of identity within the program context, which, in turn, promotes long-term participation in the activity (Barber et al., 2005).

As the nature and quality of youth OST activity involvement is so critical to positive development, it is important to delineate the precise features of programs that serve as crucial developmental assets for youth. Youth development (YD) programs are an example of a domain of OST activities. YD programs are defined as structured activities having a theory of change that associates program characteristics and activities with positive developmental outcomes (Lerner, 2004). Eccles and Gootman (2002) suggested eight program characteristics that were conceptually linked to proving a positive developmental setting: physical and psychological safety, appropriate structure, supportive relationships, opportunities to belong, positive social norms, support for efficacy and mattering, opportunities for skill building, and integration of family, school, and community efforts. Subsequent reviews and meta-analyses (Blum, 2003; Roth & Brooks-Gunn, 2003) reduced these features to three (coined "The Big Three"; Lerner, 2004).

YD programs often contain these "Big Three" program characteristics, that is, (1) positive and sustained (for at least one year; Rhodes, 2002) adult–youth relations; (2) youth life-skill building activities; and (3) youth participation in and leadership of valued community activities (Lerner, 2004). Examples of YD programs are 4-H Clubs and after-school programs, Big Brothers Big Sisters, Boys and Girls Clubs, YMCA, and Boy Scouts and Girl Scouts. These programs incorporate the Big Three characteristics and provide a structured environment serving as a developmental asset that encourages youth to take leadership of (agency in) their development (Eccles & Gootman, 2002; Larson, 2000) and to develop needed and useful life skills (Mahoney, Larson, Eccles, & Lord, 2005). Greater participation in such programs has been linked to indicators of PYD (Balsano, Phelps, Theokas, Lerner, & Lerner, 2009; Mahoney et al., 2009), and to the growth of positive outcomes such as higher grades, school value, self-esteem, and resiliency (Fredricks & Eccles, 2005).

In addition to examining the structure of an activity (such as a YD program) as well as youth engagement in the program, it is also important to examine youth patterns of participation. These patterns can include duration of participation, the intensity or frequency with which a youth is involved in activities, and breadth of involvement in various types of programs (Mahoney et al., 2009). Duration, or consistency of participation over time, in a YD program has been shown to predict positive outcomes (Kiely, 2010; Zaff et al., 2003). A similar impact on positive outcomes exists in regard to intensity of involvement (especially when there is also high duration of participation; Gardner, Roth, & Brooks-Gunn, 2008). In sum, these findings point to the importance of including conceptually predicated and evidence-based structure and content in OST activities (not just for YD programs, but in any OST activity), so as to provide the support necessary to promote positive developmental outcomes.

II. Individual ↔ Context Relations in OST Activities: Findings from the 4-H Study of PYD

It is clear from the extant research that activity involvement constitutes an important developmental ecological asset for youth. However, the specific facets of participation, including type of activity and patterns of participation, require nuanced research to delineate the most adaptive practices for aligning the strengths of youth with the assets provided by program participation. Further, it is critical for such research to be framed in a relational, developmental systems, PYD perspective if it is to elucidate the specific patterns of individual ↔ context relations that account for the array of outcomes associated with OST activities that eventuate in PYD (or not) among diverse youth.

The 4-H Study of PYD is a longitudinal study that exemplifies a developmental systems approach to PYD research. The 4-H Study of PYD is a longitudinal investigation that initially studied a cohort of fifth graders and now includes information through the twelfth grade (Bowers et al., 2010; Lerner et al., 2005; Phelps et al., 2007, 2009). The purpose of this study was to explore the various ways in which individual strengths align with ecological developmental assets to promote PYD.

A. INTENTIONAL SELF-REGULATION SKILLS

When examining youth activity participation, a key task in assessing the alignment of individual skills with ecological assets is to explore if there are in fact particular characteristics of youth that may be linked to effectively engaging adolescents in programs in ways that maximize the probability of PYD. Gestsdóttir and colleagues (Gestsdóttir & Lerner, 2007, 2008; Gestsdóttir, Lewin-Bizan, von Eye, Lerner, & Lerner, 2009) have suggested that intentional self-regulation behaviors, involving the *selection* of positive or developmentally beneficial goals, acting to *optimize* the resources needed to make such goals a reality, and possessing the ability to *compensate* effectively when goals are blocked, are thecharacteristics that youth need to seek out and use maximally the resources in the environment, such as those represented by (or found within) youth programs. These selection (S), optimization (O), and compensation (C) skills (i.e., SOC skills) provide the architecture for an individual to contribute to mutually beneficial relations with his or her context, in other words, to engage in adaptive developmental regulations (i.e., adaptive individual ↔ context relations). The SOC model offers a framework for understanding adolescents' abilities to influence or select from and use the resources in the context of the program that is, in turn, influencing them (Freund & Baltes, 2002; Gestsdóttir & Lerner, 2008; Lerner, Freund, De Stefanis & Habermas, 2001).

Research from the 4-H Study of PYD has indicated that SOC skills are in fact predictive of PYD outcomes (Gestsdóttir & Lerner, 2007; Zimmerman, Phelps, & Lerner, 2007), such that high SOC scores are associated with the highest PYD trajectories (Zimmerman, Phelps, & Lerner, 2008). Therefore, it is reasonable to expect that if the OST program experiences of youth were structured to provide the developmental assets of positive adult relationships, skill building, and leadership opportunities, then, when such program features are aligned with individual strengths, such as intentional self-regulation, these programs should constitute an ideal setting for promoting positive individual ↔ context relations and should result in PYD.

In fact, there is empirical support for the notion that participation in high-quality, structured YD programs, when aligned with individual intentional self-regulation skills, may also promote Contribution, the purported "Sixth C" of PYD, and, theoretically, a key outcome of PYD (Lerner, 2004, 2009). Contribution (e.g., contribution to self, family, community, society; Lerner et al., 2005) is often regarded as an important outcome related to PYD (Lerner, 2004), and one that YD programs (such as 4-H) often focus on in particular. For instance, using data from Grades 8–10 of the 4-H Study of PYD, Mueller et al. (in press) found that YD program participation and intentional self-regulation skills in Grades 8 and 9 predicted Contribution in Grade 10. As well, Grade 8 YD participation predicted Grade 9 intentional self-regulation skills, which, in turn, predicted Grade 10 PYD and Contribution. These findings suggested that there is a relationship between the contextual resource of YD programs and the individual asset of intentional self-regulation skills, such that YD programs may in fact be promoting the intentional self-regulation skills that are believed to be critical in youth thriving (Gestsdóttir & Lerner, 2008).

B. PATTERNS OF ACTIVITY PARTICIPATION

In addition to assessing the role of individual skills in affecting outcomes associated with youth activity participation, it is also important to examine various patterns of participation and how the configurations of activities youth are involved in may differentially affect developmental outcomes. Consistent with other work on activity involvement and PYD (Linver, Roth, & Brooks-Gunn, 2009), Zarrett and colleagues found that for youth in Grades 5–7, the benefits of participating in sports were different depending on the other types of activities in which youth also participated (Zarrett, Peltz, Fay, Li, & Lerner, 2007). In fact, youth who participated in sports along with a YD program showed the highest levels of PYD and the lowest levels of risk behaviors, even when controlling for the total time youth spent in activity participation and duration of participation (Zarrett et al., 2007, 2009).

While research on OST programs suggests that, in general, increased participation in OST activities is linked to positive developmental outcomes (e.g., Mahoney et al., 2009), Zarrett et al. (2009) suggests that a more nuanced relationship exists. For example, in some instances, high participation can lead to higher PYD, but also to higher risk of depression, perhaps due to increased parental pressure or issues of time management that could arise from being highly engaged in multiple activities (Zarrett et al., 2009).

These findings point to the complexity of the ways in which youth may be influenced by their participation in OST activities and suggests that a more nuanced approach is necessary, one that establishes how much and what kind of programs are beneficial to youth of particular characteristics.

C. NEIGHBORHOOD EFFECTS AND ACTIVITY INVOLVEMENT

From a relational, developmental systems perspective, it is important to consider the multiple contexts that influence YD, including the neighborhoods in which youth live. Neighborhoods potentially provide opportunities for youth to find meaningful ways to actively participate in processes that affect their development (Benson et al., 2006; see also, Benson et al., 2011). All youth can benefit from involvement in supportive ecologies, contexts, and relationships (Benson et al., 2006); however, depending on an individual's social location and individual characteristics (such as self-regulation), the strategies for promoting these assets may differ. For example, the quality of neighborhood resources such as recreational and social programs (parks, community centers, and sports programs), schools, and social services may mediate the effects of neighborhoods on youth well-being (Leventhal & Brooks-Gunn, 2000; Leventhal, Dupere, & Brooks-Gunn, 2009).

Using data from Grades 5–7 of the 4-H Study of PYD, Urban et al. (2009) found that the relationship between activity involvement and neighborhood assets was such that girls living in lower asset neighborhoods exhibited higher levels of PYD and lower levels of depressive symptoms and risk behaviors when they engaged in extracurricular activities, whereas boys living in lower asset neighborhoods exhibited lower levels of PYD and higher levels of risk behaviors when engaged in moderate to high levels of extracurricular activities. However, this pattern did not emerge for youth living in higher asset neighborhoods. Girls living in higher asset neighborhoods exhibited lower levels of PYD and higher levels of depressive symptoms and risk behaviors when engaged in moderate to high levels of extracurricular activities, and boys living in higher asset neighborhoods exhibited higher levels of PYD and lower levels of risk behaviors when engaged in moderate to high levels of extracurricular activities.

In order to gain a better understanding of the potential links between individual self-regulatory processes and the characteristics of the ecology in which the person is embedded, Urban, Lewin-Bizan, and Lerner (2010) focused on youth living in neighborhoods characterized as having lower ecological assets to assess how an individuals' ability to self-regulate interacts with participation in extracurricular activities to affect the course of PYD. Again using data from Grades 5–7 of the 4-H Study of PYD, Urban et al. (2010) found that, in general, youth living in lower asset settings who had the greatest capacity to self-regulate benefited the most from involvement in extracurricular activities, as exhibited by higher levels of PYD. Girls in these lower asset settings also tended to exhibit lower levels of depressive symptoms and risk behaviors, whereas, for boys, no significant relationships were found between self-regulation, extracurricular activity involvement, and scores for depressive symptoms and risk behaviors.

Consistent with a relational, developmental systems approach, the findings reported by Urban et al. (2009, 2010) illustrate that the individual strengths of youth and the assets available in their neighborhood contexts contribute to thriving. Youth living in lower asset neighborhoods may find it particularly difficult to access extracurricular activities and, therefore, those youth with the greatest capacity to self-regulate may have the ability to secure and take advantage of opportunities needed to enhance their positive development. In addition, intentional self-regulation may influence the kinds of activities in which youth choose to participate and the peers with whom they choose to interact. Youth who are better able to self-regulate may choose higher quality programs that better fit their individual needs and more positive peer groups. However, future research must explore why the evidence supporting the relational, developmental systems approach appears to be stronger for girls than for boys. In addition, continued longitudinal analyses should examine whether these patterns persist through adolescence, or whether the neighborhood context takes on additional meaning as youth mature and access to neighborhood resources is brokered less by parents and more by adolescents' own ability to self-regulate. These ideas about specific foci of future research allow us to consider more generally the scholarly agenda that should be engaged to enhance the understanding about, and application of knowledge pertinent to, the links between OST activities and PYD.

III. Toward Further Advances in Research and Application

There is a good deal of research exploring how various types and patterns of OST activity participation, located in diverse contexts, for individuals with differing characteristics, may promote developmental outcomes. However, the breadth of such research presents a challenge when attempting to synthesize findings and to develop cohesive recommendations for application to policy and youth-serving programs. What does the current body of research tell us about the direction of future research on the impact of youth activity involvement as an

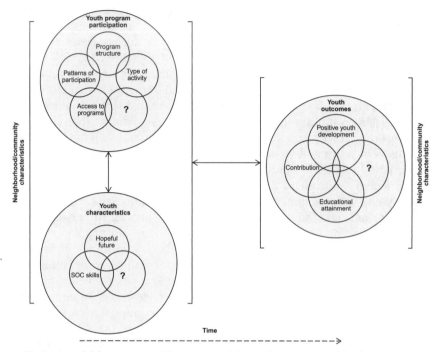

Fig. 1. A model for current and future research in youth program participation.

important contextual resource, and how would such future research inform practical application in optimizing PYD?

Figure 1 may be a useful frame for developing programs of research aimed at addressing this admittedly complex question. In taking a relational, developmental systems-based, PYD approach to research, the goal is to identify patterns of adaptive individual ↔ context relationships that lead to positive outcomes for youth. In this regard, it is critical for future research on youth activity involvement to identify more clearly the individual, contextual, and programmatic factors that promote positive, mutually beneficial individual ↔ context relations.

As depicted in Figure 1, the existing research suggests that there is complexity in the link between activity participation and positive developmental outcomes for youth. The nature of the activity (e.g., quality and structure of program, content of activity, presence of adult mentors) is critical in determining what outcomes are associated with participation (Mahoney et al., 2009; Roth & Brooks-Gunn, 2003). Further, patterns of participation in multiple types of activities and the amount of participation in those activities can differentially affect development (Zarrett et al., 2007, 2009). In addition to programmatic features, various individual factors, such as intentional self-regulation skills (Kiely, 2010; Mueller et al., in press) and gender (Urban et al., 2009), can also affect how youth participate in activities and how they benefit from participation. As represented in Figure 1, these individual characteristics interact in a mutually influential way with the nature of youth program participation to affect youth outcomes. In addition, the bidirectional relationships between individual characteristics and elements of youth program participation develop within the context of the neighborhood and community. In fact, existing literature supports the importance of contextual influences, such as neighborhood assets (Urban et al., 2009, 2010), in impacting the influence of activity participation. Finally, as indicated in Figure 1, there are likely important youth characteristics, elements of program participation, and youth outcomes involved in these relationships that have yet to be identified.

The next critical step in the research on youth activity participation is to further explore how we can better understand patterns of adaptive individual ↔ context relationships through engaging youth in high-quality programs. Practically speaking, we need to more clearly identify the issues of access to high-quality programs and determine how to encourage youth to become involved and stay involved in such programs. As previously noted, practitioners have observed that youth from low-resource backgrounds are not participating in youth programs as frequently as other youth (A. Roberts, personal communication, January 18, 2011). For example, youth who are living in low-resource neighborhoods, where access to high-quality programs may be limited, may need additional support to find and to remain involved with such programming. Youth may need assistance finding high-quality programs that are accessible and/or they may require assistance with transportation. Alternatively, a higher concentration of high-quality programming may be needed in those communities that are otherwise lacking in resources. Although the issues of access and barriers to participation were not the focus of this chapter, it is nevertheless a critical task of future research to better identify what patterns of participation in particular activities, in what contexts, for what individuals, promote positive developmental outcomes, with a particular focus on assessing the barriers to participation for populations who do not typically participate in longitudinal research.

While it is clear that participation in high-quality OST programs is beneficial, we need to more carefully examine why some youth are more involved than others. What are the individual characteristics that may be associated with how youth engage in and benefit from activities? For example, it may be that youth who are better able to self-regulate are more likely to seek out and benefit from high-quality programs. If so, then it may be beneficial to help youth learn how to develop better self-regulation skills. In turn, programs that help youth develop critical skills in selecting and optimizing goals, as well as compensating when they meet barriers to goal attainment, may be particularly beneficial for youth who struggle with these skills.

In addition to self-regulation skills, there might be other individual characteristics that are particularly relevant in regard to youth activity participation? Youth perceptions of, and feelings about, their hope for the future have been associated with intentional self-regulation skills in promoting positive developmental outcomes (Schmid, Phelps, & Lerner, in press; see also Schmid & Lopez, 2011). Given this link, it is reasonable to expect that an individual's hopeful future expectations might affect his or her motivation to engage in activities that are relevant to these expectations as a means of achieving future goals. Therefore, it will be important for future research to explore the role of hopeful future expectations as an important individual characteristic that might be an important factor shaping youth activity participation in a way that contributes to mutually beneficial individual ↔ context relations.

In order to advance research and application related to youth activity involvement, an important next step is to synthesize what we do already know about the features of programs, assets of individuals, characteristics of communities, and how these systems interact and affect developmental outcomes. As represented in Figure 1, there may be currently unidentified OST program, individual, or contextual factors that affect the way in which adaptive individual ↔ contextual relationships develop for youth. By synthesizing the existing research about how these systems coalesce, future research may be able to identify how youth activity participation can best be implemented to optimize PYD.

IV. Conclusions

Future research needs to identify more precisely which youth are participating in high-quality OST activities and which youth are not participating. For the youth who are not participating, what are the barriers to participation? In order to better serve the needs of all youth, we must work to assess the system of relationships that play a part in involving youth in OST program experiences. These factors may range from issues of funding and access for such programs to parental involvement and support, to neighborhood facilities and safety, and ultimately to funding policies (Leventhal et al., 2009).

Given the importance of OST activity participation in promoting positive developmental outcomes for diverse youth, the increased focus on research in this area is both timely and crucial. In order to develop programs and policies that seek to optimize the lives of youth, it will be critical to develop and execute research that builds upon past findings to create comprehensive, relational, developmental systems-oriented approaches to identifying the patterns of programmatic experiences that are most conducive to promoting positive developmental outcomes. For example, systems science methodologies, such as system dynamics, agent-based modeling, and network analysis, are particularly well suited for integrating large bodies of existing research at various levels of analysis and can address the complexity inherent in studying change across the life span (Urban, Osgood, & Mabry, 2011). In particular, these modeling approaches can prove extremely valuable when trying to evaluate various policy or programmatic options and determine the trade-offs between various courses of action. Further, we must focus on identifying individual and contextual factors that are preventing youth from participating in positive programmatic experiences. Researchers need to work with policy makers and practitioners to provide evidence about how best to enhance access to and engagement by diverse youth in the developmental assets constituted by OST activities.

Acknowledgments

The preparation of this chapter was supported in part by grants from the National 4-H Council, the John Templeton Foundation, the Thrive Foundation for Youth, and the National Science Foundation (Grant A150001 NSZ004).

REFERENCES

Balsano, A. B., Phelps, E., Theokas, C., Lerner, J. V., & Lerner, R. M. (2009). Patterns of early adolescents' participation in youth development programs having positive youth development goals. *Journal of Research on Adolescence, 19*(2), 249–259.

Barber, B. L., Stone, M. R., Hunt, J. E., & Eccles, J. S. (2005). Benefits of activity participation: The roles of identity affirmation and peer group norm sharing. In L. Mahoney, R. W. Larson & Js. S. Eccles (Eds.), *Organized activities as contexts of development: Extracurricular activities, after-school and community programs* (pp. 185–210). Mahwah, NJ, USA: Lawrence Erlbaum Associates Publishers.

Benson, P. L., Scales, P. C., Hamilton, S. F., & Sesma, J. A. (2006). Positive youth development: Theory, research and applications. In R. M. Lerner & W. Damon (Eds.), *Handbook of child psychology: Vol. 1. Theoretical models of human development* (6th ed., pp. 894–941). Hoboken, NJ: Wiley.

Benson, P. L., Scales, P. C., & Syvertsen, A. K. (2011). The contribution of the developmental assets framework to positive youth development theory and practice. In

R. M. Lerner, J. V. Lerner, & J. B. Benson (Eds.), *Advances in child development and behavior*, Vol. 41 (pp. 197–230). Amsterdam: Elsevier Inc.

Blum, R. W. (2003). Positive youth development: A strategy for improving health. In F. Jacobs, D. Wertlieb & R. M. Lerner (Eds.), *Handbook of applied developmental science: Vol. 2. Promoting positive child, adolescent, and family development through research, policies, and programs* (pp. 237–252). Thousand Oaks, CA: Sage.

Bowers, E. P., Li, Y., Kiely, M. K., Brittian, A., Lerner, J. V., & Lerner, R. M. (2010). The Five Cs model of positive youth development: A longitudinal analysis of confirmatory factor structure and measurement invariance. *Journal of Youth and Adolescence, 39*, 720–735.

Dearing, E., Wimer, C., Simpkins, S. D., Lund, T., Bouffard, S. M., Caronogan, P., et al. (2009). Do neighborhood and home contexts help explain why low-income children miss opportunities to participate in activities outside of school? *Developmental Psychology, 45* (6), 1545–1562.

Dworkin, J. B., Larson, R., & Hansen, D. (2003). Adolescents' accounts of growth experience in youth activities. *Journal of Youth and Adolescence, 32*(1), 17–26.

Eccles, J. S., & Gootman, J. A. (Eds.), (2002). *Community programs to promote youth development: Committee on community-level programs for youth.* Washington, DC: National Academy Press.

Erikson, E. H. (1968). *Identity: Youth and crisis.* Oxford, England: Norton & Co.

Fredricks, J. A., & Eccles, J. S. (2005). Developmental benefits of extracurricular involvement: Do peer characteristics mediate the link between activities and youth outcomes? *Journal of Youth and Adolescence, 34*(6), 507–520.

Freund, A. M., & Baltes, P. B. (2002). Life-management strategies of selection, optimization and compensation: Measurement by self-report and construct validity. *Journal of Personality and Social Psychology, 82*, 642–662.

Gardner, M., Roth, J., & Brooks-Gunn, J. (2008). Adolescents' participation in organized activities and developmental success 2 and 8 years after high school: Do sponsorship, duration, and intensity matter? *Developmental Psychology, 44*(3), 814–830.

Gestsdóttir, S., & Lerner, R. M. (2007). Intentional self-regulation and positive youth development in early adolescence: Findings from the 4-H study of positive youth development. *Developmental Psychology, 43*, 508–521.

Gestsdóttir, S., & Lerner, R. M. (2008). Positive development in adolescence: The development and role of intentional self-regulation. *Human Development, 51*, 202–224.

Gestsdóttir, S., Lewin-Bizan, S., von Eye, A., Lerner, J. V., & Lerner, R. M. (2009). The structure and function of selection, optimization, and compensation in middle adolescence: Theoretical and applied implications. *Journal of Applied Developmental Psychology, 30*(5), 585–600.

Hall, G. S. (1904). *Adolescence: Its psychology and its relations to physiology, anthropology, sociology, sex, crime, religion, and education* (Vols. 1 and 2), New York: Appleton.

Hansen, D. M., & Larson, R. W. (2007). Amplifiers of developmental and negative experiences in organized activities: Dosage, motivation, lead roles, and adult-youth ratios. *Journal of Applied Developmental Psychology, 28*(4), 360–374.

Hansen, D. M., Larson, R. W., & Dworkin, J. B. (2003). What adolescents learn in organized youth activities: A survey of self-reported developmental experiences. *Journal of Research on Adolescence, 13*(1), 25–55.

Kiely, M. K. (2010). *Intentional self-regulation and participation in 4-H programs: Individual and contextual bases of positive youth development and contribution.* Unpublished Master's Thesis, Medford, MA: Tufts University.

Larson, R. W. (2000). Toward a psychology of positive youth development. *The American Psychologist, 55*(1), 170–183.

Larson, R. W., & Brown, J. R. (2007). Emotional development in adolescence: What can be learned from a high school theater program? *Child Development*, *78*(4), 1083–1099.

Larson, R. W., Hansen, D. M., & Moneta, G. (2006). Differing profiles of developmental experiences across types of organized youth activities. *Developmental Psychology*, *42*(5), 849–863.

Larson, R. W., & Rusk, N. (2011). Intrinsic motivation and positive development. In R. M. Lerner, J. V. Lerner, & J. B. Benson (Eds.), *Advances in child development and behavior*, Vol. 41 (pp. 89–130). Amsterdam: Elsevier Inc.

Lerner, R. M. (1984). *On the nature of human plasticity.* New York: Cambridge University Press.

Lerner, R. M. (2004). *Liberty: Thriving and civic engagement among American youth.* Thousand Oaks, CA: Sage Publications.

Lerner, R. M. (2005). *Promoting positive youth development: Theoretical and empirical bases.* White paper prepared for the Workshop on the science of adolescent health and development, National Research Council/Institute of Medicine. Washington, DC: National Academies of Science.

Lerner, R. M. (2009). The positive youth development perspective: Theoretical and empirical bases of a strength-based approach to adolescent development. In C. R. Snyder & S. J. Lopez (Eds.), *Oxford handbook of positive psychology* (2nd ed., pp. 149–163). Oxford, England: Oxford University Press.

Lerner, R. M., Freund, A. M., De Stefanis, I., & Habermas, T. (2001). Understanding developmental regulation in adolescence: The use of the selection, optimization, and compensation model. *Human Development*, *44*, 29–50.

Lerner, R. M., Lerner, J. V., Almerigi, J., Theokas, C., Phelps, E., Gestsdóttir, S., et al. (2005). Positive youth development, participation in community youth development programs, and community contributions of fifth grade adolescents: Findings from the first wave of the 4-H study of positive youth development. *Journal of Early Adolescence*, *25*(1), 17–71.

Lerner, J. V., Phelps, E., Forman, Y., & Bowers, E. P. (2009). Positive youth development. In R. M. Lerner & L. Steinberg (Eds.), *Handbook of adolescent psychology: Vol. 1. Individual bases of adolescent development* (3rd ed., pp. 524–558). Hoboken, NJ: Wiley.

Lerner, R. M., Lerner, J. V., & Benson, J. B. (2011). Positive youth development: Research and applications for promoting thriving in adolescence. In R. M. Lerner, J. V. Lerner, & J. B. Benson (Eds.), *Advances in child development and behavior*, Vol. 41 (pp. 1–17). Elsevier Inc.

Leventhal, T., & Brooks-Gunn, J. (2000). The neighborhoods they live in: The effects of neighborhood residence on child and adolescent outcomes. *Psychological Bulletin*, *126*(2), 309–337.

Leventhal, T., Dupere, V., & Brooks-Gunn, J. (2009). Neighborhood influences on adolescent development. In R. M. Lerner & L. Steinberg (Eds.), *Handbook of adolescent psychology: Vol. 2. Contextual influences on adolescent development* (3rd ed., pp. 411–443). Hoboken, NJ: Wiley.

Li, Y., Bebiroglu, N., Phelps, E., & Lerner, R. M. (2009). Out-of-school time activity participation, school engagement and positive youth development: Findings from the 4-H study of positive youth development. *Journal of Youth Development*, *3*(3), DOI: 080303FA001.

Linver, M. R., Roth, J. L., & Brooks-Gunn, J. (2009). Patterns of adolescents' participation in organized activities: Are sports best when combined with other activities? *Developmental Psychology*, *45*(2), 354–367.

Mahoney, J. L., Cairns, B. D., & Farmer, T. W. (2003). Promoting interpersonal competence and educational success through extracurricular activity participation. *Journal of Educational Psychology*, *95*(2), 409–418.

Mahoney, J. L., Larson, R. W., & Eccles, J. S. (Eds.), (2005a). *Organized activities as contexts of development: Extracurricular activities, after-school and community programs* Mahwah, NJ, USA: Lawrence Erlbaum Associates Publishers.

Mahoney, J. L., Larson, R. W., Eccles, J. S., & Lord, H. (2005b). Organized activities as development contexts for children and adolescents. In J. L. Mahoney, R. W. Larson & J. S. Eccles (Eds.), *Organized activities as contexts of development: Extracurricular activities, after-school and community programs* (pp. 3–22). Mahwah, NJ, USA: Lawrence Erlbaum Associates Publishers.

Mahoney, J. L., Lord, H., & Carryl, E. (2005c). An ecological analysis of after-school program participation and the development of academic performance and motivational attributes for disadvantaged children. *Child Development, 76*(4), 811–825.

Mahoney, J. L., Vandell, D. L., Simkins, S., & Zarrett, N. (2009). Adolescent out-of-school activities. In R. M. Lerner & L. Steinberg (Eds.), *Handbook of adolescent psychology: Vol. 2. Contextual influences on adolescent development* (3rd ed., pp. 228–269). Hoboken, NJ: Wiley.

Mueller, M. K., Phelps, E., Bowers, E. P., Agans, J. P., Urban. J. B., & Lerner, R. M. (in press). Youth development program participation and intentional self-regulation skills: Contextual and Individual bases of pathways to positive youth development. *Journal of Adolescence.*

National Institute of Out-of-School Time. *How afterschool programs can most effectively promote positive youth development as a support to academic achievement.* (2003). www.nysan.org. New York State Afterschool Network. (2008). The value of afterschool. Retrieved January 26, 2009 from.

Overton, W. F. (2010). Life-span development: Concepts and issues. In R. M. Lerner (Ed-in-chief) & W. F. Overton (Vol. Ed.), *The handbook of life-span development: Vol. 1. Cognition, biology, and methods* (pp. 1–29). Hoboken, NJ: Wiley.

Phelps, E., Balsano, A., Fay, K., Peltz, J., Zimmerman, S., Lerner, R. M., et al. (2007). Nuances in early adolescent development trajectories of positive and of problematic/risk behaviors: Findings from the 4-H study of positive youth development. *Child and Adolescent Clinics of North America, 16*(2), 473–496.

Phelps, E., Zimmerman, S., Warren, A. E. A., Jelicic, H., von Eye, A., & Lerner, R. M. (2009). The structure and developmental course of positive youth development (PYD) in early adolescence: Implications for theory and practice. *Journal of Applied Developmental Psychology, 30*(5), 571–584.

Plomin, R. (1986). *Development, genetics, and psychology.* Hillsdale, NJ: Erlbaum.

Rhodes, J. E. (2002). *Stand by me: The risks and rewards of mentoring today's youth.* Cambridge, MA: Harvard University Press.

Roth, J. L., & Brooks-Gunn, J. (2003). What exactly is a youth development program? Answers from research and practice. *Applied Developmental Science, 7*, 94–111.

Rowe, D. C. (1994). *The limits of family influence: Genes, experience, and behavior.* New York: Guilford Press.

Schmid, K. L., & Lopez, S. (2011). Positive pathways to adulthood: The role of hope in adolescents' constructions of their futures. In R. M. Lerner, J. V. Lerner, & J. B. Benson (Eds.), *Advances in child development and behavior,* Vol. 41 (pp. 69–88). Amsterdam: Elsevier Inc.

Schmid, K. L., Phelps, E., & Lerner, R. M. (in press). Constructing positive futures: Modeling the relationship between adolescents' hopeful future expectations and intentional self-regulation in predicting positive youth development. *Journal of Adolescence.*

Sherrod, L. R., & Lauckhardt, J. (2009). The development of citizenship. In R. M. Lerner & L. Steinberg (Eds.), *Handbook of adolescent psychology: Vol. 2. Contextual influences on adolescent development* (3rd ed., pp. 372–407). Hoboken, NJ: Wiley.

Simpkins, S. D., Vest, A. E., & Becnel, J. N. (2010). Participating in sport and music activities in adolescence: The role of activity participation and motivational beliefs during elementary school. *Journal of Youth and Adolescence, 39*, 1368–1386.

Stoneman, D. (2002). The role of youth programming in the development of civic engagement. *Applied Developmental Science, 6*, 221–226.

Theokas, C., & Lerner, R. M. (2006). Observed ecological assets in families, schools, and neighborhoods: Conceptualization, measurement and relations with positive and negative developmental outcomes. *Applied Developmental Science, 10*(2), 61–74.

Urban, J. B., Lewin-Bizan, S., & Lerner, R. M. (2009). The role of neighborhood ecological assets and activity involvement in youth developmental outcomes: Differential impacts of asset poor and asset rich neighborhoods. *Journal of Applied Developmental Psychology, 30*(5), 601–614.

Urban, J. B., Lewin-Bizan, S., & Lerner, R. M. (2010). The role of intentional self regulation, lower neighborhood ecological assets, and activity involvement in youth developmental outcomes. *Journal of Youth and Adolescence, 39*(7), 783–800. doi:10.1007/s10964-010-9549-y.

Urban, J. B., Osgood, N., & Mabry, P. (2011). Developmental systems science: Exploring the application of non-linear methods to developmental science questions. *Research in Human Development, 8*(1), 1–25. doi:10.1080/15427609.2011.549686.

Wigfield, A., Eccles, J. S., Schiefele, U., Roeser, R. W., & Davis-Kean, P. (2006). Development of achievement motivation. In N. Eisenberg, W. Damon & R. M. Lerner (Eds.), *Handbook of child psychology: Vol. 3. Social, emotional, and personality development* (6th ed., pp. 933–1002). Hoboken, NJ, US: John Wiley & Sons Inc.

Wood, D., Larson, R. W., & Brown, J. R. (2009). How adolescents come to see themselves as more responsible through participation in youth programs. *Child Development, 80*(1), 295–309.

Zaff, J. F., Moore, K. A., Papillo, A. R., & Williams, S. (2003). Implications of extracurricular activity participation during adolescence on positive outcomes. *Journal of Adolescent Research, 18*, 599–630.

Zarrett, N., Fay, K., Carrano, J., Li, Y., Phelps, E., & Lerner, R. M. (2009). More than child's play: Variable- and pattern-centered approaches for examining effects of sports participation on youth development. *Developmental Psychology, 45*(2), 368–382.

Zarrett, N., Peltz, J., Fay, K., Li, Y., & Lerner, R. M. (2007). Sports and youth development programs: Theoretical and practical implications of early adolescent participation in multiple instances of structured out-of-school (OST) activity. *Journal of Youth Development, 2*, DOI: 0702FA001.

Zimmerman, S., Phelps, E., & Lerner, R. M. (2007). Intentional self-regulation in early adolescence: Assessing the structure of selection, optimization, and compensations processes. *European Journal of Developmental Science, 1*, 272–299.

Zimmerman, S., Phelps, E., & Lerner, R. M. (2008). Positive and negative developmental trajectories in U.S. adolescents: Where the PYD perspective meets the deficit model. *Research in Human Development, 5*, 153–165.

MEDIA LITERACY AND POSITIVE YOUTH DEVELOPMENT

Michelle J. Boyd* and Julie Dobrow[†]

* INSTITUTE FOR APPLIED RESEARCH IN YOUTH DEVELOPMENT,
TUFTS UNIVERSITY, MEDFORD, MASSACHUSETTS, USA
[†] COMMUNICATIONS AND MEDIA STUDIES PROGRAM, TUFTS UNIVERSITY,
MEDFORD, MASSACHUSETTS, USA

Abstract

This chapter explores the links among media literacy (specifically news media literacy), civic engagement, and positive youth development (PYD). We begin by providing an overview of the literature on PYD and media literacy, and go on to discuss media literacy in the context of civic development. We also explore the existing literature on the associations between news media use, news media literacy, and civic indicators. In addition, we discuss the promotion of media literacy (with a focus on news media literacy) and PYD in educational, extracurricular, and home settings. We conclude with a discussion of the current research in this nascent and interdisciplinary area and, as well, consider directions for future research.

One of the more salient characteristics of the world in which twenty-first century young people are growing up is the wall-to-wall media culture that envelops them. Adolescents' increasing use of and dependence on

Advances in Child Development and Behavior
Richard M. Lerner, Jacqueline V. Lerner and Janette B. Benson : Editors

various forms of media will inevitably affect their development, attitudes, and behavior.

Most indicators suggest that adolescents today are exposed to an astonishing amount of media. According to a 2010 Kaiser Family Foundation study, exposure to television content (although not necessarily viewing television in real time) has increased to an average of over 4 h a day; young people spend at least an hour and a half per day online; and as the number and percentage of young people with access to mobile electronic devices have increased, so too has the amount of time they spend in front of various types of screens (Rideout, Foehr, & Roberts, 2010). Youth spend almost ten and a half hours per day on average involved with various forms of media, although this figure is conflated because some of that time is spent "media multitasking" (such as listening to an iPod while surfing the Internet and using a social networking site such as Facebook) (Rideout et al., 2010). Media use among minority youth in the Rideout et al. (2010) sample showed the greatest increase, compared to youth in previous Kaiser Family Foundation assessments.

By some metrics, social networking use, especially Facebook, has become a significant part of American adolescents' daily lives: one organization that tracks Facebook use reported an 88.2% increase between 2009 and 2010 among 13- to 17-year-olds (Corbett, 2010). A Pew Foundation Report found that among all forms of media, cell-phone texting has become the most preferred channel of basic communication between teenagers and their friends. About 75% of 12- to 17-year-olds now own cell phones, up from 45% in 2004, and more than half of the teens in their large national sample reported texting daily, half of them sending 50 or more text messages a day, or 1500 texts a month, and one in three sending more than 100 texts a day, or more than 3000 texts a month (Lenhart, Ling, Campbell, & Purcell, 2010).

Concerns about the amount of media to which adolescents are exposed to must also be seen in the context of their already having grown up with very significant amounts of screen time. With the increase of electronic media, including television programming, developed for infants and toddlers in the past few decades, children are becoming media consumers at a very early age and spending considerable amounts of time using media (Wartella & Robb, 2007). Despite recommendations from the American Academy of Pediatrics that discourage screen time altogether for children younger than 2 years of age and suggest a maximum of 2 h of total media time for older children, in actuality, many young children have considerable exposure to media (American Academy of Pediatrics, 2001; Rideout & Hamel, 2006). Thus, by the time a child reaches adolescence, he or she will already have conceivably accrued thousands of hours of exposure to television, video games, the Internet, and other forms of media and been socialized into environments in which it is possible that media behaviors are patterned, media images fully engrained, and effects of media well established (Strasburger, Wilson, & Jordan, 2009).

Given this degree of media use among young people, many educators and advocates have renewed calls for a more systemic inclusion of media literacy curricula in formal education. For example, Rheingold (2008) suggests that "As increasing numbers of young people seek to master the use of media tools to express themselves, explore their identities, and connect with peers—to be active creators as well as consumers of culture—educators have an opportunity to encourage young media makers to exercise active citizenship" through getting them to be more media literate (p. 1). Others have posited that increased media use by young people, and the potential to harness the power of media in their lives, makes media literacy a critical twenty-first century civic engagement skill (Fedorov, 2003; Livingstone, 2004).

In this chapter, we will explore the links among media literacy, civic engagement, and positive youth development (PYD). We will provide an overview of the literature on PYD and media literacy, and discuss issues involved in promoting PYD and media literacy in the home as well as in educational and extracurricular settings. Then, by exploring some of the existing literature on the use of news literacy as an indicator of civic outcomes, we will consider how media literacy about news might become an important indicator of PYD as a significant predictor of civic engagement among young people. Finally, we will assess where research in this nascent and interdisciplinary area stands and consider some directions for future research.

I. Overview of the PYD Perspective

PYD is a perspective that utilizes a strength-based approach to understand youth development. This perspective holds that all young people have strengths, as exemplified by their great capacity for systematic change, or "plasticity," and that those strengths, when aligned with ecological resources that nurture or enhance these strengths, and direct them toward healthy and positive behaviors, enhance the probability that youth may be put on a more positive life path (Lerner, 2009; Lerner, Phelps, Forman, & Bowers, 2009). Benson, Scales, Hamilton, and Semsa (2006; see also Chapter 8) term these ecological resources "developmental assets." In short, proponents of the PYD perspective believe that youth are resources to be developed (Roth & Brooks-Gunn, 2003).

The PYD perspective informs practice within a number of fields, including education, public health, social work, and medicine (Benson et al., 2006). PYD can serve as a guide for researchers, practitioners, and policy makers in their efforts to describe, explain, and optimize adolescent development (e.g., Floyd, 2010; Porter, 2010). PYD may be operationalized as an approach that involves identifying indicators that define youth thriving. A leading, empirically validated framework for such operationalization of PYD is referred to as the "Five Cs"—Competence, Confidence, Connection, Character, and Caring. When a young person exhibits these qualities across time, then he/she is "thriving" (King et al., 2005; Lerner, Phelps, et al., 2009; Lerner, von Eye, Lerner, & Lewin-Bizan, 2009; Lerner, von Eye, Lerner, Lewin-Bizan, & Bowers, 2010). The young person is on a course toward a positive adulthood, where a sixth "C" emerges, Contribution—to self, family, community, and institutions of civil society (Jeličić, Bobek, Phelps, Lerner, & Lerner, 2007). This framework can be applied to individuals of various ages; however, most of the empirical work or research on PYD has focused on adolescents.

This conception of PYD is directly influenced by relational, developmental systems theories (DSTs) of human behavior. These theories explain human development in terms of bidirectional, mutually influential, individual–context relations (Lerner, 2002), represented as individual ↔ context relations. That is, DST emphasizes that the individual and his or her environment (e.g., family, peer groups, schools, after-school programs, neighborhoods and communities, media, and culture) influence each other. This mutually influential relationship allows the individual to contribute to his or her own development. In addition, as noted earlier, the individual has the potential for systematic change or "plasticity" across adolescence and as well throughout life. We have already pointed to the fact that plasticity is a fundamental strength of human development. Because of this strength, practitioners, policy makers, and researchers can be optimistic about their ability to promote changes in the trajectories of youth by attempting to understand and adjust the course of youth development through rigorous research, interventions, community-based programs, and social policies.

As suggested by Benson et al. (2006) and, as well, by Lerner, Phelps, et al. (2009), PYD can be promoted by aligning individual strengths (e.g., creativity, intrinsic motivation, leadership skills, and resilience) with the developmental assets of the environment of youth (e.g., home, school, and community). These ecological developmental resources may entail support from adults, effective out-of-school-time (OST) activities, and opportunities for young people and adults to work together on valued community activities (Theokas & Lerner, 2006). The PYD perspective enhances the ability of schools, teachers, communities, mentors, and parents to capitalize on youth strengths while simultaneously decreasing youth engagement in problematic behaviors.

Interventions and programs that utilize a deficit approach to youth development tend to target a small body of troubled or "at-risk" youth and to focus efforts on reducing specific problem behaviors (e.g., alcohol use, delinquency, and mental health problems). However, such programs fail to acknowledge that youth who are problem-free are not necessarily fully prepared to become active, productive, and successful adults (Benson, Mannes, Pittman, & Ferber, 2004; Pittman, Irby, Tolman, Yohalem, & Ferber, 2001). That is, a young person might not exhibit violent behavior, take drugs, or become a teenage parent, but the absence of these outcomes does not mean that a young person is on a trajectory to lead a productive and meaningful life. Lerner (2004) points out that:

> "All too often in the United States we discuss positive development in terms of the absence of negative or undesirable behaviors...As such, when we describe a successful young person we speak about a youth whose problems have been managed or are, at best, absent...America as a nation must do a better job of talking about the positive attributes of our young people. We must talk to our youth about what they should and can become, not only about what they must not be. We must then act on our statements, and work with young people to promote their positive development. In the context of nurturing and healthy adult-youth relationships we need to offer young people the opportunities to learn and use the skills involved in participating actively in their communities and in making productive and positive contributions to themselves and their families and society" (pp. 1, 4).

In the most obvious sense, encouraging PYD prepares youth to become engaged, contributing members of society. Youth who have higher levels of PYD are more likely to make positive contributions to their families, schools, and communities (Benson & Pittman, 2001; Damon, 2004; Lerner, 2004). In addition, building strengths in one youth tends to reverberate among peers, families, schools, and communities. For example, when youth recognize and are able to capitalize on their own assets, they tend to bring these assets and the tools for enhancing them into interactions with peers, teachers, and community and family members (Benson, 2007). When youth are capitalizing on their strengths, they are more effectively accessing the assets that exist in their environment (Lerner et al., in press).

Sherrod (2007) described youth civic engagement "as an expression of PYD" and discusses how it relates to all of the Cs of PYD, but especially to Contribution. To illustrate, he discussed how external assets can promote the development of civic engagement and, in turn, how a youth's civic engagement can support the development of these ecological assets. Sherrod concluded by describing how media-focused research, programs, and policies are needed to understand how media might relate to civic engagement, specifically "the impact of the media on knowledge about and attitudes to civic engagement in young people" (Sherrod, 2007, p. 71). A true media literacy perspective, consistent with the PYD perspective, acknowledges the young person as an active agent in his or her development (Hobbs & Jensen, 2009). By linking the PYD perspective with the promotion of media literacy, such agency can lead to empowerment and be directed toward efforts of social contribution.

II. Overview of Media Literacy Approach

Media literacy was once simply defined as "the ability to access, analyze, evaluate, and create media in a variety of forms," but with a constantly changing and expanding media landscape, this definition has also evolved (Thoman & Jolls, 2003, p. 21). A more elaborate definition set forth by the Center for Media Literacy (CML), a pioneering organization in the area of media literacy education, is as follows: "Media Literacy is a 21st century approach to education. It provides a framework to access, analyze, evaluate and create messages in a variety of forms—from print to video to the Internet. Media literacy builds an understanding of the role of media in society as well as essential skills of inquiry and self-expression necessary for citizens of a democracy" (Thoman & Jolls, 2003, p. 21). Building upon this definition, media literacy also "refers to analytical, reflective understanding of print and electronic mass media, including film, their aesthetic components, institutional structures, socioeconomic contexts, and an ability to interact with media in preparing audiovisual products and in influencing media decision makers" (Brown, 2001). Media literacy is an approach that can be regarded as a new literacy or an expansion of how we have traditionally defined literacy (Hobbs, 2001, 2008). Those promoting the importance of media literacy acknowledge the ubiquitous nature of media in our lives, and the fact that media is a part of modern culture; therefore, often the emphasis is not placed on protecting or secluding young people from media and its messages (Hobbs & Jensen, 2009; Thoman & Jolls, 2003) but instead on recognizing the role of the mass media and its subsequent influence while encouraging people to become "competent, critical, and literate in all media forms" (Thoman & Jolls, 2003, p. 21). Media literacy training should empower individuals and provide them with the ability to become critical consumers and creators of media.

The Federal Communications Commission (FCC) 2009 Notice of inquiry (NOI) on "Empowering Parents and Protecting Children in an Evolving Media Landscape" gave one measure of how widely recognized media literacy's potential importance may be. The commissioners asked for public comment on the effectiveness of media literacy programs, their availability, and the ability of schools and other organizations to deliver this critical information to children toward the goal of making them more careful and critical consumers of the vast amounts of media products to which they are exposed in this "evolving media landscape" (Federal Communications Commission, 2009).

In general, media literacy programs within an educational setting, with a particular focus on television content, have been categorized by three levels based on the foci of instruction and study (Anderson & Ploghoft, 1993; Brown, 2001, p. 684), which include media production in an effort to understand the underlying production operations, media studies with a focus on how "social, economic, political, and ethical" factors influence media products, and "critical analysis of media content," respectively (see Table I).

Table I

Levels of Media Literacy Programs

Level	Description of level/level foci	Stage of schooling
1	"The modes and methods of production" (Anderson & Ploghoft, 1993, p. 89) "Learning to produce media presentations ... to deconstruct how media operate and develop programs, including the 'codes' of image-sound forms and formats" (Brown, 2001, p. 684)	Usually not offered until middle school, then high school and college
2	"The nature and character of media industries" (Anderson & Ploghoft, 1993, p. 89) Studying "media industries" and the "social, economic, political, and ethical contexts to learn about forces shaping media content, including advertising economics and governmental regulation and public interest groups" (Brown, 2001, p. 684)	Offered mostly at upper secondary and college
3	"The critical analysis of media texts" (Anderson & Ploghoft, 1993, p. 89) Critically analyzing "media content, including 'text' of story lines, dialog, images, sounds, and other codes or forms of media presentation" to examine "meaning" (including the intentions of the creators and distributors as well as individual viewers' perceptions and interpretations) (Brown, 2001, p. 684)	Offered in early grades, through middle and high school and college

Optimally, media literacy programs would have components representing each level outlined in Table I and, as well, such instruction would begin as early as possible in a person's life, especially given that initial exposure to media often occurs early in one's life (Rideout & Hamel, 2006).

Formal media literacy programs exist in many school systems worldwide, including throughout Canada, Australia, New Zealand, and many European countries, including Great Britain (Frau-Meigs & Torrent, 2009; Hobbs, 1996, 1998; Lederer, 1988). In some cases, media literacy programs are sanctioned and sponsored by the government; in other cases, they have been developed by and advocated for by international organizations and coalitions, such as UNESCO (United Nations Educational, Scientific, and Cultural Organization) and the Alliance of Civilizations (Frau-Meigs & Torrent, 2009). Recent years have seen an increase in international interest in such programs and related policy which is evident by such developments as the First Conference on Media Education in the Middle East in 2007, the First Africa Media Literacy Conference in 2008, and the International Media Literacy Research Forum (Frau-Meigs & Torrent, 2009). Frau-Meigs and Torrent (2009) stated,

> The importance of media education is being gradually recognized worldwide. After the time of the lonesome innovators isolated in their classrooms, after the time of extended communities of practice around researchers and field practitioners working at the grassroots level, the moment of policy makers has arrived. A threshold has been reached, where the body of knowledge concerning media literacy has matured, where the different stakeholders implicated in education, in media and in civil society are aware of the new challenges developed by the so-called "Information Society", and the new learning cultures it requires for the well-being of its citizens, the peaceful development of civic societies, the preservation of native cultures, the growth of sustainable economies and the enrichment of contemporary social diversity (p. 15).

Yet, for all of the attention media literacy training and education appears to have received in many places around the world, formal media literacy education in the U.S. public schools has lagged. Some analysts suggest a number of possible explanations for this, including the historically autonomous role of individual school districts and classroom teachers in determining curricula in American schools, a long-standing bias toward print and away from visual media in American education, and the increasing influence of "standards-based learning" and the necessity of testing students to retain state and federal funding in public schools (Buckingham, 2003; Considine, 2003; Kubey, 2001). Due to lack of resources, including funding, allocated time, and teacher training, media education has often been adopted by a minority of teachers and administrators, limited in scope, and incorporated into preexisting courses or classroom instruction (Brown, 2001).

Nevertheless, we believe that media literacy has become an important skill for young people to develop in this evolving media world in which they live. The 2009 FCC NOI which called for information on media literacy queried, "To what extent is media literacy a required part of school curricula throughout the nation? Is media literacy education in schools particularly critical for those at-risk children whose parents are either unaware of the benefits and harms of media consumption or choose not to become involved in monitoring their children's media use? At what age should children begin to be taught media literacy? Is it critical for such education to begin early in a child's development? What roles do the Department of Education and other government or private organizations play in this area?" (Federal Communications Commission, 2009, p. 21). By acting to address these key questions, the United States as well as nations around the world may undertake an important approach to create educational systems to promote media literacy.

Given the level of exposure and access to media during developmentally formative years, it is reasonable to hypothesize that media is a substantive contextual influence on the development of youth. Based on research agendas and public discussion regarding mass media and developmental issues, there is a clear concern for better understanding what media youth use, the patterns and purposes of such media use, and the nature and range of the outcomes related to such media use. These interests should also include theoretically and empirically exploring the role of media literacy in civic development.

III. Media Literacy and Civic Development

We have noted that civic engagement can be described as an instantiation of PYD, especially as it relates to contribution (Sherrod, 2007)—that is, to the contributions that a young person can make to civil society. Those contributions, which may be termed civic engagement, can take on a variety of forms, and any conception or evaluation of civic engagement should take into account indicators that are not only behavioral in nature (e.g., civic participation) but also related to various forms of cognition (e.g., civic knowledge, civic skills, and efficacy) and socioemotional functioning (e.g., a sense of civic duty or responsibility).

Such a multifaceted conception of civic engagement is in accordance with the continued efforts of scholars to differentiate components of civic engagement. For instance, Sherrod and Lauckhardt (2009) proposed distinguishing between knowledge and understanding, participation and behaviors, and attitudes and beliefs. Flanagan and Faison (2001) similarly defined these components as civic literacy, skills, and attachment, respectively. In addition, Sherrod (2003) argued that political attitudes can be a type of civic engagement, even if the individual is not a political participant, and that political attitudes can serve as an earlier representation of civic engagement that precedes political behavior in the development of citizenship.

As knowledge, including knowledge acquisition, and understanding are key conceptual attributes of civic development, and are potentially related to one's attitudes and behavior, it is important to consider the ways in which exposure to civic information (e.g., concerning public and community affairs, political issues, and current events) and indicators of civic engagement are related (Flanagan & Faison, 2001; Sherrod, 2003; Sherrod & Lauckhardt, 2009). At the same time, we should focus on the potential of media literacy education and training for developing young people as critical (with regard to processing and understanding the information) and efficient (with regard to acquiring information) consumers of such information.

Proponents of enhancing media literacy education contend that such efforts provide individuals with the necessary skills to be active and engaged citizens (e.g., Hobbs & Jensen, 2009; Moeller, 2009). In providing a rationale for the funding of media literacy training efforts, Moeller (2009) stated, "[Media literacy training] helps people understand the value of news, defend their access to free information, decipher the messages they receive, use their rights of free expression to make their voices heard, and participate in the process of governing ... A media literate citizenry is essential to building and sustaining a democracy" (p. 4). Compiled by members of the media literacy education community in 2007, the *Core Principles of Media Literacy Education in the United States* declare "that the purpose of [media literacy education] is to develop informed, reflective, and engaged participants essential to a democratic society" and further, media literacy education has a "role in supporting active democratic citizenship, as opposed to simply creating informed consumers of mass media and popular culture" (Hobbs & Jensen, 2009, p. 7).

IV. News Media Literacy

Theoretically and conceptually, the development of media literacy skills may be a critical component of one's civic development and socialization, especially as it relates to becoming news literate. Because of its salience for democratic values and institutions, this area of media scholarship warrants further exploration, especially an assessment of how news media literacy can promote civic development and socialization among young people (Raynes-Goldie & Walker, 2008; Rheingold, 2008).

Potter (2011) provided a useful overview and description of what constitutes news media literacy. When approaching news content, Potter emphasized that one must understand that news is not a reflection of reality or actual events but a construction that is undoubtedly shaped by "constraints" and "influences." Of course, actual events spark news coverage; however, as Potter stated, "But what we see presented as news by the media are not the events themselves. Instead, the media present us with stories *about* the events, and those stories are constructed by journalists who are influenced by constraints that are largely outside of their control. Journalists are also profoundly influenced by other factors that frame what gets presented as news" (p. 139).

According to Potter, those constraints include deadlines (which are less of an issue for certain media, including the Internet), resource limitations (including the inefficient use of such fixed resources), and geographical focus (regardless of local, national, and global coverage, there are biases concerning what locales and regions are considered newsworthy). In addition to such constraints, Potter states that "news-framing influences" also potentially sway journalists and impact what is ultimately covered as news content. One such force or factor to consider is the commercial nature of many news organizations. Thus, a goal of these organizations is to produce content that will draw large audiences in an effort to generate advertising revenue. The degree to which a news organization is focused on attracting audiences and advertisers could influence what is being presented as news (e.g., choosing to avoid publishing or featuring news content which might offend the audience and/or advertisers). Such constraints and influences shape what Potter referred to as the overall "news perspective." Further, Potter (2011) noted that one must consider the degree to which journalists can actually be objective in their presentation of information. In the most obvious sense, fabricating details of a story clearly violates journalistic standards. However, biased (e.g., in presenting certain stories but ignoring others), partial (e.g., not covering a particular story over an extended period of time even in light of future relevant developments), decontextualized (e.g., not presenting adequate background information to evaluate the story), and unbalanced (e.g., not presenting viewpoints from multiple perspectives) reporting are less apparent and more ambiguous instances of actions wherein journalistic standards are in question.

The earlier, seminal sociological research and work of Gans (1979) also support an analysis of news content that emphasizes that judging and comprehending the news involves understanding the news organizations and journalism professionals who provide such information. For example, this may include acknowledging an organizations' efforts to earn profits (e.g., by attracting and retaining advertisers and audiences) and compete with other media organizations. This may also include organizations and professionals' values and perceived societal roles and functions. Other factors include judgments concerning, for example, "the availability and suitability of sources, story importance or interest, as well as novelty [and] quality" (Gans, 1979, p. 280).

Due to such constraints and influences as well as the potential framing (Tewksbury & Scheufele, 2009) and agenda-setting function of the news media (McCombs & Reynolds, 2009), individuals must consciously attend to news coverage to ensure that they are becoming well informed. According to Potter (2011), "the key is to develop higher media literacy with more elaborated knowledge structures, more well-developed skills, and a strong personal locus that drives us to analyze news and hold it to a higher standard that we have in the past" (p. 155). Potter (2011) organized such skills along four dimensions—cognitive (e.g., "ability to analyze a news story to identify key points of information"), emotional (e.g., "ability to analyze the feelings of people in the news story"), aesthetic (e.g., "ability to analyze the craft and artistic elements in the story"), and moral (e.g., "ability to evaluate the ethical responsibilities of the journalists on this story")—and provides representative examples of each (p. 156). Similarly, he suggested strategies for further developing or expanding one's "knowledge structures," which include analyzing the news perspective, searching for context, developing alternative sources of information, being skeptical of public opinion, and exposing oneself to more news (Potter, 2011, p. 156). For instance, while consuming news content, one should be continually aware of possible constraints and influences or the overall news perspective of the overarching news organization presenting the information and be critical of such information. As well, one must consider the difference between news and information, respectively. Although there can be overlap, Potter defined news as what is deviant or out of the norm and can often be sensationalized; however, adequate contextualization of a news event can provide information that is of value to consumers.

One who aims to be media literate should seek more relevant contextualized information, not just sensationalized, surface reporting of events. When such contextual information is not adequately provided by media outlets, then the media literate individual should seek out sources of such information from diverse viewpoints and perspectives. In addition, one should develop some degree of skepticism toward what is considered public opinion, due to the fact that public opinion will be skewed if many people lack an opinion or are unsure about their opinion. Finally, limited exposure to news and information does not allow one to expand his or her knowledge pool and thus have the informational resources needed to fully evaluate the coverage of a particular issue or event.

A. NEWS MEDIA USE, NEWS MEDIA LITERACY, AND CIVIC INDICATORS

There is evidence of direct and indirect effects of media use, specifically news media use, on civic and political indicators. Previous research on older adolescents and young adults has found links between informational uses of media and civic indicators, such as increased participation in civic activities, higher levels of political awareness, and higher levels of civic knowledge (Amadeo, Torney-Purta, & Barber, 2004; Lopez et al., 2006; Pasek, Kenski, Romer, & Jamieson, 2006). For instance, watching national television news was positively associated with both participation in civic activities and political awareness, using the Internet for information was significantly associated with higher levels of political awareness, and listening to news on the radio was associated with increased participation in civic activities (Pasek et al., 2006). Youth and young adults who regularly followed the news, regardless of medium, were more likely to be members of political groups, regular voters, and workers on a community problem, than those who did not follow the news (Lopez et al., 2006). Based on data from a civic education study of 14- and 17-year-olds, those who watched more news on television and read newspapers had higher average levels of civic knowledge (Amadeo et al., 2004). Further, those students who more frequently read newspapers were also more likely to indicate that they expected to vote in national elections as adults compared to students who read newspapers less frequently. Using a sample of high-school students, Hoffman and Thomson (2009) found that local television news viewing had a positive effect on civic participation when mediated by political efficacy.

Ashley, Poepsel, and Willis (2010) provide some evidence that among a college student population, knowledge about media ownership (e.g., concentration of ownership or consolidation) increased skepticism toward media products (i.e., print news articles). The authors stated that the goal of media literacy education should be "not to simply generate distrust, cynicism, or apathy" but "to teach critical thinking skills that will help citizens evaluate media content and make judgments based on a more complete understanding on how the news is produced" (Ashley et al., 2010, p. 43). In another study, high-school students, who were instructed in critically analyzing media messages, were found to have improved analysis skills when compared to students who received no such instruction, including the ability to recognize omitted information while reading and viewing news content (Hobbs & Frost, 2003). Such findings illustrate the importance of further identifying how news media use relates to civic development and socialization, especially for youth. However, the goal should also be to further the theoretical and empirical understanding of the role of media literacy skills, particularly news literacy, in strengthening the links between news media consumption and civic indicators.

If we contend that knowledge and understanding are key components of civic engagement (Flanagan & Faison, 2001; Sherrod & Lauckhardt, 2009) and that an informed citizenry is needed to maintain a thriving democracy, then researchers must aim to elucidate the mechanisms by which media literacy education supports civic development. Resolving internal conflicts and tensions concerning "new literacies" (Hobbs, 2008), as well as clearly defining and assessing the features of media literacy and their contribution to civic outcomes, could aid in validating and strengthening the arguments in support of this approach.

B. MEDIA LITERACY AND NEWS MEDIA LITERACY WITHIN EDUCATIONAL, EXTRACURRICULAR, AND HOME SETTINGS

In light of the limitations of the traditional school setting for providing media literacy education and training discussed earlier in the chapter, organizations, such as the Action Coalition for Media Education, National Association for Media Literacy Education, and the CML, have the potential to serve as useful resources and contacts for media education activities pursued outside of the traditional school setting. If implemented properly, such OST activities and programs, including after-school clubs and youth development programs, can provide a forum for building youth strengths and supporting their positive development. One characteristic of effective youth development programs is that young people are given the opportunity to participate in structured activities that enable them to develop valued life skills (Lerner, 2007). Arguably, becoming media literate is one such skill. And when such program education and training particularly pertain to news media literacy, organizations such as Fairness and Accuracy in Reporting and the Center for Media and Public Affairs can provide valuable information that specifically relates to news coverage.

Parental mediation has been a suggested approach for promoting media literacy skills within the home. This mechanism "relies on parents to mediate their children's media use by talking with them about media, enforcing rules regarding media use, and/or watching or using content with them," generally described as active mediation, restrictive mediation, and co-viewing, respectively (Chakroff & Nathanson, 2011, pp. 552–553). However, mediation is multifaceted, and due to variation in its conceptualization and operationalization, the resulting body of the literature is difficult to integrate. Typically, unlike media literacy interventions, mediation approaches do not require structured lesson plans for parents to follow and thus must be considered as a distinct concept separate from media literacy education (Chakroff & Nathanson, 2011).

With regard to parental mediation and news content, much discussion has focused on how exposure to news-related information and images can negatively affect young news consumers. For example, news reports that detail violent acts (e.g., crime reports) and tragedies (e.g., terrorist attacks) can elicit discomforting emotional reactions (e.g., stress, fear, and anxiety) from youth of all ages, and adults as well (American Academy of Child and Adolescent Psychiatry, 2002; Kaiser Family Foundation, 2003; Walsh, 2001). Despite a parent or a caregiver's efforts to shield his or her child from such news coverage, it is likely that young people will have some exposure to such information and images, being that, as youth get older they spend less time with their parents (Furstenburg, 2000; Larson & Richards, 1991; Larson, Richards, Moneta, Holmbeck, & Duckett, 1996) and due to their increasing independence, they have greater opportunities to make their own media consumption choices. Accordingly, such emotion-laden instances of media content provide an opportunity for both adults and young people to become more media literate by practicing and further developing relevant skills. In addition to caring adults providing assurances and listening to the concerns of young people in light of such upsetting reports, one way to approach such news coverage is to encourage teens to be aware and critical in evaluating the content (Walsh, 2001). In other words, action steps here may include guiding youth in monitoring their sources of information. For instance, caregivers may act to encourage youth to attend to media that is informative and that will help them better understand and make sense of the situation or issue, and avoid media that is sensational and simply plays upon their emotions (Walsh, 2001). Previous research suggests that when parents have media literacy training, and thus are equipped with appropriate strategies for discussing the news with their children, they can help their children better cope with threat-related news (i.e., terrorism-related news in this case) (Comer, Furr, Beidas, Weiner, & Kendall, 2008). Similarly, such training helped the parents cope with the anxiety-provoking news coverage as well (Comer et al., 2008).

Unfortunately, the bulk of research on media literacy as well as mediation interventions has been atheoretical in nature and falls short at explaining the underlying mechanisms that are associated with certain outcomes (Chakroff & Nathanson, 2011). Chakroff and Nathanson (2011) suggest several priorities for future research, including the use of rigorous, systematic program evaluations for assessing effectiveness, and further examination of restrictive mediation. A review of the literature shows that evaluations of media literacy curricula are lacking. As a result, curricula are being implemented without sound assessments of their effectiveness. The authors contend that "research on media literacy needs to begin to create theoretically driven curricula which are then systematically implemented in order to allow a thorough evaluation. By evaluating each part of a program individually, researchers would be able to make more informed recommendations to parents and educators" (Chakroff & Nathanson, 2011, p. 568). As well, Chakroff and Nathanson (2011) suggest that a developmental focus as well as longitudinal research would benefit the research by determining effectiveness at different developmental stages and across time. Similarly, mediation-related research is lacking in that restrictive mediation has been understudied compared to active mediation and co-viewing, thus the concept and its effects are not fully understood.

We resonate with the calls for theory-based, longitudinal research linking media literacy, youth development, and key outcomes of such development. Indeed, the ideas of Chakroff and Nathanson (2011) enable us to draw conclusions about the future role of a relational, DST-based approach to understand the relation between media literacy and youth contributions to civil society through their civic engagement.

V. Discussion and Conclusions

In this chapter, we have presented pieces of a puzzle. We know that youth today are exposed to and utilize daily an astonishing amount of media. We know that PYD is a theoretical and practical approach toward understanding and enhancing the lives of adolescents that can empower young people in their development. Research has shown that media literacy training is an approach that can similarly empower young people, making them into more careful and critical consumers of the huge amount of media they absorb. Finally, there are indications from the research literature that consuming news on a regular basis, and becoming more news literate, are positively associated with various indicators of civic engagement.

When we begin to put the disparate pieces of this puzzle together, we would posit that one could utilize the theoretical frameworks and empirical measures of PYD and apply them to the case of news media literacy. As such, we hypothesize that greater news literacy would, in turn, be a predictor of both measures of civic engagement and measures of PYD. Research on this relation is needed. We suggest as well that media literacy training in young people will result in youth empowerment, positive life paths and practices, and greater participation in civic outcomes such as voting, more civic knowledge, and greater involvement in community organizations and endeavors. Again, research to test this expectation is needed.

To be sure, there are challenges, both in terms of research and in terms of policy, with regard to further elucidation of the links between media literacy and PYD. Developing appropriate methodologies to assess these relationships may be difficult because they would involve interdisciplinary research, which tends to be difficult to fund and is not undertaken by many researchers due to the disciplinary culture of many academic departments. Longitudinal work, which might perhaps best assess these relationships, is difficult to fund and to execute. In addition, we have discussed in this chapter challenges to systemic inclusion of media literacy programs in many American public schools. In an era of "standards-based learning," it seems unlikely that, unless and until media literacy education is included in state curricula and assessed in schools, it will be widely taught.

Despite these challenges, we believe that it is important to develop ways to systematically investigate the relationships between media literacy and PYD. We also believe that the media culture into which young people today are born and in which they grow up necessitates the investment of intellectual capital to understand these relationships and, as well, the investment of resource capital to educate young people in ways that empower them to use media to be active and engaged citizens.

Acknowledgment

This chapter was supported in part by grants from the National 4-H Council and the Thrive Foundation for Youth.

REFERENCES

Amadeo, J., Torney-Purta, J., & Barber, C. H. (2004). *Attention to media and trust in media sources: Analysis of data from the IEA civic education study [Fact sheet].* Retrieved from The Center for Information and Research on Civic Learning and Engagement website: http://www.civicyouth.org/PopUps/FactSheets/FS_Attention_To_Media_Trust_Sources.pdf.

American Academy of Child and Adolescent Psychiatry. (2002). *Children and the news [Facts for Families No. 67].* Retrieved from http://www.aacap.org/galleries/FactsForFamilies/67_children_and_the_news.pdf.

American Academy of Pediatrics, Committee on Public Education. (2001). Children, adolescents and television. *Pediatrics, 107((2),* 423–426.

Anderson, J. A., & Ploghoft, M. E. (1993). Children and media in media education. In G. L. Berry & J. K. Asamen (Eds.), *Children and television: Images in a changing sociocultural world.* Newbury Park, CA: Sage.

Ashley, S., Poepsel, M., & Willis, E. (2010). Media literacy and news credibility: Does knowledge of media ownership increase skepticism in news consumers? *Journal of Media Literacy Education, 2*(1), 37–46.

Benson, P. (2007). Developmental assets: An overview of theory, research and practice. In R. K. Silbereisen & R. M. Lerner (Eds.), *Approaches to positive youth development.* Thousand Oaks, CA: Sage.

Benson, P. L., Mannes, M., Pittman, K., & Ferber, T. (2004). Youth development, developmental assets, and public policy. In R. M. Lerner & L. Steinberg (Eds.), *Handbook of adolescent psychology* (2nd ed., pp. 781–814). Hoboken, NJ: Wiley.

Benson, P. L., & Pittman, K. (2001). *Trends in youth development: Visions, realities, and challenges.* Norwell, MA: Kluwer Academic Publishers.

Benson, P. L., Scales, P. C., Hamilton, S. F., & Semsa, A., Jr., (2006). Positive youth development: Theory, research, and applications. In R. M. Lerner (Ed.), *Handbook of child psychology. Theoretical models of human development* (6th ed., Vol. 1, pp. 894–941). Hoboken, NJ: Wiley.

Brown, J. A. (2001). Media literacy and critical television viewing in education. In D. G. Singer & J. L. Singer (Eds.), *Handbook of children and the media* (pp. 681–697). Thousand Oaks, CA: Sage.

Buckingham, D. (2003). *Media education: Literacy, learning and contemporary culture.* Cambridge, UK: Polity Press.

Chakroff, J. L., & Nathanson, A. I. (2011). Parent and school interventions: Mediation and media literacy. In S. L. Calvert & B. J. Wilson (Eds.), *The handbook of children, media, and development* (pp. 552–576).

Comer, J. S., Furr, J. M., Beidas, R. S., Weiner, C. L., & Kendall, P. C. (2008). Children and terrorism-related news: Training parents in coping and media literacy. *Journal of Consulting and Clinical Psychology, 76*(4), 568–578.

Considine, D. (2003). Weapons of mass distraction? Media literacy, social studies and citizenship. *Visions/revisions: Moving forward with Media Education,* Retrieved from http://www.frankwbaker.com/Considinearticle_final.pdf.

Corbett, P. (2010). *Re: Facebook demographics and statistics report, 2010 [Web log message].* Retrieved from http://www.istrategylabs.com/2010/01/facebook-demographics-and-statistics-report-2010-145-growth-in-1-year/.

Damon, W. (2004). What is positive youth development? *The ANNALS of the American Academy of Political and Social Science, 591,* 13–24. doi:10.1177/0002716203260092.

Federal Communications Commission. (2009). *Notice of inquiry: Empowering parents and protecting children in an evolving media landscape (MB Docket No. 09–194).* Retrieved from http://hraunfoss.fcc.gov/edocs_public/attachmatch/FCC-09-94A1.pdf.

Fedorov, A. (2003). *Media education and media literacy: Experts' opinions.* UNESCO: MENTOR. A Media Education Curriculum for Teachers in the Mediterranean. The Thesis of Thessaloniki, First Version, 1–17. Retrieved from http://www.european-mediaculture.org/fileadmin/bibliothek/english/fedorov_experts/fedorov_experts.pdf.

Flanagan, C. A., & Faison, N. (2001). Youth civic development: Implications of research for social policy and programs. *Social Policy Report, 15*(1), 3–14.

Floyd, D. T. (2010). Invited commentary: A practitioner's journey into developmental research. *Journal of Youth and Adolescence, 39*(7), 836–838.

Frau-Meigs, D., & Torrent, J. (Eds.), (2009). *Mapping media education policies in the world: Visions, programmes and challenges.* Retrieved from http://ec.europa.eu/culture/media/literacy/docs/global/mapping_media_education.pdf.

Furstenburg, F. F. (2000). The sociology of adolescence and youth in the 1990s: A critical commentary. *Journal of Marriage and the Family, 62,* 896–910.

Gans, H. J. (1979). *Deciding what's news: A study of CBS evening news, NBC nightly news, Newsweek, and Time.* New York: Pantheon Books.

Hobbs, R. (1996). Teaching media literacy. In E. Dennis & E. Pease (Eds.), *Children and the media* (pp. 103–111). New Brunswick: Transaction Press. Retrieved from http://www.medialit.org/reading-room/teaching-media-literacy-yo-are-you-hip.

Hobbs, R. (1998). Building citizenship skills through media literacy education. In M. Salvador & P. Sias (Eds.), *The public voice in a democracy at risk* (pp. 57–76). Westport, CT: Praeger Press. Retrieved from http://www.medialit.org/reading-room/building-citizenship-skills-through-media-literacy-education.

Hobbs, R. (2001). Expanding the concept of literacy. In R. Kubey (Ed.), *Media literacy in the information age: Current perspectives* (Vol. 6, pp. 163–183). New Brunswick, New Jersey; Transaction Publishers.

Hobbs, R. (2008). Debates and challenges facing new literacies in the 21st century. In K. Drotner & S. Livingstone (Eds.), *The international handbook of children, media and culture* (pp. 431–447). Thousand Oaks, CA: Sage.

Hobbs, R., & Frost, R. (2003). Measuring the acquisition of media-literacy skills. *Reading Research Quarterly, 38*(3), 330–355.

Hobbs, R., & Jensen, A. (2009). The past, present, and future of media literacy education. *Journal of Media Literacy Education, 1,* 1–11.

Hoffman, L. H., & Thomson, T. L. (2009). The effect of television viewing on adolescents' civic participation: Political efficacy as a mediating mechanism. *Journal of Broadcasting and Electronic Media, 53*(1), 3–21. doi:10.1080/08838150802643415.

Jeličić, H., Bobek, D., Phelps, E., Lerner, J. V., & Lerner, R. M. (2007). Using positive youth development to predict contribution and risk behaviors in early adolescence: Findings from the first two waves of the 4-H Study of Positive Youth Development. *International Journal of Behavioral Development, 31*(3), 263–273.

Kaiser Family Foundation. (2003). *Children and the news: Coping with terrorism, war, and everyday violence [Publication No. 3210].* Retrieved from http://www.kff.org/entmedia/upload/Key-Facts-Children-and-the-News.pdf.

King, P. E., Dowling, E. M., Mueller, R. A., White, K., Schultz, W., Osborn, P., et al. (2005). Thriving in adolescence: The voices of youth-serving practitioners, parents, and early and late adolescents. *Journal of Early Adolescence, 25*(1), 94–112.

Kubey, R. (Ed.), (2001). *Media literacy in the information age: Current perspectives.* New Brunswick, NJ: Transaction Books.

Larson, R., & Richards, M. H. (1991). Daily companionship in late childhood and early adolescence: Changing developmental contexts. *Child Development, 62*(2), 284–300.

Larson, R. W., Richards, M. H., Moneta, G., Holmbeck, G., & Duckett, E. (1996). Changes in adolescents' daily interactions with their families from ages 10 to 18: Disengagement and transformation. *Developmental Psychology, 32*(4), 744–754.

Lederer, L. (1988). *What are other countries doing in media education?* Retrieved from http://www.medialit.org/reading-room/what-are-other-countries-doing-media-education.

Lenhart, A., Ling, R., Campbell, S., & Purcell, K. (2010). *Teens and mobile phones.* Retrieved from Pew Internet and American Life Project website: http://www.pewinternet.org/~/media//Files/Reports/2010/PIP-Teens-and-Mobile-2010-with-topline.pdf.

Lerner, R. M. (2002). *Concepts and theories of human development* (3rd ed.). Mahwah, NJ: Lawrence Erlbaum Associates.

Lerner, R. M. (2004). *Liberty: Thriving and civic engagement among America's youth.* Thousand Oaks, CA: Sage.

Lerner, R. M. (2007). *The good teen: Rescuing adolescents from the myths of the storm and stress years.* New York: The Crown Publishing Group.

Lerner, R. M. (2009). The positive youth development perspective: Theoretical and empirical bases of a strength-based approach to adolescent development. In C. R. Snyder & S. J. Lopez (Eds.), *Oxford handbook of positive psychology* (2nd ed., pp. 149–163). Oxford, England: Oxford University Press.

Lerner, J. V., Phelps, E., Forman, Y. E., & Bowers, E. (2009). Positive youth development. In R. M. Lerner & L. Steinberg (Eds.), *Handbook of adolescent psychology Individual bases of adolescent development* (3rd ed., Vol. 1, pp. 524–558). Hoboken, NJ: Wiley.

Lerner, R. M., von Eye, A., Lerner, J. V., & Lewin-Bizan, S. (2009). Exploring the foundations and function of adolescent thriving within the 4-H Study of Positive Youth Development: A view of the issues. *Journal of Applied Developmental Psychology, 30* (5), 567–570.

Lerner, R. M., von Eye, A., Lerner, J. V., Lewin-Bizan, S., & Bowers, E. P. (2010). Special issue introduction: The meaning and measurement of thriving: A view of the issues. *Journal of Youth and Adolescence, 39*(7), 707–719.

Lerner, R. M., Lerner, J. V., Bowers, E. P., Lewin-Bizan, S., Gestsdottir, S., & Urban, J. B. (2011). Self-regulation processes and thriving in childhood and adolescence: A view of the issues. In R. M. Lerner, J. V. Lerner, E. P. Bowers, S. Lewin-Bizan, S. Gestsdottir, & J. B. Urban (Eds.), *Thriving in childhood and adolescence: The role of self-regulation processes. New Directions for Child and Adolescent Development, 133,* 1–10.

Livingstone, S. (2004). Media literacy and the challenge of new information and communication technologies. *The Communication Review, 7*(1), 3–14. doi:10.1080/10714420490280152.

Lopez, M. H., Levine, P., Both, D., Kiesa, A., Kirby, E., & Marcelo, K. (2006). *The 2006 civic and political health of the nation: A detailed look at how youth participate in politics and communities.* Retrieved from The Center for Information and Research on Civic Learning and Engagement (CIRCLE) website: http://www.civicyouth.org/PopUps/2006_CPHS_Report_update.pdf.

McCombs, M., & Reynolds, A. (2009). How the news shapes our civic agenda. In J. Bryant & M. B. Oliver (Eds.), *Media effects: Advances in theory and research* (3rd ed., pp. 1–16). New York: Routledge.

Moeller, S. D. (2009). *Media literacy: Understanding the news.* Retrieved from Center for International Media Assistance website: http://cima.ned.org/sites/default/files/CIMA-Media_Literacy_Understanding_The_News-Report.pdf.

Pasek, J., Kenski, K., Romer, D., & Jamieson, K. H. (2006). America's youth and community engagement: How use of mass media is related to civic activity and political awareness in 14- to 22-year-olds. *Communication Research, 33*(3), 115–135.

Pittman, K., Irby, M., Tolman, J., Yohalem, N., & Ferber, T. (2001). *Preventing problems, promoting development, encouraging engagement: Competing priorities or inseparable goals?* Washington, DC: The Forum for Youth Investment.

Porter, R. I. (2010). Invited commentary: The positive youth development perspective is an exciting direction for adolescent and family policies and programs. *Journal of Youth and Adolescence, 39*(7), 839–842.

Potter, W. J. (2011). *Media literacy* (5th ed.). Thousand Oaks, CA: Sage.

Raynes-Goldie, K., & Walker, L. (2008). Our space: Online civic engagement tools for youth. In W. Lance Bennett (Ed.), *Civic life online: Learning how digital media can engage youth.* (pp. 161–188). Cambridge, MA: The MIT Press. doi:10.1162/dmal.9780262524827.161.

Rheingold, H. (2008). Using participatory media and public voice to encourage civic engagement. In W. Lance Bennett (Ed.), *Civic life online: Learning how digital media can engage youth.* (pp. 97–118). Cambridge, MA: The MIT Press. doi:10.1162/dmal.9780262524827.097.

Rideout, V., Foehr, U. G., & Roberts, D. F. (2010). *Generation M²: Media in the lives of 8- to 18-year-olds.* Retrieved from Kaiser Family Foundation website: http://www.kff.org/entmedia/upload/8010.pdf.

Rideout, V., & Hamel, E. (2006). *The media family: Electronic media in the lives of infants, toddlers, preschoolers, and their parents.* Retrieved from Kaiser Family Foundation website: http://www.kff.org/entmedia/upload/7500.pdf.

Roth, J., & Brooks-Gunn, J. (2003). What exactly is a youth development program? Answers from research and practice. *Applied Developmental Science, 7*(2), 94–111.

Sherrod, L. R. (2003). Promoting the development of citizenship in diverse youth. *PS: Political Science and Politics, 36*(2), 287–292.

Sherrod, L. R. (2007). Civic engagement as an expression of positive youth development. In R. K. Silbereisen & R. M. Lerner (Eds.), *Approaches to positive youth development* (pp. 59–74). Thousand Oaks, CA: Sage.

Sherrod, L. R., & Lauckhardt, J. (2009). The development of citizenship. In R. M. Lerner & L. Steinberg (Eds.), *The handbook of adolescent psychology* (3rd ed., pp. 372–407). Hoboken, NJ: Wiley.

Strasburger, V., Wilson, B., & Jordan, A. (2009). *Children, adolescents, and the media* (2nd ed.). Thousand Oaks, CA: Sage.

Tewksbury, D., & Scheufele, D. A. (2009). News framing theory and research. In J. Bryant & M. B. Oliver (Eds.), *Media effects: Advances in theory and research* (3rd ed., pp. 17–33). New York: Routledge.

Theokas, C., & Lerner, R. M. (2006). Observed ecological assets in families, schools, and neighborhoods: Conceptualization, measurement and relations with positive and negative developmental outcomes. *Applied Developmental Science, 10*(2), 61–74.

Thoman, E., & Jolls, T. (2003). *Literacy for the 21st century: An overview & orientation guide to media literacy education.* Retrieved from Center for Media Literacy website: http://www.medialit.org/sites/default/files/01_MLKorientation.pdf.

Walsh, D. (2001). Helping children cope with war and terrorism. *Telemedium: The Journal of Media Literacy, 47*(3), 32–33.

Wartella, E., & Robb, M. (2007). Young children, new media. *Journal of Children and Media, 1*(1), 35–44.

ADVANCES IN CIVIC ENGAGEMENT RESEARCH: ISSUES OF CIVIC MEASURES AND CIVIC CONTEXT

Jonathan F. Zaff, Kei Kawashima-Ginsberg, and Emily S. Lin

TUFTS UNIVERSITY, MEDFORD, MASSACHUSETTS, USA

I. WHAT DO WE MEAN WHEN WE SAY "CIVIC ENGAGEMENT?"
  A. DIGGING DEEPER INTO CIVIC ENGAGEMENT BY DIGGING INTO "ENGAGEMENT"
  B. DEVELOPMENTAL TRAJECTORIES OF CIVIC ENGAGEMENT
  C. DEVELOPMENT OF CIVIC ENGAGEMENT WITHIN RELATIONAL MODELS OF DEVELOPMENT
  D. STUDYING CULTURAL, SOCIOECONOMIC, AND RACIAL VARIATIONS IN CIVIC ENGAGEMENT
  E. RELATIONSHIP BETWEEN DEVELOPMENTAL CONTEXT AND DEVELOPMENT OF CIVIC ENGAGEMENT
  F. MEANING AND PREDICTORS OF CIVIC ENGAGEMENT IN DIVERSE CULTURAL CONTEXTS

II. WHERE WE GO FROM HERE

REFERENCES

Abstract

Civic engagement has gained prominence over the past two decades as an important topic in developmental science. Much has been learned about what civic engagement means, how it is measured, and how young people develop civic engagement. In this chapter, we discuss emerging areas of research for civic engagement and core questions that we believe need to be explored. In particular, we focus on a broader conceptualization of civic engagement beyond behavioral measures, consider the relevance of cultural and political contexts on the development of civic engagement among under-served populations, and discuss the implications of advancing the civic engagement field on the civic participation of youth in the United States and throughout the world.

The development of civic engagement has emerged over the past two decades as a substantive subfield within developmental science (Flanagan, 2008; Hart & Kirshner, 2009; Youniss, 2009; Zaff, Boyd, Li, Lerner, & Lerner, 2010; Zaff, Hart, Flanagan, Youniss, & Levine, 2010). Much has

Advances in Child Development and Behavior
Richard M. Lerner, Jacqueline V. Lerner and Janette B. Benson : Editors

been learned about the formative experiences that lead to civic participation and to other civic attitudes and competencies (Sherrod, 2007; Watts & Flanagan, 2007; Youniss, McLellan, & Yates, 1997; Zaff, Boyd, et al., 2010; Zaff, Hart, et al., 2010). Best practices for promoting participation, attitudes, and competencies have been drawn from cross-sectional, longitudinal, and randomized studies of individual and contextual factors (Zaff & Michelsen, 2001). This research has been incredibly informative for policymakers and practitioners who seek to encourage civic participation, whether the U.S. government's Corporation for National and Community Service, corporate social responsibility offices of Fortune 500 companies, nonprofit organizations, such as City Year and Hands On, and elementary, secondary, and postsecondary schools. All of these entities recognize on some level that, consistent with de Tocqueville (2002), a vibrant democracy is reliant on the participation of its citizenry and the well-being of any society, regardless of political structure, is based on the civic actions of individuals and groups.

We define civic as more than fulfilling the rights and responsibilities of citizenship, such as following the rule of law and voting in local and national elections. Instead, we consider civic to be synonymous with being part of the social fabric of a nation, which can be expressed on the national, state, or local level. Civic actions, then, are those that strengthen the social fabric. Although these acts could support the status quo, these acts do not by any means need to sustain the status quo or in any way support ruling entities, whether political, corporate, or otherwise. Individuals could very well act to disrupt aspects of the social fabric that are seen to be unjust or otherwise maladaptive to the well-being of individual citizens. This definition is consistent with a social justice or liberation psychology perspective (Watts & Flanagan, 2007). In addition, as we discuss more fully below, civic participation is not the same as having a deep commitment to civic action. For our purposes in this chapter, then, we examine the development of civic engagement, which is a coupling of civic participation with a motivation, duty, and/or commitment to civic participation.

Considering the plethora of high-quality primary research articles and syntheses that have been published, our chapter is not meant to be an exhaustive discussion of the civic field. Rather, we focus here on key areas where we believe research is headed and where we believe core questions about civic engagement need to be fleshed out. Our hope is that the reader will come away from this chapter with a greater understanding of the definitions of measurement of civic engagement, the ontogenetic development of civic engagement (by examining trajectories of components of civic engagement), and how civic engagement develops among under-researched populations (e.g., disadvantaged youth, youth from other countries). As we discuss more deeply later in this chapter, we conceptualize the development of civic engagement through a developmental systems theoretical lens, that is, civic engagement development defined as a person–context interaction. We end the chapter with a consideration for the implications of the current state of knowledge about civic engagement and how advancing the field could impact the more widespread and more in depth civic participation of youth in the United States and throughout the world.

I. What Do We Mean When We Say "Civic Engagement?"

Civic engagement has typically had a *de facto* definition of civic behaviors, that is, participation in civic activities. These actions could include behaviors ranging from volunteering in the community, such as in a soup kitchen, to leading a civic enterprise, such as being the head of a soup kitchen; to advocating for policy changes, such as policies that address issues of hunger; to working on a political campaign, running for political office, or voting. We say *de facto* because, although much research has used behavioral measures in civic engagement research (see Zaff, Boyd, et al., 2010; Zaff, Hart, et al., 2010), these same studies have used much more comprehensive theories that include such constructs as character and morality. In this chapter, we note that we do not discuss other forms of prosocial behavior, such as to the family. Although prosocial behaviors in support of one's family provides support to the family's well-being and is formative for the youth, our focus is on civic contributions, that is, actions that benefit the broader and more distal community and polity.

The breadth of civic activity types, which have been delineated in national surveys (e.g., Center for Information and Research on Civic Learning and Engagement, 2006), brings together distinct types of actions, such as direct service (e.g., volunteering), advocacy (e.g., protesting or boycotting for a cause), and political participation (voting, working on a campaign). Although these behaviors could be considered discrete categories, they have more recently been discussed as overlapping categories, as individuals often participate in more than one category. In this regard, Westheimer and Kahne (2003) considered three categories of civic action: the *responsible citizen*, who takes part in individual acts such as volunteering; *the participatory citizen*, who becomes involved in the political process with the goal of addressing issues seen in the community; and the *justice-oriented citizen*, who takes more of a leadership role to combat social injustice.

We define civic engagement as more than taking actions enhancing the greater good, whether through community action, advocacy, or political participation. A young person (or older person for that matter) could participate in an activity because they were mandated to participate by school requirements, because their parents told them to participate, or because their friends were participating and the activity seemed fun. None of these reasons, however, speak to a deeper level of commitment to the activity. Thus, our conceptualization includes the motivation, commitment, and/or duty to engage in such civic behaviors, the definition being the realized activity of civic motivation. This consideration of civic engagement is consistent with the school engagement literature (Fredericks, Blumenfeld, & Paris, 2004) and with conceptualizations within broader engagement (e.g., Larson, 2000, 2010) and identity (Erikson, 1963) theories that implicitly, or explicitly, integrate behavioral, emotional, and cognitive factors within the individual. Youniss (2008), Erikson (1963), and action theorists (e.g., Brandtstädter, 2006; Freund & Baltes, 2002) consider the dynamic interplay between cognitive processes, emotions, and behaviors, such that motivations would be considered to be interconnected with behaviors. Action theorists stress the mutually beneficial relations between actions of the individual on the context and the actions of the context on the individual. Although any participation has the potential to benefit the individual and the greater society, we argue, based on the broader engagement and identity literatures mentioned, that developing a civic engagement, beyond behaviors, is key to maximizing individual positive outcomes and to influencing one's community.

In our formulation of civic engagement, we do not put a value on the type of civic action in which one is committed, whether volunteering for a community-based nonprofit organization, taking a leadership role on an advocacy campaign, or running for public office. An open, pluralistic society is inevitably in need of individuals who will take on a variety of civic roles. Indeed, a nation could not thrive if everyone wanted to be the leader, and there was no one passionate about working on the ground on community issues. The important point is that someone is committed to some type of civic action.

A. DIGGING DEEPER INTO CIVIC ENGAGEMENT BY DIGGING INTO "ENGAGEMENT"

As we noted, civic engagement, the realized civic activity of civic motivation, should be distinguished from civic participation, which is solely behavioral. In the school engagement literature, simply attending school is not synonymous with school engagement, nor should participation in a volunteer or political activity be synonymous with civic engagement. Research on engagement builds on prior work on motivation—an emotional and cognitive construct—but explicitly integrates motivation with action (e.g., Fredericks et al., 2004; Zaff, Boyd, et al., 2010; Zaff, Hart, et al., 2010), consistent with developmental systems theory (Ford & Lerner, 1992) and German Action Theories (Brandtstädter, 2006). Motivation has been considered as a drive to fulfill a hierarchy of needs (Maslow, 1954); the consequence of one's feelings of self-efficacy (Bandura, 1977); distinct sets of intrinsic and extrinsic factors (Deci & Ryan, 2000; Malone & Lepper, 1987); a system that can be "turned on" by interpreting experiences as evidence of personal competence, linking actions to potential futures (Larson, 2010); or a feeling of connection to a sense of purpose (Damon, 2008). Larson's (2000) conceptualization of intrinsic motivation (what he called "initiative"; but see Chapter 5) is most closely aligned with our definition of engagement. He proposed that initiative is the ability to direct oneself in an ordered and sustained way toward achieving a challenging goal.

In considering civic engagement within a motivation/action theoretical frame, with a basis in the key motivation theories (e.g., Catalano & Hawkins, 1996; Deci & Ryan, 2000; Larson, 2000; Wigfield & Eccles, 2000), we would posit that civic engagement develops if there is a fit between contextual opportunities and the individual's own values, abilities, and interests. This fit is bidirectional, such that the individual's values are not just passively waiting for the right context, but, rather, are evolving to take in and integrate appropriate values, norms, and regulations from the context. Research on school engagement supports this general model, where student internalization of the school or classroom's values and behavioral norms is associated with higher school participation, more positive feelings toward school, and fewer problematic behaviors (Ryan, Stiller, & Lynch, 1994). Similarly, the development of young people's engagement in out-of-school time activities is associated with person–context fits, such as personal identification with a program's mission or the extent to which adult leaders in the programs facilitated the exercise of youth responsibility (Larson & Hansen, 2005; Pearce & Larson, 2006). And, thus, with regard to civic engagement, Youniss and Yates (1997) observed that both the experience of being efficacious in a service context and the active interpretation of one's efficacy through a moral or ideological lens are equally important in developing one's civic engagement.

Some empirical evidence does exist to indicate a relation between civic engagement and school engagement that is based on similarities in contextual factors. For instance, young people's trust and commitment to civil society and school community has been found when students' perceptions of norms of their school culture (e.g., a civic climate or sense of solidarity with peers at school) align with their perceptions of norms of the larger society (Flanagan, Bowes, Jonsson, Csapo, & Sheblanova, 1998). If young people are able to develop engagement in out-of-school settings like civic leadership programs, then we might expect that they have internalized particular cultural norms from those settings. If schools similarly operate on those norms, or could be interpreted by students to do so, then a young person who has become civically engaged in one context could find him- or herself more engaged with school, as well, as a result of this internalization. This bidirectional cross-context relation can be further seen in schools where youth are often given opportunities to learn about civics, participate in class discussions of current events, and become involved in student government and community service (Niemi & Chapman, 1998).

While a "taking in" of external norms, either through connecting to innate psychological needs or through the influence of social bonds, explains why engagement might exist in different contexts as long as those contexts share features like similar cultural norms, engagement as a general construct may also develop through other processes. For example, in a case study of one particularly active youth organization, Larson, Hansen, and Walker (2005) found that initiative—a long-term, goal-driven version of motivation—can be developed through metacognitive processes. By distinguishing initiative from less reflective "industry" as something that can be learned (e.g., learning to understand that time can be organized strategically), Larson and colleagues laid out a pathway for transfer of engagement. If initiative is developed in a favorable context, the metacognitive abilities it produces do not disappear but can be applied in new contexts, as well. Through this lens, we can begin to see that engagement could be developed not just through socialized internalization but through active learning. Indeed, in a recent analysis (Zaff, Li, & Lin, 2011), we find that civic engagement and school engagement trajectories are intertwined, such that those who are in a high and stable civic engagement trajectory across adolescence are nearly ensured that they will be in a high and stable school engagement trajectory (and likewise for low engagement groups). There is basically a zero-percent chance that a high civic engagement youth will be a low school engagement youth. Youniss, Yates and Su (1997) found consistent results among a nationally representative sample of high-school seniors, with more school-oriented youth much more likely to engage in civic activities than students with less school orientation.

To this point, we have focused on the realized activity of motivation. Building on this idea, we considered the multiple constructs that could define a more actualized form of civic engagement. In our exploration of a more actualized form of civic engagement, we include civic participation, civic self-efficacy, civic duty, and neighborhood connection. Through an empirical analysis of these constructs, we find that these constructs load onto a second-order factor, which we call Active and Engaged Citizenship

(AEC; Bobek, Zaff, Li, & Lerner, 2009; Zaff, Boyd, et al., 2010; Zaff, Hart, et al., 2010). Actions that enhance the community in this way will likely feed back to the individual, thus supporting his/her positive development (Lerner, 2004; Lerner, Alberts, & Bobek, 2007). And, thus, our conception of this civic construct is one in which the individual would participate in civic activities (action) and focus more intensely on a civic enterprise (engaged). Note that "active and engaged" does not necessarily refer to subjective or objective success in a civic action. For instance, a young person who advocates for the closing of sweat shops in Vietnam might not be successful in changing or enacting policies or programs. Theiss-Morse and Hibbing (2004) suggest that failure in civic activities can be an important component of civic development.

1. Cross-contextual Engagement

Psychologists have extensively studied engagement and its associated outcomes in particular contexts, but little is known about the relationships between engagement in different contexts. For example, if an adolescent is highly engaged in school, will he also be engaged socially? In after-school programs? In community life? And if he or she is, can we generalize and now call that adolescent an "engaged person?" We hypothesize that "engagement," a form of self-regulation (see Larson, 2000, for a discussion of initiative, a form of self-regulation that is closely aligned with our concept of engagement), can develop as a construct across contexts (Geldhof, Little, & Colombo, 2010). Aspects of self-regulation have been empirically and theoretically connected across time and across contexts. For example, children who are better able to delay gratification as preschoolers show greater resilience as well as better test performance as adolescents (Mischel, Shoda, & Peake, 1988; Shoda, Mischel, & Peake, 1990). Forms of self-regulation are also cumulative and cross-pollinating, such that improvement in one's self-regulatory competencies begets further improvement in those self-regulatory competencies, and one's development of a particular kind of self-regulation can translate across contexts (Cunha & Heckman, 2009). Thus, engagement can be understood as an aspect of self-regulation in which one's emotions, thoughts, and actions are coordinated toward achieving positive results not just in a single context but across contexts. Unlike other forms of self-regulation, the development of engagement across contexts has not been examined empirically.

As a next step in the research on civic engagement and civic engagement, we consider the intersection of civic engagement and school engagement, two seemingly complementary constructs that predict positive outcomes in adolescence and into adulthood. However, in modern society, school engagement and civic development often seem to be kept carefully separate. Young people's minds are educated in schools, but their civic engagement is largely developed in out-of-school settings (Gibson & Levine, 2003). An empirical question arises about how engagement in these domains might come together, such that those who are engaged with the academic domain are also engaged in the civic. The answer to this question has potentially important implications for children's development of academic and civic competencies and connections. Research is scarce on the relation between the development of civic engagement (i.e., participating in and having a commitment to participating in civic activities) and the development of school engagement (i.e., having a social, cognitive, and behavioral connection to academic work). Although both school and civic engagement represent important pathways toward positive youth development, previous research has not looked at the relation between the two using a pattern-centered approach. By studying both the individual and the dual trajectories of these constructs, we can better understand how these two forms of engagement function within the individual and, on a practical level, begin to understand how to influence the pathways toward the positive outcomes that are associated with them. In a study by two of the chapter authors (Zaff et al., 2011), civic and school engagement trajectories were analyzed across the adolescent years (from 8th to 11th grades). Using a dual trajectory analysis, we found that the trajectories were highly related to each other, such that those who were high on civic engagement throughout adolescence were also highly engaged in school. Likewise, for those low on civic engagement, they were also low on school engagement. The results suggest that intentional efforts are needed to take young people off of low engagement pathways. However, much more research is needed to replicate these findings using other data sets (the analysis was done using the 4-H Study of Positive Youth Development, which skews to a more advantaged and engaged sample) and to understand how external and internal factors work in concert with civic and school engagement.

B. DEVELOPMENTAL TRAJECTORIES OF CIVIC ENGAGEMENT

There is limited understanding of the ontogenesis of civic engagement. Without this understanding, there is little known about normative developmental trajectories of civic engagement and how plastic an individual's civic engagement can be. Research on the developmental trajectories of civic engagement mainly uses time-lag designs to examine how individuals of different ages develop across years. For instance, those transitioning to adulthood have become increasingly less likely to engage in a variety of civic behaviors over the past three decades (Flanagan, Levine, & Settersten, 2009; Syvertsen, Wray-Lake, Flanagan, Osgood, & Briddell, 2011). Few studies have examined the developmental trajectories of civic engagement for individuals over time, which provide insights into the ontogenetic development of civic engagement, not just the effect of interventions or life experiences that alter young people's civic paths.

The vast majority of intraindividual trajectory studies have focused on whether one's participation in civic activities, not deeper civic engagement, at one time point is linked to future civic participation. In their life span study of civic development, Jennings and Stoker (2002, 2004) followed a sample of youth for more than 30 years, examining how and why individuals participated in civic activities and developed civic competencies and attitudes. The researchers found that stability in political attitudes was more a norm than an exception, with those who were civically active earlier in life having more stability throughout life. In other studies, student activists have been found to continue to participate in an array of political activities and to show persistent in political attitudes and ideology two or more decades later (Braungart & Braungart, 1990; Fendrich & Lovoy, 1988; McAdam, 1989). Others have conducted long-term longitudinal studies, with data typically collected once every 10 years, showing high persistence in partisanship and ideology well into adulthood (Alwin, Cohen, & Newcomb, 1991; Alwin & Krosnick, 1991; Sears & Funk, 1999).

A few researchers have studied the continuity of civic engagement from adolescence into young adulthood, consistently showing that participation during early, middle, or late adolescence is related to civic participation in young adulthood, whether volunteering in one's community or participating in electoral politics (Hart, Donnelly, Youniss, & Atkins, 2007; Metz & Youniss, 2005; Smith, 1999; Zaff, Malanchuk, & Eccles, 2008). Further, a recent cross-sectional study found civic participation, knowledge, skills, efficacy, and interest plateau at approximately age 16 (Hart & Atkins, 2010).

As seen in the above studies on stability, what we know about civic trajectories is primarily based on studies of trajectories of civic participation (and political ideology) that typically include only one or two time points during adolescence. Understanding the ways that multiple aspects of civic engagement develop throughout adolescence might provide clues into effective ways to optimize civic engagement during adolescence, which, as suggested by the stability studies, should result in life-long civic engagement. In an analysis of the trajectories of AEC and its components using data from the 4-H Study of Positive Youth Development (Zaff, Kawashima-Ginsberg, Lin, Lamb, & Balsano, in press), the various components of AEC (civic participation, civic duty, civic self-efficacy, and neighborhood connection) had different starting points in early

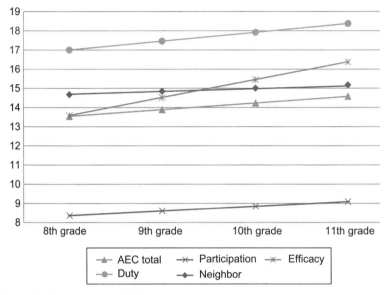

Fig. 1. Predicted values of AEC outcomes by time.

adolescence as well as different slopes (see Figure 1). The components all showed relatively gradual upward slopes, with civic efficacy having the steepest slope and neighborhood connection not changing significantly over the four waves of data. Interestingly, civic participation had a much lower starting point than the other constructs, illustrating the benefit of considering multiple components of civic engagement. By the 11th grade, youth appear to believe that they have a duty to effect change in their communities as well as feeling efficacious to effect change. However, the slope for civic participation is not very steep and stays well below the levels for the other AEC components. Thus, there might be a gap between connection to one's neighborhood, sense of duty to effect change in that neighborhood, and sense of efficacy to effect that change on the one hand and actual participation on the other hand. In a separate analysis of the same data, Zaff et al. (2011) found, using pattern-centered trajectory analysis, that youth followed a high stable, medium stable, or low stable civic engagement path throughout adolescence. That is, once youth were on a civic path, they did not deviate from that path, consistent with the other stability studies that those who are engaged remain engaged.

Taken together, these studies of stability or persistence show that those who are civically active at one period in their lives are very likely to remain civically active throughout their lives. Although these studies have not necessarily examined whether other aspects of civic engagement have similar stability within individuals, we would hypothesize that this level of stability suggests deeper engagement. The question arises, then, why do some individuals begin on these trajectories of civic activity, while others do not? Because civic attributes and experiences during adolescence predict continued civic engagement into later adulthood (Jennings & Stoker, 2004), adolescence may provide a unique opportunity to encourage civic engagement throughout the life course. In the following section, we consider the theories for understanding the development of civic engagement and the factors that appear to predict this development.

C. DEVELOPMENT OF CIVIC ENGAGEMENT WITHIN RELATIONAL MODELS OF DEVELOPMENT

Several theoretical frameworks have been used to frame the development of civic engagement. Flanagan (2004) described two prevailing theories of civic development as the political socialization model and the generational model. In the political socialization model, parents and other adults in a child's life pass down civic understanding, ideologies, and a level of trust in the current system of the time. What is not explicit in the socialization model is the role of the individual in his or her development. That is, the assumption in this theoretical model is that youth take in the civic attitudes and allegiances of their adult models, but their individual characteristics do not influence the way that they interpret and react to the socializing factors. The social uprisings that have occurred throughout history, whether against racial oppression in the United States or against autocratic governments such as more recently in Egypt, exemplify this notion that young people do indeed respond to the prevailing civic structures based on external factors (e.g., modernization, lack of trust of government, and simply being fed up with how one is being treated by society) and enablers (e.g., technology to help mobilize thousands and/or a charismatic leader) as well as by internal factors (e.g., social-cognitive processes that lead to interpreting oppression as a wrong that needs to be addressed). Somewhat differently, the generational theoretical model focuses on the transition to adulthood as a defining moment in a young person's life during which civic attitudes and behaviors are realized. The work cited above by Jennings and Stoker (2002, 2004) provides evidence for the stabilization of attitudes and behaviors during this time period. However, this theoretical model does not account for development that occurs before the transition to adulthood, influenced by the family, the school, and out-of-school time contexts.

To address the shortcomings of these theoretical models, researchers have begun to consider civic engagement within a fuller developmental framework that considers the internal and external influences across the life span and, importantly, considers the dynamic interaction between the individual and the various contexts within which the individual develops. Thus, based on relational theories of development, such as developmental systems theory and the bioecological theory of development (Bronfenbrenner & Ceci, 1993; Ford & Lerner, 1992), and on culturally rich developmental theories that focus on social justice, such as Watts' theory of sociopolitical development (Watts & Flanagan, 2007), our theoretical model of civic development recognizes that factors which exist both in the youth, such as values, and external to the youth, such as socializing agents, work in concert to encourage or deter civic engagement. This composite of individual and contextual variables can be considered to comprise a civic context. Consistent with relational theorists (Bronfenbrenner & Ceci, 1993; Eccles, Midgley, & Wigfield, 1993; Eccles, Midgley, Wigfield, Buchanan, et al., 1993; Vygotsky, 1978), an age-appropriate civic context should be in place throughout childhood in order to encourage the development of civic engagement.

More specifically, Zaff, Youniss and Gibson (2009) provide the following tenets for this theoretical model:

- *Civic engagement is a process and develops over time.* Civic engagement does not suddenly emerge at age 18 with voting eligibility or with an AmeriCorps experience after college. Rather, civic engagement is developed through multiple experiences during childhood and adolescence that cumulate and build into these later experiences and opportunities.
- *A wide and diverse array of proximal and distal factors influence young people's civic development* (proximal factors include families, communities, faith traditions, peer groups, the media, schools, and out-of-school activities, and more distal factors include social disorganization, presence of a civic infrastructure, and isolation). Civic engagement is not solely influenced by one factor.
- *All young people are capable of becoming civically engaged.* Just as positive youth developmental researchers emphasize the strengths of all youth (Lerner, 2004), young people, regardless of background, have the potential to become agents of change in their communities, in their country, and even throughout the world. However, in order to realize this potential, there must be adequate opportunities and resources.

Thus, civic engagement is deeply embedded in and interconnected among individual, social, economic, and political contexts. Without considering these variables together, an incomplete picture of the development of civic engagement will emerge. Therefore, cultural, socioeconomic, political, and historical variations should be considered theoretically central to our understanding of the development of civic engagement. The next section discusses this contextual side of the developmental equation.

D. STUDYING CULTURAL, SOCIOECONOMIC, AND RACIAL VARIATIONS IN CIVIC ENGAGEMENT

Traditionally, research on youth civic engagement has focused on predominantly middle-class, non-Hispanic white youth; the current thinking about the definition and development of civic engagement relies heavily on the findings from these studies. While preexisting studies and resulting knowledge provide a valuable foundation of civic theory, relational metatheories of development underscore the fact that civic theory is incomplete without considering the diversity of the youth population in the United States and globally. This contextually framed conceptualization of civic engagement is consistent with the Society for Research in Child Development's initiative to promote the study of the "majority" population in the world, that is, based on samples outside of White America and Europe. In this section, we discuss the research on civic engagement among those majority cultures, with an emphasis on traditionally disadvantaged groups in the United States. We then highlight the little research available on other, non-Western nations.

Many studies have examined the differences in civic engagement *levels* between the mainstream youth and others, such as youth who come from lower socioeconomic backgrounds, immigrant youth, Hispanic youth, and urban African American youth, to name a few (e.g., Center for Information and Research on Civic Learning and Engagement, 2006; Hart & Atkins, 2003; Verba, Schlozman, & Brady, 1995). Though there are important exceptions, these studies generally examine these differences from a deficit model, in which findings indicate that nonmainstream youth are generally less engaged than their mainstream peers, based on conventional measures of civic engagement such as voting, volunteering, monetary donation, and discussion of political issues. While examining disparities in levels of engagement is crucial in order to come up with solutions, future research on youth civic engagement should place stronger emphasis on at least two additional areas: (a) how variations in developmental contexts affect civic engagement development and (b) capturing conventional and unconventional forms of engagement and broadening our understanding of *civic engagement* to fit in with the diversity of contexts in U.S. society and abroad.

E. RELATIONSHIP BETWEEN DEVELOPMENTAL CONTEXT AND DEVELOPMENT OF CIVIC ENGAGEMENT

There is much research on the factors within various contexts that promote or discourage civic engagement. Parents, other adults, peers, schools, extracurricular programs, civic engagement programs, and neighborhood-level factors have all been found to affect the civic development of youth and young adults (see Zaff, Boyd, et al., 2010; Zaff, Hart, et al., 2010; Zaff et al., 2009 for reviews). Parents can serve as models and help to encourage young people to become involved in civic activities (and sometimes sign them for such activities). Peers create norms within peer groups, which can include civic norms, such as volunteering for civic organizations, working on a political campaign, or taking part in school government. Schools have (or do not have) democratic cultures that service as microcosms of democracy as well as providing (or not providing) opportunities to engage in civic activities within and outside of the school walls. Neighborhoods may be filled with civic institutions that align with the needs of a community or could be dissonant with their needs (e.g., overly aggressive police, nonreactive local government, etc.). Civic engagement programs and more general extracurricular programs can be avenues for exploring and developing civic attitudes and civic skills, but overall have mixed results, suggesting that certain practices are necessary to optimize a program's impact. The purpose of this section is not to rehash these contextual findings. Rather, we focus on how contexts interact with the individual, with an emphasis on those from more disadvantaged backgrounds.

1. Societal Disparities and Poverty

As noted earlier, action theory (Brandtstädter, 2006) and the broader engagement theory suggest that individual's cognitive, emotional, and behavioral tendencies interact with the context in which actions occur. In other words, civic engagement development occurs within a specific context that is unique to each person (Rubin, 2007; Rubin & Hayes, 2010), and action is likely to occur if there is clear benefit to taking action within that particular context and less likely to occur if a person's context does not signal clear benefit to one's action. Our society is marked by significant social and economic disparities that affect development of civic engagement (Abu El-Haj, 2009; Levinson, 2007, 2009). These social disparities, largely driven by economic hardship and related factors, have a strong influence on youth's developmental contexts (family, schools, neighborhoods, relationships, and civic institutions) and on the ways in which youth develop their civic identity and, importantly, develop trust in authority and civic institutions in which a young person may choose to participate or not. Marginalized youth not only show lower levels of engagement but often express a sense of hopelessness or inefficacy when asked about their participation (Stepick, Stepick, & Labisierre, 2008; Swartz, Blackstone, Uggen, & Mclaughlin, 2009). Poverty, at various levels of developmental context (e.g., family, community), exerts a complex web of effects on development of civic engagement by affecting all residents in that community and the resources that the community has to offer to its youth, such as positive adult role models (Hart & Atkins, 2003) and a lack of social trust and social capital among residents (Hart & Atkins, 2002).

Rubin (2007) articulates how youth's experiences of societal disparities interact with their civic development based on her extensive work with marginalized students. Rubin (2007) defined four typologies of civic efficacy and subsequent behavioral intent by two dimensions: youth's experiences in relation to the learned ideals of the United States (congruence vs. disjuncture) and youth's attitudes toward civic participation (active vs. passive). Rubin (2007) defines disjuncture as disconnect between what they learn as fundamental democratic principles of our country (e.g., Bill of Rights) in school and what they actually experience in their daily lives. Youth who experience disjuncture tend to be discouraged ("nothing I do would make a difference"), while youth who experience congruence may be complacent, because they see no need for drastic change. These youth in different developmental contexts might respond to different approaches in mobilizing them, as they have very different experience with the principles of democracy and authority in their daily lives (Table I).

Rubin and Hayes (2010) document a striking example of how high-school students attending schools in economically advantaged and disadvantaged communities differed dramatically in attitudes toward civic participation and personal perception of the democratic ideals of the United States, which led to differences in the way students decided to work on civic issues as a class. Students attending the advantaged school picked an issue that was specific and occurred within the school—carrying a backpack during the hall pass. In their case, the problem solved itself because the new administration decided that the rule was irrelevant, shortly after students chose this issue and abolished this rule. Students were highly engaged in the issue identification phase of the project but soon lost interest and did not actively advocate for the change. When the rule was abolished, students still felt empowered and efficacious and noted that this was a good experience. Even though they did not actively advocate for the change themselves, many of them came away feeling that they did something to make the change.

Table I

Congruence and Disjuncture of Youth Civic Attitudes

		Youth's experience in relation to the learned ideals of the society	
		Congruence	Disjuncture
Youth's attitudes toward civic participation	Active	*Aware*: there is a need for change toward equity and fairness Have experienced congruence, recognize their privilege, and are aware that disjunctures exist	*Empowered*: change is a personal and community necessity Have experienced disjuncture Believe in their ability to use the system to bring about justice Know about civic rights and processes Have been encouraged to critique
	Passive	*Complacent*: no change is necessary; all is well Have experienced congruence Support preservation of status quo Do not know about or recognize disjunctures experienced by others (Rubin, 2007)	*Discouraged*: no change is possible; life is unfair Have experienced disjuncture Express deep cynicism about the possibility of using the system to make changes

Students in the disadvantaged school chose to work on a much different issue that affected their entire neighborhood and daily lives, drugs and murders. Working on the chosen issues was infinitely complicated at this school: students knew that some of their peers were contributing to the problem on which they worked (by dealing drugs themselves) and they were constantly challenged by complexity of choices that were involved in personal and community civic actions. For example, reporting on incidents of drug sales to the authorities (the "civil thing" to do) was accompanied by great personal risks. Despite the fact that students were challenged and even ambivalent at times, they became more and more committed to making the change and followed through with the project for the entire year. Students reported feeling proud of their involvement in something so meaningful even though no immediate changes were observed (Rubin & Hayes, 2010).

In this particular example, students in both schools concluded the year with at least some sense of accomplishment and positive feeling toward the project. However, developmental trajectories of their civic engagement differed dramatically. From programmatic and educational perspectives, the difference in youth's relationship to developmental context (disjunctures vs. congruence) has important implications to how they can be supported in developing positive civic identities. Youth experiencing congruence are far more likely to accept ideals of a civil society as a genuine reality and show more predictable, smooth development over time. Students experiencing disjunctures have more challenges and also opportunities for critical learning because the issues they experience are often the very problems that plague this society. Thus, students may feel deep personal commitment to the issue on which they work and see meaningful difference in their own view of self and the community. Civic learning, both in school and in out-of-school settings, must account for the social, political economic contexts in which youth development takes place. It is also important to note that schools within economically disadvantaged neighborhoods are less likely to have a civic culture or teachers who push students to be civically minded. For instance, schools in low-income neighborhoods are less likely to have student government or to engage students in school-level decision making (McFarland & Starrmans, 2007; Verba et al., 1995). The lack of either type of experience or the lack of open classrooms where students are encourage to voice their opinions diminish the opportunity for students to develop critical thinking skills or to be involved in what Torney-Purta and Amadeo (2011) have called emergent citizenship—the practicing of civic skills and actions in civic microcosms.

2. Civic Ecology of Families Experiencing Economic Hardship

Although youth's socioeconomic status is generally defined by both parental educational attainment and income, some researchers argue that income itself and related economic hardship is an independent predictor of civic participation, particularly voting (Pacheco & Plutzer, 2007). Qualitative research suggests that economic strains related to jobs, income, and childcare availability act as a barrier for low-income parents to actively participate in civic activities (Obradovic & Masten, 2007; Safrit & Lopez, 2001; Smetana & Metzger, 2005). This, in turn, affects the child's civic engagement, as parents serve as critical role models for civic behavior (Janoski & Wilson, 1995). The children in poor families are far more likely to have parents with lower levels of education, which, in turn, affect civic knowledge and identity development (Pacheco & Plutzer, 2007; Verba, Burns, & Schlozman, 2003), possibly as a result of spending precious time on essential actions to earn money to put food on the table and roof over the family's head. Participating in civic activities becomes a luxury (Gauthier & Furstenberg, 2005). [Singapore, South Korea, and Taiwan are examples of economies that created a nation of middle-class families, which enabled those families to become concerned with political actions (Jones & Smith, 2007).]

3. Community Context and Trust in Authority, Fellow Residents, and Humanity

Flanagan (2003) posits that young people's general sense of trust, a sense that people are basically good and trustworthy, is a crucial foundation for civic participation and therefore a democratic society. A child's experience in interacting with other members of his or her family or community has an impact on formation of trust and subsequently civic development. In the aforementioned study by Rubin and Hayes (2010), students in the advantaged community felt that their community is a "good place to live" and had positive view of adults and authority figures. On the contrary, students in the disadvantaged community, where violence and drugs were daily reality, felt that the civic institutions that were designed to protect its citizens were not functioning as they should and had low levels of trust toward virtually all authority figures, including their own teachers. The difference in the level of trust in authority and adults, in general, has clear implications in the way youth will interact with their community (Kelly, 2009).

The child's perspective does not only reflect his or her direct experiences (e.g., mistreatment by police, low-quality educational experiences) but also those of family and community members. For example, parents who experience prejudice and discrimination are more likely to tell their own children that other people may not be trustworthy (Hughes & Chen, 1997; Hughes et al., 2006; Thornton, Chatters, Taylor, & Allen, 1990). Findings indeed suggest that levels of social capital and trust are substantially lower among adults in urban centers than suburban areas (Hart & Atkins, 2002).

Thus, in a developmental context where citizens are unable to trust civic institutions and each other, children are less likely to receive messages about trust in others, or receive opportunities to work with others toward a common goal, as they would in a community project or in a community-based organization. This dynamic is exacerbated when there is a high youth-to-adult ratio, called a "youth bulge," the result being a lack of human and social capital with which to positively guide youth's civic development (Hart, Atkins, & Youniss, 2005).

Ethnographic research about youth in urban communities further suggests that young people in urban communities feel a sense of civic political disempowerment, many youth describing it as a feeling of "them versus us" (Solomon & Steinitz, 1979; Stepick et al., 2008). This mind-set, which includes hostility toward authority and subsequently a limited understanding of the potential impact they could make, deters young people from being engaged in their communities (O'Donoghue & Kirshner, 2003) and gain formative experiences where they could build trust through positive experiences (see Flanagan, Gill, & Gallay, 2005; Putnam, 2000; Youniss & Yates, 1999). Along with encouraging participation in civic-related activities, civic role models in adolescence are a crucial part in youth civic development (Smith, 1999). Consistent with this idea, Zaff et al. (2008) posit that "living within a civic context contributes to the development of civic engagement from early adolescence into adulthood." An important aspect of such a civic context is an opportunity to *consistently* participate in substantive and formative civic activities (Youniss & Yates, 1999; Zaff et al., 2008).

4. School as a Context for Civic Development

School plays important roles in the development of civic engagement, both by providing youth with civic knowledge and by acting as a microcosm of the larger society that can empower or disempower youth the same way their communities can. In other words, schools have a potential to provide youth with crucial civic knowledge and skills and instill positive beliefs and values toward civic engagement by providing students with experiences appropriate to the youth's age and appropriate to the youth's life situation. There are, however, significant challenges in providing youth with developmentally and contextually appropriate experiences. As noted earlier, students who experience a disjuncture between what school teaches and what they experience in their daily lives can feel disempowered and unmotivated (Rubin, 2007; Rubin & Hayes, 2010; Rubin, Hayes, & Benson, 2009). Teaching in such a context becomes unauthentic and ineffective. At the same time, schools have the potential to provide youth with a context in which they can directly experience the ideals of a democratic society, such as fairness in school policies, the openness of classrooms to discussion (Campbell, 2005; Flanagan, Gallay, Gill, Gallay, & Nti, 2005), and meaningful learning experience such as high-quality service learning that includes thoughtful reflection and community-embedded experiential learning (Billig, Root, & Jesse, 2005; Eyler & Giles, 1999; Hart et al., 2007).

Challenge lies in providing high-quality civic education and civic experience to students of various backgrounds and economic resources. Students attending schools in economically advantaged communities are more likely to be exposed to "best practices" of civic education (Campbell, 2005; Kahne & Middaugh, 2008) or civic education at all (Center on Education Policy, 2006). Research further suggests that quality of civic education is uneven across race, ethnicity, income, and parental educational attainment (Lutkus & Weiss, 2007). Another related, but distinct challenge is that students from ethnic minority backgrounds receive little support in their academic curriculum which gives them understanding of their own lives in a civic context (Abu El-Haj, 2009; Roberts, Bell, & Murphy, 2008). As an already and increasingly diverse society, schools are challenged to provide high-quality civic education that considers the diversity in both social status and cultural background of each student (Junn, 2004) and researchers are challenged to uncover the most effective practices.

5. Urban Communities as a Fertile Ground for Civic Development
Though research has consistently shown that living in urban, poor neighborhoods is related to lower civic engagement levels and more barriers to developing positive civic identity, a number of studies have demonstrated that urban neighborhoods and an ecology of poverty can be a "developmental ground for children's civic attitudes" (McBride, Sherraden, & Pritzker, 2006). Well-implemented case studies and ethnographic studies suggest that, given meaningful, empowering, and challenging opportunities, young people often rise to the opportunities and develop a deep sense of commitment for social or civic causes (Berg, Coman, & Schensul, 2009; Dawes & Larson, 2011; Foreman & Neal, 2004; Ginwright & Cammarota, 2007; Kirshner, 2009; Rubin & Hayes, 2010). Particularly for urban, ethnic minority youth who contend with discrimination and prejudice daily and learn to become "invisible" in all forms of public life (Cohen, 2006), a change from passive observant to active participant represents a transformational change (Kirshner, 2009). Emerging research also recognizes an important role for personal connection and a sense of safety and competency in transforming youth who have low civic attitudes into highly committed civic actors (Borden & Serido, 2009; Dawes & Larson, 2011). For example, Ginwright and Cammarota (2007) suggest that it is the activities in local youth organizations that can facilitate "critical civic praxis" among youth and facilitating a process whereby young people engage in solving community and school conditions that impact their lives.

The role of community-based organizations in mobilizing traditionally disengaged and marginalized youth is being increasingly recognized (Dawes & Larson, 2011; Ginwright & Cammarota, 2007), and research continues to show that it is indeed possible to engage these youth (Andolina, Jenkins, Zukin, & Keeter, 2003; Dawes & Larson, 2011). These community organizations and youth groups use various strategies to involve and retain youth, but especially for those marginalized youth who experience disjunctures on a daily basis (Rubin, 2007), the kind of experiences that help youth become aware of larger societal issues that affect them daily, the process termed "civic praxis" by Ginwright, seems to be helpful. Ginwright and Cammarota (2007) theorize that through organizational processes, young people experience critical civic praxis and comprehend the full, humanistic potential to create social change. This notion marks a significant departure from the standard social capital literature that more often fails to recognize both the individual and collective agency and how social networks ultimately foster critical consciousness. Research shows that once given the opportunity to participate (e.g., through a CBO) youth gain an understanding of their stake in both the larger community as well as the overall community needs (Borden & Serido, 2009; Rubin & Hayes, 2010; Safrit & Lopez, 2001).

Although urban centers can provide rich civic experiences for young people, relatively little longitudinal data exist on ways that urban youth become civically engaged. Considering the structural barriers to civic participation, such as fewer civic institutions than more advantaged communities, civic entry points for youth and young adults have diminished. More needs to be learned about ways to work within this new normal of urban centers, a normal that includes low high-school graduation rates, high unemployment, and low levels of social trust.

6. Religious Institutions and Spirituality as a Context for Civic Development

Involvement in religious organizations and frequent attendance at religious services are associated with volunteering among minority youth and youth who are traditionally less likely to volunteer, such as noncollege youth (National Conference on Citizenship, 2008). Religiosity in early- and late adolescents predicts more positive civic orientation (Crystal & DeBell, 2002) and religious attendance in early adolescence predicts civic engagement in later on in early adulthood (Zaff et al., 2008) for youth of all income ranges. This remains true specifically for middle-class African Americans and civic involvement, but not political involvement (Smetana & Metzger, 2005). According to Verba et al. (1995), churches and religious organizations are particularly helpful for those who are otherwise less likely to participate because churches provide opportunities for skill building and the kind of social networks that can build adolescents' trust toward authority. Further, churches played a critical role as a stage for the civil rights movement in America and therefore have an important place in civic development among African American youth. Harris (1994) posits that religious organizations are fertile ground for civic development, particularly for African Americans, because

> The churches' communication networks, their capacity to stimulate social interaction, provide material resources, and give individuals the opportunity to learn organizing skills, and perhaps most importantly, their sustainability over time and physical space made them the only black institutions consistently promoting the collective resistance of African Americans through several historical periods, shifting political alliances, and interests, and vastly differing opportunity structures for activism. (279)

Though findings suggest that religious organizations facilitate civic participation for many reasons, the process by which youth develop from passive observant to civic actor as they continue to affiliate with religious organizations is not yet understood well. Park and Smith (2000) offer four different sources of "religious capital" that might facilitate volunteerism — religiosity or a person's behaviors and value toward the religion, religious socialization (being exposed to religious values and behaviors during formative years), religious identity (sense of belonging to a specific movement or a set of values), and religious social networks (affiliation with others who hold similar values toward volunteering). Findings suggest that frequency of church activities and social network consistently predict higher levels of volunteering (in and out of their own church) among adults. Whether these findings apply to youth is not known. Further, even less is known about youth who identify as religious minorities, such as Arab youth in the United States, and how their religiosity may influence civic identity development, particularly if they also feel that their religious affiliation can place them in a marginalized position in the society. Future research should examine the processes by which youth who affiliate with religious organizations become active civic participants, and whether *all* types of religious affiliations have the same effect on youth civic development.

F. MEANING AND PREDICTORS OF CIVIC ENGAGEMENT IN DIVERSE CULTURAL CONTEXTS

Though relatively few formal studies have been done on the variations in concept of civic engagement or the behaviors that constitute civic engagement across cultural contexts, some researchers argue that cultural practice—such as the types of activities that are considered part of the norm, and materials and tools (e.g., religious texts) and symbols that represent the cultural group (e.g., rituals for welcoming a new member to the community)—plays an important role in youth's moral and civic development (Nasir & Kirshner, 2003). Again, civic development, including what it means to be civically engaged, would be defined in terms of interactions between youth's social position (e.g., minority status, religious affiliation), cultural practice, and larger societal context.

For instance, in Nasir and Kirshner's case study, students in a Muslim school within a black community learned about morality and activism through Qu'ran and hip-hop. In youth programs for urban, economically disadvantaged such as the one documented by Ginwright and Cammarota (2007) and also by Nasir and Kirshner (2003), programs actively highlight societal inequalities that directly affect them rather than simply engaging youth in service to "help those who are in need." For the youth in these programs, the concept of civic engagement may or may not include community service. In qualitative studies that one of the authors (Kawashima-Ginsberg) is involved in, young, urban, predominantly African American adults who have not attended college and generally live in a challenging developmental context (e.g., high crime rates, economic hardship, distrust of authority), participants defined civic engagement differently and used different terms. Some young people spoke of "service" as something that triggers a sense of disempowerment, as in mandatory community service as a form of punishment, or something that they or their parents did for a living (e.g., cleaning up, picking up garbage). Many also expressed skepticism toward the ideals of democracy, much like the students with whom Rubin and Hayes (2010) interacted, and they opted not to vote, even during the 2008 presidential election, which mobilized many urban African American youth (Center for Information and Research on Civic Learning and Engagement, 2009). As such, most young people in these studies would have said that they did not engage in many "civic" activities that are included in conventional surveys. However, many young people were helping others and giving back to the community in meaningful ways, such as mentoring neighborhood children, visiting and helping out in a local homeless shelter, or providing a place to live for someone who needed it. Although some of the activities fall well under what we consider as "conventional" forms of civic engagement, these young people did not see these activities as "volunteering" or "community service." Further, even the youth who opted not to vote were often highly engaged in political discussions with their coworkers and friends. Once again, a survey item about voting would have missed this form of civic engagement.

Social context and cultural practices dictate whether what we in the United States and Western Europe think of as "good citizenship" is a goal for positive youth development. Findings from a recent U.S. study (Lee, Purcell, & Smith, 2011) suggest that young adults who are active in online groups are also more active offline. However, in a study of Columbians who use the Internet technologies for civic purposes, findings suggest that the connection between online and offline is nonexistent (Rojas & Puig-i-Abril, 2009). In a society where active and formal political participation (e.g., collectively demonstrating, contacting a public official) may accompany some risks (Rojas & Puig-i-Abril, 2009), online civic engagement should be seen as a legitimate form of participation, rather than a mere pathway to more formal, offline participation. In one of the few youth civic program evaluations in China to date (Johnson, Johnson-Pynn, & Pynn, 2007), youth participants expressed mixed views of the government's support for nongovernmental organizations to protect the environment and stated that the community viewed their civic activities with suspicion.

We have so far discussed the important role of one's community or neighborhood in the developmental process in this chapter, with American youth in mind. However, the idea of "community" itself is not universal across the world. For example, displaced refugees living in a camp show far less attachment to the community and willingness to contribute compared to the residents of equivalent financial status living in their home village (Townley, Kloos, Green, & Franco, 2011). For urban and rural Chinese adults, "social capital," an important predictor of virtually all forms of civic engagement in Western contexts, does not predict participation in local politics; instead, more informal connection with neighbors and perceived support predict participation (Xu, Perkins, & Chow, 2010). The researchers argue that the Western definition of social capital might not resonate with Chinese citizens because the conventional definition of social capital implies that individuals build networks with others and belong to groups as a personal choice, which may not fit in well with more collectivistic Chinese society (Xu et al., 2010). Further, citizens of a nondemocratic society such as China may see less benefit in taking individual action against or for a cause for fear of being singled out as a rebel in their sociocultural context.

Little is known about the development of civic engagement in non-Western settings, and really, little is known about the development of civic engagement among non-U.S. populations. Two notable cross-sectional studies, the IEA Civic Education Study (IEA) and the social contract study, used nationally representative samples from multiple countries to understand the civic attitudes and competencies of youth in mostly

Western nations. The IEA study (Torney-Purta & Amadeo, 2003) surveyed 90,000 14-year-olds across 28 countries in 1999, with a focus on individual-, classroom-, and school-level predictors and outcomes of civic engagement. The social contract study (Flanagan et al., 1998) included more than 5500 12- to 18-year-olds in seven countries (three stable and three transitional democracies, including the United States, Australia, and eastern and western European countries). In both studies, the researchers found country-level sociocultural and political effects on civic engagement. In the IEA study, classroom and school effects were also found. Although the findings become quite nuanced, a general theme seems to be that more open and democratic societies and institutions tend to predict higher levels of civic attitudes, knowledge, and competencies. Although there are other studies that have examined the impact of civic engagement programs (including, among others, national service programs in Germany, Israel, and Italy) and have analyzed country-level civic attitudes (e.g., Dejaeghere & Hooghe, 2009), the majority of studies on youth civic engagement have been documentations of civic participation (see Perold, Stroud, & Sherraden, 2003; World Bank and Innovations in Civic Participation, 2008; Yates & Youniss, 1998). Considering the diversity in the ways that civic engagement is defined within and outside the United States, and considering that civic engagement should be examined through a developmental systems lens, we argue that gaining a deeper understanding of the ways that civic engagement is promoted and expressed throughout the world is essential to the promotion of a global, active, and engaged citizenry.

One powerful sign of civic engagement that cuts across cultures and contexts occurs when young people drive and sustain large-scale social movements. From the civil rights movement in the United States of the 1950s and 1960s, to the student riots that marked the beginning of the end of apartheid in South Africa, to the recent popular uprising and ousting of Hosni Mubarak in Egypt, students and youth in their teens and early 20s have been responsible for generating the strategy, will, and collective action necessary to create globally momentous shifts in social and political structures. Kuhn (1962) described revolutions in the scientific domain as being driven by paradigm shifts, which only become possible when "normal science" within the existing paradigm fails to accommodate a critical mass of anomalous information, and a new scientific paradigm (and often with it, new scientists) arises, within which normal science can again be practiced. In social revolutions, then, young people can be seen as natural catalysts for similar kinds of paradigm shifts, having both the critical eye to observe social anomalies (e.g., institutionalized segregation in a democratic state) and the hopeful heart to believe that their actions can create a new paradigm in which such anomalies no longer exist (e.g., institutionalized integration and equal protection of civil rights) (Ganz, 2010).

Because such shifts require creating collective power that is commensurate with or even greater than the currently dominant power, large numbers of organized participants are needed to drive effective social movements. Collective action at this scale requires developing leadership and engagement at all levels of participation (Ganz, 2002). Thus, youth involvement in large-scale social change can take place at many levels. For example, in Egypt, some youth leaders had been strategizing, learning, and teaching tactics of nonviolent resistance for years before the January 25, 2011 march; others—inspired by the success of peers in Tunisia, where another uprising was occurring—spent the week before the planned protest posting video blogs and Facebook updates calling on others to march with them against a tyrannical president; and many others only joined on the day of the protest when they decided, crucially, to come out of their homes and schools and march to Tahrir Square and other public venues around the country with the thousands of other people demanding Mubarak's resignation (Shukrallah, 2011).

Along with recent events like these, historical accounts and scholarly research tell us that large-scale social movements driven by young people can have a transformational impact on social and political structures. However, from a developmental perspective, many open questions remain about the reciprocal and sustained impact of those movements on the young people who lead and engage in them. For example, given the distributed leadership model necessary for organized collective action, one might hypothesize that individuals at different levels of social movements display different trajectories in future civic engagement. McAdam (1988) described continued and high levels of social activism among educated white participants in "Freedom Summer" who chose to leave their own communities and act on behalf of unknown others. But, little is known about the African American youth for whom participation in the civil rights movement was a matter of daily survival, who were engaged by their pastors, peers, and neighbors to stay off the buses they rode every day or to sit down in the restaurants they had always passed by but never dared to enter. We do not know, for instance, whether these youth remained active in political movements in later years, whether their future civic engagement took some other form, or whether their engagement disappeared altogether.

From an interventionist perspective, we may also ask, "How can we scaffold the civic development of young people so that they can be successful in their collective social justice efforts?" Emerging lines of research on effective adult support for developing youth activists (e.g., Kirshner, 2008; Shah & Mediratta, 2008; Zeldin, Larson, Camino, & O'Connor, 2005) could be integrated with the theoretical and empirical literature on teaching leadership for collective civic action and social change (e.g., Andrews, Ganz, Baggetta, Han, & Lim, 2010; Freire, 1970; Ganz & Lin, in press) in order to begin exploring the developmental antecedents and consequences of participating in large-scale social movements.

Such an agenda poses exciting theoretical and methodological challenges to developmental scientists. Existing case studies of youth organizing—what Camino and Zeldin (2002) have called a "new pathway" for civic development—point the way toward potential future directions for this research. Many of these case studies focus on community-organizing efforts to advocate for local policy changes, such as increasing funding for school programs (Warren, Mira, & Nikundiwe, 2008), improving curriculum offerings (Shah & Mediratta, 2008), and integrating youth voice into program- or city-level decision making (Christens & Dolan, 2010; Kirshner, 2007). Although this body of research has mostly been conducted in the context of "small wins" (Foster-Fishman et al., 2006), it also yields a number of theoretical frameworks linking individual-level development to community impacts and larger social shifts. For researchers working in the context of large-scale social movements, these frameworks could be inverted, such that participating in *big win* political changes like the overthrow of a national government can be related to within-person development and between-person differences in that development, particularly because big win changes are the result of multiple small wins strategically organized to build upon each other. No such developmental models currently exist, possibly because of the difficulty of *catching* a large-scale political change within a scientific research design. Though this challenge is substantial, developmental scientists may find guidance in the political science literature, which contains useful examples of real-time research within evolving social movements (e.g., Han & Hudgens, 2010).

II. Where We Go From Here

The past two decades have seen an influx in research on civic participation, civic attitudes, and civic competencies. This research has crossed disciplines, including psychologists, sociologists, political scientists, economists, and anthropologists. Even with this influx and with a much greater understanding about what civic engagement means and the factors that promote civic engagement, there is still much that the civic engagement field needs to uncover. From a measurement perspective, researchers need to continue to develop measures that assess the more holistic nature of civic engagement, getting away from solely using behavioral measures as proxies. We presented ideas around two concepts of civic engagement (blending participation and motivation as well as a more actualized form that includes social connection and self-efficacy, AEC). We are not convinced that our measures are the "right" measures for all young people in the world, nor do we think they capture the breadth of experiences that comprise civic engagement. Not only does civic measure need to be refined but they also need to be tested among diverse groups of youth, who represent differences in race/ethnicity, educational trajectory and attainment, income, and geography. The measures should also be tested for longitudinal measurement invariance to confirm that the measures can be used for youth of all ages, or whether more than one measure is needed to assess civic engagement throughout the first two decades of life. The differences in life experience should not be confined to the United States. Countries throughout the world provide unique contexts for encouraging and discouraging civic development. Without measurement refinement, research on these less advantaged populations will be invalid, at best.

The globalization of connections across the world—and the continuing immigration of families from one nation to another—provides an opportunity to understand the dynamics of civic engagement in a variety of countries, including countries that have not historically been a part of cross-national studies, particularly emergent democracies and nondemocratic societies. For instance, within nondemocratic countries, what factors result in having an engaged citizenry that believes in the rights and freedoms of the given country's citizens and which leads to civic actions to improve the citizens' well-being? Given that the United States' evolution over the past 50 years, including the decreased membership in unions, has dealt researchers a set of complexities to understand the intersection of society and individuals, one can only imagine the complexities of civic engagement in countries such as China that have undergone a transformation of their economies, which have opened up opportunities for citizens to engage with various economic and noneconomic institutions. The assimilation of immigrants into their new home countries is an issue with which countries struggle and has immense implications for the continued strength of a country's democracy (as immigrants tend to leave nondemocratic countries and move to more democratic countries) and the well-being of local communities, as social connection appears to be related to civic participation.

A civic person–context fit—that is, providing a fit between the individual's attitudes, temperament, and beliefs, and the sociopolitical contexts that intersect with the individual characteristics—undergirds much of what is needed from researchers to address the above issues. This relational developmental approach strongly suggests that the information about civic functioning to date, focused primarily on Western democracies, cannot be the end to the civic engagement story. By developing culturally relevant civic measures and exploring the ways that civic engagement can be encouraged in a breadth of contexts, practitioners and policymakers will be better informed about ways to encourage national and community-level civic action, and individuals and groups in democratic and nondemocratic countries will be empowered to work toward more just societies.

REFERENCES

Abu El-Haj, T. R. (2009). Becoming citizens in an era of globalization and transnational migration: Re-imagining citizenship as critical practice. *Theory into Practice, 48*, 274–282.

Alwin, D. F., Cohen, R. L., & Newcomb, T. M. (1991). *Political attitudes over the life span: The Bennington Women after fifty years.* Madison: University of Wisconsin Press.

Alwin, D. F., & Krosnick, J. A. (1991). Aging, cohorts, and the stability of sociopolitical orientations over the life span. *The American Journal of Sociology, 97*, 169–195.

Andolina, M., Jenkins, K., Zukin, C., & Keeter, S. (2003). Habits from home, lessons from school: Influences on youth civic engagement. *PS: Political Science and Politics, 36*, 275–280.

Andrews, K. T., Ganz, M., Baggetta, M., Han, H., & Lim, C. (2010). Leadership, membership, and voice: Civic associations that work. *The American Journal of Sociology, 115* (4), 1191–1242.

Bandura, A. (1977). *Social learning theory.* New York: General Learning Press.

Berg, M., Coman, E., & Schensul, J. J. (2009). Youth action research for prevention: A multilevel intervention designed to increase efficacy and empowerment among urban Youth American. *Journal of Community Psychology, 43*, 345–359.

Billig, S., Root, S., & Jesse, D. (2005). *The impact of participation in service learning on high school students' civic engagement.* (CIRCLE Working Paper #33). Retrieved February 17, 2011, at www.civicyouth.org.

Bobek, D. L., Zaff, J., Li, Y., & Lerner, R. M. (2009). Cognitive, emotional, and behavioral components of civic action: Towards an integrated measure of civic engagement. *Journal of Applied Developmental Psychology, 30*, 615–627.

Borden, L., & Serido, J. (2009). From program participant to engaged citizen: A developmental journey. *Journal of Community Psychology, 37*, 423–438.

Brandtstädter, J. (2006). Action perspectives on human development. In R. M. Lerner (Ed.), *Theoretical models of human development. Volume 1 of handbook of Child Psychology.* (6th ed., pp. 516–568). Hoboken, NJ: Wiley.

Braungart, M. M., & Braungart, R. G. (1990). The life course development of left-and right-wing youth activist leaders from the 1960s. *Political Psychology, 11*, 243–282.

Bronfenbrenner, U., & Ceci, S. J. (1993). Heredity, environment, and the question "how" In R. Plomin & G. McClearn (Eds.), *Nature nurture & psychology.* (pp. 313–324). Washington, DC: APA Books.

Camino, L., & Zeldin, S. (2002). From periphery to center: Pathways for youth civic engagement in the day-to-day life of communities. *Applied Developmental Science, 6*(4), 213–220.

Campbell, D. E. (2005). *Voice in the classroom: How open classroom environment facilitates adolescents' civic development.* CIRCLE Working Paper # 28. Retrieved February 15, 2011, at www.civicyouth.org.

Catalano, R. F., & Hawkins, J. D. (1996). The social development model: A theory of antisocial behavior. In J. D. Hawkins (Ed.), *Delinquency and crime: Current theories.* New York: Cambridge University Press.

Center for Information and Research on Civic Learning and Engagement. (2006). *The 2006 Civic and Political Health of the Nation: A detailed look at how youth participate in politics and communities.* Retrieved February 16, 2011, at www.civicyouth.org.

Center for Information and Research on Civic Learning and Engagement. (2009). *Key findings about civic engagement among non-college youth from Baltimore focus groups.* Unpublished manuscript.

Center on Education Policy, (2006). *From the capital to the classroom: Year four of the No Child Left Behind Act.* Washington, DC: Center on Education Policy.

Christens, B. D., & Dolan, T. (2010). Youth development, community development, and social change through youth organizing. *Youth and Society,* 1–21. doi:10.1177/0044118X10383647.

Cohen, C. (2006). *African American youth: Broadening our understanding of politics, civic engagement, and activism.* New York: Social Sciences Research Council.

Crystal, D. S., & DeBell, M. (2002). Sources of civic orientation among American youth: Trust, religious valuation, and attributions of responsibility. *Political Psychology, 23,* 113–132.

Cunha, F., & Heckman, J. J. (2009). The economics and psychology of human inequality and development. *Journal of the European Economic Association, 7,* 320–364.

Damon, W. (2008). *The path to purpose.* New York: The Free Press.

Dawes, N. P., & Larson, R. W. (2011). How youth get engaged: Grounded-theory research on motivational development in organized youth programs. *Developmental Psychology, 47,* 259–269.

de Tocqueville, A. (2002). *Democracy in America.* Washington, DC: Regnery Publishing.

Deci, E. L., & Ryan, R. M. (2000). The "what" and "why" of goal pursuits: Human needs and the self-determination of behavior. *Psychological Inquiry, 11,* 227–268.

Dejaeghere, Y., & Hooghe, M. (2009). Citizenship concepts among adolescents: Evidence from a survey among Belgian 16-year olds. *Journal of Adolescence, 32,* 723–732.

Eccles, J. S., Midgley, C., & Wigfield, A. (1993). Development during adolescence: The impact of stage-environment fit on young adolescents' experiences in schools and in families. *The American Psychologist, 48,* 90–101.

Eccles, J. S., Midgley, C., Wigfield, A., Buchanan, C. M., Reuman, D., Flanagan, C., et al. (1993). Development during adolescence: The impact of stage-environment fit on adolescents' experiences in schools and families. *The American Psychologist, 48,* 90–101.

Erikson, E. H. (1963). *Childhood and society.* New York: WW. Norton & Co.

Eyler, J., & Giles, D. E. (1999). *Where's the learning in service learning?* New York: Jossey-Bass.

Fendrich, J. M., & Lovoy, K. L. (1988). Back to the future: Adult political behavior of former student activists. *American Sociological Review, 53,* 780–784.

Flanagan, C. (2003). Trust, identity, and civic hope. *Applied Developmental Science, 7,* 165–171.

Flanagan, C. A. (2004). Volunteerism, leadership, political socialization, and civic engagement. In R. M. Lerner & L. Steinberg (Eds.), *Handbook of adolescent psychology* (pp. 721–746). Hoboken, NJ: Wiley.

Flanagan, C. (2008). Civil Societies as developmental contexts for civic identity formation. In L. Arnett Jensen (Ed.), *Bridging cultural and developmental psychology: New syntheses in theory, research and policy*. New York: Oxford University Press.

Flanagan, C. A., Bowes, J. M., Jonsson, B., Csapo, B., & Sheblanova, E. (1998). Ties that bind: Correlates of adolescents' civic commitments in seven countries. *Journal of Social Issues, 54*, 457–475.

Flanagan, C. F., Gallay, L. S., Gill, S., Gallay, E., & Nti, N. (2005). What does democracy mean? Correlates of adolescents' views. *Journal of Adolescent Research, 20*, 193–218.

Flanagan, C. A., Gill, S., & Gallay, L. S. (2005). Social participation and social trust in adolescence: The importance of heterogeneous encounters. In A. Omoto (Ed.), *Processes of community change and social action*. (pp. 149–166). Erlbaum, New York, NY.

Flanagan, C., Levine, P., & Settersten, R. (2009). *Civic engagement and the changing transition to adulthood*. Medford, MA: Center for Information and Research on Civic Learning and Engagement.

Ford, D. L., & Lerner, R. M. (1992). *Developmental systems theory: An integrative approach*. Newbury Park, CA: Sage.

Foreman, M., & Neal, M. A. (Eds.), (2004). *That's the joint! The hop-hop studies reader*. New York: Routledge.

Foster-Fishman, P. G., Fitzgerald, K., Brandell, C., Nowell, B., Chavis, D., & Van Egeren, L. A. (2006). Mobilizing residents for action: The role of small wins and strategic supports. *American Journal of Community Psychology, 38*, 143–152.

Fredericks, J. A., Blumenfeld, P. C., & Paris, A. H. (2004). School engagement: Potential of the concept, state of the evidence. *Review of Educational Research, 74*, 59–109.

Freire, P. (1970). *Pedagogy of the oppressed*. New York: Herder and Herder.

Freund, A. M., & Baltes, P. B. (2002). Life-management strategies of selection, optimization and compensation: Measurement by self-report and construct validity. *Journal of Personality and Social Psychology, 82*, 642–662.

Ganz, M. (2002). What is organizing? *Social Policy, 33*, 16–17.

Ganz, M. (2010). Leading change: Leadership, organization, and social movements. In N. Nohria & R. Kharuna (Eds.), *Handbook of leadership theory and practice*. (pp. 527–568). Boston: Harvard Business School Press.

Ganz, M., & Lin, E. S. (in press). Learning to lead: A pedagogy of practice. In N. Nohria, R. Kharuna, & Snook, S. (Eds.), *The SAGE handbook for teaching leadership*. London: SAGE Publications.

Gauthier, A. H., & Furstenberg, F. Jr., (2005). Historical trends in patterns of time use among youth in developed countries. In R. A. Settersten, F. F. Furstenberg & R. G. Rumaut (Eds.), *On the frontier of adulthood*. (pp. 150–176). Chicago, IL: University of Chicago Press.

Geldhof, G. J., Little, T. D., & Colombo, J. (2010). Self-regulation across the life span. In A. M. Freund & M. E. Lamb (Eds.), *Social and emotional development across the life span: Vol. 2, Handbook of life-span development*. (pp. 116–157). Hoboken, NJ: John Wiley & Sons.

Gibson, C., & Levine, P. (2003). *The civic mission of schools*. Report for Carnegie CorporationNew York: Carnegie Corporation.

Ginwright, S., & Cammarota, J. (2007). Youth activism in the urban community: Learning critical civic praxis within community organizations. *International Journal of Qualitative Studies in Education, 20*, 693–710.

Han, H., & Hudgens, J. (2010). *A report assessing the September 2009 youth organizing trainings in Colorado and Florida*. Washington, DC: The Center for Community Change.

Harris, F. C. (1994). Something within: Religion as a mobilizer of African-American political activism. *Journal of Politics, 56,* 42–68.

Hart, D., & Atkins, R. (2002). Civic competence in urban youth. *Applied Developmental Science, 6,* 227–236.

Hart, D., & Atkins, R. (2003). Neighborhoods, adults and the development of civic identity in urban youth. *Applied Developmental Science, 7,* 156–164.

Hart, D., & Atkins, R. (2010). American sixteen- and seventeen-year-olds are ready to vote. *The Annals of the American Academy of Political and Social Science, 633,* 201–222.

Hart, D., Atkins, R., & Youniss, J. (2005). Knowledge, youth bulges, and rebellion. *Psychological Science, 16,* 661–662.

Hart, D., Donnelly, T. M., Youniss, J., & Atkins, R. (2007). High school community service as a predictor of adult voting and volunteering. *American Educational Research Journal, 44,* 197–219.

Hart, D., & Kirshner, B. (2009). Promoting civic participation and development among urban adolescents. In J. Youniss & P. Levine (Eds.), *Engaging young people in civic life.* Nashville, TN: Vanderbilt University Press.

Hughes, D., & Chen, L. (1997). When and what parents tell children about race: An examination of race-related socialization among African American families. *Applied Developmental Science, 1,* 200–214.

Hughes, D., Rodriguez, J., Smith, E. P., Johnson, D. J., Stevenson, H. C., & Spicer, P. (2006). Parents' ethnic-racial socialization practices: A review of research and directions for future study. *Developmental Psychology, 42*(5), 747–770.

Janoski, T., & Wilson, J. (1995). Pathways to volunteerism: Family socialization and status transmission models. *Social Forces, 74,* 271–292.

Jennings, M. K., & Stoker, L. (2002). *Generational change, life cycle processes, and social capital.* Paper prepared for a workshop on Citizenship on Trial: Interdisciplinary Perspectives on the Political Socialization of Adolescents. McGill University, Montreal, Canada.

Jennings, M. K., & Stoker, L. (2004). Social trust and civic engagement across time and generations. *Acta Politica, 39,* 342–379.

Johnson, L. R., Johnson-Pynn, J. S., & Pynn, T. M. (2007). Youth civic engagement in China: Results from a program promoting environmental activism. *Journal of Adolescent Research, 22,* 355–386.

Jones, D. M., & Smith, M. L. R. (2007). Constructing communities: The curious case of East Asian regionalism. *Review of International Studies, 33,* 165–186.

Junn, J. (2004). Diversity, immigration and the politics of civic education,. *PS: Political Science and Politics, 37,* 253–255.

Kahne, J., & Middaugh, E. (2008). *Democracy for some: The civic opportunity gap in high school.* CIRCLE Working Paper No. 59. Retrieved February 1, 2011, at www. civicyouth.org.

Kelly, D. C. (2009). In preparation for adulthood: Exploring civic participation and social trust among young minorities. *Youth and Society, 40,* 526–540.

Kirshner, B. (2007). Supporting youth participation in school reform: Preliminary notes from a university-community partnership. *Children, Youth and Environments: Pushing the Boundaries: Critical International Perspectives on Child and Youth Participation, 17*(2), 354–363.

Kirshner, B. (2008). Guided participation in three youth activism organizations: Facilitation, apprenticeship, and joint work. *The Journal of the Learning Sciences, 17*(1), 60–101.

Kirshner, B. (2009). "Power in numbers": Youth organizing as a context for exploring civic identity. *Journal of Research on Adolescence, 19,* 414–440.

Kuhn, T. S. (1962). *The structure of scientific revolutions.* Chicago: University of Chicago Press.

Larson, R. W. (2000). Towards a psychology of positive youth development. *The American Psychologist, 55*, 170–183.

Larson, R. W. (2010). *Positive development in a disorderly world. Journal of Research on Adolescence, 21*, 317–334.

Larson, R., & Hansen, D. (2005). The development of strategic thinking: Learning to impact human systems in a youth activism program. *Human Development, 48*, 327–349.

Larson, R., Hansen, D., & Walker, K. (2005). Everybody's gotta give: Adolescents' development of initiative and teamwork within a youth program. In J. Mahoney, R. Larson & J. Eccles (Eds.), *Organized activities as contexts of development: Extracurricular activities, after-school and community programs.* (pp. 159–183). Hillsdale, NJ: Lawrence Erlbaum Associates.

Lee, R., Purcell, K., & Smith, A. (2011). *The social side of the Internet.* Pew Internet & American Life Project. Retrieved February 20, 2011 at http://www.pewinternet.org/Reports/2011/The-Social-Side-of-the-Internet.aspx.

Lerner, R. M. (2004). *Liberty: Thriving and civic engagement among America's youth.* Thousand Oaks, CA: Sage Publications.

Lerner, R. M., Alberts, A. E., & Bobek, D. (2007). Thriving youth, flourishing civil society— How positive youth development strengthens democracy and social justice. In Bertelsmann Stiftung (Ed.), *Civic engagement as an educational goal.* (pp. 21–35). Gutersloh, Germany: Verlag Bertelsmann Stiftung.

Levinson, M. (2007). *The civic achievement gap.* (CIRCLE Working Paper #51). Medford, MA: Center for Information and Research on Civic Learning and Engagement. Retrieved February 1, 2011, from www.civicyouth.org.

Levinson, M. (2009). Taking action: What we can do to address the civic achievement gap. *Social Studies Review, 48*, 33–36.

Lutkus, A., & Weiss, A. (2007). *The nation's report card: civics 2006.* (NCES 2007–476) Washington, DC: U.S. Government Printing Office, U.S. Department of Education, National Center for Education Statistics.

Malone, T., & Lepper, M. (1987). Making learning fun: A taxonomy of intrinsic motivations of learning. In R. E. Snow & M. J. Farr (Eds.), *Aptitude, learning, and instruction: Vol. 3. Conative and affective process analyses.* (pp. 223–253). Hillsdale, NJ: Lawrence Erlbaum.

Maslow, A. H. (1954). *Motivation and personality.* New York: Harper & Row.

McAdam, D. (1988). *Freedom summer.* New York: Oxford University Press.

McAdam, D. (1989). The biographical consequences of activism. *American Sociological Review, 54*, 744–760.

McBride, A. M., Sherraden, M. S., & Pritzker, S. (2006). Civic Engagement among low-income and low-wealth families: In their words. *Family Relations, 55*, 151–162.

McFarland, D. A., & Starrmans, C. (2007). Student government and political socialization. *Teachers College., 111*, 27–54.

Metz, E., & Youniss, J. (2005). Longitudinal gains in civic development through school-based required service. *Political Psychology, 26*, 413–437.

Mischel, W., Shoda, Y., & Peake, P. (1988). The nature of adolescent competencies predicted by preschool delay of gratification. *Journal of Personality and Social Psychology, 54*, 687–696.

Nasir, N., & Kirshner, B. (2003). The cultural construction of moral and civic identities. *Applied Developmental Science, 7*, 138–147.

National Conference on Citizenship. (2008). *2008 Civic health index.* Washington, DC: National Conference on Citizenship. Retrieved February 11, 2011, via www.ncoc.net.

Niemi, R. G., & Chapman, C. (1998). *The civic development of 9th- through 12th-grade students in the United States: 1996.* Washington, DC: U.S. Department of Education, National Center for Education Statistics.

Obradovic, J., & Masten, A. (2007). Developmental antecedents of young adult civic engagement. *Applied Developmental Science, 11,* 2–19.

O'Donoghue, J. L., & Kirshner, B. R. (2003). Urban youth's civic development in community-based organizations. In: *International conference on civic education.*

Pacheco, J. S., & Plutzer, E. (2007). Stay in school, don't become a parent: Teen life transitions and cumulative disadvantages for voter turnout. *American Politics Research, 35,* 32–56.

Park, J. Z., & Smith, C. (2000). "To whom much has been given...": Religious capital and community volunteerism among churchgoing protestants. *Journal for the Scientific Study of Religion, 39,* 272–286.

Pearce, N. J., & Larson, R. W. (2006). How teens become engaged in youth development programs: The process of motivational change in a civic activism organization. *Applied Developmental Science, 10,* 121–131.

Perold, H., Stroud, S., & Sherraden, M. (Eds.), (2003). *Service enquiry: Service in the 21st century.* Johannesburg: Global Service Institute and Volunteer and Service Enquiry South Africa.

Putnam, 2000.Roberts, R., Bell, L. A., & Murphy, B. (2000). Flipping the script: Analyzing youth talk about race and racism. *Anthropology & Education Quarterly, 39,* 334–354.

Roberts, R. A., Bell, L. A., & Murphy, B. (2008). Flipping the script: Analyzing youth talk about race and racism. *Anthropology & Education Quarterly, 39,* 334–354.

Rojas, H., & Puig-i-Abril, E. (2009). Mobilizers mobilized: Information, expression, mobilization and participation in the digital age. *Journal of Computer Mediated Communication, 14,* 902–927.

Rubin, B. (2007). "There's still not justice": Youth civic identity development amid distinct school and community contexts. *Teachers College record, 109,* 449–481.

Rubin, B. C., & Hayes, B. (2010). "No backpacks" vs. "Drugs and murder": The promise and complexity of youth civic action research. *Harvard Educational Review, 80,* 149–175.

Rubin, B., Hayes, B., & Benson, K. (2009). "It's the worst place to live": Urban youth and the challenge of school- based civic learning. *Theory into Practice, 48,* 213–222.

Ryan, R. M., Stiller, J., & Lynch, J. H. (1994). Representations of relationships to teachers, parents, and friends as predictors of academic motivation and self-esteem. *Journal of Early Adolescence, 14,* 226–249.

Safrit, D. R., & Lopez, J. (2001). Exploring Hispanic American involvement in community leadership through volunteerism. *Journal of Leadership Studies, 7,* 3–19.

Sears, D. O., & Funk, C. L. (1999). Evidence of the long-term persistence of adults' political predispositions. *Journal of Politics, 61,* 1–28.

Shah, S., & Mediratta, K. (2008). Negotiating reform: Young people's leadership in the educational arena. *New Directions for Youth Development, 117,* 43–59.

Sherrod, L. (2007). Civic engagement as an expression of positive youth development. In R. Silbereisen & R. Lerner (Eds.), *Approaches to positive youth development.* London: Sage.

Shoda, Y., Mischel, W., & Peake, P. (1990). Predicting adolescent cognitive and self-regulatory competencies from preschool delay of gratification: Identifying diagnostic conditions. *Developmental Psychology, 26,* 978–986.

Shukrallah, S. (2011). *Egypt revolution youth form national coalition.* Ahram Online. Retrieved from http://english.ahram.org.eg/~/NewsContent/1/64/5257/Egypt/Politics-/Coalition-of-The-Revolutions-Youth-assembled.aspx.

Smetana, J., & Metzger, A. (2005). Family and religious antecedents of civic involvement in middle class African American late adolescents. *Journal of Research on Adolescence, 15,* 325–352.

Smith, E. S. (1999). The effects of investments in the social capital of youth on political and civic behavior in young adulthood: A longitudinal analysis. *Political Psychology, 20,* 553–580.

Solomon, E. R., & Steinitz, V. (1979). Toward an adequate explanation of the politics of working-class youth. *Political Psychology, 1,* 39–60.

Stepick, A., Stepick, C. D., & Labisierre, Y. (2008). South Florida's immigrant youth and civic engagement: Major engagement, minor differences. *Applied Developmental Science, 12,* 57–65.

Swartz, T., Blackstone, A., Uggen, C., & McLaughlin, H. (2009). Welfare and citizenship: The effects of government assistance on young adult's civic participation. *The Sociological Quarterly, 50,* 633–665.

Syvertsen, A. K., Wray-Lake, L., Flanagan, C. A., Osgood, D. W., & Briddell, L. (2011). *Thirty year trends in American adolescents' civic engagement: A story of changing participation and educational differences. Journal of Research on Adolescence,* 1–9. doi: 10.1111/j.1532-7795.2010.00706.x.

Theiss-Morse, E., & Hibbing, J. R. (2004). Citizenship and civic engagement. *Annual Review of Political Science, 8,* 227–249.

Thornton, M. C., Chatters, L. M., Taylor, R. J., & Allen, W. R. (1990). Sociodemographic and environmental correlates of racial socialization by Black parents. *Child Development, 61,* 401–409.

Torney-Purta, J., & Amadeo, J. (2003). A cross-national analysis of political and civic involvement among adolescents. *PS: Political Science and Politics, 36,* 269–274.

Torney-Purta, J., & Amadeo, J. (2011). Participatory niches for emergent citizenship in early adolescence. *The Annals of the American Academy of Political and Social Science, 633,* 180–200.

Townley, G., Kloos, B., Green, E. P., & Franco, M. M. (2011). Reconcilable differences? Human diversity, cultural relativity, and sense of community. *American Journal of Community Psychology, 47,* 69–85.

Verba, S., Burns, N., & Schlozman, K. (2003). Unequal at the starting line: Participatory inequalities across generations and among groups. *The American Sociologist, 34,* 45–69.

Verba, S., Schlozman, K. L., & Brady, H. E. (1995). *Voice and equality: Civic voluntarism in American politics.* Cambridge, MA: Harvard University Press.

Vygotsky, L. S. (1978). *Mind and society: The development of higher psychological processes.* Cambridge, MA: Harvard University Press.

Warren, M. R., Mira, M., & Nikundiwe, T. (2008). Youth organizing: From youth development to school reform. *New Directions for Youth Development, 117,* 27–42.

Watts, R., & Flanagan, C. (2007). Pushing the envelope on youth civic engagement: A developmental and liberation psychology perspective. *Journal of Community Psychology, 35,* 1–14.

Westheimer, J., & Kahne, J. (2003). What kind of citizen? Political choices and educational goals. *Campus Compact Reader, Winter 2003,* 1–13.

Wigfield, A., & Eccles, J. S. (2000). Expectancy: Value theory of motivation. *Contemporary Educational Psychology, 25,* 68–81.

World Bank & Innovations in Civic Participation, (2008). *Measuring the impact of youth voluntary service programs: Summary and conclusion of the international experts' meeting.* Washington, DC: Author.

Xu, Q., Perkins, D., & Chow, J. (2010). Sense of community, neighboring, and social capital as predictors of local political participation in China. *American Journal of Community Psychology, 45,* 259–271.

Yates, M., & Youniss, J. (1998). Community service and political identity development in adolescence. *Journal of Social Issues, 54,* 495–512.

Youniss, J. (2008). Reshaping a developmental theory for political-civic development. In P. Levine & J. Youniss (Eds.), *Youth civic engagement: An institutional turn.* Medford, MA: Circle.

Youniss, J. (2009). Why we need to learn more about youth civic engagement. *Social Forces, 88*, 971–975.

Youniss, J., McLellan, J. A., & Yates, M. (1997). What we know about engendering civic identity. *The American Behavioral Scientist, 40*, 620–631.

Youniss, J., & Yates, M. (1997). *Community service and social responsibility in youth.* Chicago: University of Chicago Press.

Youniss, J., & Yates, M. (1999). Youth service and moral-civic identity: A case for everyday morality. *Educational Psychology Review, 11*, 363–378.

Youniss, J., Yates, M., & Su, Y. (1997). Social integration: Community service and marijuana use in high school seniors. *Journal of Adolescent Research, 12*, 245–262.

Zaff, J. F., Boyd, M., Li, Y., Lerner, J. V., & Lerner, R. M. (2010). *Active and engaged citizenship: Multi-group and longitudinal factorial analysis of an integrated construct of civic engagement. Journal of Youth & Adolescence, 39*, 736–750.

Zaff, J. F., Hart, D., Flanagan, C. A., Youniss, J., & Levine, P. (2010). Developing civic engagement within a civic context. In A. M. Freund & M. E. Lamb (Eds.), *The handbook of life-span development, Vol. 2.* Hoboken, NJ: Wiley.

Zaff, J. F., Li, Y., & Lin, E. S. (2011). *The engaged youth: A dual trajectory analysis of civic engagement and school engagement.* Working PaperMedford, MA: Institute for Applied Research in Youth Development.

Zaff, J. F., Malanchuk, O., & Eccles, J. S. (2008). Predicting positive citizenship from adolescence to young adulthood: The effects of a civic context. *Applied Development Science, 12*, 38–53.

Zaff, J. F., & Michelsen, E. (2001). *Background for community-level work on positive citizenship among adolescents: A review of antecedents, programs, and investment strategies.* Report prepared for the John S. and James L. Knight Foundation. Washington, DC: Child Trends.

Zaff, J. F., Youniss, J., & Gibson, C. M. (2009). *An inequitable invitation to citizenship: Non-college-bound youth and civic engagement.* Denver, CO: Philanthropy for Active Civic Engagement.

Zaff, J. F., Kawashima-Ginsberg, K., Lin, E. S., Lamb, M. E., & Balsano, A. (in press). Developmental trajectories of civic engagement across adolescence: Disaggregation of an integrated construct. *Journal of Adolescence.*

Zeldin, S., Larson, R., Camino, L., & O'Connor, C. (2005). Intergenerational relationships and partnerships in community programs: Purpose, practice, and directions for research. *Journal of Community Psychology, 33*(1), 1–10.

SHORTRIDGE ACADEMY: POSITIVE YOUTH DEVELOPMENT IN ACTION WITHIN A THERAPEUTIC COMMUNITY

Kristine M. Baber[*,1] *and Adam Rainer*[†,2]

* UNIVERSITY OF NEW HAMPSHIRE, EMERITUS, NEW HAMPSHIRE, USA
† SHORTRIDGE ACADEMY, MILTON, NEW HAMPSHIRE, USA

Abstract

This chapter presents a case example of the implementation of Positive Youth Development (PYD) at a therapeutic boarding school including the theoretical, conceptual, and empirical information about PYD,

[1] Present address: Kristine Baber is now at KMB Research & Consulting, Dover, New Hampshire, USA
[2] Adam Rainer is Founder and President of Shortridge Academy

309

adolescent brain development, authoritative communities, and youth-adult partnerships that guided this work. Specific examples demonstrate how key concepts and underlying principles of PYD were put into practice. The chapter provides information about parents' perceptions of the school's effectiveness and explains a theory of change approach used to develop the program evaluation. The chapter concludes with a discussion of challenges and opportunities experienced in the development and implementation of the program.

Positive Youth Development (PYD) provides an optimistic and proactive approach to working with adolescents and their families. Increased interest and understanding of the possibilities of such a perspective over the past decade resulted in a growing appreciation for this alternative to deficit-based approaches and an expansion of research on the topic. Efforts now have turned to the task of evaluating the effectiveness of PYD-influenced programs and practices. This work is complicated by the fact that programs that employ or endorse PYD frequently operate within larger systems in the community that prioritize problem reduction and control, rather than engagement, of adolescents. The PYD effects of afterschool programs that serve students a few hours each day, for example, might be attenuated by longer hours spent in schools, families, and other contexts that are authoritarian or see adolescents as problems to be managed or contained.

This chapter presents a case example of the implementation of a PYD framework at a therapeutic boarding school, Shortridge Academy (Shortridge). Although it has been proposed that conjoint efforts among parents, teachers, counselors, and other caring adults would be most beneficial in promoting aspects of positive development, such efforts have been exceedingly rare (Kirschman, Johnson, Bender, & Roberts, 2009). Shortridge is private and residential and includes both clinical and academic services, thereby providing a setting where a PYD approach can pervade the environment of the students' day-to-day lives. Education and support for parents, both integral parts of the school's agenda, increase the likelihood of greater consistency in students' interactions at school and with families.

The implementation of PYD at Shortridge is very much in process even though initial efforts began over 3 years ago. Shortridge is an existing school making the transition to a new theoretical approach to the way it functions. The transformation has required a complete review of all aspects of the school, an explicit commitment to adopting such an approach, the development of a logic model, the training of staff, the orientation of parents, decisions about how to include and engage students in the process, and the creation of an evaluation plan. Some of this work is completed, but much is ongoing. It is important to keep in mind, also, that at the same time that this innovation is being undertaken, the school must continue to function as a therapeutic environment attending to the day-to-day demands of educating and supporting developing youth and their families.

Zeldin and Petrokubi (2006) proposed that there are at least three stages that organizations go through in implementing innovative programs. These three stages—start-up, growth, and sustainability—each have their own characteristics and challenges. In the start-up phase, there is a cost/benefit analysis regarding undertaking such an implementation and a focus on generating ideas for putting the theory into practice. The growth stage involves balancing existing practices with new approaches. Managers simultaneously are determining how to restructure existing programming to accommodate new or revised practices and actually running the program. This stage also includes the development of accountability systems. The third stage, sustainability, assumes a mature and productive program where challenges include making the new approach standard practice while continuing to review and refine the program to address current issues and evolving knowledge. Using Zeldin and Petrokubi's stage model, we would see the implementation process at Shortridge to be in the growth stage.

The chapter begins with an introduction to the school and presents the theoretical, conceptual, and empirical information about PYD, adolescent brain development, and authoritative communities that guided the implementation of the approach used at Shortridge. We then discuss how we used a PYD perspective to review, refine, and integrate the work of the school. Using specific examples, we demonstrate how some of the key concepts and underlying principles of PYD are put into practice. We also explain how we are using a theory of change approach to develop a systematic program evaluation of Shortridge and include some preliminary information about parents' perceptions of the school's effectiveness. The chapter concludes with a discussion of some of the challenges and opportunities experienced in the development and implementation of the program that should be useful to others contemplating the implementation of such a comprehensive PYD program.

I. The School

Shortridge is an accredited, coeducational, therapeutic boarding school serving bright, creative, yet struggling teenagers in grades 9–12. The first student enrolled at Shortridge in November 2002. In 2003, its first full year, Shortridge enrolled 20 students. Currently, between 50 and 65 students attend each year, entering on a rolling basis and remaining at the school for 14–16 months. The school is situated on 350 acres in a rural New England setting and offers playing fields, miles of trails, and a basketball court. The campus includes a main building with classrooms, a music room, workout facilities, a yoga/dance room, common rooms, office space, a kitchen, and a dining room. Students live in single-sex dormitories that have adjoining faculty apartments. Several of the dorms have activity spaces used for the recording studio, a bike shop, and meetings. There are also two faculty homes on campus and an on-site Health Center.

Students attend classes, academic activities, or groups from 9 a.m. to 5 p.m. on weekdays. Each student participates in at least 1 hour of individual counseling and three group sessions each week. Depending on the topic, group sessions are facilitated by master's level clinicians, teachers, and/or residential staff and are either thematic or focus on peer interactions and issues. One group each week is devoted to health and wellness. There also are groups specifically designed for girls and for students who experienced adoption. All students participate in PRIME for Life (Daugherty & O'Bryan, 2004), an alcohol and drug risk reduction and prevention program. Those with substance abuse issues receive additional therapeutic interventions. Students also participate in several, day-long workshops during their stay at Shortridge to process why they are at the school and their plans for the future. The workshops are experiential, therapeutic, and educational, and students report they value them most because they encourage bonding among peers and with staff members. Students remain on campus for the duration of their stay at Shortridge except for planned off campus, family visits that begin after the first month, home visits that occur after about 5 months, and organized trips with school staff members. A three-phase system is used to acknowledge progress through the program. Students apply to "move up" from Phase I to Phase II and then to Phase III through written documentation and interviews that include reflection on their growth and achievements. They secure letters of support from staff and peers. Counselor, teacher, and parent assessments also are included in the decision that a student is ready to "move up."

A. SHORTRIDGE ACADEMY STAFF

The management team at the school consists of an executive director, a clinical director, an academic director, a residential program director, and an admissions director. The executive director joined Shortridge in 2010 bringing many years of experience directing and managing therapeutic schools and programs. The executive director replaced the second author (Rainer) freeing him to focus on long-term planning, strategizing for the future, and serving as research liaison. The clinical director is a board-certified clinical specialist in child and adolescent psychiatric mental health nursing. She supervises six full-time counselors, provides individual and family therapy, directs the Health Center, and does medication management. The clinical director is assisted by a part-time licensed, clinical social worker who supervises MSWs on staff, does assessments, and provides individual and family therapy for students who need more intensive services.

The academic director supervises nine teachers, a guidance counselor, and an academic day manager who supports the day-to-day aspects of the academic program. The residential program director supervises full- and part-time residential staff whose primary responsibilities are to manage the milieu evenings and weekends, including activities and behavior management. In addition to handling admissions, the admissions director has special training in adoption work. She also is certified as a licensed clinical mental health counselor.

Transition and Alumni Services at Shortridge provide transition support and coaching to all students and families as they prepare to leave the school. Also offered and recommended through this department is an optional postgraduate transitional support service to complement any home-based counseling services or supports. Approximately 2 months before their scheduled graduation, students begin attending transition groups, have focused time to discuss their transition plans, and do more in-depth work with their families. The home transition contract facilitated by transition and alumni services allows parents and their child opportunities to collaboratively set boundaries, negotiate, power share, and partner in important decisions about their future.

B. SHORTRIDGE STUDENTS

A typical Shortridge student is bright, creative, and has a recent history of making what some parents and adults view as risky or unhealthy decisions. Students come to Shortridge as the result of poor decision making, risky behaviors, academic difficulties, or problems in parent–child relationships. These circumstances often result from loss, trauma, or other unfortunate life events coupled with psychosocial issues. Many of the students, upon enrollment, are experiencing mood disorders, ADD/ADHD, substance use/abuse, mild learning differences, adoption/identity issues, oppositional or behavioral problems, lack of motivation, and/or low self-esteem. For example, it can be expected that at any point in time, over half of the students will be diagnosed with a mood disorder, over one-third with ADHD, and about half with substance abuse or dependence. Most of the students carry more than one diagnosis.

A typical student might be adopted and living with parents who are very permissive. She may be dealing with identity issues, using alcohol and other drugs, and struggling in school. Her parents probably have attempted to set boundaries but have been ineffectual in enforcing them resulting in their feeling that their daughter is "out of control." Another student might be one who comes to Shortridge after his mother's death. He is dealing with grief, is depressed, has stopped attending school on a regular basis, is disengaged from family and friends, and spends most of his time alone in his room on his computer. His father is concerned about his son but is still dealing with his own grief and does not know how to help his child.

Despite their psychosocial and family challenges and normative developmental issues, the students at Shortridge are young people with various personal strengths and abilities. Most of the students are intelligent, personable, and enjoyable to be around. They are often socially adept, know how to be respectful, and have a good sense of humor.

1. Decision to Attend Shortridge

Most students do not enter Shortridge totally voluntarily, but do so because their parents decided that their child needs a different environment and additional assistance to get back on track. Parents generally work with an educational consultant to identify therapeutic settings appropriate for their son or daughter. The majority of the students attend Shortridge after completing a wilderness program. Wilderness programs usually last between 3 and 10 weeks and vary in structure and focus, but most have therapeutic and assessment components. Some programs emphasize backpacking and hiking, spending most of the time out in the field. Others have campus buildings for dorms, classes, and meals creating an experience that combines outdoor-based trips with traditional academic coursework. Through different therapeutic and clinical strategies, wilderness programs identify issues that both the child and the family need to address. New skills are introduced to move the family forward in a more productive manner, and a plan for the future, such as residence at Shortridge, is developed to support continued growth for the adolescent and the family.

2. Students from Affluent Families

The students at Shortridge are mostly from more affluent families—those who are able, in one way or another, to afford the tuition at a residential, therapeutic school. Students such as these rarely are the focus of research or programming. Most programs and most research with a PYD focus have targeted what are traditionally identified as "at risk" or disadvantaged students, youth from middle-income groups, or youth participating in out-of-school-time groups such as 4-H clubs. Although PYD is theorized to better prepare all young people for a healthy, productive adulthood, there has been little consideration given to the potential benefits of such an approach for students from relatively affluent families. Laub, Doherty, and Sampson (2007) argue that there is much to be learned about what youth need to stay connected and engaged from both concentrated poverty and concentrated affluence.

The very small body of research on affluent youth, most of it by Luthar and her colleagues (Luthar & Becker, 2002), found surprisingly high levels of internalizing distress and substance abuse among this group. Substance use (more frequent use of cigarettes, alcohol, marijuana, and other illicit drugs) was reported at higher rates by affluent students than by their inner-city counterparts (Luther & Latendresse, 2002) apparently as a means of self-medicating for anxiety and depression. The researchers attributed their findings to affluent parents' overemphasis on achievements and visible accomplishments complicated by the isolation of adolescents from parents who often are distracted by their own busy lives and demanding careers. Some research has suggested, for example, that 10–12-year-olds in affluent families are more likely to be unsupervised than are their peers from families with fewer resources.

Based on the minimal research available on more affluent youth and the basic assumptions of PYD, we expect that the Shortridge experience will be effective in facilitating the development of the students involved. Clearly, their family resources and some of their issues are different than those of adolescents who have been the usual participants in PYD research and programming. However, we believe that the research that is part of this PYD implementation will provide a greater understanding about youth from affluent families and broaden supporting evidence for the effectiveness of this theoretical perspective.

C. SHORTRIDGE PARENTS

The family's commitment to the Shortridge experience is a critical ingredient in their child's positive growth. At enrollment, Shortridge parents tend to possess several common characteristics: a deep concern and care for their child's well-being, a sadness or guilt about their own parenting decisions and behaviors, a dwindling sense of hope for their future, and an uncomfortable realization that outside help is needed. Even in light of these emotions, however, most parents remain resolute in their commitment and caring for their child. Many parents feel that Shortridge is the last chance "to get their son or daughter back," and most become partners in that process. They are willing to make considerable investment of money, time, availability, self-reflection, and affection.

Typically well educated and successful professionally, Shortridge parents often connect the need for help for their child and family with a sense of personal failure. This dynamic can be difficult to reconcile when they, like their children, may have experienced their own sense of loss and struggle through divorce, the death of a loved one, or substance abuse. In addition, many parents face a unique set of challenges related to their child's adoption.

Perhaps as the result of life circumstances or individual upbringing, Shortridge parents often use permissive or authoritarian parenting styles. Most Shortridge parents, however, desire and actively seek out information that will help them better support the positive development of their child. While at the school, they have an opportunity to learn about PYD, reflect on parenting styles, understand concepts of authoritative parenting, and practice new skills during phone calls and visits.

II. Positive Youth Development

PYD is a strengths-based approach to working with young people that has roots in positive psychology, developmental psychology, developmental epidemiology, and prevention sciences (Lerner, 2009; Roth & Brooks-Gunn, 2003; Silbereisen & Lerner, 2007). This perspective encourages adults to go beyond problem prevention and deterrence to support the development of skills and abilities that prepare all youth for healthy, happy, and productive adulthood. This approach focuses more on understanding, educating, supporting, and engaging youth rather than correcting or treating them (Commission on Positive Youth Development, 2005). PYD draws upon the notion of plasticity of developmental trajectories and the idea that if adolescent strengths can be aligned with environmental resources, optimal functioning can occur and young people will thrive. According to the Commission on PYD, a thriving youth is "a young person who experiences more positive affect than negative affect, is satisfied with his or her own life as it has been lived, who has identified what he or she does well and uses these talents and strengths in a variety of fulfilling pursuits; and is a contributing member of a social community" (p. 508).

Among the key concepts of PYD are the five "Cs" (*competence, confidence, caring, connection,* and *character*). Working definitions of these concepts capture many of the most positive characteristics of thriving young people and continue to be refined (Gavin, Catalano, & Markham, 2010; Hamilton, Hamilton, & Pittman, 2004; Lerner, 2007; Pittman, Irby, Tolman, Yohalem, & Ferber, 2003; Roth & Brooks-Gunn, 2003). Competence refers to the knowledge and skills that help a young person function effectively and accomplish identified goals. Competence includes emotional, social, behavioral, and vocational competence, as well as cognitive and academic achievement. Confidence is concerned with an overall sense of self-worth and self-efficacy; a clear and positive identity; and belief in, and hope for, the future. Caring involves a sense of sympathy, empathy, and compassion for others, as well as caring for oneself. A related concept, connection, focuses on positive bonds developed with parents and other caring adults, peers, and institutions such as schools and community. Character includes the development of an internal framework to guide behavior and includes respect for social and cultural rules and standards; an ability to assess what is just, right, and good and respond appropriately; and a sense of moral justice and integrity. It also includes increased self-control and a decrease in problematic and health-compromising behaviors.

Lerner et al. (2005) in their 4-H Study provided the initial evidence for the five "Cs" and the sixth "C" of contribution which draws upon the other "Cs" and encourages the young person to give to others including family, school, community, and society. Subsequent results from this longitudinal study have indicated positive relationships among these six concepts and inverse relationships between the "Cs" and risky behaviors (Lerner, 2009).

A. ENGAGEMENT OF YOUTH

One of the key tenets in a PYD approach is the inclusion and engagement of adolescents in planning, decision making, and implementation of activities, policies, and programs that affect them. Pittman et al. (2003) have provided the PYD mantra that "problem free is not fully prepared and that fully prepared is not fully engaged" (p. 9). They argued that development is triggered by engagement and stress the importance of "choice and voice" (p. 6) for youth. They urged that organizations commit to engaging youth in all aspects of decision making. Allowing adolescents to participate in these meaningful processes acknowledges that youth are active agents who can help shape their own development, not just recipients of services, and also can result in programs that are more responsive, attractive to adolescents, and effective (Hamilton et al., 2004). "Bringing youth to the table" (Huber, Frommeyer, Wisenbach, & Sazama, 2003, p. 297) can result in opportunities for mentoring, leadership, and the development of competence and confidence for the youth involved. It also can offer fresh perspectives and ideas, as well as students' connections with their peers that may be leveraged to encourage broader participation and investment.

There are a variety of ways to include youth as participants. Mitra (2006) suggests a three-level, hierarchical model that begins with listening to students—the most common and basic level. At this level, students' voices are heard through activities such as focus groups, surveys, and interviewing about their experiences and how structures and functions might be improved. Mitra claims that in order to encourage positive development, we need to go beyond just listening to young people to the next two levels—collaborating with youth to bring about change and building their capacity for leadership. This involves allowing them to influence the issues that matter to them and giving them opportunities to prepare for and assume leadership.

Even though intergenerational collaboration is emerging as an important strategy in youth development and a growing body of research suggests that these actions promote many positive outcomes, programs that take seriously youth–adult partnerships remain scarce in the United States (Zeldin & Petrokubi, 2006). Many professionals are trained to work *for* rather than *with* their adolescent clients. Welcoming youth as partners, which if done authentically involves some power sharing, is often difficult for adults. Finding the optimal balance between letting youth take leadership and providing adult guidance is challenging. Larson (2007) identifies an "intentionality paradox" noting that for adults to be intentional in supporting an adolescent's development, they have to support the youth's own intentionality. He notes that "youth are most empowered to engage in developmental change when adults strike an optimal balance between encouraging youth agency and providing structure and support that keep youth on track (p. 288)." Attaining this balance requires the adults involved to simultaneously be thinking about their responsibilities in maintaining a safe, supportive environment; considering the longer-term goals they are trying to promote by including youth; and facilitating the process through which the adolescents are meaningfully included. In addition, it is generally necessary to *scaffold* youth, structuring opportunities in such a way that they are challenged, but balancing this with just the needed amount of support.

Historically, adults at Shortridge made decisions regarding policies and procedures at the school. One of the most powerful shifts made during PYD implementation had to do with the degree of student inclusion. Power sharing, already an idea accepted to some extent at the school, became intentional and integral to the opportunities for student growth. Decisions about dress codes, program length of stay, home visits, music, computers, all very important topics to students, were shaped with their advice. Students' awareness of staff attempts to include them in decision making and to facilitate their contributions to the school community was confirmed when a student providing a tour of the campus for the parent of a prospective student was overheard to say, "If you have a good idea to improve Shortridge, the school will work with you to get it done."

B. THE IMPORTANCE OF ATMOSPHERE IN MAXIMIZING POSITIVE DEVELOPMENT

The atmosphere within which programs are implemented is an important contributor to success, and various authors have identified the components of a desirable environment for maximizing the positive development of young people (Eccles & Gootman, 2002; Gavin et al., 2010; Roth & Brooks-Gunn, 2003). These characteristics included a physically and psychologically safe, stable environment with strong linkages among family, school, and community that offer adolescents supportive relationships with adults, and opportunities to feel connected and valued as they develop a strong moral structure and build confidence. Ideally, activities will be carried out in an environment that not only includes and empowers young people but also communicates expectations for positive behavior. PYD programs provide an atmosphere of empowerment when they involve and engage youth in useful roles and important decisions, help them learn about and practice self-determination, and develop the skills they need to clarify their goals for the future.

In order to provide some definition of youth development programs, Roth and Brooks-Gunn (2003) reviewed effective programs serving youth and identified three features: program goal, atmosphere, and activities that distinguished youth development programs from other types of programs. Their findings indicated that the program goals and atmosphere, rather than specific activities, were the most important factors. They concluded that the programs that truly fostered youth development went beyond building specific competencies and aimed for broader developmental goals. These programs encouraged development by providing an empowering atmosphere that supported youth in participating in useful roles, practicing self-determination, and developing goals for the future.

Schools are particularly important environments for supporting positive development because most adolescents spend a substantial amount of time in these settings. Although most work focused on PYD and schools does not address therapeutic boarding schools, conceptual contributions such as those of Zeigler (2004) can be useful in implementing PYD approaches in settings such as Shortridge. Zeigler noted that students want to learn and be challenged and recommended that schools be dynamic and interactive, involving students in new ways in their own education. He explained that transforming schools requires changing the ways that the staff thinks about adolescents and being willing to share power with youth in determining what happens at the school. Administrators need to have vision to provide leadership in advocating for students, listening to them, and letting them into the process. Zeigler sees such a school—one that shares a vision of what youth can become; that holds high expectations; that is open to change, risk, and experimentation; and that can maintain optimism as the transformation proceeds—to be one that is likely to enhance learning and positively prepare young people for adulthood. With a unified and clear vision of how to build and maintain this type of atmosphere at Shortridge, the management team is actively transforming the school.

C. ADOLESCENT BRAIN DEVELOPMENT

The implementation of PYD at Shortridge Academy also integrated the quickly evolving body of research on adolescent brain development (Casey, Getz, & Galvan, 2008; Steinberg, 2008a, 2010a, 2010b; Steinberg et al., 2008; Weinberger, Elvevag, & Giedd, 2005). This research suggests that the "remodeling" process that is going on in the teen brain with the pruning of unused synapses and the myelination of neural circuits, the increased dopaminergic activity around puberty, and the increased connectivity between prefrontal and other brain regions contributes to the cognitive changes that occur during adolescence and influence behaviors. A critical finding is that the prefrontal cortex, the region of the brain responsible for controlling impulses, planning ahead, weighing costs and benefits, and improving emotional regulation, does not complete development until at least the mid-20s. Risky behavior, seemingly normative among adolescents, appears to be due to the heightened dopaminergic activity that encourages reward-seeking behaviors associated with the limbic and paralimbic areas of the brain that tend to outpace the development of the cognitive control centers of the brain including the prefrontal and parietal cortices (Steinberg, 2010b; Steinberg et al., 2008). Particularly in complicated and high arousal situations, if there is conflict between limbic and cognitive control functions, teens may participate in risky behaviors even when they have the information to "know" better.

The reward system of the brain is of considerable interest during adolescence because of its centrality to decision making, specifically the way that costs and benefits are assessed (Giedd, 2009). Changes in reward processing by the neural system may influence substance use, accidents, and risky sexual behavior, as well as increase affective disorders during adolescence (Holm et al., 2009). Holm and colleagues offer evidence that lowered reactivity in the reward systems of adolescents may contribute to increased risk taking because the pubertal adolescent may require higher levels of sensation and rewards to achieve the same level of neural activation as younger children. It is believed that the increase, reduction, and redistribution of dopamine receptors during puberty increase sensation seeking as a way to boost reactivity in the reward system (Steinberg et al., 2008). Steinberg and colleagues found different developmental trajectories in sensation seeking and impulsivity in young people aged 10–30 years. Sensation seeking, the tendency to seek out novel, varied, and highly stimulating experiences, and being willing to take risks to achieve them were found to follow an inverted U curve peaking between ages 12 and 15. Impulsivity, the lack of self-control and response inhibition that leads to reactive, unplanned behavior, showed a linear decline through adolescence and into young adulthood.

We know conclusively that the adolescent brain differs structurally and functionally from brains of children or adults (Steinberg, 2010a). It appears that adolescence is not only a period of increased plasticity in terms of brain development but also a time of greater vulnerability to psychopathology and risk taking. Based on the latest research in this area, it is believed, but not known for sure, that the context of an adolescent's life influences neural development, therefore offering opportunities for intervention. So important does Steinberg see the emerging neuroscientific perspective to be that he claims, "it has the potential to structure a new overarching model of normative and atypical adolescent development" (p. 162). If parents and professionals who work with adolescents have information about normative adolescent brain development, they should be better able to respond authoritatively when interacting with youth.

D. AUTHORITATIVE PARENTING AND COMMUNITIES

Few areas of research on adolescence are as consistent in their results as that regarding effective parenting (Steinberg, 2008b). The scheme of defining parenting types through combinations of parental responsiveness and demandingness (Baumrind, 1978; Maccoby & Martin, 1983) developed decades ago continues to be useful today in demonstrating the effectiveness of authoritative over authoritarian, indulgent, or permissive approaches to parenting. Authoritative parenting refers to warm but firm parenting that includes high, age-appropriate expectations and discipline techniques that rely primarily on discussion and explanation. This means dealing with teens in a rational, inclusive manner and providing flexible guidance with verbal give and take. Authoritative parents have realistic expectations about the abilities of their adolescents, and these expectations change over time as their children move toward adulthood. By providing a balance between restrictiveness and autonomy, authoritative parents monitor, rather than control, their teens and include them in making decisions about rules and consequences for infractions. Authoritative parents seek to support the development of self-reliance and self-monitoring without ceding their ultimate responsibility as parents.

Adolescents raised by authoritative parents display a variety of social, psychological, and academic benefits (Steinberg, 2008b). These positive outcomes include strong parent/teen attachments, increased competence and self-reliance, more developed behavioral and emotional autonomy, increased curiosity and creativity, higher social skills, and greater success in school. This approach to parenting also enhances reasoning skills, role taking, empathy, and moral judgment. All these outcomes are consistent with the definition of youth who are thriving.

It has been suggested that a community of authoritative parents might have a positive, cumulative effect if there are mutually agreed upon expectations and standards of behavior for adolescents that all parents support and enforce (Bradshaw & Garbarino, 2004). The approach used by authoritative parents also can be implemented in schools and communities. By engaging youth in age appropriate ways; encouraging them to accept challenges, but providing the support they need to be successful; being flexible, but setting clear boundaries; and offering positive adult role models, we can create environments where youth can thrive.

Even greater benefits might be realized through more formally designed "authoritative communities" where there is consensus about expectations and behaviors as well as how best to respond to situations where adolescents violate standards. The Shortridge community, which includes students and staff and extends beyond the campus to the families living around the country, offers a model for this effort. Combining knowledge about PYD and adolescent brain development with authoritative parenting skills should offer an optimal environment for youth to acquire the skills and abilities they need for adulthood.

III. A Comprehensive Implementation of PYD

The challenges presented by integrating theory and research from several substantive areas and bridging this integration into practice are significant. The process at Shortridge began by one of us (Baber) meeting individually with staff members and with a group of students to identify ways that the school could be strengthened. There was agreement that there needed to be a shared understanding of the therapeutic grounding of the school that could guide staff and also could be consistently and clearly articulated. There also was a desire for greater integration between the academic and counseling aspects of the school. These stated needs appeared to be in part a consequence of the school's guiding philosophy of emotional growth which was in place at that time. This perspective did not provide a common language for staff and lacked an explicit theory of change that could unite all components of the school to serve one mission.

Follow-up discussions between the two authors, the first a faculty member at a nearby university with expertise in normative adolescent development and PYD as well as skills in program design, implementation, and evaluation and the second the founder and director of the school, ensued. We concluded that Shortridge offered an extraordinary opportunity to implement PYD and related evidence-based practices in a way that would add value to the school and also would contribute to our understanding of the developmental consequences of using this approach in such a controlled environment. An enhanced understanding of PYD at Shortridge would build upon the school's existing foundation that promoted strength development rather than a focus on problem reduction. Although the paradigm shift that would be required would take considerable time, resources, and the open-mindedness of the leadership team, staff, and faculty, PYD would provide a common language and a structure that could channel energy and creativity toward advancing the Shortridge mission. We believed that if an explicit PYD approach was implemented thoughtfully and systematically at the school, Shortridge would become an example of an educational community deeply grounded in PYD.

Working with the management team at Shortridge Academy, the authors began the development of a logic model for the school to guide practices and decision making, as well as to provide a concise overview for parents and educational consultants of the goals of the school and how staff members work to achieve those goals. Logic models not only serve as a guide when decisions are being made and priorities are being set but also help keep all constituencies aware of the principles to which programs adhere. The process of developing the logic model can be almost as useful as the finished product because it involves activities that require staff to examine their attitudes and beliefs about the work they are doing. The process also encourages staff to determine what they see as their most important goals and how they expect to achieve these goals. The process at Shortridge took many months and included extended discussions through which values were clarified, implicit beliefs and goals were made explicit, and a greater understanding of the implications of a PYD approach was realized.

Among the goals of this step in the project were to enhance consistency among the professionals at the school, to ensure that practices were evidence based whenever possible, to identify needs for additional staff development, and to make the school's philosophy about working with students and their parents as transparent as possible. In addition, the process was designed to lay the foundation for a sustainable evaluation component to document the effectiveness of the school.

A hybrid logic model that includes aspects of theory, activities, and outcome models was developed for Shortridge. This encouraged the staff to clarify and validate their mission, theory of change, goals, and long- and short-term objectives. The mission statement identifies the program's theoretical grounding in PYD, the population the school serves, and the staff's commitment to including students and parents in the process of supporting healthy development.

> Shortridge Academy Mission Statement
> Guided by a Positive Youth Development perspective, Shortridge Academy provides a therapeutically supportive and inspiring educational community. We support the cognitive, emotional, and social development of bright yet struggling adolescents by utilizing clearly-defined, goal-directed plans, evidenced-based strategies, and a rigorous college preparatory curriculum. Joining with families, our trained staff engages students to identify their strengths and encourages the development of skills and knowledge that will prepare them for healthy and productive adulthood.

The school's stated theory of change focuses upon the use of evidence-based practices, well-trained and supervised staff, and positive peer influence to promote emotional healing, fulfillment of academic potential, character building, improved family relations, and the development of interpersonal and decision-making skills. Individualized Positive Development Plans (PDPs) systematically developed by therapists, counselors, teachers, and parents that build on the strengths of each student guide the use of programmatic, academic, and therapeutic strategies and activities. Shortridge believes that the structured residential environment provides a nurturing, intentional community where staff provides positive role modeling and the scaffolding students need to succeed. Students are empowered to work as partners with parents and staff to develop competence and confidence in making positive choices and planning for their future.

A. MAJOR GOALS

The goals of Shortridge Academy also are linked closely to the commonly agreed upon characteristics of thriving adolescents: competence, confidence, caring, connection, and character. Although contribution is a sixth "C" that has been identified as a possibility after the achievement of the other five (Lerner, 2009), the implementation at Shortridge included this as a primary characteristic conceptualizing it as one that interacts with, and can help build, the other five. After reviewing what they believed to be the common implicit goals of the work being done at the school, the management team identified what they saw to be the seven most significant goals consistent with a PYD approach. These included:

(1) *Build positive decision-making skills.* This goal includes critical thinking skills, developing a positive personal value system to guide thoughtful decision making, and seeking adult assistance when necessary. Activities and strategies related to the objectives of this goal are expected to build competence and character.

(2) *Establish and maintain trusting relationships.* This includes developing mutually supportive relationships with family, peers, and other adults and the use of effective communication skills. This goal is associated with the development of connection, competence, and caring.

(3) *Embrace and implement healthy lifestyle changes.* This goal focuses on healthy eating and regular exercise, having a healthy attitude toward one's body and one's sexuality, and managing risk-seeking impulses in positive ways. Achievement of this goal is expected to contribute to the growth of competence, character, and caring for oneself.

(4) *Recognize and develop individual leadership potential.* This includes understanding good leadership skills, developing one's own ability to lead, and seeking out leadership opportunities. It is expected that this will lead to further development of competence, confidence, character, connection, as well as contribution.

(5) *Create personal goals and identify the resources and strategies to attain them.* This includes identifying short- and long-term goals, plans to achieve those goals, and the development of a healthy transition plan

to life after Shortridge. This goal is related to the development of competence, character, and connection.

(6) *Develop resilience and self-efficacy.* This includes developing self-confidence, self-esteem, coping skills, and the ability to respond to situations rather than to react, as well as seeking help when needed. This goal is related to the development of competence, confidence, character, and connection.

(7) *Understand, navigate, and enhance family relations.* This includes identifying the students' role in their family systems and how this role contributes to the dynamics of the family. This relates to the development of competence, caring, confidence, character, connection, and contribution.

B. STRATEGIES FOR ACHIEVING OUTCOMES

Each of these seven overarching goals has a set of concrete and measurable outcomes associated with it. These outcomes are, in turn, linked to a variety of strategies and activities that staff members use to facilitate students' development. For example, to help students build positive decision-making skills (Goal 1), with the desired outcome that they will "demonstrate decision making consistent with commitments they have made," activities might involve identifying and assessing "trigger" interactions that lead to less than productive decisions. Students would then develop an action plan to help them manage the situations. Strategies and activities are designed to include the opportunity to reflect upon and discuss outcomes either in group or in individual counseling or therapy sessions. For example, in this case, the outcomes of decisions and behaviors in relation to the student's personal goals might be discussed in individual counseling.

The strategies and activities designed to facilitate a particular outcome vary by phase. For example, to address the goal of establishing and maintaining trusting relationships with a desired outcome of understanding and being able to articulate how their actions affect others, a Phase I student might interview 10 different people (students from different phases and staff) regarding the positive and negative effects of the student's actions. In Phase II, the student might be expected to support at least one Phase I student in their development by reviewing their writing assignments, helping them stay in agreement with consequences of rule violations, or assisting them in other aspects of the program. The specific goals and outcomes on which a student will focus during a particular period are identified in his or her PDP.

C. INDIVIDUALIZED PDPS

In keeping with the theoretical grounding of PYD, we made a decision to transform the notion of a traditional "treatment plan" for each student at Shortridge into something less deficit focused and more positive. The tenets of PYD and specific goals for each student are implemented through an ongoing plan for which we coined the term "Positive Development Plan." These plans are developed jointly among the student, the counselor, the parents, and the clinical and academic directors. The plans include traditional clinical information such as DSM IV-R diagnostic material and a clinical assessment, as well as an academic assessment. The rest of the PDP provides a personalized approach for working toward the seven goals and facilitating the development of the six "Cs" of PYD. Integrated into the PDP are the most relevant outcomes on which the student will focus for a particular period of time and the related therapeutic/programmatic strategies and activities linked to achieving those outcomes.

The PDP is developed approximately 1 month into the student's stay at the school, but the groundwork is laid for it as early as the parents' enrollment application to the school when they are asked to provide their social and emotional goals for their child. The PDPs are supervised by the clinical director and are reviewed and revised regularly by staff, parents, and students. The PDP is available electronically to all staff working with a student and guides the work of counselors, teachers, and parents. This PDP also serves as the basis for how progress is communicated to families, both in conference calls and in written reports, and how objectives for the next period are determined. In addition, PDPs will provide data for the outcome evaluation.

D. ACTIVELY ENGAGING AND INVOLVING STUDENTS

Shortridge is committed to including and engaging students whenever possible with an understanding that the adults are always ultimately responsible for maintaining boundaries that help ensure safety and maximize positive development. Staff members are encouraged to keep in mind the overarching goals of the school and what we know about adolescent development when including youth and developing partnerships. Students participate in choosing activities, making school policies, and creating new programming. Students have the opportunity to present ideas to the management team or to come to staff meetings to make a proposal. As a result, staff members report that students begin to see themselves as competent and capable individuals who have the ability to set and achieve goals that will allow them to thrive in the future.

An aspect of actively engaging and involving students that is widely used at Shortridge is the enlisting of peers in positive interventions. Peers can enhance one another's development, help one another process feedback, react to conflict and problems in positive ways, and promote positive qualities and behavior (Karcher, Brown, & Elliott, 2004). With adult oversight, students act as tutors, mentors, guides, and support persons. Experiences such as these help develop the competence, confidence, caring, connections, and character of both students while providing an opportunity for the more experienced student to contribute to others.

1. Involving Students in the Academic Environment

Shortridge provides students an intellectually stimulating learning environment that is flexible and sensitive to students' learning needs. Curriculum and instruction at Shortridge is designed to motivate and engage all students to reach their academic potential and become lifelong learners. Faculty members are experienced, skilled teachers who use multimodal approaches to learning emphasizing classroom discussion, collaboration, problem solving, and active learning. These instructional approaches are effective in engaging and challenging gifted students, as well as supporting those with a range of learning needs and challenges from ADHD to mild learning disabilities.

Students are actively engaged in creating their learning environment. Teachers talk to students about how to have an environment that facilitates learning. Some teachers choose books for class with input from students. Others talk with students about their preferences for structuring of assignments and how they would like to demonstrate their ability to apply their knowledge using writing, projects, presentations, or some other format. Students can assume the role of teaching assistants if they want to be more challenged in a class. This might involve reading ahead and helping design and facilitate lessons or serving as a peer tutor.

The emphasis is on developing higher-order thinking skills and enhancing executive functions. Scaffolding of students is done as needed. To assist a student with a project that might take a month to complete, a teacher might use graphic organizers and help students divide the assignment into smaller segments. A great deal of time is spent talking about future goals and identifying the steps to reach those goals. Students' struggles are seen as opportunities. If students get off track, such as not turning in homework or earning falling grades, teachers assist students in developing a plan to get back on track.

Teachers also emphasize creating community in their classrooms. In one situation, a teacher was responding to a highly distracted English class. By asking students to come up with a plan for keeping students more engaged, a plan was developed for a "tea club" in class. Each student has her or his own cup and has tea during English. The students sip their (noncaffeinated) tea, feel more adult-like, and are more engaged because the solution was their idea.

2. Involving Students in Clinical Care

The clinical director uses a variety of inclusive and educational approaches when introducing or adjusting a student's medications. Using diagrams, a book on the brain, and online psychopharmacology information, she might explain to students and parents how an antidepressant is believed to work and about different neurotransmitters. By increasing students' knowledge and competence about medications, they can more confidently become a partner in managing their own medications. Students are more able to determine whether they are being helped or having an adverse event and can contribute to decisions about discontinuing medication.

The clinical director also talks with students and families about normative adolescent brain development and neural plasticity. This information, along with a book on the adolescent brain and addiction, helps address substance abuse. She also explains testing and assessment to students and parents, providing information in easily digestible amounts. The approach she advocates is "caretive rather than curative" with the goal of optimizing strengths rather than getting rid of something. By providing a safe emotional and psychological environment and establishing a sense of trust, the clinical director provides examples of how both PYD and positive parental development are supported at the school.

3. Involving Students in Activities

Under the management team's direction, Shortridge staff actively promotes the type of school that Zeigler (2004) envisioned. The school leadership opens itself to innovation, change, and experimentation as the students are listened to and brought into the process. Activities suggested by students frequently reflect the dynamics of adolescent brain development. Attaching skis to a mountain bike to sled the front hill, taking field trips to play paintball, or starting a sky diving club are just a few ideas suggested by students over the years. Historically, without a wealth of knowledge regarding research on the adolescent brain, Shortridge viewed many suggestions as too dangerous for the school to endorse. Some ideas sounded good but were simply seen as too risky.

However, as the staffs' understanding of PYD and brain development grew, so did the number of student ideas converted into implemented activities. The knowledge that all teenagers, and certainly those at Shortridge, are influenced by their peers and at times make choices more on impulse than through thoughtful introspection encouraged staff to reevaluate the importance of extracurricular activities and give them higher priority. Student ideas became opportunities for inclusion, role modeling, sharing of decisions, and the building of relationships. In addition, staff–student collaboration provided an environment that nurtured strengths while providing healthy risk-taking opportunities. So, for example, when a group of students sought to build a small terrain park for skiing and snowboarding on the campus, staff realized this provided an opportunity for staff and student partnership to be maximized and discussions between teenagers and adults followed. Together they addressed safety issues, developed supervision plans, determined student eligibility, and finalized other relevant details. The student-generated plan took shape and became a reality at the next snowfall.

The Shortridge surfing program provides an example of another collaborative effort intended to contribute to students' long-term, healthy life styles. Some Shortridge students wake up before sunrise weekly for 10 of the 12 months of the year and head to the coast. With wet suits, surfboards, and thrills needing to be satisfied, students plunge into the beautiful, yet icy, water to ride a few waves. Their faces project their exhilaration as they emerge from the ocean. If surfing does not catch students' interest, there are many other activities from which they can choose. Some students choose mountain biking on 6 miles of student-made trails, rock climbing at a local gym, participating on a hike or backpacking trip in the White Mountains, or "jamming" in the recording studio. Regardless of the activity choices, the common themes are building on student ideas and interests and encouraging healthy risk taking. The consistent results are increased student competence and confidence, as well as richly nuanced stories about staff and students joined in negotiation, collaboration, and friendship.

A somewhat deeper challenge for engaging students is demonstrated by student-driven projects requiring capital budgets. To take an idea from conceptualization to implementation requires curiosity, thought, planning, passion, persistence, and a variety of other resources. For many students at the school, inclusion on this level of the creative process represents a new experience. These more complicated projects provide particularly powerful opportunities to build strengths and introduce key concepts and competencies relevant to entrepreneurship. One initiative, the first of this nature at Shortridge, occurred a few years ago when a student with a passion for the guitar requested that staff create a space where students could play and record music. The student's primary goal was to enhance his musical talents. The staff's aim was to include the student in as many ways as possible, hoping thereby to strengthen his competence and confidence. The student prepared an initial proposal with diagrams, created a detailed budget, and presented these items to the administration. He not only influenced decisions about which equipment and materials to purchase but also helped to install and build the recording studio. Navigating roadblocks with skill and growing competence, the student met with the fire department to discuss sprinklers and egress issues, the electrical contractors for code purposes, the administration about supervision issues, and with the director regarding the budget. Discussing alternative ways to approach budgetary challenges offered possibilities for growth in character and connection. After months of hard work, the student's contribution resulted in a recording studio that took music in a new direction for the Shortridge community.

The most capital-intensive, student/staff project to date, the skateboard park, ultimately provided a $50' \times 50'$ leveled, paved area for students to stay connected with one of their passions. In addition to the site work, students managed a budget and chose skateboards, helmets, pads, and skate park elements. Students and staff drafted parent releases and generated safety protocols through conference calls with the school's attorney. Finally, with a student-created and supervised system in place that was based on demonstrated ability, students enjoyed the park in an organized and safe manner. To the student body, the skateboard park symbolized an explicit shift on the administration's part, a shift that further encourages students to voice ideas and to move those ideas forward.

Examples abound of ways that students participate in the development of new activities that not only provide entertainment and involvement for the students but also foster connections with other students and staff, support the development of new competencies, and provide opportunities to build confidence. Including students in the process of developing or refining policies at the school involves a different level of power sharing with students.

4. Developing and Refining Policies

Engaging students through revising old or creating new policies, a responsibility usually reserved for senior administrators, is a relatively new practice at Shortridge. Most adults at the school enthusiastically provide scaffolding to students participating in this process where decisions are weighed, relationships tested, and intellects challenged. In part, that opportunity to guide students in work such as this is what attracts many faculty and staff to the school's mission. Therefore, when Shortridge began viewing students not only as resources to be developed but also as individuals possessing insights that could aid and help with decision making, inclusion took on a deeper meaning.

As previously discussed, students are very involved in the creation and revision of their PDPs. Students also are engaged in designing and reviewing the dorm head role and helping to develop their home visit agreements. Shortridge uses the term "agreement" to describe the school's boundaries and explicit codes of conduct. The thinking is that the concept of *agreements*, as opposed to *rules*, better includes students and families and encourages negotiation while emphasizing the concept of "power sharing." As is the case with authoritative parenting, the degree to which students and families shape agreements is influenced by the nature of the topic. For example, agreements involving student safety are much less negotiable than those pertaining to music, dress, or family visit.

Involving students in the process of developing or revising agreements has become routine at Shortridge. A recent example is when the residential program director included students in the revision of the policy on dealing with violations of community agreements and behavioral issues. As a result of this collaboration between staff and students, the term *consequences* replaced *restrictions* to denote a response to agreement violations more consistent with PYD. A new Consequences Guidelines document reviewed by students requires anyone violating an agreement to reflect on his or her violation and determine how to resolve the consequences of that behavior. The student is encouraged to write about what happened, why they think it happened, what aspect of their PDP they need to focus on to recover from the violation, and what or who might assist them. Those who violate agreements also are asked to develop an action apology relevant to the infraction and determine what self-imposed restrictions might be appropriate. Peers and staff members will participate in this process to assist students in thinking through the effects of the violation and determining meaningful consequences. The idea is that students violating community agreements would be encouraged to think about the effects of their actions on others and how they might make amends. In this way, they may internalize responsibility, rather than merely have externally imposed consequences that they must satisfy. This approach is expected to not only build character and increase caring but also improve competence in dealing with difficult situations, raise awareness of one's effects on the community, and help students realize what resources might be needed to recover from a difficult situation.

Shortridge uses a variety of vehicles for listening to students and therefore clearly has moved beyond Mitra's (2006) first level of youth participation, and is involved in integrating the next two levels into practice by collaborating with students to bring about change and giving them opportunities to assume and develop leadership skills. An example of how youth are involved at all three levels can be seen in a recent project that took place at a regularly scheduled group meeting at the school. The project was entitled "You Speak, We Listen" and included all students, teachers, and counselors. The project was led by a leadership group of six students who received scaffolding by the authors. The six students met to identify what they thought were indicators of progress in students at Shortridge and what the school could do to better support that progress. They generated ideas about these topics and, in a follow-up meeting, discussed how similar ideas might be collected from all students at the school. They decided to use a three-phase process all of which took place during the 2-hour group session. The process involved first having students respond anonymously and individually in writing to three questions focused on what they might like to change about the school, what they saw as indicators of progress for themselves or other students, and what they thought were the strengths of the school. This process helped students organize their thoughts and share ideas they might feel uncomfortable verbalizing. Next, students broke into dyads and discussed four topics identified by the six-student leadership group: nutrition, health, and fitness; decision making and self-control; activities and entertainment; and maintaining a positive environment and respectful community. Students were provided with some guiding questions for each topic. After a short discussion among the dyads, students moved into three larger groups for discussion. Each group discussion was led by two of the students from the leadership group. Identified staff members who attended a preparatory session with the leadership group served as an adult back up and scribes. Other staff members attended the discussions but primarily listened to the students.

Students participated actively and provided a vast amount of information that was content analyzed and presented to the management team. Some of the student ideas, such as wanting more variety in food at breakfast or more opportunities to individualize their rooms in the dorms, were relatively straightforward and easily addressable. However, many of the suggestions from the students required more reflection and/or funding and also offered new possibilities for youth–staff partnerships. For example, there was a recommendation from the students for the school to make available food they thought was healthier and would meet the needs of vegetarians. In the discussion, the idea of students planning meals and meal times was brought up, as well as the idea of bringing back the garden.

Another request that students had was in regard with having more control in decision making. Students wanted to make more decisions themselves. One group suggested that students should be able to decide when to eat, when to go to sleep, and when to go to dorm based on phase. They thought students should earn these privileges and that making decisions such as these will teach them how to handle their day and to make better decisions in general. Suggestions such as these offer multiple possibilities for youth–adult partnerships whether it be researching healthy eating, menu planning, gardening, and food preparation or working together to think about how to better address the students' growing desire for autonomy and ability to practice decision making as they progress at the school. To address these requests, the management team plans to develop staff–student partnerships to explore several of the topics and determine how they might work together to respond to students in a way that further promotes positive development.

E. PREPARING STAFF AND PARENTS

An important component in the success of any PYD program is the readiness of the adults involved to facilitate the continued growth of the students. For Shortridge, this means that staff and parents need to have a good understanding of PYD concepts, adolescent brain development, and authoritative parenting. The belief is that for the school to be effective and for the students to thrive, it is important to do *positive staff development* and *positive parental development* as well. This means determining and building upon the strengths of staff and family members, as well as those of the students.

1. Positive Staff Development

Training and orientation of staff members is an ongoing process as each individual considers the implications of a PYD approach for his or her own practice. A mix of large group and smaller seminar-type sessions provided conceptual and empirical information on PYD and adolescent brain development. On some occasions, staff with the same areas of responsibility, such as teachers, would come together to share challenges and ideas for addressing those challenges. Other times, staff with different responsibilities would meet for a more general discussion. Efforts were made to ensure that any presentation made to parents, for example, one on helping teens make better decisions, also would be presented to relevant staff. Time at administrative team meetings regularly would be allocated to new information about PYD, thinking about research, and addressing challenges related to involving students in new ways at the school. The assumption is that the directors are the primary trainers and educators of other staff as they supervise teachers, counselors, and residential staff providing leadership and mentoring. The authors provide necessary scaffolding for the directors who, in turn, provide scaffolding useful to staff members. Additional training on specific topics is secured through a variety of professional organizations in which staff members participate.

2. Positive Parental Development

Including and educating parents is central to the family work that supports the students' progress. If families understand and practice a PYD approach, they become partners with the staff in the therapeutic process providing consistent expectations, authoritative discipline, and nurturing environments for their daughters and sons. Parents are engaged even during the application process in identifying their child's strengths as well as challenges and in sharing their own expectations about long-term goals. Parent conferences are held twice a year during which parents spend 3 days interacting with staff and their adolescents, attending both educational and experiential sessions, and making contact with other parents who have children at Shortridge. Time at these conferences is devoted to providing information about PYD, authoritative parenting, and the academic program as well as learning about new developments at the school and listening to panels of students talk about their experiences. Each family is provided with their own copy of *The Good Teen* (Lerner, 2007).

In response to parent requests, new parent orientation seminars began recently. In order to fully embrace the strengths-based approach of PYD and to complement the biannual Parent Conferences, Shortridge staff designed a 1-day seminar for parents of newly enrolled students. The current plan is to hold these seminars every other month to provide information on the counseling, academic, and residential life components. The seminars also will build parents' skills in being effective partners in their child's PDP during the 14–16-month program. Elements of authoritative parenting, the roles of Shortridge staff and parents in setting limits, providing scaffolding to their student's healthy decision making, and facilitating positive change will be discussed. An experiential activity and dinner with their son/daughter on campus concludes the day.

F. PROGRAM EVALUATION

The implementation of PYD at Shortridge involved consideration of evaluation from the beginning. Undertaking an evaluation of a program as complex as this requires extensive time, energy, expense, and patience. Conducting a program evaluation that employs experimental or even quasi-experimental techniques is unfeasible. Therefore, we are using a *theory of change approach* (Connell & Klem, 2000; Izzo, Connell, Gambone, & Bradshaw, 2004) because it is appropriate for youth development initiatives and draws upon current research, best practices, and local experiences. The theory of change approach provides a working theory by which a program is developed and the evaluation planned. This approach is designed to determine the effectiveness of a program during and after implementation providing immediate, intermediate, and ultimate outcomes.

Shortridge's theory of change met Connell and Klem's (2000, pp. 94–95) criteria for a high-quality theory of change. It needed to be seen as plausible, doable, testable, and meaningful. In other words, stakeholders believe the logic of the model is correct; that the resources available are sufficient to implement the action strategies in the theory; that there are credible ways to discover whether predicted results are achieved; and that the outcomes are important and worth the effort to pursue.

The theory of change approach is assumed to be collaborative and iterative (Izzo et al., 2004). So at Shortridge, the theory of change and overarching, ultimate goals were developed over a period of many months by administrators, directors in consultation with frontline staff, and the evaluator. Continuing collaborations with staff identified the expected shorter-term goals and the strategies and activities to be used to achieve the expected outcomes. We currently are in the process of collaborating with stakeholders to select the most useful indicators to measure change. For example, staff members were individually interviewed to get their perceptions of indicators of progress and how they currently assess that progress. Students participated by sharing their ideas in the You Speak, We Listen project. Parents also were consulted about their ideas regarding positive indicators of movement toward the goals.

We currently are continuing to elaborate the logic model, identifying indicators and making final commitments to instrumentation and procedures. Management has taken the position that program evaluation will take place, but that the process should draw upon existing data as much as possible so that the instruments serve academic and therapeutic, as well as research purposes. In order to achieve this goal, it has been necessary to not only review all existing sources of data but also determine in collaboration with the staff how existing documentation might be revised to serve these dual purposes. A Research Advisory Committee constituted by Shortridge will review the final evaluation protocol, and it then will be submitted to the IRB at the university with which the first author is affiliated.

In the interim, and as a strategy for including parents and their perceptions in the transition process, we conducted parent surveys in 2009 and 2010. The survey instrument included demographic questions; forced-choice items through which respondents provided the extent of their agreement, satisfaction, or perception of change in response to a series of statements; and open-ended questions that allowed them to provide their individual observations and comments.

Parents saw PYD to be a positive aspect of the school, and they had a growing understanding of the promise of such an approach. As one mother of a Phase III student noted, Shortridge provides "Chances for students who have 'failed' in many situations to be successful and to be given the chance to mentor newer students." Another Phase III parent commented on staff using such an approach. "Counseling staff and faculty are amazing, both in personal dedication and effectiveness. They meet each student where they are and find ways to connect and help them own their personal growth." Other parents were more effusive in their praise.

> In the nine months that our son has been at Shortridge, we have developed a deeper understanding of our son's strengths and needs. If we had been able to create a school designed specifically for our son, we could not have conceived a more perfect match in environment and philosophy than Shortridge Academy and Positive Youth Development.
> Thank you for C[6]. (Phase II Parent)

However, as parents' understanding of PYD becomes more sophisticated, their expectations about its implementation rise, also. One Phase II father explained that "The more I have experienced Shortridge, the greater my expectations have grown. The more you understand, the more you expect." Parents who made critical comments in 2010 did not voice concerns so much about the theoretical approach itself, but rather about the way, or the extent to which, it was being implemented. For example, one Phase II father said, "I would create a more structured and measurable path for students to develop in the areas of competence, confidence, connection, character, caring, & contribution."

In one section of the survey, parents rated the amount of change they observed in their child since entering Shortridge Academy in regard to the following strengths: caring, competence, connection, character, confidence, and contributions. They rated change on 18 items using a Likert-type scale. For example, under confidence, parents rated the extent of perceived change for *improved self-esteem, belief in the future,* and *believe goals can be achieved.* Statistically, significant changes were found among Phase I, Phase II, and Phase III parents on 14 of the 18 items. These results need to be interpreted cautiously because they are based on cross-sectional data, but parents' responses indicated a clear pattern of perceived positive change from Phase I to Phase II, and then to Phase III. Parents whose children have been at Shortridge longer perceive greater improvement in all the strength categories.

A confirmatory factor analysis run on the 20 original PYD items in 2009 indicated that, except for two items focused on siblings, all items loaded on the same factor. Deleting these two items resulted in a PYD index with a potential range of 18–90 to measure parents' perception of overall change in regard to these strength items. An ANOVA of PYD index scores indicated a significant difference by Phase in parents' perceptions of change. Follow-up testing revealed the significant difference was between Phase I ($M = 55.58$, $SD = 10.18$) and Phase III parents ($M = 72.38$, $SD = 12.27$), suggesting that parents whose children had been in the school longer perceived greater strengths in regard with competence, confidence, character, caring, connections, and contributions.

IV. Discussion

The implementation of PYD at Shortridge Academy has been exhilarating, challenging, informative, and demanding. Although the population of students and parents involved in the school are not typical of those generally associated with youth programs, we believe that there are a variety of ways this case example can inform the efforts of others implementing PYD programs. Among the most important ingredients in moving an institution through change of this magnitude is leadership and collaboration. We are convinced that there needs to be at least one person in a leadership position committed enough to maintain the vision of desired long-term outcomes so that the project will keep moving forward despite setbacks that inevitably occur. This person must be in close enough contact with staff that the pace of change can be modulated as necessary to take advantage of opportunities for moving forward without overwhelming staff.

We also believe that it is valuable for programs to seek out expertise in theory, research, and program development early in the process. The development of a logic model, though often a demanding experience, helps organize all activity in the program, serves as a touchstone when decisions need to be made, and lays the foundation for determining whether the program is effective. In the case of Shortridge, the translation of the research on adolescent brain development and authoritative parenting into workshops and training for staff and parents helped them better understand adolescent behavior and decision making so they could more effectively respond to the students using PYD-consistent approaches. Our experience suggests that a basic understanding of the dynamics of adolescent brain development combined with the rather conclusive evidence supporting the benefits of authoritative parenting (Steinberg, 2010a) helped staff and parents understand *why* PYD approaches used at Shortridge could be expected to facilitate the students' positive development. The information also helped them respond more productively to seemingly incomprehensible behavior of students who were making great progress and then appeared to be backsliding into risky activities.

A few people with a vision and information do not make a program such as this possible, however. Connell and Klem (2000) point out that, "core and systemic actions are necessary to improve critical outcomes" (p. 116). To us, this emphasized the need for a collaborative approach that included all members of the Shortridge community. We were able to draw upon the staff's expertise, dedication to the students, and trust in one another and the management team to move the implementation forward in a way that worked at the school. Caring, trusting relationships allow the concept of scaffolding to be heavily utilized. The authors, in leading the project, scaffold each other and the management team, which, in turn, scaffolds one another and the staff. The staff provides scaffolding for the parents and students, and students scaffold one another. The management team and staff are informed by parent and student feedback which provides a different type of scaffolding to help refine and improve the program. Shortridge's model of providing support also has resulted in parents forming groups among themselves to assist one another. Again, all of these efforts contribute to the positive development of not only the adolescents but also the staff and parents.

A. CHALLENGES AND OPPORTUNITIES

We encountered a variety of challenges in conceptualizing and implementing a comprehensive PYD program at Shortridge, but we chose to define these as opportunities rather than problems. Among these were the efforts involved in the theoretical shift, attitude shifts in regard with power sharing, administrative demands, and the complexities of evaluating such an extensive intervention.

1. Theory Shift

Early assessment at Shortridge indicated that there was an implicit strengths-based approach that pervaded much of the staffs' work with students and that a strong focus on community, caring relationships, self-study by students, and student leadership existed. Therefore, the philosophical acceptance of PYD by most staff was relatively easy. What proved more challenging is helping staff reach the point where a PYD approach is their primary response to interacting with students in all situations making it their "instinctual" response. Thinking about building on strengths is relatively easy if one is designing an activity or a new experience for students. It is less intuitive when responding to situations where students are involved in prohibited behavior or have taken actions that some staff members see as needing "punishment." It is also not intuitive for most staff to have students involved in designing their own consequences for infractions of agreements. We have had to remind staff that PYD is not just an approach that is useful in creating fun opportunities for students to be involved but is a perspective that can have universal utility.

Implementing a pervasive change such as that which is happening at Shortridge is challenging for staff on a daily basis as they not only work to respond in PYD consistent ways to students but also work to *not* respond in ways they traditionally might have. Connell and Klem (2000) note the importance of staff supporting one another "to choose change making over work that is comfortable and familiar" (p. 116). They suggest that the challenge for administrators is to support staff in following through on commitments and persisting in change making despite setbacks that are likely to occur. We saw this occurring at Shortridge at times where there were serious behavioral issues, and the reaction from staff was that "maybe we should let PYD go for a while and tighten up some," suggesting also that some staff saw PYD as being a "loose" or "soft" way of dealing with adolescents when things got difficult.

The challenges of bringing about a theory shift have provided opportunities for a review of all policies, procedures, and activities at Shortridge encouraging everyone to reflect on not only what they are doing but also why they are doing it. There is an explicit consensus about the philosophy that guides the school and the identified goals for students, both individually and collectively. The work involved in making the theory shift means that the functioning of the school now is relatively transparent and can be communicated clearly to parents, students, and educational consultants. The process of expected change is demystified.

2. Power Sharing

One of the greatest challenges in comprehensively implementing PYD at Shortridge involved the extent to which staff felt comfortable including students in decision making at the school. Almost all staff endorsed the idea of student participation, but as in most programs, considerable diversity existed regarding where individuals would "draw the line." As Zeldin and Petrokubi (2006) point out, the belief that adolescents can work as partners on very important issues "runs counter to prevailing societal norms, public policies, structures, and standards of practice" (p. 11). Youth often are not seen to have the necessary values or competence. This, however, may be because professionals have little experience with true power sharing with adolescents. Zeldin and Petrokubi emphasize the challenges of building both the will and the capacity to integrate youth–adult partnerships and caution implementers to "go slow and do it right" (p.14).

The attitudes and demeanor of staff toward students are critical components in the atmosphere of a PYD program, and some staff members will be required to rethink and reconstruct attitudes and beliefs developed through prior personal, educational, and vocational experiences. This is probably particularly true when the youth involved are identified by some as troubled, at risk, or behavior problems. At Shortridge, where a history of youth involvement existed, youth–adult partnership opportunities continue to develop as staff, through experience, feel more comfortable working with students and sharing power even in regard with what some see as the most important and serious aspects of the school, such as governance and control. In the process, the adults have benefited by learning more about the ideas and perspectives of the adolescents and increased their appreciation for the students' abilities, initiative, and humor.

PYD approaches for encouraging and facilitating students' positive and creative ideas came quite "naturally" for staff at the school because of the history of building on strengths. However, using a PYD lens to respond to student problems or poor decisions that staff saw as requiring disciplinary measures proved more difficult. For those adults with a more authoritarian than authoritative orientation, personal belief systems often clashed with a philosophy that focuses more on building strengths and internal controls than disciplining or punishing. For example, in a situation where a student was involved in an act of theft or destruction of property, one course of action might be to enforce negative consequences or punishments. It might be argued that a loss of privileges at the school store and work chores such as shoveling the front walk would teach the student not to take others' belongings. Another vantage point could focus on opportunities for the student to develop character and improve decision making by reflecting on the situation and the effects of the student's actions on others and the community as a whole. Including the student in an authoritative manner in identifying appropriate consequences and apologies, as well as alternative strategies for dealing with problematic decisions or impulsiveness in the future, would be more in line with PYD. It is the latter viewpoint to which the community has shifted, but only through extensive consideration and discussion.

Effective power sharing requires that staff carefully think through the boundaries of such a partnership, considering the implications for achievement of goals, understanding the risks and benefits that might be involved, and being willing to let go of a certain amount of control. The orchestration of successful power sharing through youth–adult partnerships not only contributes to the development of the students involved but also extends the positive development of staff and provides a model for how parents can interact authoritatively with their adolescents.

3. Administrative Demands

Implementing a PYD program requires a massive amount of time, energy, thought, and discussion. Even without including a program evaluation, the financial costs might be more than a traditional program, as well. There is not a packaged PYD program or curriculum, so activities and strategies need to be carefully considered for their relevance to program goals and a strengths- and youth-centered approach. Particularly at the beginning, most staff members find that they have to stop and think before they respond to youth if they want to maximize the educational and developmental benefits of a particular situation. This may feel artificial or inefficient. However, working with a distracting student in the classroom, a disrespectful student in the dorm, or a "rule breaker" are challenges that staff might face that can be defined as opportunities for PYD. The manner in which students will be included in the governance of the school demands ongoing discussions as the management team struggles with how to provide meaningful inclusion of students and still maintain the boundaries that ensure safety and signal to students and parents that the adults maintain ultimate responsibility and are "at the helm."

The consensus among the director and the management team was that steering the Academy's philosophical approach in a new direction, even when that new direction did not require a major compass change, took tremendous effort. First introduced to the staff and faculty close to 4 years ago, PYD was well received. Shortridge had already been implementing many aspects of this positive perspective, and at first glance, PYD seemed like a "common sense" approach. The first major challenge did not surface until about 1 year later when the PYD emphasis began to test personal perspectives. Some faculty and staff have found the move toward a more explicit implementation of PYD easier than have others. However, everyone, regardless of comfort level with PYD, found they could enhance their understanding of how best to promote positive development in students, particularly when confronted with difficult situations. To support this growth, the staff needed scaffolding, just as it is provided to students and parents. Trainings, information, and forums to debrief school events all received more in-depth preparation in regard to stressing PYD strategies and opportunities. The majority of Shortridge staff thrived with this type of support. Only a small number of individuals found the shift too difficult to embrace and ultimately moved on from the school emphasizing the importance of carefully screening candidates for new staff openings in the future.

Shortridge Academy faced, and continues to face, several obstacles while on a path toward making PYD more visible and part of its daily habits. Resources like time, money, commitment, support from the Board, and an open mind on the part of the school's leadership, have all been crucial. The use of external expertise helped to nurture and sustain this creative and entrepreneurial undertaking. Due in part to its proximity to major colleges and universities, Shortridge Academy's leadership developed relationships with experts in the areas of research and adolescent development. Guidance from these relationships helped make the challenges surmountable and the expectations for progress realistic. Further, because of these connections, much of the staff scaffolding such as training and education were readily available.

4. Evaluation

Program evaluation offers one of the greatest challenges and greatest opportunities in this project. One of the challenges of evaluating any PYD program is that the vast majority of standardized instruments tend to focus on problems and negative outcomes leaving much work to be done in regard to developing measures of positive constructs (Commission on Positive Youth Development, 2005). The few instruments developed to measure positive constructs linked to PYD (e.g., Lerner et al., 2005) have not been used with adolescents the age of those at Shortridge

(Phelps et al., 2009) and assume adolescents are free living in the community. Therefore, even these instruments will need to be revised or used partially.

Another challenge has to do with decisions about data collection and follow-up assessment. Collecting data may involve staff assessing students in different ways and at different times than they have in the past. We need to strike a balance between collecting adequate, valid, reliable data for program evaluation and ensuring that data collection does not impede the functioning of the school.

Timing of data collection is always a critical decision. How early might we validly collect "baseline" data from students considering that they may not be voluntary participants at the school? We expect that there may be positive changes that do not manifest themselves until after students have graduated (Izzo et al., 2004) or that there might be results that are curvilinear. In the case of Shortridge, where students are moving back into the community after living in a very structured environment for over a year, how frequently and for how long do we do follow-up assessment?

We anticipate that the evaluation process will provide a variety of opportunities to develop new measures to supplement standardized instruments we will use. Bringing staff, students, and parents into the evaluation process not only has helped to identify existing information that might be used to document student progress but also has helped to invest all constituencies in the evaluation effort. Parents and educational consultants want to know if and for whom Shortridge Academy is effective. Staff members want to be able to confidently offer evidence that their work is having the intended results.

There has been little research completed to indicate *how* PYD programs work and for whom they may or may not be effective (Commission on Positive Youth Development, 2005). For example, there has been little research done to determine if PYD is effective for adolescents already experiencing psychological problems. We anticipate that the evaluation of Shortridge will address some of these gaps in our knowledge.

V. Final Reflections

We are encouraged and take great pride in the progress that the entire Shortridge community has made toward implementing the PYD perspective. Particularly important has been the flexibility and the open-mindedness of all Shortridge staff that allowed them to question their personal perspectives about how best to support young people, even when this might be uncomfortable, and contribute to this joint undertaking.

We believe that this case example demonstrates how theory and research can guide institutional change. The combination of leadership with vision and the collaboration among all constituencies have resulted in a school that is now clearer in its mission, has well-defined goals, and speaks a common language. Shortridge also is well situated to begin a formal program evaluation. Each aspect of the process is documented and recorded, increasing the consistency at the school and improving communication. The examples provided for how youth can be brought to the table and given voice are only a sampling of those occurring on a regular basis at Shortridge. These examples illustrate how adults and youth can partner to share power and bring about meaningful change.

The emphasis on trusting and caring relationships among students, peers, their families, and the Shortridge staff in conjunction with a guiding theory offers a unique opportunity to see an authoritative community in action. The connectedness felt in relationships throughout the Shortridge experience is often captured in the speeches at graduation ceremonies. It is not unusual for a student's speech to include a comment such as "the friends I have here are the best friends I have ever made." In addition, many students and their families refer to Shortridge as their second home and family.

The positive perceptions of parents, our own and staff observations, and anecdotal evidence give us confidence that Shortridge is supporting the positive development of its students. However, we will not know the true effectiveness of the work at the school until we have results from the formal evaluation. We look forward to reporting on that next chapter in the Shortridge story. In the meantime, we believe that providing this example, even as it is evolving, may encourage and assist others to use PYD to support the positive development of the adolescents with whom they work.

Acknowledgments

The authors would like to acknowledge Kathy Patch, Sarah Wagner, and Brian Laing for their examples of PYD at Shortridge Academy. The authors especially thank Philip Zaeder for his careful reading of, and useful comments on, the chapter.

REFERENCES

Baumrind, D. (1978). Parental disciplinary patterns and social competence in children. *Youth and Society, 9*, 239–276.

Bradshaw, C. P., & Garbarino, J. (2004). Using and building family strengths to promote youth development. In S. F. Hamilton & M. A. Hamilton (Eds.), *The youth development handbook: Coming of age in American communities.* (pp. 170–192). Thousand Oaks, CA: Sage.

Casey, B. J., Getz, S., & Galvan, A. (2008). The adolescent brain. *Developmental Review, 28*, 62–77.

Commission on Positive Youth Development. (2005). The positive perspective on youth development. In D. L. Evans, E. B. Foa, R. E. Gur, H. Hendin, C. P. O'Brien, M. E. Seligman & B. T. Walsh (Eds.), (2005). *Treating and preventing adolescent mental health disorders.* (pp. 497–527). New York: Oxford University Press.

Connell, J. P., & Klem, A. M. (2000). You can get there from here: Using a theory of change approach to plan urban education reform. *Journal of Educational and Psychological Consultation, 11*, 93–120.

Daugherty, R., & O'Bryan, T. (2004). *PRIME for life.* Lexington, KY: Prevention Research Institute.

Eccles, J. S., & Gootman, J. A. (Eds.), (2002). *Community programs to promote youth development.* Washington, DC: National Academy Press.

Gavin, L. E., Catalano, R. F., & Markham, C. M. (2010). Positive youth development as a strategy to promote adolescent sexual and reproductive health. *The Journal of Adolescent Health, 38*, S1–S6.

Giedd, J. N. (2009). Linking adolescent sleep, brain maturation, and behavior. *The Journal of Adolescent Health, 45*, 319–320.

Hamilton, S. F., Hamilton, M. A., & Pittman, K. (2004). Principles for youth development. In S. F. Hamilton & M. A. Hamilton (Eds.), *The youth development handbook: Coming of age in American communities.* (pp. 3–22). Thousand Oaks, CA: Sage.

Holm, S. M., Forbes, E. E., Ryan, N. D., Phillips, M. L., Tarr, J. A., & Dahl, R. E. (2009). Reward-related brain function and sleep in pre/early pubertal and mid/late pubertal adolescents. *The Journal of Adolescent Health, 45*, 326–334.

Huber, M. S. Q., Frommeyer, J., Weisenbach, A., & Sazama, J. (2003). Giving youth a voice in their own community and personal development. In F. A. Villarruel, D. F. Perkins, L. M. Borden & J. G. Keith (Eds.), *Community youth development.* (pp. 297–323). Thousand Oaks, CA: Sage.

Izzo, C. V., Connell, J. P., Gambone, M. A., & Bradshaw, C. P. (2004). Understanding and improving youth development initiatives through evaluation. In S. F. Hamilton & M. A. Hamilton (Eds.), *The youth development handbook: Coming of age in American communities.* (pp. 301–326). Thousand Oaks, CA: Sage.

Karcher, M. J., Brown, B. B., & Elliott, D. W. (2004). Enlisting peers in developmental interventions: Principles and practices. In S. F. Hamilton & M. A. Hamilton (Eds.), *The youth development handbook: Coming of age in American communities.* (pp. 193–215). Thousand Oaks, CA: Sage.

Kirschman, K. J. B., Johnson, R. J., Bender, J. A., & Roberts, M. C. (2009). Positive psychology for children and adolescents: Development, prevention, and promotion. In S. J. Lopez & C. R. Snyder (Eds.), *Oxford handbook of positive psychology.* (2nd ed., pp. 133–148). New York: Oxford University Press.

Larson, R. (2007). From "I" to "we": Development of the capacity for teamwork in youth programs. In R. K. Silbereisen & R. M. Lerner (Eds.), *Approaches to positive youth development.* (pp. 277–292). Thousand Oaks, CA: Sage.

Laub, J. H., Doherty, E. E., & Sampson, R. J. (2007). Social control and adolescent development: A view from life-course criminology. In R. K. Silbereisen & R. M. Lerner (Eds.), *Approaches to positive youth development.* (pp. 173–188). Thousand Oaks, CA: Sage.

Lerner, R. M. (2007). *The good teen: Rescuing adolescence from the myths of the storm and stress years.* New York: Crown.

Lerner, R. M. (2009). The positive youth development perspective: Theoretical and empirical bases of a strengths-based approach to adolescent development. In S. J. Lopez & C. R. Snyder (Eds.), *Oxford handbook of positive psychology.* (2nd ed., pp. 149–163). New York: Oxford University Press.

Lerner, R. M., Lerner, J. V., Almerigi, J., Theokas, C., Phelps, E., Gestsdottir, S., et al. (2005). Positive youth development, participation in community youth development programs, and community contributions of fifth grade adolescents: Findings from the first wave of the 4-H Study of Positive Youth Development. *The Journal of Early Adolescence, 25,* 17–71.

Luthar, S. S., & Becker, B. E. (2002). Privileged but pressured? A study of affluent youth. *Child Development, 73,* 1593–1610.

Luther, S. S., & Latendresse, S. J. (2002). Adolescent risk: The costs of affluence. In In: R. M. Lerner, C. S. Taylor & A. von Eye (Eds.), *New directions for youth development: Theory, practice, and research: Pathways to positive youth development among diverse youth* (Vol. 95, pp. 101–121). (pp. 101–121). San Franscisco: Jossey Bass.

Maccoby, E., & Martin, J. (1983). Socialization in the context of the family: Parent-child interaction. In E. M. Hetherington (Ed.), *Handbook of child psychology: Socialization, personality, and social development* (Vol. 4, pp. 1–101). (pp. 1–101). New York: Wiley.

Mitra, D. (2006). Increasing student voice and moving toward youth leadership. *The Prevention Researcher, 13*(1), 7–10.

Phelps, E., Zimmerman, S., Warren, A. E. A., Jeličić, H., von Eye, A., & Lerner, R. M. (2009). The structure and developmental course of Positive Youth Development (PYD) in early adolescence: Implications for theory and practice. *Journal of Applied Developmental Psychology, 30,* 571–584.

Pittman, K., Irby, M., Tolman, J., Yohalem, N., & Ferber, T. (2003). *Preventing problems, promoting development, encouraging engagement: Competing priorities or inseparable goals?* Washington, DC: Forum for Youth Investment.

Roth, J. L., & Brooks-Gunn, J. (2003). Youth development programs: Risk, prevention, and policy. *The Journal of Adolescent Health, 32,* 170–182.

Silbereisen, R. K., & Lerner, R. M. (2007). Approaches to positive youth development: A view of the issues. In R. K. Silbereisen & R. M. Lerner (Eds.), *Approaches to positive youth development.* (pp. 3–30). Thousand Oaks, CA: Sage.

Steinberg, L. (2008a). A social neuroscience perspective on adolescent risk-taking. *Developmental Review, 28,* 78–106.

Steinberg, L. (2008b). *Adolescence.* Boston: McGraw Hill.

Steinberg, L. (2010a). A behavioral scientist looks at the science of adolescent brain development. *Brain and Cognition, 72,* 160–164.

Steinberg, L. (2010b). A dual systems model of adolescent risk-taking. *Developmental Psychology, 52,* 216–224.

Steinberg, L., Albert, D., Cauffman, E., Banich, M., Graham, S., & Woolard, J. (2008). Age differences in sensation seeking and impulsivity as indexed by behavior and self-report: Evidence for a dual systems model. *Developmental Psychology, 44,* 1764–1778.

Weinberger, D. R., Elvevag, B., & Giedd, J. N. (2005). *The Adolescent brain: A work in progress.* Washington, DC: The National Campaign to End Teen Pregnancy Retrieved from http://www.thenationalcampaign.org/resources/pdf/BRAIN.pdf.

Zeigler, J. M. (2004). Can high schools foster youth development? In S. F. Hamilton & M. A. Hamilton (Eds.), *The youth development handbook: Coming of age in American communities.* (pp. 127–146). Thousand Oaks, CA: Sage.

Zeldin, S., & Petrokubi, J. (2006). Understanding innovation: Youth-adult partnerships in decision-making. *The Prevention Researcher, 13,* 11–15.

INTEGRATING THEORY AND METHOD IN THE STUDY OF POSITIVE YOUTH DEVELOPMENT: THE SAMPLE CASE OF GENDER-SPECIFICITY AND LONGITUDINAL STABILITY OF THE DIMENSIONS OF INTENTION SELF-REGULATION (SELECTION, OPTIMIZATION, AND COMPENSATION)

Alexander von Eye, Michelle M. Martel,[†] Richard M. Lerner,[‡]
Jacqueline V. Lerner,[§] and Edmond P. Bowers[¶]*

[*] MICHIGAN STATE UNIVERSITY, EAST LANSING, MICHIGAN, USA, AND UNIVERSITY
OF VIENNA, AUSTRIA
[†] UNIVERSITY OF NEW ORLEANS, NEW ORLEANS, USA
[‡] INSTITUTE FOR APPLIED RESEARCH IN YOUTH DEVELOPMENT, TUFTS UNIVERSITY,
MEDFORD, MASSACHUSETTS, USA
[§] COUNSELING, DEVELOPMENTAL, AND EDUCATIONAL PSYCHOLOGY DEPARTMENT,
BOSTON COLLEGE, CHESTNUT HILL, MASSACHUSETTS, USA
[¶] ELIOT-PEARSON DEPARTMENT OF CHILD DEVELOPMENT, TUFTS UNIVERSITY,
MEDFORD, MASSACHUSETTS, USA

I. THE CONCEPTS OF SELECTION, OPTIMIZATION, AND COMPENSATION

II. THE BIFACTOR MODEL
   A. TECHNICAL ELEMENTS OF THE BIFACTOR MODEL
   B. THE MULTIGROUP BIFACTOR MODEL
   C. A LONGITUDINAL BIFACTOR MODEL

III. DATA EXAMPLES

IV. CROSS-SECTIONAL BIFACTOR MODELS FOR THE PYD DATA OF
THE 4-H STUDY
   A. RESULTS FOR GRADE 10
   B. RESULTS FOR GRADE 11

V. GENDER DIFFERENCES IN THE STRUCTURE OF SOC

VI. LONGITUDINAL CHARACTERISTICS OF THE SOC STRUCTURE

VII. DISCUSSION

VIII. CONCLUSIONS

REFERENCES

Advances in Child Development and Behavior
Richard M. Lerner, Jacqueline V. Lerner and Janette B. Benson : Editors

Abstract

The study of positive youth development (PYD) rests on the integration of sound developmental theory with rigorous developmental methods. To illustrate this link, we focused on the Selection (S), Optimization (O), and Compensation (C; SOC) model of intentional self regulation, a key individual-level component of the individual context relations involved in the PYD process, and assessed the dimensional structure of the SOC questionnaire, which includes indices of Elective Selection, Loss-Based Selection, Optimization, and Compensation. Using cross-sectional and longitudinal data from Grades 10 and 11 of the 4-H Study of PYD, we estimated three models through bifactor data analysis, a procedure that allows indicators to load both on their specific latent variables and on a superordinate factor that comprises the construct under study. The first model estimated was a standard bifactor model, computed separately for the 10th and 11 graders. In both samples, the same model described the hypothesized structure well. The second model, proposed for the first time in this chapter, compared multiple groups in their bifactor structure. Results indicated only minimal gender differences in SOC structure in Grade 10. The third model, also proposed for the first time in this chapter, involved an autoregression-type model for longitudinal data, and used data from the 609 participants present in both grades. Results suggested that the SOC bifactor structure was temporally stable.

The study of positive youth development (PYD) has evolved both theoretically and methodologically (Lerner, Lerner, & Benson, 2011). Among the key theoretical ideas of PYD has been the use of a relational, developmental systems conception (Overton, 2010) to assess the coupling of the strengths of youth with resources in their ecology in the shaping of positive trajectories across the adolescent decade (Benson, 2003; Larson, 2000; Lerner, Phelps, Forman, & Bowers, 2009). This strengths-based conceptual approach to the understanding of youth development has brought several new concepts to the fore of developmental analysis.

The concept of PYD itself is the key idea within this literature and has been operationalized in several ways (Lerner et al., in press), one of the most prominent ones being the five Cs conceptualization of PYD (Bowers et al., 2010; Lerner et al., 2005). In addition, other concepts linked to the positive development of youth have also been constructs pertinent to the role of the individual and the role of the ecology in creating PYD trajectories. Constructs pertinent to the strengths of youth such as intentional self-regulation (e.g., Gestsdóttir & Lerner, 2007, 2008; and see Napolitano, Bowers, & Gestsdottir, 2011; Larson & Rusk, 2011), hopeful future orientation (e.g., Schmid et al., 2011; and see Chapter 4), and school engagement (e.g., Li, Lerner, & Lerner, 2010; and see Li, 2011) have been assessed at the individual level. In turn, the growth-promoting resources found in schools, homes, and communities, and, specifically, out-of-school-time (OST) programs (see Chapter 9) have been assessed as well (e.g., Theokas & Lerner, 2006). Moreover, the outcomes of PYD have been operationalized by constructs such as community contributions of youth (e.g., Jelicic, Bobek, Phelps, Lerner & Lerner, 2007) or active engaged citizenship (e.g., Zaff, Boyd, Li, Lerner, & Lerner, 2010; and see Chapter 11).

This burgeoning conceptual work has been coupled with the development of measures pertinent to all of these constructs, and, as well, with methods useful for understanding the mutually influential relationships between individuals and contexts that shape PYD trajectories and structure their implications for the development of individuals. Key methodological contributions have involved a burgeoning of procedures for person-centered analyses, and for indexing the role of the active individual in engaging the context in shaping the developmental trajectories of youth (e.g., Li & Lerner, 2011; Zimmerman, Phelps, & Lerner, 2008). The purpose of the present chapter is to illustrate how the conceptual and methodological work involved in the PYD perspective unfolds for the mutual benefit of our theoretical understanding of PYD and the enhancement of our methodological tools to study this facet of development.

Accordingly, to provide this illustration, this chapter will use the sample case of gender specificity of the dimensions of a key measure of intentional self-regulation in adolescence (Lerner, Freund, De Stefanis, & Habermas, 2001), that is, the measure of Selection, Optimization, and Compensation (SOC; Baltes, 1997; Freund, 2008; Freund & Baltes, 2002; Lerner, Dowling, & Roth, 2003). We ask three questions concerning these dimensions. First, we ask whether these dimensions can be established in an adolescent sample. The original studies on SOC focused on samples of advanced adult age. Second, we ask whether these dimensions exhibit gender-specificity. Specifically, we ask whether the same dimensions can be established for the two gender groups, in adolescence. Third, we ask whether the SOC dimensions show longitudinal stability. For each of the questions, we hypothesized that a bifactor model would allow one to represent the dimensions of SOC. Earlier attempts at assessing the structure of the dimensions of intentional self-regulation present in the SOC measure (e.g., Gestsdottir, Bowers, von Eye, Napolitano, & Lerner, 2010; Gestsdottir, Lewin-Bizan, von Eye, Lerner, & Lerner, 2009) have considered first- and second-order factor structures, and the present sample case seeks to extend this literature with innovative methodological approaches to data analysis.

To provide this sample case, this chapter is organized into three sections. The first section provides an overview of the theoretical basis of the SOC model of intentional self-regulation and of the SOC measure from a dimensional perspective. In the second section, we describe the bifactor model of SOC. Two of the contributions of this chapter are the extensions of the bifactor model to accommodate hypotheses about (1) group differences and (2) autoregressive characteristics of the latent variables of a bifactor model. The third section of this chapter describes the results of an application of the bifactor model to the dimensions of SOC, their possible gender specificity, and their temporal stability. Finally, our conclusions pertain both to the use of the methodology we have employed to enhance the conceptualization of the SOC measure of intentional self-regulation and, more generally, to the links between theory and method in the study of PYD.

I. The Concepts of Selection, Optimization, and Compensation

Psychological concepts are, in most theories, considered *multidimensional*, that is, they are thought of as comprising a finite, typically small number of subdimensions. Classical examples of such concepts include psychometric intelligence and personality. Among the first theories of intelligence that used multiple dimensions was Thurstone's (1938). Based on Spearman's unidimensional g-factor model, Thurstone proposed the existence of seven orthogonal factors, verbal comprehension, word fluency, number facility, spatial visualization, associative memory, perceptual speed, and reasoning. These seven factors have become known as the primary mental abilities. More recent theories of intelligence have also adopted a multidimensional perspective (see, e.g., Horn & Cattell, 1966; Sternberg, 1985).

Similarly, theories of personality have always been multidimensional. Examples include Eysenck's (1967) Theory of Extraversion and Neuroticism, and McCrae and Costa's (1987) theory of the Big Five Factors of personality: extraversion, agreeableness, conscientiousness, neuroticism, and openness. Being broad categories of personality characteristics, these dimensions are supposed to be universal and developmentally stable. That is, every human being can meaningfully be placed on these dimensions, the dimensions are supposed to exist over the course of development during the adult years, and an individual's ranking among peers is supposed to remain stable.

The concept of PYD within the applied developmental science of adolescence can also be seen as multidimensional. PYD is located on the interface between individual and environmental factors. It is defined as comprising the Five Cs of competence, confidence, connection, character, and caring (Lerner, von Eye, Lerner, Lewin-Bizan, & Bowers, 2010). Lerner and collaborators hypothesize that when a young person manifests high levels of the Five Cs over time, that is, when the youth is thriving, he or she will show development marked by integrated and mutually reinforcing contributions to self, family, community, and the institutions of civil society. As explained in the literature associated with the approach to PYD taken by investigators involved in the 4-H Study of PYD (Lerner et al., 2010, in press; Lerner, Phelps, et al., 2009), the constructs associated within both the contextual and individual components of these mutually influential relations (represented as individual ↔ context relations) are also multidimensional in character. Developmental assets supporting PYD (Benson, Scales, Hamilton, & Sesma, 2006; Theokas & Lerner, 2006) are composed of such sources of support as individuals, institutions, social networks, and paths of access to resources. In turn, the person-based components of these individual ↔ context relations involve intentional self-regulation characteristics (Gestsdóttir & Lerner, 2008) and have been operationalized in the 4-H Study through the measure associated with Freund and Baltes' (2002; see also Baltes, 1997) SOC model. In this chapter, we focus on the theoretical and methodological issues pertinent to the SOC model and measure, respectively.

The SOC model is an instance of action theory (Brandtstädter, 1998). Within this theory, it is assumed that the amount of resources (time, energy, etc.) available to the individual is limited. Because of these limitations, not all goals can be pursued, and a *selection* of goals is needed. To be able to optimize the pursuit of a goal, or to be able to optimally function, the use of resources is needed. That is, resources need to be acquired, refined, and employed, or, in one word, *optimized*. If goals, or level of functioning, suffer because of losses of resources, other resources must be employed in a compensatory manner (see the discussion of Compensation, below).

The concept of *Selection* consists of two dimensions, *elective selection* and *loss-based selection*. Elective selection occurs when goals are specified, a hierarchy of goals is established, goals are contextualized, and the individual commits to goals. Loss-based selection occurs in response to losses, for example, when the individual focuses on the most important goals that remain after losses of resources, when the individual reconstructs his or her goal hierarchy, or when a search for new goals is undertaken.

The dimension of *Optimization* (of goal-relevant means) involves seizing the right moment, persistence, acquiring new skills and resources, practicing of skills, the distribution of effort and energy, the allocation of time, and modeling successful others. At this point in the process of the development of the theory of SOC, Optimization does not consist of subdimensions.

The dimension of *Compensation* involves activities such as the substitution of means (that are no longer available), the help of others, the acquisition of new skills and resources, an increase in effort, an increase in allocated time, the modeling of others who successfully compensate, or the neglect of optimizing other means. As with Optimization, Compensation is a one-dimensional concept. Based on these definitions, instruments that measure SOC consist of questions that indicate the two dimensions of Selection, and one dimension each of Optimization and Compensation (e.g., Baltes, Baltes, Freund, & Lang, 1999).

In this chapter, we ask whether the dimensional structure of SOC can be represented by a bifactor model. We also ask whether the bifactor model is gender-specific in the sense that the latent variables of the model are invariant across the two gender groups. Third, we ask whether an autoregressive bifactor model adequately represents short-term development of the SOC structure. All these questions are answered using data from the 4-H Study of PYD (Bowers et al., 2010; Lerner et al., 2005). We discuss first the bifactor model.

II. The Bifactor Model

In this section, we first present technical elements of the bifactor model. Then, we present two extensions of the model, the multigroup bifactor model and the autoregressive bifactor model.

A. TECHNICAL ELEMENTS OF THE BIFACTOR MODEL

For the following introduction to the bifactor model, we use the notation of the statistical model of LISREL (Jöreskog & Sörbom, 1989). Consider the general LISREL model

$$\eta = B\eta + \Gamma\xi + \zeta,$$

where η is the $m \times 1$ random vector of latent dependent variables, B is an $m \times m$ matrix of coefficients of the η variables, Γ is an $m \times n$ matrix of coefficients of the ξ variables, ξ is an $n \times 1$ vector of latent independent variables, and ζ is an $m \times 1$ vector of factor residuals (random disturbances) in the structural relationship between η and ξ. Factor models can, in LISREL, be specified on the x-side of the model, that is, solely in terms of independent latent variables, on the y-side of the model, that is, solely in terms of dependent latent variables, and on both the x- and the y-sides. In the following description, we focus on the y-side of the LISREL model. The measurement model for y is

$$y = \Lambda_y \eta + \varepsilon,$$

where y is a $p \times 1$ vector of observed variables, Λ_y is a $p \times m$ matrix of coefficients of the regression of y on η, and ε is a $p \times 1$ vector of residuals in y.

Without any loss of information, we can simplify the general LISREL model by using LISREL Submodel 3b. Consider the general LISREL model which is defined by the first of the two above equations. This model can be cast as model with no x-variables (Submodel 3a). Going one step farther, this model can also be cast as a model with no ξ-variables. The resulting model is Submodel 3b, or

$$\eta = B\eta + \zeta$$

and y can be expressed as

$$y = \Lambda_y(I - B)^{-1}\zeta + \varepsilon,$$

where I is the $m \times m$ identity matrix. A well-known paradox is that LISREL Submodel 3b is more general than the full LISREL model that was given in the first equation above. It holds that every LISREL model can be equivalently re-cast as a model with only y- and η-variables.

Now, to introduce the bifactor model, consider the standard factor model, in which p variables load on m factors such that every variable loads on only one factor, and every variable loads on a factor. The corresponding model is

$$\Sigma = \Lambda_y \Phi \Lambda'_y + \Theta,$$

where Σ is the $p \times p$ covariance matrix of the p y-variables, Φ is the $m \times m$ variance–covariance matrix of the η-variables, and Θ is the $p \times p$ variance–covariance matrix of residuals of the y-variables. To give an example, consider the five variables y_1, y_2, y_3, y_4, and y_5. Let the first two of these variables load on η_1 and the remaining three on η_2. The matrix of this loading pattern is

$$\Lambda_y = \begin{bmatrix} 1 & 0 \\ 1 & 0 \\ 0 & 1 \\ 0 & 1 \\ 0 & 1 \end{bmatrix},$$

where the 1s indicate parameters to be estimated.

The bifactor model leaves the original loading pattern of a factor model intact. However, it adds one latent variable such that each y-variable is constrained to have a nonzero loading on this additional latent variable, and a second nonzero loading on the latent variable it had been loading on in the original model. In other words, the bifactor model adds to an existing standard factor model a general, superordinate factor that all *y*-variables are supposed to load on. The loading pattern matrix in the above example becomes, in a bifactor model,

$$
\Lambda_y = \begin{bmatrix} 1 & 1 & 0 \\ 1 & 1 & 0 \\ 1 & 0 & 1 \\ 1 & 0 & 1 \\ 1 & 0 & 1 \end{bmatrix},
$$

where the first column represents the new, superordinate factor. This formulation allows researchers to test the hypothesis that each variable (item) loads on a specific factor while still belonging to a superordinate latent variable that is universal in the sense that every variable loads on it.

The idea of the bifactor model was first proposed by Holzinger and Swineford (1937). Tucker (1958) discussed this model in the context of exploratory, and Jöreskog (1969) discussed it in the context of confirmatory, factor analysis. At the level of items, the bifactor model was discussed by Muthén (1989), Gibbons and Hedeker (1992), and Maydeu-Olivares and Coffman (2006). Gibbons and Hedeker (1992) also discuss issues of estimation of parameters of the bifactor model at the item level. The issue of scale or domain scores was addressed using bifactor models by Reise, Moore, and Haviland (2010) and Yao (2010). Only recently, the model has found applications, in particular in health research (Reise, Morizot & Hays, 2007), developmental research (Kim, Deater-Deckard, Mullineaux, & Allen, 2010), and clinical psychological research (Martel, Roberts, Gremillion, von Eye, & Nigg, 2010; Martel, von Eye, & Nigg, 2010).

The idea that carries research on and with the bifactor model relates to the multidimensionality of psychological concepts. Individual variables are hypothesized to play two roles. The first is that they are indicators of a particular factor such as a dimension of intelligence (e.g., verbal comprehension) or one of the four SOC dimensions. This role is indistinguishable from the role a variable plays in standard confirmatory factor models. The second role is that the same variable is an indicator of a superordinate, overarching factor such as intelligence, PYD, or SOC. So far in the literature and in the development of psychological theories, superordinate latent variables were defined in terms of higher order factor models. The role played by individual variables or items was that they were indicators only of their specific factors. These first-order factors then served as indicators of the higher order factor(s). In contrast, *in the bifactor model, individual variables are also indicators of the superordinate factor.*

This structure has two interesting characteristics. First, it can be determined whether the individual variable or item also loads significantly and strongly on the superordinate factor. Second, the superordinate factor is specified at the same level as the specific factors. It typically is also a first-order factor. By implication, the superordinate factor then does not explain the interrelations among the specific first-order factors (cf. Chen, West, & Sousa, 2006). These interrelations can be modeled more specifically and separately for each pair of specific first-order factors. The superordinate factor thus explains the covariation among all variables or items. The specific factors explain the covariation among items in particular domains.

In the following sections, we present two extensions of the bifactor model. The first allows one to compare two or more groups. The second allows one to test hypotheses about autoregression in longitudinal designs.

B. THE MULTIGROUP BIFACTOR MODEL

Multigroup models are of interest when researchers ask whether structures are the same in more than one population or, in different terms, whether a structure is specific to a particular population. In the literature, there is no general agreement on the conditions that must be fulfilled for a structure to be considered "the same" for two or more groups. For example, DeShon (2004) maintains, in the context of measurement equivalence, that measures are not invariant without error variance equivalence. In other words, even the error structure must be invariant across groups for a measure to be considered equivalent over these groups. Not surprisingly, other researchers support different perspectives.

In longitudinal developmental research, this discussion takes an interesting twist. If measures or, more generally, structures, are not equivalent over time in DeShon's sense, there may be at least two reasons that need to be explored, since these two reasons that can be confounded. One reason is standard lack of equivalence. Two populations do not share the exact same structure. The other reason is that development has taken place. Measures may change their characteristics over the course of the development of those responding to the measure. If the respondents are administered the instrument repeatedly, the well-known problems with repeated administration and developmental changes may be reasons for lack of measurement equivalence. If respondents from different cohorts are given the instrument, cohort-specific characteristics of structures may play a role in addition to development.

In the present context, we ask whether the structure of the four SOC dimensions is invariant over the two gender groups (factor equivalence).

We attempt to answer the question of equivalence of a bifactor structure by defining a two-group model.

In the following specification of a two-group bifactor model, we focus on the elements that are specific to the bifactor model. These are (1) the specific first-order factors that are indicated by groups of manifest variables and (2) the general, superordinate first-order factor that is indicated by all variables. If the two groups are equivalent in regard to this structure, the following hypotheses hold for a model that is formulated on the y-side:

$$\Lambda_y^{(1)} = \Lambda_y^{(2)},$$

where (1) and (2) indicate the two comparison groups,

$$\Theta_\varepsilon^{(1)} = \Theta_\varepsilon^{(2)},$$

$$\Psi^{(1)} = \Psi^{(2)},$$

and

$$B^{(1)} = B^{(2)}.$$

The first of these four hypotheses states that the two loading matrices are the same, the second states that the two error structures are the same, the third states that the matrices of factor covariances are the same, and the fourth states that the matrices of structural relationships among the first-order factors are the same. As was indicated before, depending on a researcher's definition of *equivalent*, the constraints imposed on a model may differ. Four options exist that can be applied to entire matrices but also to individual parameters or groups of parameters.

(1) A matrix has the *same pattern* of fixed and free (estimated) elements as the corresponding matrix in the comparison group.
(2) An estimation run begins, for a particular matrix, with the same *starting values* for the iteration as the corresponding matrix in the comparison group.
(3) An estimation run begins with the *same pattern* and the same *starting values* for the iteration as the corresponding matrix in the comparison group.
(4) A matrix is *invariant* over the comparison groups.

These four options are hierarchically ordered. The order is ascending, from the most liberal to the most strict. The last option places the strictest constraints on a model. All parameters of a matrix have the same pattern of fixed and estimated elements, and all elements that are estimated are the same in the comparison groups. *The same* implies, in the present context, that the parameters are numerically the same, not just nonsignificantly different. This definition of model equivalence of a bifactor model can be extended to involve more than two comparison groups.

C. A LONGITUDINAL BIFACTOR MODEL

In the domain of latent growth curve modeling, a large number of models has been proposed (see, e.g., Bollen & Curran, 2006; Preacher, Wichman, MacCallum, & Briggs, 2008; von Eye & Clogg, 1994). For the present purposes, we focus on autoregressive models. These are models in which latent or manifest variables predict themselves over time. Autoregression effects are typically the strongest in a longitudinal model (for the study of effects that go beyond autoregression, see von Eye, Mun, & Bogat, 2009).

The models we consider here are recursive. The autoregressive effects are expressed using the B matrix. Consider again the introductory example to this section. In this example of a bifactor model, we had two specific and one superordinate first-order latent variables. In a two-wave design, one can test the hypothesis that each of these latent variables predicts itself from the first to the second wave. The corresponding B matrix will then be

$$B = \begin{bmatrix} 0 & 0 & 0 & 0 & 0 & 0 \\ 0 & 0 & 0 & 0 & 0 & 0 \\ 0 & 0 & 0 & 0 & 0 & 0 \\ 1 & 0 & 0 & 0 & 0 & 0 \\ 0 & 1 & 0 & 0 & 0 & 0 \\ 0 & 0 & 1 & 0 & 0 & 0 \end{bmatrix}.$$

In this matrix, the first three rows represent the three latent variables at Time 1, and the second three rows represent the same latent variables at Time 2. The 1s in Cells 4 1, 5 2, and 6 3 indicate that autoregressive parameters are estimated for each of the three latent variables such that each predicts itself over time. Additional within- and cross-time regression parameters can be considered.

III. Data Examples

The following examples use data from the 4-H study of PYD (Lerner et al., 2005, 2010; Lerner, Lerner, von Eye, & Lewin-Bizan, 2009; Phelps et al., 2009). The 4-H Study of PYD began in 2002 with a sample of about 1700 5th grade youth and about 1100 of their parents from 13 states in the United States (Lerner et al., 2005). The study uses a form of cohort sequential longitudinal design (Baltes, Reese, & Nesselroade, 1977; Collins, 2006), and as such, the sample size increases across successive waves of testing. That is, data from fifth graders were gathered in Wave 1 of the study (the 2002–2003 school year), and these fifth graders were the initial cohort in the study. However, to maintain at least initial levels of power for within-time analyses and to assess the effects of retesting, subsequent waves of the study involved the addition of a "retest control" cohort of youth (and a sample of their parents). Participants in the added "retest control" cohort were then followed longitudinally. In Wave 2, the grade level of the initial cohort was Grade 6. As such, a "retest control" group of sixth graders was added to the study, and these youth became members of the second longitudinal cohort, Cohort 2. Both the original cohort of fifth graders and the added cohort of sixth graders were followed into Grade 7, and a new cohort of seventh graders was added to the sample (along with their parents). In subsequent waves of testing, this process was followed.

At this writing, the 4-H study includes 6885 youth from 41 states. Participants reside in rural, suburban, and urban areas in different parts of the country and represent a diverse array of racial, ethnic, and religious backgrounds and a range of socioeconomic levels.

This study was designed to establish the concept of PYD and its usefulness. As described by Lerner et al. (2005), several measures derived from the overall measurement model of the 4-H Study of PYD were used to index PYD, operationalized through the assessment of the Five Cs. Each of the Cs of PYD—competence, confidence, character, connection, and caring—comprises a number of well-validated scales designed to assess the essential elements of the definition of the construct. A PYD score for each participant was computed as the mean of Five Cs, with higher scores representing higher levels of the Cs and PYD. Within the 4-H Study, the SOC questionnaire, devised by Baltes, Baltes, Freund, and colleagues (e.g., Baltes, 1997; Baltes & Baltes, 1990; Freund & Baltes, 2002), was selected to conceptualize and measure intentional self-regulation. Items on the SOC questionnaire are administered using a forced-choice format, where each item consists of two statements. One statement for each item describes a behavior reflecting one of the four SOC constructs (e.g., elective selection, loss-based selection), while the other describes a non-SOC related behavior. Participants then select which statement is more similar to how they would behave. This measure includes six items per subscale. Higher scores on each subscale indicate higher levels of self-regulatory skills. For the present examples, we used data from Grades 10 and 11 (Waves 6 and 7). On average, the respondents were 15.73 years of age in Wave 6, and 16.80 years in Wave 7.

IV. Cross-sectional Bifactor Models for the PYD Data of the 4-H Study

In this section, we describe the results of estimating cross-sectional bifactor models for the SOC data from Grades 10 and 11 of the 4-H study. We use data from 2,343 respondents for each wave. Both models were estimated using ML in LISREL. Admissibility checks were on, and the number of iterations was restricted to a maximum of 200.

A. RESULTS FOR GRADE 10

When the model for the Grade 10 data (Wave 6) was first estimated, the model converged, but model fit was poor (RMSEA = 0.66). Therefore, we estimated additional parameters of two kinds. First, we allowed residual covariances of individual items to be estimated. Selection was guided by interpretability and the relative magnitude of modification indices. Second, we allowed the first-order factors that are specific to the SOC dimensions to correlate. We did not allow the specific factors to correlate with the superordinate factor. In all, we allowed nine residual covariances to exist which represents 3.3% of all possible residual covariances. We also allowed four correlations among first-order factors to exist, which represents 40% of all possible factor correlations. The final model describes the data well (minimum fit function $X^2 = 10,183.89$, df = 215, $p < 0.01$; RMSEA = 0.045, 90% CI = [0.045; 0.046]; CFI = 0.91; GFI = 0.96). Figure 1 displays the model (standardized coefficients given; all parameters are significant).

Figure 1 shows an interesting pattern of results. None of the following results could have been obtained using standard second-order factor modeling.

First, some of the items make a stronger contribution to the superordinate factor than to their specific factors. Examples include Items 8, 13, and 15. This indicates that these items are more strongly related to the overall concept of SOC than to their specific concepts.

Second, some of the items show negative loadings on their specific factors and positive loadings on the superordinate factor (and vice versa).

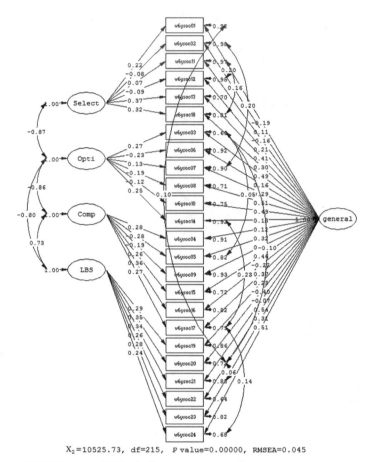

X₂=10525.73, df=215, P value=0.00000, RMSEA=0.045

Fig. 1. SOC bifactor model Grade 10.

At first, this may be confusing. However, considering that the wording of items is mixed (see the mixed signs of the loadings of the items on the specific factors), signs can be hard to interpret. Reverse coding of some items so that the coding goes not only in the same direction for the specific factors but also for the superordinate factor may help. Researchers may wish to reconsider including an item in the analysis if it systematically loads with opposite signs on its specific and the superordinate factors.

Third, the estimated correlations among the SOC factors are all strong. This supports the notion that the four SOC dimensions speak to the same underlying concept. However, one may wonder whether an alternative factor structure can be found that explains the same portion of variance.

An example of such a structure is a model with a second-order factor. However, although such a model would describe the present structure well, we focus, in the present context, on the bifactor solution because it has interpretational characteristics not found in the second-order factor model.

B. RESULTS FOR GRADE 11

When estimating the bifactor model for the data from Grade 11, we performed only a single run. This run was done with the hope that exactly the same model specification would describe the data well again. This was the case. Model fit indices support this model (minimum fit function $X^2 = 6977.63$, df $= 215$, $p < 0.01$; RMSEA $= 0.053$, 90% CI $= [0.052; 0.054]$; CFI $= 0.89$; GFI $= 0.95$). Therefore, no model modifications were undertaken. Figure 2 depicts the model.

As one might expect, the fit of this model can be improved by estimating additional residual covariances or factor intercorrelations. We decided against attempting to improve the model. Most of the changes would be purely cosmetic, the structural elements of the model would remain unchanged, and the similarity between the two models would be watered down.

Now, in spite of the strong similarities between the models for Grades 10 and 11, there are differences. For example, the fourth and the fifth indicator loadings of the optimization factor are negative for Grade 10 and close to zero and positive for Grade 11. Similarly, the first loading on the superordinate SOC factor is positive for Grade 10 and close to zero and negative for Grade 11. Given the characteristics of the data used to estimate the present models, it is impossible to conclude that these differences reflect developmental changes or cohort differences. Reasons for this problem include the confounding of cohort and time, and the fact that some of the respondents at Grade 10 is also in the sample of Grade 11.The remaining respondents were included to replenish the sample with the goal of obtaining a sample size that is large enough for analyses of the kind presented here. Removing the cases that were included to keep the sample size large would reduce the sample size. It would, however, allow one to talk about developmental changes (see Section VI). Nevertheless, there would be no way to disentangle the multiple causes for these changes. The changes could be cohort-specific, developmental, or both.

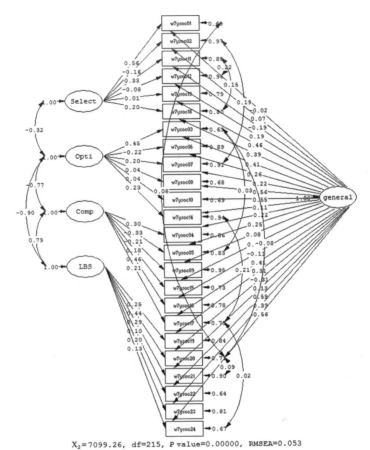

$X_2 = 7099.26$, df=215, P value=0.00000, RMSEA=0.053

Fig. 2. SOC bifactor model Grade 11.

V. Gender Differences in the Structure of SOC

We now ask whether the structure of SOC is invariant across the two Gender groups. To answer this question, we split the sample by Gender and estimated a two-group bifactor model as described above. To determine the degree of similarity, we start from the strictest of models, the one in which all patterns of parameters are the same and the estimates are also exactly the same. If this model fails, there is the option to estimate parameters so that they can vary across the comparison groups. Most typically, one allows the error structure to be group-specific first and then the loadings and structural elements.

When splitting the sample, we obtained 854 male and 1489 female respondents. These samples are certainly large enough for the proposed model. However, the program (LISREL 8.8) indicated that the covariance matrix to be analyzed is not positive definite which prohibits estimation with maximum likelihood or generalized least squares methods. Therefore, the models to be described here were estimated using unrestricted least squares.

As in the comparison of the structures found for Grades 10 and 11 in the last section, we attempted to specify the gender-comparison model so that it is as similar as possible to the models presented in the last section. We therefore started with the exact same model specification as for the two previous models.

The first model that was estimated was the one in which all parameter matrices were specified to be invariant across the two Gender groups. Without reporting every detail, we note that this model converged and fit well. However, there was room for improvement. Therefore, we allowed the matrix of residual variances and covariances of the manifest variables to be estimated so that the estimates were group-specific. In contrast, the pattern of freed and fixed elements in this matrix was specified to be invariant across the comparison groups. Figure 3 shows this model for the male respondents (the graph of the model for the female respondents can be requested from the authors).

The fit of the two-group model is very good, suggesting that the two Gender groups do not differ systematically in adolescence, at age 15.73 (normal theory weighted least squares $X^2 = 750.30$, df $= 486$, $p < 0.01$; RMSEA $= 0.007$, 90% CI $= [0.006; 0.008]$; CFI $= 1.00$; GFI $= 0.97$).

When compared to the model for Grade 10 in the last section, small differences can be found again. Specifically, four of the six loadings on the Selection factor changed sign, and so did the sign of the correlation of the Selection factor with the Optimization factor. At this point and without additional information, we would have to speculate about the reasons for these differences. One reason could be that different estimation methods were used. However, it may also be that the aggregate-level results presented in the last section fell prey to the phenomenon of ecological fallacy, so that the signs of the aggregate-level analysis differ from the signs of the individual-level analysis. This possibility would be interesting and certainly worth an in-depth analysis. This analysis will be performed and reported in a different context. In most other respects, particularly concerning the parameter estimates for the superordinate factor, the models for the aggregate at Grade 10 and the two-group analysis are very similar, and there is no reason to worry about other instances of distorted estimates.

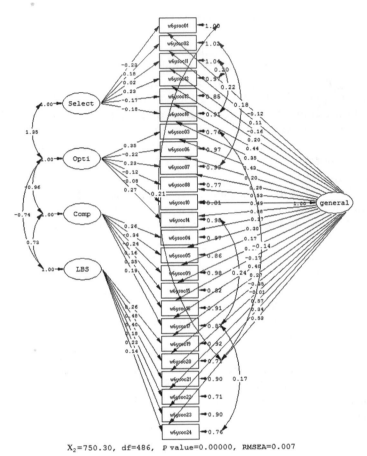

$X_2 = 750.30$, df=486, P value=0.00000, RMSEA=0.007

Fig. 3. SOC bifactor model for male adolescents in two-group Comparison, Grade 10.

For Grade 11, the same analyses were performed, and extremely similar results were obtained. The overall model fit was even better (normal theory weighted least squares $X^2 = 524.43$, df = 486, $p = 0.11$; RMSEA = 0.004, 90% CI = [0.000; 0.006]; CFI = 1.00; GFI = 0.96). We noticed that the correlation between Selection and Optimization was positive again. From this result, we conclude that the difference in this correlation between the aggregate-level and the group-specific results may not be a fluke, and assume that, for this particular parameter, the hypothesis of ecological fallacy may be entertained.

VI. Longitudinal Characteristics of the SOC Structure

In this section, we examine the longitudinal stability of the SOC structure. The model that is estimated was described in the section on the longitudinal bifactor model above. The sample that is used for the present analyses is the same as for the analyses in the last two sections. However, only the 609 cases were included for which complete data exist for Grades 10 and 11. The same variables are included as in the first two bifactor models in this chapter. The final Model is depicted in Figure 4.

For the present analyses, maximum likelihood estimation was possible again. Overall model fit is good, suggesting that the SOC structure is time-invariant when examined over Grades 10 and 11. The overall goodness-of-fit estimates provide a mixed picture (normal theory weighted least squares $X^2 = 72{,}695.46$, df $= 1002$, $p < 0.01$; RMSEA $= 0.051$, 90% CI $= [0.050; 0.051]$; CFI $= 0.82$; GFI $= 0.90$). However, in order to keep a model that is maximally similar to the ones in the previous sections of this chapter, we again refrained from further embellishing the estimates by estimating additional parameters. (We tried and improved the model considerably, but we had to free a large number of residual covariances. These attempts are not reported here.) The command file for this model appears in the Appendix to this chapter.

The aspects of the model that are most interesting in the present context concern the cross-time characteristics. Temporal stability, in the present context, is represented in three model characteristics. The first of these characteristics is that the four first-order SOC factors are regressed onto themselves. As expected, the autoregression effects were strong: t-values ranged from 12.49, for the autoregression of Optimization, to 23.37, for the autoregression of Compensation. The second characteristic concerns the autoregression of the superordinate factor onto itself. This effect was even stronger, with a t-value of 67.97. These results suggest that the rank orders of adolescents in this age group (age 16/17) are highly stable.

The third characteristic concerns cross-time residual covariances of individual items. The cross-time relationships of Items 4, 9, 14, and 16 were not adequately represented by the longitudinal bifactor model. Therefore, the corresponding residual covariances were freed. The first of these four items is an indicator of Optimization, the other three are indicators of Compensation. The four items are:

Item 4: When something does not work as well as before, I get advice from experts or read books.

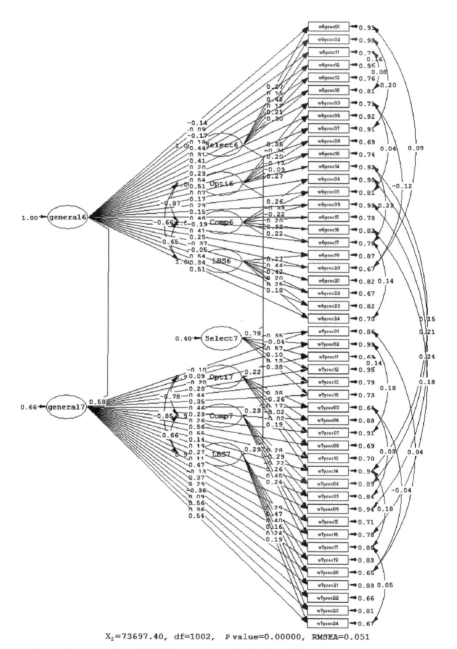

X_2=73697.40, df=1002, P value=0.00000, RMSEA=0.051

Fig. 4. Autoregression SOC bifactor model, Grades 10 and 11.

Item 9: When things aren't going so well, I accept help from others.
Item 14: When I want to get ahead, I also look at how others have done it.
Item 16: When I can't do something as well as I used to, then I ask some-
one else to do it for me.

However, despite being associated with either Optimization (Number
14) or Compensation (Numbers 4, 9, and 16), all items share a common
characteristic, that is, all items involve getting help from other people.

VII. Discussion

Concepts as general as those used in the SOC model often share two
characteristics. First, as was discussed in the introduction, they are multidimensional. In the present chapter, the four-dimensional nature of the
SOC model is confirmed. Second, these concepts are time-invariant. In
other words, as soon as the concepts are fully developed, they tend to stay
unchanged over the course of later development. In the present chapter,
we show that, by Age 15, the SOC structure can be considered fully developed and time-stable, for at least 1 year.

Naturally, one can ask whether development can still take place when a
mental structure is fully developed. The answer is clearly yes. A fully
developed structure does not imply that all other parameters are time-
invariant. As was implied earlier (in Section VI), the strong
autoregressions in the space of the five first-order factors of the concepts
studied here suggest that the rank order of individuals is time-stable.
However, even if a rank order is stable, means can change, and the
corresponding increases or decreases do not even have to be the same. Earlier work with the SOC scale suggested that the means on the four
dimensions do change over the course of adolescence, but that these
mean changes were not differentiated by gender, that is, girls tend to always
have higher SOC scores than boys (Gestsdóttir et al., 2009; Zimmerman
et al., 2008). The present results do show gender differences, but these
differences do not affect the rank order of individuals in any of the four
latent dimensions or the superordinate factor. This finding notwithstanding,
person-oriented data analysis may suggest that subgroups exist in the population that show subgroup-specific developmental trajectories. Future
research will have to identify these subgroups.

From a methodological perspective, this chapter proposed multiple
group and autoregression versions of the bifactor model. The application
showed that these models can be estimated even at the item level. Gener-
alizations are conceivable. For example, when data from more than two

waves are available, simplex models or latent growth curve models can be considered. The latter impose a particular structure, mostly polynomial trajectories, onto the data, and one asks whether this structure can be used to represent the data. Considering the earlier results (e.g., Gestsdòttir, et al., 2009), according to which there are mean differences in SOC dimensions between the two gender groups, means models can also be devised.

The main advantage of a bifactor model is that, instead of using second-order factors that explain the covariation among first-order factors, it specifies a superordinate factor that explains the covariation among the indicators of the first-order factors. This element has the effect that the contribution that the individual indicator makes to the superordinate concept can be directly understood, on the basis of the loadings of an indicator on the superordinate factor. The present chapter shows that this method is useful both in group-comparative and longitudinal models.

VIII. Conclusions

The purpose of this chapter was to demonstrate the links between innovative developmental methodology and the theoretical foundations of developmental theory, in general, and the relational, developmental systems model of PYD. Using the sample case of gender specificity and longitudinal stability of the dimensions of a key measure of intentional self-regulation in adolescence, the SOC measure (Baltes, 1997; Freund, 2008; Freund & Baltes, 2002; Lerner et al., 2001, 2003), we were able to demonstrate that SOC dimensions could be established in adolescence, and that they do exhibit stability and gender specificity without affecting the rank order of individuals.

Accordingly, our sample case indicates that developmental scientists studying PYD must attend both to establishing the change-sensitivity and the characteristics of development they are studying and, at the same time, to the differences that may exist between individuals in these developing characteristics. The integration of facets of development that remain the same with those that change is a hallmark of the relational, developmental systems model of PYD. The findings presented in this chapter illustrate the importance of developing methods that enable identification of both intraindividual change and of interindividual differences in intraindividual change among equivalent measures across the adolescent years.

Appendix. LISREL Command File for the Autoregression Bifactor Model

```
Longitudinal Bifactor analysis SOC Waves 6 and 7
DA NI=50 NO=609 MA=cM
RA FI=waves6and7first609longit.psf
SE
3 4 13 14 15 20
5 8 9 10 12 16
6 7 11 17 18 19
21 22 23 24 25 26
27 28 37 38 39 44
29 32 33 34 36 40
30 31 35 41 42 43
45 46 47 48 49 50 /
MO NY=48 NE=10 BE=FU,fi PS=SY,fi TE=SY
LE
Select6 Opti6 Comp6 LBS6 general6 Select7 Opti7 Comp7
LBS7 general7
 pa ly
 6(1 0 0 0 1 0 0 0 0 0)
 6(0 1 0 0 1 0 0 0 0 0)
 6(0 0 1 0 1 0 0 0 0 0)
 6(0 0 0 1 1 0 0 0 0 0)
 6(0 0 0 0 0 1 0 0 0 1)
 6(0 0 0 0 0 0 1 0 0 1)
 6(0 0 0 0 0 0 0 1 0 1)
 6(0 0 0 0 0 0 0 0 1 1)
 fi ps 1 1 ps 2 2 ps 3 3 ps 4 4 ps 6 6 ps 7 7 ps 8 8 ps 9 9 ps 5 5
ps 10 10
 va 1 ps 1 1 ps 2 2 ps 3 3 ps 4 4 ps 6 6 ps 7 7 ps 8 8 ps 9 9 ps 5 5
ps 10 10
 FR TE(6,3) TE(9,2) TE(14,7) TE(18,12) TE(20,7) te 4 3
te 24 18 te 20 1
 fr te 33 26 te 38 31 te 42 36 te 44 31 te 28 27 te 48 42 te 44
25
 fr te 39 15 te 37 13 te 36 12 te 41 17
 fr ps 4 3 ps 3 2 ps 4 2
 fr ps 9 8 ps 8 7 ps 9 7
 fr be 10 5
 fr be 6 1 be 7 2 be 8 3 be 9 4
 PD
 OU RS mi me=ml
```

REFERENCES

Baltes, P. B. (1997). On the incomplete architecture of human ontogeny: Selection, optimization, and compensation as foundation of developmental theory. *American Psychologist, 52*, 366–380.

Baltes, P. B., & Baltes, M. M. (1990). Psychological perspectives on successful aging: The model of selective optimization with compensation. In P. B. Baltes & M. M. Baltes (Eds.), *Successful aging: Perspectives from the behavioral sciences* (pp. 1–34). New York: Cambridge University Press.

Baltes, P. B., Baltes, M. M., Freund, A. M., & Lang, F. R. (1999). *The measurement of selection, optimization, and compensation (SOC) by self report: Technical report 1999*. (Materialien aus der Bildungsforschung No. 66). Berlin: Max-Planck-Institut für Bildungsforschung.

Baltes, P. B., Reese, H. W., & Nesselroade, J. R. (1977). *Life-span developmental psychology: Introduction to research methods*. Monterey, CA: Brooks/Cole.

Benson, P. L. (2003). Toward asset-building communities: How does change occur? In R. M. Lerner & P. L. Benson (Eds.), *Developmental assets and asset-building communities: Implications for research, policy, and practice*. New York, NY: Kluwer Academic/Plenum Publishers.

Benson, P. L., Scales, P. C., Hamilton, S. F., & Sesma, J. A. (2006). Positive youth development: Theory, research and applications. In W. Damon & R. M. Lerner (Editors-in-chief) & W. Damon & R. M. Lerner (Eds.), *Handbook of Child Psychology: Vol. 1. Theoretical models of human development*. (6th ed, pp. 894–941). Hoboken, NJ: Wiley.

Bollen, K. A., & Curran, P. J. (2006). *Latent curve models: A structural equation approach*. Hoboken, NJ: Wiley.

Bowers, E. P., Li, Y., Kiely, M. K., Brittian, A., Lerner, J. V., & Lerner, R. M. (2010). The Five Cs Model of Positive Youth Development: A longitudinal analysis of confirmatory factor structure and measurement invariance. *Journal of Youth and Adolescence, 39*(7), 720–735.

Brandtstädter, J. (1998). Action perspectives on human development. In W. Damon & R. M. Lerner (Eds.), *Handbook of child psychology, Vol. I: Theories and models of human development* (5th ed, pp. 807–863). New York: Wiley.

Chen, F. F., West, S. G., & Sousa, K. H. (2006). A comparison of bifactor and second-order models of quality of life. *Multivariate Behavioral Research, 41*, 189–225.

Collins, L. M. (2006). Analysis of longitudinal data: The integration of theoretical model, temporal design, and statistical model. *Annual Review of Psychology, 57*, 505–528.

DeShon, R. P. (2004). Measures are not invariant without error variance equivalence. *Psychology Science, 46*, 137–149.

Eysenck, H. J. (1967). *The biological basis of personality*. Springfield, IL: Charles C. Thomas.

Freund, A. M. (2008). Successful aging as management of resources: The role of selection, optimization, and compensation. *Research in Human Development, 5*, 94–106.

Freund, A. M., & Baltes, P. B. (2002). The adaptiveness of selection, optimization, and compensation as strategies of life management: Evidence from a preference study on proverbs. *Journals of Gerontology: Psychological Sciences*, P426–P434.

Gestsdóttir, S., Bowers, E. P., von Eye, A., Napolitano, C. M., & Lerner, R. M. (2010). Intentional self regulation in middle adolescence: The emerging role of loss-based selection in Positive Youth Development. *Journal of Youth and Adolescence, 39*(7), 764–782.

Gestsdóttir, S., & Lerner, R. M. (2007). Intentional self-regulation and positive youth development in early adolescence: Findings from the 4-H Study of Positive Youth Development. *Developmental Psychology, 43*(2), 508–521.

Gestsdóttir, S., & Lerner, R. M. (2008). Positive development in adolescence: The development and role of intentional self-regulation. *Human Development, 51,* 202–224.

Gestsdóttir, S., Lewin-Bizan, S., von Eye, A., Lerner, J. V., & Lerner, R. M. (2009). The structure and function of selection, optimization, and compensation in adolescence: Theoretical and applied implications. *Journal of Applied Developmental Psychology, 30*(5), 585–600.

Gibbons, R. D., & Hedeker, D. R. (1992). Full-information item bi-factor analysis. *Psychometrika, 57,* 423–436.

Holzinger, K., & Swineford, F. (1937). The bi-factor method. *Psychometrika, 2,* 41–54.

Horn, J. L., & Cattell, R. B. (1966). Refinement and test of the theory of fluid and crystallized general intelligences. *Journal of Educational Psychology, 57,* 253–270.

Jelicic, H., Bobek, D., Phelps, E. D., Lerner, J. V., & Lerner, R. M. (2007). Using positive youth development to predict contribution and risk behaviors in early adolescence: Findings from the first two waves of the 4-H Study of Positive Youth Development. *International Journal of Behavioral Development, 31*(3), 263–273.

Jöreskog, K. G. (1969). A general approach to confirmatory maximum likelihood factor analysis. *Psychometrika, 34,* 183–202.

Jöreskog, K. G., & Sörbom, D. (1989). *LISREL 8: User's reference guide.* Lincolnwood, IL: Scientific Software International, Inc.

Kim, J., Deater-Deckard, K., Mullineaux, P. Y., & Allen, B. (2010). Longitudinal studies of anger and attention span: Context and informant effects. *Journal of Personality, 78,* 419–440.

Larson, R. (2000). Toward a psychology of positive youth development. *American Psychologist, 55,* 170–183.

Larson, R. W., & Rusk, N. (2011). Intrinsic motivation and positive development. In R. M. Lerner, J. V. Lerner, & J. B. Benson, (Eds.), *Advances in Child Development and Behavior: Positive youth development: Research and applications for promoting thriving in adolescence.* Elsevier Publishing. 87–128.

Lerner, J. V., Phelps, E., Forman, Y. E., & Bowers, E. (2009). Positive youth development. In R. M. Lerner & L. Steinberg (Eds.), *Handbook of adolescent psychology (3rd ed.): Vol. 1, Individual bases of adolescent development.* (3rd ed., pp. 524–558). Hoboken, NJ: Wiley.

Lerner, R. M., Dowling, E., & Roth, S. L. (2003). Contributions of lifespan psychology to the future elaboration of developmental systems theory. In U. M. Staudinger & U. Lindenberger (Eds.), *Understanding human development: Dialogues with lifespan psychology.* (pp. 413–422). Dordrecht, The Netherlands: Kluwer Academic.

Lerner, R. M., Freund, A. M., DeStefanis, I., & Habermas, T. (2001). Understanding developmental regulation in adolescence: The use of the selection, optimization, and compensation model. *Human Development, 44,* 29–50.

Lerner, R. M., Lerner, J. V., Almerigi, J., Theokas, C., Phelps, E., Gestsdóttir, S., et al. (2005). Positive youth development, participation in community youth development programs, and community contributions of fifth-grade adolescents: Findings from the first wave of the 4-H Study of Positive Youth Development. *Journal of Early Adolescence, 25,* 17–71.

Lerner, R. M., Lerner, J. V., & Benson, J. B. (2011). Research and applications for promoting thriving in adolescence: A view of the issues. In R. M. Lerner, J. V. Lerner, & J. B. Benson, (Eds.), *Advances in Child Development and Behavior: Positive youth development: Research and applications for promoting thriving in adolescence.* Elsevier Publishing. 1–17.

Lerner, R. M., Lerner, J.V., Lewin-Bizan, S., Bowers, E. P., Boyd, M. B., Mueller, M. K., et al. (in press). Positive youth development: Processes, programs, and problematics. *Journal of Youth Development.*

Lerner, R. M., von Eye, A., Lerner, J. V., & Lewin-Bizan, S. (2009). Exploring the foundations and functions of adolescent thriving within the 4-H study of positive youth development: A view of the issues. *Journal of Applied Developmental Psychology, 30* (5), 567–570.

Lerner, R. M., von Eye, A., Lerner, J. V., Lewin-Bizan, S., & Bowers, E. P. (2010). The meaning and measurement of thriving: A view of the issues. *Journal of Youth and Adolescence, 39,* 707–719.

Li, Y. (2011). Intrinsic motivation and positive development. In R. M. Lerner, J. V. Lerner, & J. B. Benson, (Eds), *Advances in Child Development and Behavior: Positive youth development: Research and applications for promoting thriving in adolescence.* Elsevier Publishing. 87–128.

Li, Y., & Lerner, R. M. (2011). Trajectories of school engagement during adolescence: Implications for grades, depression, delinquency, and substance use. *Developmental Psychology, 47,* 233–247.

Li, Y., Lerner, J. V., & Lerner, R. M. (2010). Personal and ecological assets and academic competence in early adolescence: The mediating role of school engagement. *Journal of Youth and Adolescence, 39*(7), 801–815.

Martel, M. M., Roberts, B., Gremillion, M., von Eye, A., & Nigg, J. T. (2010). *External validation of bifactor model of ADHD: Explaining heterogeneity in psychiatric comorbidity, cognitive control, and personality trait profiles. Psychological Assessment.* In press.

Martel, M. M., von Eye, A., & Nigg, J. T. (2010). Revisiting the latent structure of ADHD: Is there a "g"-factor? *Journal of Child Psychology and Psychiatry, 51,* 905–914.

Maydeu-Olivares, A., & Coffman, D. L. (2006). Random intercept item factor analysis. *Psychological Methods, 11,* 344–362.

McCrae, R. R., & Costa, P. C. Jr., (1987). Validation of the five-factor model across instruments and observers. *Journal of Personality and Social Psychology, 52,* 81–90.

Muthén, B. (1989). Latent variable modeling in heterogeneous populations. Presidential address to the Psychometric Society, July, 1989. *Psychometrika, 54,* 557–585.

Naploitano, C. M, Bowers, E. P., & Gestsdottir, S. (2011). The development of intentional self regulation in adolescence: Describing, explaining, and optimizing its link to positive youth development. In R. M. Lerner, J. V. Lerner, & J. B. Benson, (Eds.), *Advances in Child Development and Behavior: Positive youth development: Research and applications for promoting thriving in adolescence.* Elsevier Publishing. 17–36.

Overton, W. F. (2010). Life-span development: Concepts and issues. In W. F. Overton (Ed.), Cognition, biology, and methods across the lifespan. Volume 1 of the Handbook of life-span development. (pp. 1-29) Editor-in-chief: R. M. Lerner. Hoboken, NJ: Wiley.

Phelps, E., Zimmerman, S., Warren, A. A., Jelicic, H., von Eye, A., & Lerner, R. M. (2009). The structure and developmental course of positive youth development (PYD) in early adolescence: Implications for theory and practice. *Journal of Applied Developmental Psychology, 30,* 571–584.

Preacher, K. J., Wichman, A. L., MacCallum, R. C., & Briggs, N. E. (2008). *Latent growth curve modeling.* Thousand Oaks, CA: Sage.

Reise, S. P., Moore, T. M., & Haviland, M. G. (2010). Bifactor models and rotations: Exploring the extent to which multidimensional data yield univocal scale scores. *Journal of Personality Assessment, 92,* 544–559.

Reise, S. P., Morizot, J., & Hays, R. D. (2007). The role of the bifactor model in resolving dimensionality issues in health outcomes measures. *Quality of Life Research: An International Journal of Quality of Life Aspects of Treatment, Care & Rehabilitation, 16*(Suppl. 1), 19–31.

Schmid, K. L., Phelps, E., M., Kiely, M. K., Napolitano, C. M., Boyd, M. J., & Lerner, R. M. (2011). The relationship between intra-individual change in Positive Youth Development and adolescents' hopeful futures: Findings from the 4-H Study of Positive Youth Development. *Journal of Positive Psychology*, 6(1), 45–56.

Sternberg, R. J. (1985). *Beyond IQ: A triarchic theory of human intelligence.* New York: Cambridge University Press.

Theokas, C., & Lerner, R. M. (2006). Observed ecological assets in families, schools, and neighborhoods: Conceptualization, measurement and relations with positive and negative developmental outcomes. *Applied Developmental Science*, 10(2), 61–74.

Thurstone, L. L. (1938). *Primary mental abilities.* Chicago: University of Chicago Press.

Tucker, L. R. (1958). An inter-battery method of factor analysis. *Psychometrika*, 23, 111–136.

von Eye, A., & Clogg, C. C. (Eds.), (1994). *Latent variable analysis: Applications for developmental research.* Thousand Oaks, CA: Sage.

von Eye, A., Mun, E. Y., & Bogat, G. A. (2009). Temporal patterns of variable relationships in person-oriented research: Prediction and auto-association models of configural frequency analysis. *Applied Developmental Science*, 13, 172–187.

Yao, L. (2010). Reporting valid and reliable overall scores and domain scores. *Journal of Educational Measurement*, 47, 339–360.

Zaff, J., Boyd, M., Li, Y., Lerner, J. V., & Lerner, R. M. (2010). Active and engaged citizenship: Multi-group and longitudinal factorial analysis of an integrated construct of civic engagement. *Journal of Youth and Adolescence*, 39(7), 736–750.

Zimmerman, S., Phelps, E., & Lerner, R. M. (2008). Positive and negative developmental trajectories in U.S. adolescents: Where the PYD perspective meets the deficit model. *Research in Human Development*, 5(3), 153–165.

Author Index

Subject Index

A

A&B. *See* Attitudes and behaviors
Adolescence. *See also* Intentional
  self-regulation, adolescence
  brain development
    decision making, 321
    dopamine receptors, 321
    neural activation, 321
    psychopathology and risk taking, 321
    "remodeling" process, 320
  thriving, PYD
    individual ↔ context relations, 5–8
    relational, developmental systems, 3–5
Attitudes and behaviors (A&B)
  DAP, 210–211
  survey, 209–210

B

Bifactor model
  advantage, 370
  cross-sectional, 4-H study
    grade 10, 361–363
    grade 11, 363
  LISREL command file, autoregression, 371
  longitudinal
    autoregressive effects, 359
    latent growth curve modeling, 359
    matrix, 359
  multigroup
    elements, 358
    longitudinal developmental research,
      357
    matrices, 358
    measurement equivalence, 357
  simplex models, 369–370
  technical elements
    confirmatory factor analysis, 356
    individual variables, 356
    LISREL model, 354–355

standard factor model, 355
  superordinate factor, 357
  y-variables, 355–356
Bronfenbrenner's bioecological theory, 3

C

Civic engagement
  behavioral measures, 275
  citizenship rights and responsibilities, 274
  civic behavior definition, 275
  cross-contextual
    engagement pathways, 279–280
    out-of-school settings, 279–280
    positive youth development, 279–280
    school engagement, 279–280
    self-regulation, 279
  cultural, socioeconomic and racial
      variations
    conventional measures, 285
    mainstream youth levels, 285
    youth population, 285
  developmental context and development
    community context and trust, 290–291
    extracurricular programs, 286
    families and economic hardship, 289–290
    religious institutions and spirituality,
      293–294
    school, 291–292
    societal disparities and poverty, 286–289
    urban communities, 292–293
    youth and young adults, 286
  developmental trajectories
    adolescence, 281–282
    AEC outcomes, 282
    competencies and attitudes, 281
    components, 281–282
    electoral politics, 281
    time-lag designs, 280–281
  diverse cultural contexts
    American adults, 295

393

Contents of Previous Volumes